Song and Circumstance

Song and Circumstance

The Work of David Byrne from Talking Heads to the Present

Sytze Steenstra

continuum

2010

The Continuum International Publishing Group Inc
80 Maiden Lane, New York, NY 10038

The Continuum International Publishing Group Ltd
The Tower Building, 11 York Road, London SE1 7NX

www.continuumbooks.com

Library of Congress Cataloging-in-Publication Data
Steenstra, Sytze.
   Song and circumstance : the work of David Byrne from Talking Heads to the present / by Sytze Steenstra.
      p. cm.
Includes bibliographical references and index.
ISBN-13: 978-0-8264-4559-9 (hardcover : alk. paper)
ISBN-10: 0-8264-4559-4 (hardcover : alk. paper)
ISBN-13: 978-0-8264-4168-3 (pbk. : alk. paper)
ISBN-10: 0-8264-4168-8 (pbk. : alk. paper) 1. Byrne, David, 1952—Criticism and interpretation. 2. New wave music—History and criticism. I. Title.

ML410.B997S74 2010
780.92—dc22   2009042865

ISBN: 978-08264-4559-9 (hardcover)
          978-08264-4168-3 (paperback)

Typeset by Pindar NZ, Auckland, New Zealand
Printed in the United States of America

Contents

List of illustrations

Introduction

1 THE WORLD IS A SONG

For several minutes a slightly unkempt face fills the screen, a man pulling faces, slowly changing from dazed and sleepy to sad, to demented grimacing, through anger to open and infective laughter, amazement, disgust, and befuddlement. Then the camera pulls back, showing the guy as he sits on a bed in a nondescript room, next to a man who holds a mop. A muffled sound is heard, distant singing, and the man with the mop gets up to check. The camera follows as he walks through long empty corridors of closed shutters, a storage warehouse, turning corners until he reaches the place where a voice sings "I wonder if you think of me, in my misery?," with a nasal emotional lilt. The janitor unlocks and lifts a shutter, revealing a narrow storage space where, facing the cardboard boxes at the back of the room, David Byrne plays a guitar and sings "There Stands The Glass." He interrupts his singing to cast a single look over his shoulder at the camera before he turns back and finishes the song, while the janitor locks up and walks away.

What would be the right facial expression to go with this classic country song by Webb Pierce? Does the maze of shuttered corridors represent the brain's neural pathways that connect the emotions in a voice to those seen on a face? If the other storage cubicles were opened, would they contain more songs in other musical genres, rock and funk and Latin and Brazilian pop, and their connections to other channels of musical performance, dance and theater and television? Would one cubicle hold boxes of books about the theoretical aspects of such questions, explaining several helpful approaches? Yes, it would, if this video were to represent the work of David Byrne. (The video is *Untitled Patton/Byrne Piece*, some six-and-a-half minutes long, and is included on the

1

first issue of *Wholphin*.[1] The man who is pulling faces is comedian/actor Patton Oswalt.)

By removing the face from the song, presenting seeing apart from hearing and placing them alongside, the clip isolates and heightens the viewer's response to them. An open, smiling face evokes a fitting response, making it hard not to smile along. A sad song invites compassion: "There Stands The Glass" evokes a sadness with a tinge of despair mixed in, and makes the listener feel sorry for the singer, a sentiment that brings up the question of how true, how autobiographical the song is. At the same time, by presenting the face and the song without an overarching story, this video is open about its own artificiality. Even while the clip is very basic, consisting of only two long takes, it is a montage. In the real world, the nondescript room where Oswalt works his face doesn't even have to be in the same city as the storage space where Byrne sings. But this knowledge doesn't detract anything at all from the infectiousness of a sad song, or from the appeal in a face.

Faces and the ways in which they impart meaning come up time and again in Byrne's work. He has, for example, used lighting from below to turn his own face into a ghoulish mask in the film "Stop Making Sense," he has rephotographed images of faces on movie posters and statues to reframe their meaning, and written about an imaginary software program, "Digital Physiognomy," that would be able to use "a sophisticated neural network to identify correlations between facial features and psychological characteristics" — which is presumably just what real people do. And he has used songs as a mask, as persona (which is the Latin word for mask), experimenting with the meanings and emotions they evoke, for example by covering a song by Whitney Houston, or even by lending his voice to a state-of-the-art singing robot with an almost-human face mask.

Experiments such as these are relatively easy to fathom, but the greater part of Byrne's work experiments with songs, stories and roles, as they are part of wider cultural contexts. Then, his cross-genre covers of songs, his unusual ways of casting, editing and composing raise puzzling questions about the ways in which sensibilities are combined, bundled into fixed identities that may turn out to be only temporary and makeshift. Both in his writing and in interviews, Byrne has often stated such matters explicitly, but he relies mostly on the suggestive and seductive forces of the arts, about which he says:

> "We have grown up understanding the grammar of movie editing, for example. A completely artificial and made up way of implying a narrative and connectivity between scenes and visual events, but one that we've agreed to, and have learned to accept. It's a language, a grammar without text, without words . . . yet is completely

understood by everyone. In the same way, we read a smile or a frown, and don't need someone to say 'I'm happy' or 'I'm angry'. And it gets much more complex. Our animal natures understand a whole host of non-verbal gestures, body signals and wordless vocal sounds and textures. These are used by advertisers, by artists, by designers and every other visually and musically oriented profession, they use these loaded colors, shapes, gestures, sounds and beats to speak to us. Yet almost none of this stuff is easily translatable into conventional language, into words and text.

Because we in the West are so text-based these non-verbal languages are considered secondary, almost as if they don't really exist unless their messages can be expressed in words. And when they are, usually unsuccessfully, translated into words then we feel like we have finally gained control over them. But in reading the translation we sense that something is wrong, that something is missing. And that missing element is what the arts have in common."[2]

As a singer-songwriter and performer, Byrne is a master in employing these "non-verbal languages." At the same time, he is a conceptual artist who is given to the explicit verbal analysis of the arts and their function. This relationship between song and circumstance is the overarching theme of all of Byrne's work. And to Byrne, this theme is literally all-encompassing:

I wouldn't be surprised if poetry — poetry in the broadest sense, in the sense of a world filled with metaphor, rhyme, and recurring patterns, shapes, and designs — is how the world works. The world isn't logical, it's a song.[3]

This book is the attempt to explain this unusual idea, the world is a song, by giving an account of the development of Byrne's work as a musician, artist and writer, paying at each step close attention to the conceptual influences that define the inner logic of Byrne's songs.

2 SINGER AND CONCEPTUAL ARTIST

There is little or no common ground between the raw emotional and intuitive appeal of rock songs and the extreme intellectualism of Art & Language, the almost sectarian group of conceptual artists whose work fascinated Byrne in the early days of Talking Heads. Struggling to combine the two, he approached his own role as front man of a rock group as if he was observing himself from a considerable distance. He would later describe this as "filtering emotion through an extremely constricting linguistic bottleneck."[4]

In the years he spent in art schools in the early 1970s, conceptual art had pulled Byrne under its spell. Conceptualism held the most outspoken intellectual position in the very diverse art scene of the late 60s and early 70s. Having its roots in the arts world, it called for a complete dismantling of the traditions of painting and sculpture, declaring that their conventions had collapsed, that their language had lost all credibility. Instead of continuing to make painting or sculpture, artists set out to make the forces that defined their lives — whether physical, social, cultural, philosophical, or political — the focus of their work, without the intervening support of established artistic conventions. In the words of Joseph Kosuth, conceptual art had the task of "dismantling the mythic structure of art as posited in the present day cultural institutions. But to do this our work must be *methodologically* creative; as artists we must continually question the conventions of our activity."[5] This questioning of conventions emphasized language and ideas as the true essence of art, and went hand in hand with the conviction that all visual experience and sensual joy were secondary and inessential to art; the more puritanically minded conceptualists would conclude that such pleasures were simply mindless and immoral.[6]

This conceptual attitude is not easily reconciled with the almost instinctive physical appeal of rock music, with its undeniably sensual and emotional potential for communication. The two just don't blend. And yet these opposing attitudes are constant presences in Byrne's work. The austere and critical attitude is a palpable factor in Byrne's work with Talking Heads, the band whose success made him a celebrity, and the insistent reflexivity, the relentless questioning of one's own art, continues in Byrne's later career as a solo musician. Byrne makes this exchange between popular music and conceptual art work in both directions. The direct appeal of non-verbal communication and of everyday vernacular forms of exchange are a crucial factor in Byrne's art books, even while these remain within the rigorously intellectual framework of conceptualism. This explains why this book doesn't treat Byrne's music and his conceptual art separately: they are always within each other's field of gravity.

Talking Heads was founded in New York in 1975 by three former art school students, David Byrne, Chris Frantz, and Tina Weymouth. They set out to become a rock band, but insisted that this could be combined with artistic sincerity. This was supported by the developments in New York's art scene around 1975, when there was a sense of kinship between minimalism and structuralism in the arts and the stripped-down and abstracted versions of rock and roll that the Velvet Underground had pioneered. Just as relevant, a new generation of performance artists began to explore combinations of the experimental attitudes of Fluxus and "happenings" with the typical forms of mass media entertainment, turning inside-out the pleasures of Hollywood movies, TV soap operas and commercials, rock music and cabaret. Talking Heads fitted right in with this mixture, and they could play their set of original songs both in rock clubs and in art venues. When they were playing in CBGB, the rock club in Manhattan's downtrodden Lower East Side, Byrne recalls he "would be excited if some of the artists whose work I knew at the time showed up, whether it was Vito Acconci, or Joseph Kosuth, or Dennis Oppenheim, Andy Warhol. It was somehow exciting, but I often didn't get to meet them. They were interested in what we were doing musically, and I was interested in what they were doing in galleries and publications. There was some kind of connection."[7] In 1976, Talking Heads also played concerts in The Kitchen, an art venue in the SoHo district that had in the 60s been the epicenter of artistic experimentation. The Kitchen was dedicated to the alternative performance arts, to experimental music, dance, theater, video, and performance art. In The Kitchen's catalogue for 1976, Talking Heads described their act in the analytical and anti-individualistic terms that conceptual art had brought into vogue:

> a group of performing artists whose medium is rock-and-roll and the pursuant "band" organization and visual presentation. The original music and lyrics are structured within the commercial accessibility of rock-and-roll sound and contemporary, popular language. Lead singer Byrne relies on Chris Frantz and Tina Weymouth to complete their anti-individualist stance as a group concept.[8]

Some of the reasons for this balancing act, half inside and half outside popular music, must also be sought in the developments in the rock scene. In the mid-1970s, the mythology that had come into being in the 1960s, when rock music symbolized personal authenticity and was a gripping vehicle for protest against war, conventionality and consumerism, still held its power, and the singers and bands that had survived the turmoil were more popular than ever. But it was clear to everyone who wanted to see it that rock had become an industry in its own right, a sound and a fashion that was fully co-opted by the rest of the entertainment industry. Rock had become part of the TV culture, with its unprecedented capability to accommodate every kind of content and to strip it of all context.

During the first years of his work as songwriter and frontman of Talking Heads, Byrne's performances exerted a peculiarly strong fascination because he was engaged in two struggles. Singing and performing were in some respects an exerting task he set himself to overcome his crippling shyness and the awkward traits in his personality which he himself has later described as bordering on Asperger's syndrome, a disorder on the mild side of the autism spectrum.[9] His singing voice, not very trained or stable to begin with, would often get choked up or squeaky, and at other times he would make his voice go from singing to declamation, and from that to outright shouting. As a performer, Byrne forced himself through an emotional bottleneck, using concerts as an opportunity for self-fashioning, the urgency of which could be riveting to the audience.

And at the same time, Byrne's work with Talking Heads was a prolonged wrestling match with the cultural force of television, fighting its domination. The tradition of television is complex, fragmented and filled with contradictions; a training to accept untruths and contradictions without further ado. The capacity to understand, accept and even revel in the attractive and disruptive flow, including its superficiality and hypocrisy, is in itself a crucial part of this tradition, a cultural force that is not to be neglected. Against this background, Byrne's statement "I want to be both outside my culture and my society and be part of them. I want to be a part of popular culture . . . to swim in the great river of shit but somehow not get any on me"[10] must be understood to have methodological value. A central quality of Byrne's work is the ongoing struggle not to project a false security.

Byrne had addressed the lure of TV in his work even before he helped found Talking Heads (the band took its name from TV cameramen jargon for close-ups of people's heads): in art school, he made a transcript of the TV quiz show "The Price Is Right" to read out aloud in coffeehouses. Many of the songs that Byrne wrote for Talking Heads have the TV as their subject. The most outspoken is perhaps "Television Man" (of the album *Little Creatures*), which sums up the overwhelming influence of the medium in the formulaic sentence "The world crashes in, into my living room: television made me what I am." This is sung to a tune that is so simple and catchy, so warm and plain as to invite everyone who hears it to join in and sing along, and the subtle choir of backing vocals assures us that we are welcome. People's intimate cultural exchanges with television are the subject of more lyrics, as in Byrne's "Make Believe Mambo" (1989): "So how can we be strangers / He's got no personality / It's just a clever imitation / Of the people on TV."[11]

Byrne has returned time and again to this theme. In 2005, he made an incisive comment in response to Werner Herzog's film *Grizzly Man*, a documentary about a man who lived the mistaken romantic notion that he could commune with grizzly bears, and as a result was killed and eaten by them. This man had used a video camera to film himself during his solitary encounters with bears, addressing the camera as if he were the presenter of a nature show. Writes Byrne:

> I wonder if there is afloat a strange notion that if one is adrift, lost, floundering in life, one can simply take on the persona of some imaginary TV personality and problem solved. [. . .] Sometimes it seems that this mythical world validates the real world for many people — things are good and important depending on how much they conform to the TV reality.[12]

The intuitive attractions, and the potentially overwhelming reality of the ongoing mimetic and sentimental exchange between the individual and TV (as symbol of the patchwork of industrially processed cultures) form Byrne's subject matter.

3 MYTHOLOGY AND METHODOLOGY

Talking Heads were a very successful band, with a career that developed steadily from small clubs to bigger venues and on to rock festivals and mega concerts in sports arenas. This means they became fully part of the rock mythology, where every aspect of a performance is enlarged and takes on symbolic meanings in which the audience takes part. At the same time the band, but especially Byrne, held on to the conceptual program of *methodological* creativity. All four members of Talking Heads — Frantz (drums), Weymouth (bass), and Byrne (vocals, guitar) had invited Jerry Harrison (guitar and keyboards) to join them before recording their first album — had a background in the arts and were open to experiments.

During the 1970s, Byrne was reading a lot of systems theory and cybernetics: books by Norbert Wiener, Stafford Beer, Gregory Bateson, and others. He tried to integrate their analytical and methodical approach into his art, into his conceptual pieces of writing and diagrams as well as into his songs.[13] This led to a fruitful collaboration with fellow musician and music producer Brian Eno, whose own trajectory in art and popular music was guided by remarkably similar interests. Indeed, Eno's conceptual and cybernetics-based approach to the recording and composing of rock music would act as a catalyst on the development of Talking Heads' music.

Brian Eno's approach to musical composition is fundamentally influenced by cybernetic management theory. Whether he acts as producer for other rock acts, makes his own rock albums, works as a theorist, or composes music that is definitely not rock, Eno applies principles of decision and control that have been developed by cybernetic thinkers. Stafford Beer, an innovative thinker and internationally recognized expert who was among the first to apply cybernetic theory to management, has had a crucial influence on Eno's work and thoughts. Beer's book *Brain of the Firm: The Managerial Cybernetics of Organization* provides a great deal of insight into Eno's artistic outlook, his "Oblique Strategies" and his use of the recording studio.

Eno theorized and practiced the use of the recording studio as a form of integrated management. Ideally, the recording process and the development of the music as well as the artistic impulses should all be controlled by one and the same structure. In one sense, this was a continuation of the increasingly prominent role of the recording studio in rock music, a prominence that can be heard in Phil Spector's "Wall of Sound" productions and in George Martin's work with the Beatles. But Eno emphatically brought a cybernetic perspective to the studio and to music. Stafford Beer had written that "the major thread unraveled by management cybernetics is the thread of variety — its generation and proliferation, its reduction and amplification, its filtering and control."[14] Following in Beer's footsteps, Eno proclaimed, in a 1976 article titled "Generating and Organizing Variety in the Arts," that this was precisely the task of the artist. Beer, a romantic anarchist at heart, proclaimed that the controller has to be part of the system under control, not a higher authority outside the system.[15] Throughout *Brain of the Firm*, Beer warns against social and cultural patterns that become traps, and against human beings who become parodies of themselves through overspecialization and because of too much introspection.[16] Eno sought for ways of composing music in the studio that would be anti-hierarchical, and wished to avoid fixed hierarchic patterns in his approach to music by using the studio as an instrument to generate new musical hybrids.

As a result, Eno used the recording studio in a manner that was the reverse of a dominant trend in 70s rock. In orchestral rock as well as in heavy metal, multi-track recording equipment was used basically to add more of the same: to flesh out already existing songs with more and more musical layers, swelling the personae that the songs projected into pompous dimensions. Opposing all that, Eno preferred to work in a way that avoided or even erased a single domineering musical personality.[17] When he collaborated with David Bowie on his albums *Low* and *Heroes*, for example, he encouraged Bowie to let go of his set persona of the glam-rock star, recording a good number of tracks that were not songs, and did without the focus that singing provides. In his own music, Eno developed the notion of "ambient music," an atmospheric or environmental music without defined focus. He was convinced that it was possible to make a form of mood music that would retain enough idiosyncratic qualities to avoid the numbing quality of "muzak," familiar songs that have been re-arranged to leave out everything that could be disturbing or unusual.[18] Another aspect of Eno's approach was an interest in treating every aspect of music as though it was just a "found object" (like Marcel Duchamp's famous notion of the "*objet trouvée*"), as that would set the composer free to reorganize the given material.

Eno wasn't very interested in writing songs that projected a strong emotion, a persona, and only rarely played live. But working with Eno as their producer, Talking Heads gradually developed an approach to the composing and recording of songs that straddled the paradoxical combination of strong emotional personae with the anti-mythological methodology that he brought to recording and songwriting. Talking Heads' album *Remain in Light* of 1980 stands out as the main result of this collaboration.

While recording *Remain in Light*, Talking Heads welcomed Eno's idea that the fixed hierarchy of instruments in rock should be abandoned. In the musical ranking that Eno saw as outmoded, bass and drums are at the bottom, rhythm guitar and piano are in the middle, while lead guitar and especially vocals stand at the top, where the lead vocal dominates, only to keep silent when a guitar solo is due. Abandoning this model, Eno put forward the approach to rock that had been pioneered by the Velvet Underground. In Eno's words, the Velvets "used all of their instruments in the rhythm role almost and the singing is a deliberate monotone, which is a deliberate non-surprise, so when you listen to the music your focus is shifting all the time because there's no ranking, which doesn't only reflect the internal structure of the music, but also the structure of your attention to it."[19] All these methods and ideas went into the recording of *Remain in Light*. Eno and Talking Heads focused on patterns of small rhythmic elements, recording layer by layer until a new texture emerged, which could then be developed further while the original layers could be erased, a ladder that could be thrown away once it had been climbed.

Just as important was an experiment that Byrne and Eno did together with 'found vocals'. They taped voices they heard on American radio, and borrowed vocals from recordings of Lebanese and Arabian singers. All these vocals had specific emotional qualities that were highlighted by isolating and repeating the most significant fragments. The resulting vocal tracks could be combined with layers of small rhythmic motifs and sonic gestures to produce a new kind of "song." Byrne and Eno began this joint experiment before the recording of *Remain in Light*, but their album would be released after the Talking Heads album, as *My Life in the Bush of Ghosts*. The latter album can't be classified as rock music. *My Life in the Bush of Ghosts* lacks the focus of a single unifying voice, the lyrics do not outline a persona in a situation that allows for emotional identification, and the music isn't organized in a chorus-and-verse pattern. Later, the working method that Eno and Byrne established for this album would often be mentioned as influential for all kinds of music that was based on assemblage, from DJ tracks and sampling to so-called "plunderphonics." For the recording of the album that would become *Remain in Light*, Byrne and Eno introduced this process of using tape tracks as a medium for collage and composition to the other members of Talking Heads. Byrne did not want to write songs and take them to the band for rehearsals and further developing; he proposed that the rehearsals should not be rehearsals of songs, but a way to sharpen their skills at composing through collective improvisation: "one person coming up with something, somebody else coming up with a part that rhythmically locks in with it."[20]

But to make a Talking Heads album, it followed that Byrne had to come up with lyrics and with a style of singing that would add emotional relevance to the recorded tracks without stamping them with a single dominant personality, as that would undo the point of the exercise. For that purpose he wrote collages of texts for which he used material from highly diverse sources. He included phrases picked up from radio preachers across the U.S.A.; a record of John Dean's testimony for the Watergate trial hearings; a record of ex-slaves telling their stories; newspaper headlines; and quotations from books that he found inspiring.

Together with Eno, he reconsidered the relationship of his singing to the music. Where he had created dramatic tension in his songs for Talking Heads' previous albums by changing the music underneath the sung melody, he now had to find another device to communicate the drama and the emotions of his vocals, because the densely woven rhythmic tracks basically repeated root patterns over and over again. Their solution was to use complex vocal arrangements, group vocals and vocals that go on top of other vocals. Moreover, they decided to add instrumental solos that weave in and out of the rhythmic pattern. The results resemble rock songs, but the album's signature tracks (the first five tracks on the album, "Born Under Punches (The Heat Goes On)," "Crosseyed And Painless," "The Great Curve," "Once In A Lifetime," and "Houses In Motion") present a combination of emotional perspectives instead of the single emotion that is typical for rock music. The effect of this, combined with the dense roiling rhythms and the disruptive instrumental solos, was startling. Where Eno had declared lyrics and vocal persona to be mostly superfluous to music, Byrne had reintroduced persona as a collage, an ongoing exchange that could be full of internal stress and strife. *Remain in Light* stands to regular rock songs as cubism stands to impressionism: there is still a recognizable subject, a persona to the songs, but it is approached from several perspectives simultaneously.

When *Remain in Light* was released, Brian Eno and David Byrne put together a small bibliography, which they added to the press material. They hoped the list would stimulate interviewers and make the press sessions more genuinely interesting. They had both read these books, and wanted to make clear that their influence had been important during the recording process. This is the list:

- John Miller Chernoff: *African Rhythm and African Sensibility. Aesthetics and Social Action in African Musical Idioms.* University of Chicago Press, 1979.
- Robert Farris Thompson: *African Art in Motion. Icon and Act.* University of California Press, 1974.
- Christopher Alexander: *The Timeless Way of Building.* Oxford University Press, 1979, together with:

- Christopher Alexander and others: *A Pattern Language. Towns, Buildings, Construction*. Oxford University Press, 1977.

While all these books — scholarly treatises published by some of the most respected academic publishers — are about forms of art and aesthetics, none of them deals with rock, or even with popular music in general. Their authors are an ethnomusicologist who studied traditional African drumming for ten years (Chernoff), an art historian specialized in African and Afro-American art (Thompson), and a professor of architecture who also holds a degree in mathematics (Alexander). Their books all share an approach to the arts from a point of view that is a far cry from the individualism of modern Western art. Not one of them is directly applicable to anything that goes on in the modern recording studio. What they have in common is the application, across cultures, of a focus on the many layers of contextual interaction that have to go together to produce a richly satisfying artistic result, whether that be music and dance, sculpture, or architecture. Each of the authors in his own way distrusts the capacities of any single artist working in isolation to replace an outmoded tradition, as it were singlehandedly, with a new design, a new form, that would still be able to accommodate as many complex circumstances as its predecessor.

To be able to play the layered rhythmic textures of *Remain in Light* on stage, Talking Heads expanded from a rock quartet to an ensemble of nine musicians, inviting experienced funk musicians to join them for concerts. Byrne was enthusiastic about this transformation of Talking Heads:

> "For me, there's more of a feeling of community — a group of people working and playing together. The kind of thing we're doing now deals with a different series of metaphors than pop music . . . The nature of the music is to inspire a mystical communion among the musicians and the audience through repetitive rhythms and so on. On a good night, it can become a transcendent experience that is mainly to do with a lot of people feeling that they're locking together and fitting together into one thing which is very different from the other music."[21]

Byrne also worked on developing gestural equivalents to the vocal collages of *Remain in Light*. He selected and imitated body movements and gestures of preachers and of persons who enter into a trance state. He then worked with choreographer and dancer Toni Basil to formulate the spasms and abrupt jolts and twitches into a dance that remained at midpoint between dance and muscular spasms, more a form of acting than of dancing per se.[22] He used elements of this repertoire of movements when singing live on stage, and included both this dance and some of the sources that had inspired it in a video clip for the song "Once In A Lifetime." Byrne and Basil had visited the anthropological film collection of the University of California in Los Angeles to study footage of dancers from different cultures, as well as preachers and people in trance. The clip for "Once In A Lifetime" includes footage from Peggy Harper's *Studies in Nigerian Dance 2*, which is shown in the background while in the foreground Byrne, costumed somewhat stiffly in suit and tie plus spectacles, makes similar movements.

As a visual equivalent to the tracks of *My Life in the Bush of Ghosts*, with their use of found vocals, Byrne invited experimental filmmaker Bruce Conner to make clips to accompany two tracks. Conner was known for making films that used only existing film footage, and he sometimes filmed the television. In his montage, Conner worked with repetition, ironic combinations, and juxtapositions. He included "meaningless" sequences in his films, such as the countdown that precedes feature films and alternating pure white and black film cells, which undermine a stable interpretation and add a certain taste of bitterness and wry distance.

All this demonstrates how Byrne developed a methodology that was able to communicate a very complex sensibility. While this method undermines surface identity and persona, it also constitutes personal identity as a field for investigation and heightened sensibility, because it conceives of such an identity as a potentially changing pattern, an assemblage to which elements may be added or removed. Because of this very basic and far-reaching point of departure, it can be applied to songwriting, singing, acting, dancing, filmmaking; in short, every art form that is to do with personality and its transformations. And yet, in its very loose combination of such sources as cybernetic management theory and the ethnomusicological study of West-African drumming, of technology and tradition, there are paradoxical aspects and contradictions to all this as well. In other words, when *Remain in Light* was released, Byrne had developed an unusually rich mixture of thematic, method and sensibility, which he could develop in many directions. His resulting portfolio of work is unusually diverse, so that a brief overview is in order.

To a considerable part of his audience, Byrne is first and foremost the singer and songwriter of Talking Heads. With Talking Heads, Byrne developed from the singer of new wave rock songs that by all means refused to emulate the emotional bathos of "classic rock," into the frontman of a band that was capable of creating the musical euphoria that was captured on film in *Stop Making Sense*, the highly successful concert documentary that was released in 1984. From there, Byrne went on to include country, gospel and Americana in his self-directed feature film *True Stories* (1986). With Talking Heads, he also made albums that emulated television pop and country and western (*Little Creatures*,

1985) and African popular music (*Naked*, 1989). As a solo artist, after Talking Heads stopped functioning as a band, Byrne recorded and toured with an orchestra that played Latin songs, and later continued to record and tour under his own name. As a solo artist, Byrne played his older songs as well as new songs that freely combined all the styles he had tried his hand at, including Brazilian pop and the new styles in dance and R&B. He collaborated on incidental songs with musicians working in many different genres, and toured regularly with his own band.

Parallel to his work in Talking Heads, Byrne entered in collaborations with other artists. He worked with a number of choreographers, filmmakers and theater directors. For choreographer Twyla Tharp, he made a score for a full-length ballet, *The Catherine Wheel* (1981). Several film directors, including Bruce Connor and Jim Jarmusch, made video clips for songs by Talking Heads or by Byrne/Eno; Jonathan Demme directed *Stop Making Sense*. Next to this busy schedule, in the 1980s Byrne also found time to work on two productions by Robert Wilson, avant-garde theater director, and to contribute music to a film by the experimental theater group Mabou Mines.

From the mid-1990s on, Byrne began to exhibit photography and other pieces in galleries and museums. The conceptual aspect of his art is brought out to its fullest in the art books he makes, where he combines photographs, diagrams and drawings with writing. Byrne is also the author of a number of occasional essays, and of numerous forewords for books by other artists. In 2004, he began to publish a journal on the internet, of which many longer entries may be considered essays in their own right. All in all, Byrne is an author and an artist, as well as a musician and singer-songwriter.

Next to all this, Byrne performed several other roles in the art world. In 1988, he started a small record label, Luaka Bop, which was successful in introducing popular genres and artists from all over the world to a Western audience. In 1989, Byrne directed a television documentary, *Ilé Aiyé: The House of Life*, about the music and rituals of Candomblé, a syncretistic religion that combines African polytheism with Catholic elements in Bahía, Brazil. This led Robert Farris Thompson, a Yale professor of art history and highly respected Africanist and ethnographer, to declare that Byrne is as much an ethnographer as he is an artist. Byrne also presented a season of the live music public television show *Sessions at West 54th*. Working as artist and curator, he has installed several public installations, as well as a small show on politicians as represented in news photography. Byrne is also a fellow of the New York Institute of the Humanities. This overview is by no means complete, but it gives a good impression of the diversity of Byrne's endeavors and the richness of his portfolio as singer and artist.

4 CONCEPTUAL ROMANTICISM

Because of this wide range of activities and perspectives, which seem to neglect the distance between mass media entertainment and high art theoretical perspectives, Byrne has often been designated a postmodern artist. He has even been singled out as "the preeminent deconstructive artist," "more so than Baudrillard,"[23] just as Talking Heads have been labeled "a properly postmodernist band."[24] Such theoretical and philosophical concepts can be important guidelines for the interpretation of an artistic body of work, which is why this introduction cannot avoid a discussion of the merits of "postmodernism": it is too restrictive a label for Byrne's work, which can only be properly understood in terms of the longer and more encompassing tradition of Romanticism. Both terms are most often used in a very vague sense, which means that some defining distinctions are in order.

Before the relevance of the distinction can be made clear, it has to be underlined that Byrne works may be characterized as that of a composer, not in the sense of the classical composer who produces written music scores, but in the contemporary sense of an artist who juxtaposes styles of performance, forms of pleasure, verbal and non-verbal "languages" in his pieces. Byrne's work is located at an imaginary intersection where performance styles mingle and clash, and where it is impossible to distinguish once and for all between high art and popular entertainment, between sophisticated and commercial, between primitive and modern, or between the politically relevant and the purely artistic. It always refers to, and belongs to, more than one performative tradition, which means that it can be interpreted from several perspectives. This produces ironic effects: a tradition is evoked together with a distancing comment on that tradition. But the irony goes together with compassion and even with an understanding for the enthusiasm that an involvement in tradition evokes, which distinguishes Byrne's work from postmodernism and post-structuralism as such.

Next to the art student's natural interest in the history of avant-gardism in the twentieth century, plus systems theory, cybernetics and conceptual art, Byrne has woven a number of other approaches to art and culture into his work. Of these, ethnography (or cultural anthropology) has already been mentioned. Next to that, Byrne acquainted himself with comparative mythology, dipping into Sir James Frazer's *The Golden Bough* and reading the more recent books by Joseph Campbell, as well as Carl Gustav Jung's psychoanalytical theories about the inevitable mythological or archetypical aspects of the human personality.

On top of that, Byrne's work and writing shows a steadfast interest in the evolutionary perspective on human behavior and on psychological phenomena, an interest that ranges from ethology and sociobiology in the 1970s to more recently neuroscience and its application to the cognitive psychology of music. These perspectives, with their emphasis on what comes naturally to all human beings, distinguish Byrne's work from the one-sided emphasis on texts and codes that is characteristic of postmodernism: after all, there is no human involvement in culture, no enthusiasm or mimetic exchange that exists completely independent from these natural foundations.

Postmodern theorizing bases its theoretical structures on the notions of signs and text, and its foundation is the idea that signs have no natural relationship to anything outside themselves. This allows postmodern authors to stand aside from the contagious stream of modern culture, shaped as it is in many respects by the suggestive force of technological mass media, the endless stream of reproductions of images, sounds, and music. The postmodern credo is Jacques Derrida's resolutely exorbitant methodological postulate: "There is nothing outside of the text."[25] While this may perhaps make room for a radical reflection on the conditions of contemporary culture, it does nothing to help with a reflection on the qualities of mimesis, enthusiasm and feeling, the many crucially important non-verbal components of culture.

Ernst Gombrich has written an elegant rebuttal of the trend to remove mimesis, the imitation of nature, from the discussion of art, and replacing it by an unparalleled degree of semiotic abstraction. In a recent preface to his well-known study *Art and Illusion*, Gombrich writes: "It seems to me a little rash to assert that what you do not like does not exist — after all, it was precisely in this century that what we call the 'entertainment industry' became [. . .] the provider of illusions, and pursued this aim systematically and with increasing success." He continues: "people had been enchanted with their black-and-white television sets, but the more they became habituated to its images, the more they were apparently captivated by the addition of colour that approximates the image even more closely to reality."[26] Gombrich then points to the improvements in the reproduction of music, from the old horned gramophone to stereo and CD and beyond. His point is that psychological factors remain of the essence.

A closely related critique of postmodernism has been formulated by anthropologist and performance scholar Michael Taussig, who writes: "Postmodernism has relentlessly instructed us that reality is artifice yet, so it seems to me, not enough surprise has been expressed as to how we nevertheless get on with living, pretending — thanks to the mimetic faculty — that we live facts, not fictions."[27] Taussig points out that mimesis is the crossroads where history and human nature meet. It is human nature to adapt, to become socialized and adult, by copying the model of the environment. This means that identities are constructed, as the theories of social construction of reality tell us. But academic conclusions that "sex is a social construction," "race is a social construction," "the nation is an invention," and so forth do not answer the pertinent question "How come culture appears so natural?"[28] As Taussig writes:

> thanks to new social conditions and new techniques of reproduction (such as cinema and mass production of imagery), modernity has ushered in a veritable rebirth, a recharging and retooling of the mimetic faculty . . . it seems to me that we are forthwith invited if not forced into the inner sanctum of mimetic mysteries where, in imitating, we will find distance from the imitated and hence gain some release form the suffocating hold of "constructionism" no less than the dreadfully passive view of nature it upholds.[29]

The arguments of Gombrich and Taussig may well be accepted as evidence that modernism and postmodernism have not been very successful in constructing a theory of culture that is based on abstraction and encoding. We are stuck, as it were, in a culture that is still intuitive and emotional. Our culture is still romantic, and a single evening spent in front of the television, with its romantic comedy and sitcoms, news shows, Hollywood films, reality shows, and commercials, will produce all the material needed to prove that human psychology has not moved beyond its natural propensities. This popular Romanticism is the culture in which Byrne swims, and by which he would rather not be too contaminated. He has pointed out the ongoing importance of Romanticism as the foundation of a lot of art and music, even while it may seem corny. "We still work from those [Romantic] assumptions, even though we might try to throw them off."[30]

Working as an artist, not a scholar, Byrne is free to neglect the disciplinary boundaries that are so important in academic life; he can cross over between genres of popular music just as he can cross over between Jungian psychology and neuroscience, or between cybernetics and comparative mythology. Over the years, he has shown an extraordinary gift for bringing to bear such approaches, as different as they may be, in his work. What all of them have in common is that they move away from the notion of a fixed centre that determines a cultural phenomenon or a personality, replacing it by an emphasis on sensibilities that are always capable of development, of change and of mimetic exchange. And that is precisely what Byrne's work has in common with the best of the Romantic legacy.

This means that Romanticism should not be reduced to the tired cliché that holds that the Romantic artist can only express his own subjective identity. Early Romantic art is in many respects the most interesting Romantic art, and it is the attempt, in the words of art historians Rosen and Zerner, "to evade the traditional distinctions between major and minor genres, between tragedy and comedy, between the sublime and the ordinary, between art and the worlds of nature and human affairs."[31] Romanticism is a permanent revolution, not a single artistic mirror of the world, but "a multiplication of mirrors," an instable and variable understanding of words, styles and actions, a progressive destruction of the distinctions between genres[32] — all of which goes for Byrne's work as well.

It is important to distinguish sharply between this early, critical and self-reflexive Romanticism and later forms of Romanticism, as epitomized by Wagner's operas and continued in Wagnerian Hollywood productions, which do not overcome the distinction between genres but simply inflate one genre, one form of symbolism, in the totalizing attempt to overcome all others. It is this later Romanticism that has given Romanticism its unhappy connotations of artistic, and often also nationalistic and chauvinistic, bathos and sentimentality, a mythologizing that doesn't leave any room for critical exchange.

The most theoretically outspoken strand of early Romanticism is the early German Romanticism of Friedrich Schlegel, Novalis, and their circle of poets and philosophers. Some recent scholars of conceptual art have pointed out the important similarities between conceptualism and this critical version of Romanticism, coining the term "romantic conceptualism" to stress this connection. Sol LeWitt's "Sentences on Conceptual Art," printed in the first issue of *Art-Language*, may be quoted in this context: "Conceptual artists are mystics rather than rationalists, they leap to conclusions that logic cannot reach."[33] To connect conceptual art with the Romantic ideas of the fragment as an impulse and of creative intersubjective exchange as a model, the practice of conceptual art has to be valued as a way to produce new possibilities.[34]

This "conceptual Romanticism," stimulating creative exchange across divisions of genre and culture, is the best model to interpret the work of David Byrne, which repeatedly crosses borders between religious and profane musical genres, between scientific and mythical experiences of reality, to develop their exchange, their reciprocal contributions to our understanding of reality. His cross-genre covers, in music as well as in films and in writing, imitate and exchange impulses where classical standards of art and culture forbid it. The model of such exchanges may be expressed as a clarifying dialogue: "I am just like you, because I imitate you; but now that I imitate you, it becomes even clearer than before how different I am." And this is reciprocated and mirrored by: "Now that you imitate me, I see myself anew."

To explain what this implies, a more detailed exposition of the premises of early German Romanticism is in order. The early Romantics developed an innovative critique of art by opening up the artwork from within to make place for language games, irony and indirect communication, combined with a sharp polemic against aesthetic absolutism. Compared to this attitude, many later artistic and aesthetic movements seem overly simple and ideological in their pretensions that a symbolic unity may be attained.[35] This Romanticism was developed in the few years from 1795 to 1801 by a small group of young poets, writers and thinkers who were excited by the new possibilities that opened up in the arts, in philosophy, and in politics. The brothers Friedrich and August Wilhelm Schlegel, with their friends Novalis, Schleiermacher, Tieck and Wackenroder, felt at that time that drastic innovations in the domain of language and art, feeling, morality, and religion were within reach, while the developments of the French Revolution were going on and the innovative ideas of the Enlightenment seemed to be suddenly implemented in history.

The work of these early Romantics is characterized by recent scholars, such as Andreas Michel and Assenka Oksiloff, as an "aesthetic turn":

> It is their express desire to confound, and thus break open, established lines of demarcation between philosophy and art, between science and morality. In their pursuit of an eternal poiesis, they do not so much posit art as the crowning achievement and overcoming of reflexive thought; rather, they regard aesthetics as a merging of the finite and the infinite; they engage in the "gay science" of mixing and relating the most heterogeneous discourses at their proposal.[36]

A fine example of this mixing of discourses can be found in a short anonymous text that reads like a manifesto for critical Romanticism.[37] It proclaims "overthrow of all superstition, persecution of the priesthood that recently has been feigning reason, through reason itself," and proclaims its conviction that "the highest act of reason is an aesthetic act, in that reason embraces all ideas," to conclude:

> At the same time, we hear so often that the masses must have a *sensuous religion*. Not only the masses, but also the philosopher is in need of it. Monotheism of reason and of the heart, polytheism of imagination and of art, that is what we need!
>
> First, I will speak of an idea that, as far as I know, has not yet occurred to anyone — we must have a new mythology, but this mythology must serve ideas, it must become a mythology of *reason*.
>
> Until we make ideas aesthetic, that is, mythological, they are of no interest to the *people* and, conversely, until mythology is reasonable, the philosopher must be ashamed of it. Thus, in the end, enlightened and unenlightened must shake hands, mythology must become philosophical, and the people reasonable, and philosophy must become mythological in order to make the philosophers sensuous.

The search that connected the early Romantics with the philosophers of their period was the wish for a correct description of subjectivity. Such a description was meant to provide, at one go, a solid foundation for metaphysical, scientific, political, and aesthetic insight. At this crucial point, the early Romantics substituted sensibility and style for the mathematical and logical chains of reasoning of Enlightenment and rationalist philosophy. They brought issues to the foreground that had been neglected by enlightened rationalism: historical experience, individual peculiarities of language, culture, artistic styles, religious experience, and the realm of the emotions. Especially Friedrich Schlegel and Novalis produced a stream of philosophical fragments, studies, essays, poems, novels, as well as literary studies and translations. Their works are tied together loosely by an ongoing series of crossovers between the subjective and the objective, resulting in the mutual permeating of opposing aspects of experience.

Schlegel and Novalis opposed the absolutist accounts of subjectivity that had been provided by modern philosophers from Descartes to Kant. They developed an alternative account of the foundation of consciousness by concentrating on the pivotal role of aesthetic experience: not as an ornamental and beautifying addition to rational certainty, but as the only self-sufficient basis for a philosophical subjectivity. They assumed that human consciousness may obtain immediate knowledge of itself not through some special philosophical form of self-insight, as their friend and philosophical mentor Fichte had argued, but simply in the process of every aesthetic experience. And they gladly accepted the implication that this subjectivity could not be absolute, did not have a special foundation within itself, and in no way resembled the Cartesian "cogito," the thinking self that provides a firm anchor to the life of the mind. They gave up that ideal for a vision of subjectivity as floating. Novalis wrote of human consciousness: "The whole rests somewhat like the players of a game in which people sit in a circle without chairs, one resting upon the other's knee."[38] The foundation of subjectivity is not to be found in an analysis or a self-perception of the thinking self, but beyond it: in a feeling, a spirit or a belief that precedes and accompanies consciousness. Art may help to illuminate the origins of subjectivity, but its illumination will always remain an interpretation, and never result in absolute and final knowledge.

Style may reveal indirectly what cannot be explained logically and systematically, using irony and allegory; philosophy has to turn to poetry to fulfill its purpose. Romanticism has accordingly been defined as "the philosophy which in its speculations abandons the pretension to reach the absolute by reflection, and which supplements this lack by the medium of art."[39] Novalis wrote: "Through the voluntary renunciation of the absolute, infinite and free activity arises within us. This activity is the only possible absolute that can be given to us and that we find through our inability to reach and recognize an absolute."[40] In philosophical terms, early Romanticism is neither a version of rationalism nor of absolute idealism, with its dialectic logic that is always able to conclude in a final synthesis, but an aesthetic that is moved by a "negative dialectic":[41] the insight that consciousness can never know itself absolutely, but only in fragments and flashes, and most clearly in the many mirrors of artworks.

Novalis and Schlegel embraced the complexity and confusion that are so typical of the aesthetic sensibility, declaring that "a good confusion has more value than a bad order,"[42] the more so since order is completed and stable, while confusion may, by means of self-enlightenment, lead to progress and further perfection.[43] Novalis expressed time and again, in many variations, that it is impossible to fixate subjectivity: "Man is . . . nothing fixed — He can and should be something determined and undetermined at the same time"; "Everything can be I and is I or should be I"; "Genius is perhaps only the result of such an inner plural"; "Man is actually *chaos*."[44] Subjective sensibility, as a part of nature, mixed up in manifold relationships, floating and free, is interpreted as a plurality and a unity at once: "genius" is the term the Romantics used to express this.[45]

According to Novalis, the human imagination as productive fantasy can relate and synthesize the most heterogeneous realms.[46] Kant, the great philosophical source of inspiration to these Romantics, had assumed that scientific knowledge is produced by the subject by the application of a fixed set of logical categories; but Novalis maintains that fiction, illusion and fantasy are the necessary means of all synthesis, that is, of all knowledge.[47] This synthesis takes place in art. Art is the representation of the inner condition of individual chaotic genius, and as such it is a crucial contribution to rationality, a form of enlightenment. In early Romantic philosophy, the value of poetry (as paradigmatic art form) is unparalleled, because poetry is the regenerative medium in which the misunderstandings and the self-ignorance of the subject may be realized and dissolved.[48] As such, art is the very precondition of rationality. Subjectivity, as a precondition of all knowledge, is not a fixed given, but a continuously developing condition. Art has the potential to develop subjectivity, to enable it to find itself, to help it recognize itself in the greatest possible diversity of phenomena. Art is not a vacation from the obligations of everyday life, but the opposite: it underpins all theoretical and ethical endeavors.

This evaluation of art differs so much from more conventional approaches that a few exemplary aspects of it require separate attention. If every act of knowing implies fiction and poetical activity, each element of knowledge becomes (at least poetically, fictionally) related to all other fields of knowledge. Novalis thought of this universal connectedness as "universal harmony," a notion that made him conceive of the different fields, disciplines, and human faculties as reciprocally illuminating each other.[49] This does not provide closure. Novalis accepted that the Golden Age of harmony would remain forever beyond reach, a project of which only fragments can be completed. "Novalis, very much like Friedrich Schlegel, conceives of the pursuit of his encyclopedic project and of magic idealism as a never-ending aesthetic activity."[50]

This project encouraged Schlegel and Novalis to experiment: they often ask of opposites to begin to resemble each other, thus inciting reality to become more harmonious than would seem possible. This procedure makes out the very heart of early Romanticism. A few quotations can help to make clear what is at stake here. Schlegel wrote that "[man and woman should] exchange roles and in childish high spirits compete to see who can mimic the other more convincingly."[51] And Novalis declared: "We naturally understand everything that is foreign only by *making* our self *foreign* — *changing our self* — observing our self;"[52] "The poet uses things and words like a keyboard and all of poesy is based on the active association of ideas — on self-activating, intentional, ideal production of chance — (chance — or free catenation)."[53] According to this theory, subjectivity at its best is in a state of flux,[54] able to experience a highly divergent and fragmented reality as if it were harmonious. Early Romanticism provides a model of aesthetic experience as participation: participation of the arts in each other, of mankind in the arts and of man in nature, etc. Making art is a playful intermingling and imitating: it is thus impossible to delineate "the" Romantic artwork. Romantic art is both imitation, which means a following of rules and the acceptance of genres of representation, and the production of new rules, the establishment of new forms, the conventions of the future. The two are inseparable.

Just as the early Romantics thought of the mimetic capacity as potentially endless, they also considered every work of art as a single reflection within the infinite medium of art. Every artwork is by definition preliminary and fragmentary: the process of reflexivity that has been condensed in the work of art deserves to be continued. The very fact that the work of art embodies a series of reflections is what gives the work its dignity, its positive value, because, according to romantic theory, "reflection does not take its course into an empty infinity, but is in itself substantial and filled."[55] In other words: the early Romantics systematically thought of artworks as reflections on the traditions of artistic production, and realized that no artwork alone embodies a complete and fulfilled tradition. Therefore, every work of art by definition has its shortcomings, its unfulfilled promises, its rough edges. The more artworks demonstrate their own fragmentary character of unfinished (and therefore ongoing) reflexivity, the greater their dignity. This does not mean that the early Romantics disliked well-rounded, finished works. But they did insist that even an immaculately formed work of art is but a stage in an ongoing reflexive process. Instead of opposing critique to art, in early Romantic theory the two are identified with each other.

Schlegel and Novalis were well aware that this philosophy of art has mystical traits. It "is a mystical . . . pervasive idea, driving us ceaselessly in all directions."[56] It dissolves the subject by emphasizing the reality of reflection over the reality of physical personal identity. As Schlegel wrote, "everything is in us . . . we are only a part of ourselves."[57] No specific form or genre is prescribed; everything can be freely mingled. Artistic reflection may freely choose its point of departure, its content and its materials, and develop its own mimetic rules. This philosophical Romanticism is quite different from the widespread notion of Romantic art as the free expression of the personality, the arbitrary subjectivity of the artist.[58]

This summary overview of early German Romanticism has to suffice here to give an impression of what is meant by "conceptual Romanticism," with its specific perspective on the Romantic themes of irony and authenticity, community and imagination.[59] Their relevance can be seen throughout Byrne's work. Because of its free mingling of the mythologies of rock and other musical genres with the theorizing of conceptual art, and with the latest scientific notions about human consciousness, it can be described as an "emotional epistemology," a term found in the title of one of his books, *Envisioning Emotional Epistemological Information*. It is another way to describe the underlying, truly Romantic notion that informs all of Byrne's work, which is that the logic of art, especially of songs, is the best approach to understand the world we live in.[60]

5 THE METHOD OF THIS BOOK

The method of this book reflects the free-floating ongoing exchange that characterizes Byrne's work. *Everything Is Connected* is the title of one of his art pieces; *Sea of Possibilities* is another.[61] This is what characterizes the work: a song is often elaborated in the form of a video clip, or leads to a story, or connects with a book, or a documentary project, and such influences also run the other way round. Byrne's work is like the autobiography of an Everyman, where everything that appears on television may make an appearance. Even details that seem at first totally unrelated may later become relevant. An example is Byrne's remark in his introduction to his book *True Stories*: "The new patriotism is also a trick. It's a real frightening, scary trick that everyone wants so badly to believe is true."[62] This diatribe follows some lighthearted insights into the nature of storytelling and filmmaking, and it isn't really elaborated anywhere in *True*

Stories or in the film of the same name, but it is intimately connected to Byrne's later opposition to the War in Iraq, and to the political nature of several of his more recent works, and certainly to many of the entries in the internet journal he has been publishing since 2004. A different example of Byrne's talent to see unexpected connections, almost chosen at random, is his original response when music videos suddenly became an enormous popular success: he believed that "here, at last, was the vindication of the earlier, more obscure, avant-garde short filmmakers I admired: Bruce Conner, Maya Deren, Vanderbeek, Warhol . . . I could go on and on."[63]

"Everything Is Connected," however, can only be a recipe for chaos and disaster when it is taken too literally as a method to organize a book. Here, Byrne's work has been organized in chronological order, as that is the most obvious way to recount the history of influences and collaborations that have shaped it. Next to this chronology, the works are grouped by medium where it proved to be expedient, so that music, film and theater, art, and writing are each discussed in separate chapters — but only when this didn't do too much damage to the chronology.

In each chapter, the work is presented in combination with the dominant conceptual influences of that period. In many instances, a summary overview of these conceptual and theoretical subjects — fields as diverse as cybernetics, African traditional drumming and contemporary experimental theater — has been provided. In each instance, care has been taken to document the actual impact of such theories in the details of Byrne's art, whether it is in music, fine art, video, or writing. The result is an ordered mosaic, now showing the patterns from some distance, now closing in on the details in a single piece.

Throughout, the emphasis is on the work, not on Byrne's biography, even though life and work are related in so far as Byrne's work is a project of self-fashioning. Most of Byrne's songs are anything but autobiographical, but even so, singing them is an emotional and even transformational act; the voice is not activated by remote control, and Byrne has often stressed in interviews how singing is a deeply personal act for him. What this means will be revealed gradually, as the chapters of the book piece the mosaic together. And since Byrne's work finds its audience mostly through the mass media, in the mass-reproduced form of records and CDs, films and books, internet and TV, emphasis is on those works, not on individual drawings and sculptures, although they are taken into account.

In the course of the research for this book, I have benefitted from conversations and correspondence with David Byrne, as well as from access to his archives. I have also benefitted greatly from encounters and conversations with Yale Evelev of Luaka Bop, with Danielle Spencer and others at Todomundo, with

Robert Farris Thompson of Yale University, and with Lauren Panzo at Pace/MacGill Gallery. Throughout the book, I have also made use of the countless published interviews with Byrne.

The purpose of this book is to explain and document how Byrne's work evokes and reorganizes sensibilities. Each chapter highlights one facet of the many exchanges that Byrne's work encompasses, and its capacity to invite forms of reciprocal exchange. If the road through conceptual art theory and philosophy may appear to lead away from the sheer fun, confusion, shock and euphoria that Byrne's works evoke, its goal is to make the experience more lasting.

Chapter 1

Stripping Down Rock Songs

1 THE TENTATIVE REJECTION OF MIMESIS

David Byrne's mature work begins with Talking Heads, but the steady artistic development of Talking Heads grew out of a period of intense preparation. The many artistic and scientific developments that Byrne made his own have remained influential throughout his career. In the years he spent in art schools, and in the years before Talking Heads became successful, Byrne soaked up all kinds of art. He experimented with bands and with new and open ways of art making, such as performance art, conceptual art and video, and read widely, especially in conceptual art and in cybernetics.

Byrne was born in 1952 in Dumbarton, a small town near Glasgow in Scotland. His father was an electrical engineer, his mother trained later in life to become a teacher in special education. His parents emigrated, first to Canada, and in 1958 to the United States. From the second grade on, Byrne went to school in Baltimore, Maryland. Throughout junior high and high school, Byrne was in rock bands. playing mostly top 40 songs, and also performing solo, with a guitar or a ukulele. He had a passion for music, borrowed all kinds of records from the library, and started experimenting with music when he was about 15. He recorded lots of sounds onto tape, then cut up the tape more or less at random and spliced it together without knowing what order the sounds were in. He also made a version of the Turtles' song "Happy Together" with Tupperware tubs for drums. His father would help with primitive electronic effects and recording technology.

Thinking about a future profession, Byrne felt equally attracted to science and to art. He was admitted to both the prestigious Carnegie Mellon University[1] and the equally prestigious Rhode Island School of Design (RISD), and chose art over science more or less intuitively. Byrne would later explain his choice as "a) the graffiti in the halls was better and b) I wouldn't have to go through at least four years of boring shit before I had the opportunity to do anything bordering on the creative."[2] Byrne spent two years in art schools, one in RISD in Providence and one in the Maryland Institute's College of Art in Baltimore. Among other things, he studied the most influential methodology of modern art, the functional design program of the Bauhaus Theory Course. Rather that studying painting, he chose to work in the most contemporary media, making disposable Xerox art, collages from Polaroid snapshots, as well as questionnaires that he put together out of lists of statements that he collected. And he widened his artistic horizon, finding that

> anything could be art and art could be anything. The Velvet Underground, James Brown, Yoko Ono, John Coltrane, Charlie Manson, Federico Fellini, Jean-Luc Godard, Ingmar Bergman, William Burroughs, Andy Warhol, Vito Acconci, Dennis Oppenheim, Marcel Duchamp, Bruce Conner, ZAP Comics, The Hairy Who, Art & Language, Terry Riley, Superstudio, Norbert Weiner and Gregory Bateson, the Last Poets, Eldridge Cleaver, Robert Frank, Larry Clark, Tantric Art, Kool & the Gang, Luis Bunuel. I could go on and on.[3]

Not very impressed with what art schools offered to students to help them deal with this chaotic cultural landscape, Byrne chose to drop out.

The next few years he bummed around the country, stayed for a while in a hippie commune, formed a duo named Bizadi with a friend, Mark Kehoe (Kehoe played the accordion, Byrne ukulele and violin), made some art video tapes featuring people talking to the camera in various languages about American popular television programs, and one consisting of shots of suburban tract homes overlaid with taped phone conversations of him and his friends talking to their parents.[4] He finally decided to move to New York rather than to get back into school, to try and make an independent career for himself as an artist. In these years, Byrne was fascinated both by the strict version of conceptualism that was put forward by Art & Language, and by cybernetics, the interdisciplinary science of control and communication. It is as if he still had not really chosen between art and science, but tried to reconcile the two.

The Art & Language movement had been founded in 1968, simultaneously in England and New York. Byrne was fascinated by this work, and "thought it was the ultimate in eliminating all the superfluous stuff in art and being left with nothing but the idea."[5] The artists who formed Art & Language were determined to oppose the anti-intellectualism and the focus on heroic artistic personalities that had been associated with painting and sculpture during the 1950s and 60s.

According to them, the expressive and perceptual aspects, the "good looks" of art, were overvalued to the detriment of the more abstract presuppositions that were embodied in artworks. They undertook a Marxist-based critique of the gallery system, with its marketing and exploitation of the artistic personality, and tried to establish forms of art production and distribution that would not fit the regular gallery-and-museum system.

Art & Language was especially opposed to the traditional division of art from criticism. Instead of "illusionist" artworks, the group produced critical texts that combined a Marxist critique of society with a Wittgensteinian critique of language and representations.[6] Accordingly, the critical analysis of the consumption of art and culture was seen as the crucial task of the artist. Art, in this view, says nothing whatsoever about the personality of the artist; this is a likely source for the "anti-individualist stance as a group concept", which Talking Heads embraced in their statement for The Kitchen quoted in the Introduction above.

Most relevant for Byrne's work was Joseph Kosuth, who at first was closely associated with Art & Language. He had disengaged himself from the group by 1976, however, feeling that it had deteriorated into an orthodox Marxist-Leninist collective.[7] To distance himself from such straitlaced premises, Kosuth developed a wider theoretical perspective, as laid down in his essay "The Artist as Anthropologist."[8] This text is a mosaic of quotations, derived from two sources. The first of these is Martin Jay's *The Dialectical Imagination* (1973), a historical account of the unorthodox and self-reflexive Marxism of the so-called "Frankfurt School" philosophers: Max Horkheimer, Herbert Marcuse, Theodor W. Adorno and Walter Benjamin. His second source was an article by cultural anthropologist Bob Scholte: "Toward a Reflexive and Critical Anthropology" (1972). Scholte was part of a self-critical movement within anthropology that pointed to the many Western assumptions upon which anthropology has often been based, and stressed the need for a decolonization of anthropology.[9] Kosuth turned to Scholte's article to argue that art cannot give itself a foundation in the logical analysis of what it means to make art: instead, artists have to "explicate, as part of our activities, the intentional process of constitutive reasoning which make both encounter and understanding possible," and thus to enter into a hermeneutic exploration.[10]

In Byrne's own early attempts, conceptualism took the form of a distanced questioning of life and of the function of art in life. He would distribute questionnaires: one example asked the receiver to "write an *objective* account of every car accident in which you have been a participant. Each account should be about one or two paragraphs in length. Please concentrate your account(s) on the actual accident(s) and the events immediately surrounding

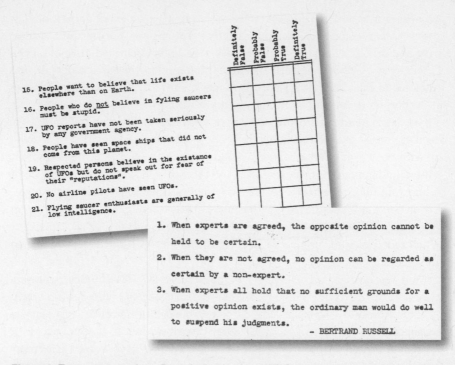

Figure 1 Two segments from Byrne's three-page *UFO Survey*, a conceptual piece from his year at the Rhode Island School of Design, 1970–71.

the accident(s)."[11] Another questionnaire consisted of a list of 21 statements about UFOs and belief in UFOs. This list was followed by a quote from the famous philosopher Bertrand Russell, a well-known summary of the skeptical position that Russell advocated.

Another piece from this period was titled *Number of Consecutive Days without Error*, with three slots in which one might put numbers, the idea being that one would come home from work at the end of the day and keep tabs on one's errors.[12] Artworks like these place their audience under the obligation to look at one's own life from a distance, with the complete detachment that is needed to judge one's accidents, errors, delusions, and prejudices objectively. This brings up the question: Is such detachment possible?

In 1975, Byrne helped an artist friend, Jamie Dalglish, who had the idea to borrow a black and white video deck to make a series of interviews.[13] Each video is a static shot of one artist in conversations with Byrne, who remained off-screen all the time, so that only his voice is heard. Byrne's part in these conversations documents his search for an art of complete honesty. In a talk with Jeff Koons (who, like Byrne, went to art school in Baltimore and could not at that time foresee his later career), Byrne tells about his conviction that art has to come across so long as it comes directly from the heart. When singing, he sometimes catches himself singing a phrase without full conviction, and then having to remedy that directly in the next word, putting himself under so much pressure that he is rushed with adrenaline. And in conversation with Vito Acconci, he explains how he finds himself caught between the impulse to become engaged in political matters and to make the world a better place, and the impulse to hack out some success for himself, and scrape his way to the top, a dilemma he doesn't know how to resolve. In other examples, he quizzes his partners in the conversation about the underlying meaning of such practicalities as furniture and fashion; what are the motives that people let themselves be guided by in their decisions to buy this rather than that?

Along these lines, Byrne was working on

"lists of statements that are thematic — statements about economics, about possibilities for the future, some of which are silly and some of which are serious. Lists about basic belief statements, not all of which I believed in, but I tried to think of and organize ones that people tend to build their lives around. Things they accept as given. I was just organizing things like that. Then I got further along to the point where I wanted to work out a sort of Nielsen rating system[14] for the visual arts, sort of cross-referencing between viewers and buyers and artists. It seemed very cold but I thought it would serve a function."[15]

Years after, in 1986, Byrne published a description of this system that deserves to be quoted at length:

When I moved to New York about 1974, [. . .] most of my time was spent working out ideas for what I called the "Nielsen Rating System for the Arts", the idea being to develop a system that would open up lines of communication between viewers and visual artists. It would work in two ways — the viewer would find out what sort of things were out there that affected and moved him or her . . . and the artists, in turn, could find out who they were talking to. If an artist would rather talk to someone else, then he or she could find out what that someone was interested in — and what kind of visual language to speak.

The whole system involved a lot of computer terminals, cross-referencing, answering multiple choice and yes/no questions, and checking true/false statements. Then, all of that information would go into a giant computer that everyone had access to, artists and viewers alike. This random selection of people would be asked questions like: What did they think visual art was for? . . . Why did they like straight lines better than squiggly lines? . . . Would they just as soon watch stuff on television? . . . Did they like art better in books or in museums? . . . Was making something ugly a way of making it romantic? . . . And so on.

In the back of my mind, I must have known that this whole system was kind of stupid and unworkable on the practical level, but on another level it did raise some interesting questions. For instance, are visual artists really interested in what the audience thinks? Do artists really believe that they are the antennae of society? Does the audience believe that? Does the audience hope the artists believe that?

The assumption behind this proposed system is that visual art has a practical and real value, that even decoration is not meaningless, and that somehow, through all this question asking and answering, the real value of this stuff to people's lives might emerge — art would turn into a product, a commodity in a kind of Marxist sense, as opposed to the current popular viewpoint in which art is valued as a rare one-of-a-kind jewel or as a religious icon, a unique expression of a savage soul. My assumption at the time was that one result of this system might be that art production would increase, and at the same time prices would drop. The visual artist might, in the course of using a system like this over a number of years, reach a wider and wider audience and do so without diluting the content or depth of his or her work.

A "functional but not craftlike" way of treating visual art might return folks to an attitude that existed in the very early part of the European medieval period — and still exists in much of the world — where such a heavy value is not placed on the individual experience. Sometimes there seems to be evidence of a slight return to this way of thinking, which might actually be a good thing . . . it might be the only way that a lot of people can live together.[16]

This shows how Byrne tried to integrate a conceptual approach with cybernetics.[17] He had eagerly read the work of Norbert Wiener, Stafford Beer, Gregory Bateson, and other scientists working in cybernetics, and their influence would be as lasting as the influence of conceptual art.

2   CYBERNETICS AS INSPIRATION

Cybernetics is the study of principles of organization, communication and control in complex systems. It is an inherently interdisciplinary field, in which "complex systems" can mean living organisms as well as machines: analogies between the behavior of a computer and that of a nervous system are central to the cybernetic imagination. Cybernetics is a complex field, and since Byrne's relationship to cybernetics is somewhat ambivalent, it has been for Byrne a positive inspiration as well as a theme that deserves to be dealt with in an ironic way.

One of the founding fathers of cybernetics was Norbert Wiener. His 1948 book *Cybernetics: Or Control and Communication in the Animal and the Machine* was a conscious attempt to establish and define the field. The key idea of cybernetics is that every flow of information, in both machines and animals, can be controlled purposively by feedback loops that try to maintain a goal state. Good examples of such feedback systems are the thermostat that regulates the function of a heating system, or a computer program for playing checkers or chess that has been programmed to include the results of played matches and to adapt its strategy according to these results. Similarly, the functioning of the heart and of the respiratory systems is regulated by biological mechanisms that work mostly autonomously, without intervention of a conscious will, producing the homeostasis that keeps the organism alive. Wiener points out that something like this is true as well for a simple action, like picking up a pencil. One may consciously will to do so, but no one knows consciously which muscles and nerves to use for it, and in which order. All that is arranged by the nervous system, which uses proprioceptive sensations (feedback on the internal status of the body, and on where the parts of the body are in relation to each other) to actually make the required movements. Generally speaking, the cybernetic approach created innovative connections between mathematics and engineering on the one hand, and biology and medicine on the other, and its emphasis on information and control provided a nearly universal and highly abstract model that may be used to build concrete machines and organizations for many specific systems and situations. Cyberneticians predicted, and helped to make possible, many of the later developments in computer sciences, information technology and related fields.[18]

Wiener introduced and concluded his book with an important warning: it is only too easy to build exaggerated expectations of the potential of cybernetics, especially since cybernetics does not lend itself very well to the understanding of human interactions, of historical, social and political matters.[19] Yet cybernetics was the outcome of a series of interdisciplinary conferences in which social scientists and psychiatrists played an important part, and cybernetics made universal claims from the beginning. In his book, Wiener freely discusses matters of society, politics, religion, mass communication, psychoanalysis, and so forth. As a result, cybernetic scientific literature often has a tinge of unreality. Science proper, the belief that science can overcome all historical restraints, science fiction, and prophecy are freely combined and mixed. A good example of cybernetics as science fiction is what Wiener wrote in a later book, *God and Golem Inc.: A Comment on Certain Points where Cybernetics Impinges on Religion* (1963): "It is conceptually possible for a human being to be sent over a telegraph line," although he quickly added that the idea is impractical for the present, and may remain impractical as long as humans exist, but is still not inconceivable.[20]

That Byrne was inspired by the cybernetic studies he read in the 70s is clear. His "Nielsen Rating System for the Arts" is evidently founded in part on the cybernetic ideas about control and communication. It is an attempt to overcome the limitations of the individual artist's consciousness, as well as the individual spectator's consciousness, by bringing the communities of artists and their audience together in a communication network that provides both sides with the necessary feedback that would organize the communication and guarantee its relevance. This means that the artist does not have the status of inspired individual or solitary genius. That was something that cybernetic thinkers had condemned in no uncertain terms. An example of this is mathematician and architect Christopher Alexander, who tried to develop, in his book *Notes on the Synthesis of Form* (1964) a general, cybernetics-inspired and computer-based approach to design and architecture. For Alexander, only an unselfconscious process has enough capacity for feedback to achieve a stable, homeostatic form of architecture. As soon as individual architects take over, this stability begins to disappear. Architectural forms that were once developed gradually, through centuries of adaptation and development, are now expected of individual architects, and "his chances of success are small because the number of factors which must fall into place is so enormous."[21]

The aversion of instability, systems out of control, animals diseased, minds unhinged, runs through all cybernetic literature, and it is coupled with an aversion for solipsistic introspection, isolated positions of managerial command, artistic dictatorship, and so forth. A lack of systematically organized communication and control is the common factor in all these instances. Take, for example, Stafford Beer, who pioneered the application of cybernetic principles in management. Beer wrote: "The first principle of control is that the controller is part of the system under control."[22] According to Beer, the control function has to evolve with the system, and needs to be diffused throughout the system. He warns: "Typically our thinking about control becomes muddled because we ourselves are very advanced systems, and we introspect too much."[23]

Characteristic of the cybernetic movement is that cybernetics is expected to provide a solution, or at the very least a crucial insight that may lead to a solution, of the great historical problems: the arms race, wars, overpopulation, pollution are but the most pressing. Stafford Beer wrote about the technical and historical developments: "The whole rate of progress is explosive, and there is hardly a human capability which remains static long enough for us to adapt to it." Sentiments like this are echoed everywhere in the cybernetics literature. Compare Norbert Wiener: "There is no homeostasis whatever. We are involved

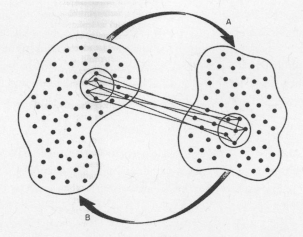

Figure 2 One of the figures from Stafford Beer's book *Brain of the Firm: The Managerial Cybernetics of Organization* (1972). A similar use of Venn diagrams can be seen in several of Byrne's artworks; cf. Illustrations 3 and 16. Moreover, the notion expressed in this figure that any individual state (represented here by a single dot) must be considered as part of a large structure, in continuous reciprocal exchange with a wider environment, is typical for much of Byrne's writing.[25]

in the business cycles of boom and failure, in the successions of dictatorship and revolution, in the wars which everyone loses, which are so real a feature of modern times."[24]

To avoid this damaging lack of homeostasis and stabilizing functions in the arts, they too have to be analyzed as part of an overreaching system. Although art is not a central subject for cybernetics in general, Gregory Bateson, who combined anthropology with a cybernetic perspective, wrote about it repeatedly. He ascertains that it is "of prime importance to have a conceptual system which will force us to see the 'message' (e.g., the art object) as *both* itself internally patterned *and* itself a part of a larger patterned universe — the culture or some part of it."[26] Art, according to Bateson, can help the individual's limited consciousness to overcome its limitations and to appreciate more fully the systemic nature of mind.[27] To illustrate by analogy what he means by "the systemic nature of mind," he compares the individual human mind to a television; just as a TV cannot show on the screen everything that goes on inside the apparatus and the entire system of studio and transmission, so consciousness is inevitably limited to a rather small portion of all mental process.[28] The artist should be able to overcome this limitation, so Bateson suggests: "We might say that in creative art man must experience himself — his total self — as a cybernetic model."[29]

This approach, insisting that the individual conscious mental process must be analyzed and understood as part of a wider system, be it an unconscious mental process or a cultural pattern, impressed Byrne deeply, as the following anecdote illustrates. In a biographical history of Talking Heads, Jerome David writes that Byrne entertained, just after he had moved to New York in 1974, a grand ambition: he wanted to make his life into a work of conceptual art. But how?

> Finally he hit on the answer: Byrne would become a *systems analyst*. He explained to Andrea [his girlfriend at that time] that he would devote his entire life to computer programming. He would call it a life system; it would be an art project. And he would do so anonymously.[30]

Twenty-five years later, in 1999, looking back on this period of his life, Byrne commented:

> "I had hopes of integrating this bizarrely analytical approach to the creation of music and art. I believe, and hope, that some of this intention was ironic — that by assuming a cool approach to hot subjects the absurdity of the whole situation would be obvious. But, to be honest, I loved the vibe and surface impression of academic texts."[31]

Still, the impersonal or more-than-just-individual, contextualizing, systemic approach of cybernetics — conceptual art raised to the level of an interdisciplinary science — has remained an influence throughout Byrne's career, and I will refer to it repeatedly in this book. Apart from its sometimes over-analytical tendencies, it stands for openness, for the capacity to see things from several perspectives at once, for a refusal to adhere to a fixed and singular point of view, and to a fixed hierarchy. This is an artistic project with a wide scope: to uncover basic aesthetic orientations that function within present society by taking into account the many important non-individualistic functions of art, design, the mass media, advertising, and so on.

At this point, just one example suffices to show Byrne's playful-yet-perfectly-serious employment of the conceptual framework of cybernetic science — in this case to explain, of all things, the functioning of CBGB, the bar where, in the mid-70s, Talking Heads and other New York new wave bands began their careers. In 2005, looking back, Byrne described CBGB as "a perfect self-actuating, self-organizing system."[32] According to Byrne, still a card-carrying conceptualist, at the start of such a system, individual creativity, original musicians and composers are not required: "There is continually and forever a pool

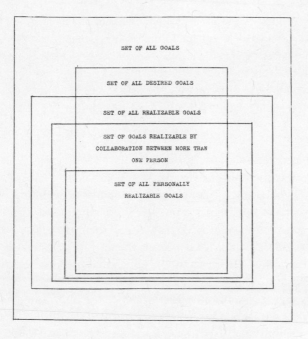

Figure 3 *Set Of All Goals* (1974), a conceptual drawing by Byrne.

of talent, energy and expression waiting to be tapped — it simply needs the right place in which to express itself." And he gives five elements for the formula to come up with innovation and success, a formula he calls in the best cybernetic fashion a "creative algorithm." (An algorithm is a full set of directions to do a specific task, or, as Stafford Beer defined it, a technical, specific rule for a specific goal.) Byrne sets out five such rules, as if the bar and music stage were to be programmed into a computer:

1) The venue must be the right size and be in the right place to present new material.
2) Musicians must get in for free, and sometimes get free beer.
3) There must be a sense of alienation from the prevailing music scene.
4) Low rents in the area must be maintained.
5) Bands must be paid fairly.

Free beer to explain the mysteries of artistic creation? Of course. It is part of the right infrastructure, and "the cybernetic answer is always structural," as Stafford Beer knew.[33] In the best structural and sociological tradition, Byrne insists that the structure surrounding the music is paramount:

It might seem dispiriting to believe that the brick and mortar determine what form of music a creative soul pours out, but I think there is an element of truth there. Songs and performances are, one hopes, absolutely heartfelt, passionate, and true — but we both consciously and unconsciously guide our feelings, passions, and ineffable creative urges to make that which is appropriate work in the given situation.[34]

3 THE FIRST YEARS OF TALKING HEADS

Is there a concept to rock music? Does it lend itself to analysis? As far as I know, Byrne is the only rock singer who would address his audience at the end of a song not just by shouting his thanks or announcing the next song, but also with the quintessential schoolish question "Are there any questions?" The point of rock is that it can move and stir, wash away, and that might raise two questions: how does the music do that, and what is there to wash away, why do people want that? From the start, Byrne wrote songs that managed to address those two questions at the same time.

Musically, Byrne, Frantz, and Weymouth relied on the simple and highly effective garage rock made in the 60s: songs that were direct, often monotonous, loud, primitive and repetitive, based on only a few chords. Such songs exude a slightly hypnotic, trance-inducing power, submerging self-conscious nervousness and inducing a flow of acceptance. (A diagrammatic representation of "music: what it is / what it's made of," published by Byrne in 2003, shows music to be made most crucially of "Frequent Repetitions," and music is first and foremost a "Personality Annihilator."[35] The diagram is ironic in its quasi-scientific simplification, but Byrne's irony here is, as it is throughout his work, a seriousness looking for the quickest way out, as if irony were the natural allegory of ineffable, pre-verbal seriousness.)

Talking Heads' version of basic rock was sparse and brittle. Their songs were organized in the verse-and-chorus pattern of the standard Top 40 tune, but the transitions in their songs were unusually abrupt. A typical early song is "I Feel It In My Heart." This was never brought out on record but was filmed when Talking Heads, still as a trio, played it in The Kitchen in 1976. Byrne's lyrics clearly present the painful process of self-examination that is the subject of many of his early songs. This is part of the refrain:

> Well I made a decision, and I revised it again
> And I saw what it meant, to both my parents and friends
> Thought it would make me feel better, well it obviously did
> To work a little bit harder, and I thought that I could,
> To keep making revisions, 'till my work satisfied me

And does it really matter, the adjustment is small
But only if I feel it in my heart

There is a contrast, almost an open contradiction, between this kind of self-searching and the moving, hypnotizing force of rock music that annuls such self-conscious doubts.

Byrne used his singing voice, an oddly choked and untrained tenor, to bring this tension to the foreground. His singing was at times close to speaking, passing on information. It lacked at all times the affectation of black "soulful" styles that typifies so many white rock singers, and because of that it has been dubbed "hyper-Caucasian," or more bluntly: "a squawk."[36] In a felicitous comparison, Byrne's high-pitched delivery has been likened to "the vocal equivalent of nervously clenching and twisting hands."[37] This is emphasized even more by Byrne's frequent use of inarticulate groans and shouts, and by his vocalizing of meaningless syllables. The unresolved tensions that Byrne's singing thus transmits focus the listeners' attention to the way in which a personal identity is created and the tensions that underlie this identity; the difficulty of selecting models to imitate.

It is the voice that defines the quality of a song's persona for the listener, since a voice stands for the person more directly than any other musical device; it offers the listener immediate access to the body that brings forth the voice, as we all recognize what it is to speak and to sing. Byrne's vocal performance, which often shifts within a song from calm to frenzied and back, suggests that it is hard to know one's own voice in the middle of the babble of different voices in which we talk to ourselves, especially when the media present so many powerful and convincing examples. Is it even feasible to have a single, stable vocal identity? Perhaps it is arbitrary to separate one part of one's vocal performances as the "real voice," the voice that really belongs to you, and to condemn the rest as funny vocal mistakes.

Byrne took both sides of the equation, the overwhelming hypnotic monotony and the analytic, fully seriously. His rock-and-roll heart was recognized very early by both Lou Reed and John Cale. Cale invited Byrne to play guitar during some of his concerts in the Lower Manhattan Ocean Club, where Reed came on stage as well.[38] The Velvet Underground was the prototype for the bands at CBGB, so that in effect Byrne had been allowed into the fold of rock history even before he had a record contract. Meanwhile, his analytic and conceptual predilection had not been lessened, and it came out in his songwriting. He wrote from an extremely formal perspective; where someone else might sing "I'm getting bored," he sang "My interest level is dropping."[39] Although the lyrics are still far from the convoluted Wittgenstein-influenced texts of the Art &

Language collective, they have a formal tinge. He wrote everything in capitals, which gave his lines a printed, more distant and impersonal look. Thirty years later, Byrne wrote about them that "these songs didn't lack emotion, but filtered it through an extremely constricting linguistic bottleneck, making the tension more pronounced, though never explicit."[40] A typical example is "Tentative Decisions," a song that doesn't identify itself with the position of someone in love, but instead presents an attempt to analyze and abstract one's way out of emotional tensions and amorous misunderstandings:

> Now that I can release my tension,
> let me make clear my best intentions.
> Girls ask: can I define decision?
> Boys ask: can I describe their function?

Generally, Talking Heads were willing to discuss every aspect of their work with the puritanical and analytical ethos of conceptual art. Every aspect of playing and performing came under close scrutiny. The function of lyrics was discussed extensively within the band:

> "We decided not to sing songs about being in a rock band. I think we decided not to sing any dance songs or any sex songs to begin with. Instead, to think of an approach to our subjects which might be interesting. We originally thought we would use conversational language instead of the "rock vocabulary" that had developed to the point where it was easy to hash out rock lyrics. Because it was so easy and so commonplace, it meant that they were not really communicating very much, if at all. [. . .] We try not to do anything distracting [on stage] because we want people to listen to our lyrics, which are kind of unique.[41]

Instead of dressing in the black leather that was more or less regular at CBGB, they decided to wear average middle-class street clothes for concerts; instead of the flashing colored lights typical of rock shows, Talking Heads opted just to leave on the house lights. Byrne explained, in the conceptual vein where aesthetics and politics are seen as very closely connected, that "in the broadest sense, it's political to go on stage and play rock music and not dress up . . . It's a political act not to place oneself above the audience."[42] Choosing not to impose a specific image on the audience, the main focus was on the songs, the lyrics, and their rendition. The band spent a lot of time discussing these. Even the name of the band was chosen to imply this. When the band members were compiling long lists of possible names, a friend, Wayne Zieve, pointed out the term "talking heads" in a *TV Guide*. It was the name of a cheap horror movie being shown on late night TV that week,[43] and also the term used by TV cameramen to describe program formats that are visually limited to face shots. As Zieve explains it, "'Talking Heads' just came from my impression of the band. David really didn't sing that much. He would yell a little bit, but it was more like he was talking, he was giving information. It seemed like a cerebral enough name for them."[44] According to Tina Weymouth, "it was the only name that had so many connotations to it that . . . the group would define the name, not the name define the group."[45]

In March 1976, nine months after their first public concert, Talking Heads were reviewed in the *New York Times*. John Rockwell, the music critic who — in an unorthodox combination — covered both classical and rock concerts for the *Times*, wrote that the formal qualities of Talking Heads' playing made for a sound "with no obvious precedent on the underground circuit — or in music itself."[46] It was the greatest possible compliment for Rockwell, who considers himself a formalist. Rockwell also mentioned in his review that Talking Heads had a reputation for being the most intellectual and most artistic band on the circuit, and quoted Byrne as saying that he did not think of himself as "an artist playing at having a band," but "as a performer — almost an entertainer." By this time, Frantz, Weymouth, and Byrne had been able to quit their day jobs, and were looking for a manager. Two weeks after the review, they wrote to Rockwell to thank him for his interest and help as a critic, and to ask him for his advice on finding a competent manager.[47] A beginning rock band asking a *New York Times* critic (Rockwell has a Ph.D. in German cultural history) for help in getting the right manager — that is definitely another example of an intellectual approach to popular music.

Without Rockwell's help, Talking Heads signed a record contract with Sire Records. They also found a fourth member, Jerry Harrison, who added parts on keyboard or guitar to make their songs a little more unified. Harrison had been in Jonathan Richman's the Modern Lovers, another Velvet Underground-influenced garage rock band, and he was able to make subtle additions to the trio's sound, gradually turning it into a quartet. Harrison had studied architecture and was bookish, which helped him to fit in. Apart from the fact that in the male-dominated world of rock it was a bit unusual to have a female bass player, the band now had a standard rock line-up: Byrne sang and played guitar, Frantz drummed, Weymouth played bass, and Harrison played guitar and keyboards. Having recorded a single as a trio, they were now ready to record their first album. They named it *77*, after the year; a basic, almost archival label, in line with their minimal-conceptual preferences.

The best-known song of that first album is "Psycho Killer." It is a song that showcases a good number of the band's characteristics: anti-autobiographical, tense, simple and direct (the introductory bass line as characteristic as the intro to the Rolling Stones' "Satisfaction"), and yet elusive. Byrne's performance of "Psycho Killer" became his trademark for years and years. He explained his motives for writing it, the first song he wrote, as an exercise:

> "Alice Cooper was really big then and I thought it'd be interesting to do a song in something approaching that mock-ghoulish vein he was pumping, but give certain twists. Alice had all these safety gauges worked out so that it wouldn't connect with anything remotely dangerous. It was all 'it's okay folks, it's only a show!'. I just liked the idea of writing a song that was more real."[48]

Byrne combined Alice Cooper's glitter rock sensationalism with the diametrically opposed approach to characterization in the songs of Randy Newman. Newman, Hollywood film composer and songwriter, excels in songs that are written — and sung — in the voice and from the unpleasant perspective of failed dramatic personae: the alcoholic, the racist bigot, the sexual pervert. By accepting the moral shapelessness of these personae as a given, Newman implicates his audience in a world of idiosyncratic cruelties, more dreadful and less entertaining than his musical vocabulary of piano-based rock and roll combined with lavish movie score-instrumentation would suggest.[49] Indeed, the casual, popular form of these songs, so easy to pick up and hum along with, adds to their impact: isn't it just as easy to fall in with the shapelessness? Byrne accordingly wrote his song from the perspective of a psychopathic character, presenting him in a non-judgmental way as oversensitive.

> I can't seem to face up to the facts.
> I'm tense and nervous and I can't relax...
> Psycho killer, q'est-ce que c'est?, fa fa fa fa fa fa
> better run run run run run run run away...
>
> You start a conversation, you can't even finish it!
> You're talking a lot, but you're not saying anything!
> When I have nothing to say, my lips are sealed
> Say something once, why say it again?
>
> Ce que j'ai fait, ce soir là.
> Ce qu'elle a dit, ce soir là.
> Réalisant mon espoir,
> je me lance, vers la gloire ... OK ...

Frantz and Weymouth helped with the French lines. Byrne explained that it was a "natural delusion that a psychotic killer would imagine himself as very refined and use a foreign language to talk to himself."[50] Avoiding the spectacular aspects of murder, Byrne highlighted a concern for polite and ordered conversation instead, and borrowed the "fa fa fa" from an old Otis Redding song ("Fa-Fa-Fa-Fa-Fa (Sad Song)), to make sure that the result was a pop song with a strong rhythmic drive that everybody could relate to. Byrne rehearsed the song tirelessly, changing the rhythm, the chords, the song structure repeatedly before recording.[51]

For an audience trying to relate to it, "Psycho Killer" is a bundle of contradictions. What does it mean to dance to the musings of a psycho killer? Is it satire or realism? Would a psychotic murderer's stream of consciousness really be made up of such uncomfortably common elements? Or is it a commentary on the world of pop, with its onset of mythical heroes and emotional role models, which may inspire fear as easily as fun?[52]

The underlying theme of the song, uniting it with the rest of the album, is the problematic relationship between language and self, or language and reality. If the "psycho killer" persona deals with this by borrowing a foreign language to speak to himself, several other songs describe a similar distance: "I want to talk like I read, before I decide what to do" ("Happy Day"); "I have to sing about the book I read" ("The Book I Read"); "I want my sentence right here, but now I'm far away"; ("Happy Day"); "Now I'm speaking out, speaking about my friends" ("New Feeling"). Even though these songs are merry and light, they are tension-filled, like the music, which is simple, light, at times with an almost skiffle-like beat, and yet projects a strong sense of urgency. These songs are full of feeling, of intuitions that are conflicting and uncontrollable, and they put across a sense that the spontaneous expression of passion, the authenticity of feeling that is so important to the Romantic ideology of rock, is not sufficient.

A number of lyrics written by Byrne portray individuals emphatically in relation to their surroundings, as part of a surrounding system or in opposition to it. "Don't Worry About The Government" from the *Talking Heads: 77* album portrays an official as part of an institutionalized world:

My building has every convenience.
It's going to make life easy for me.
It's going to be easy to get things done.
I will relax, along with my loved ones. [. . .]

I see the states across this big nation. I see the laws made in Washington, D.C.
I think of the ones I consider my favorites.

I think of the people that are working for me . . .
I'm a lucky guy to live in my building.
They all need buildings to help them along.

Byrne explained about this song that he wanted to write a rock song with pastoral imagery, and also had planned to write a critical song about the government, but got caught up for a moment in the point of view of someone who is pleased with his job, his position, the standard of living that brings him, and so on.[53] Of course, the expansion of the pastoral imagery to the entire U.S.A. and its legal system gives the song a general quality (is the government like a comfortable building, or the other way round?), while the last line turns away from the expressed contentment and presents it suddenly as questionable.

Buildings turn up in many of Byrne's songs.[54] Buildings are an easily recognized image that may stand for every structure that frames someone's life: as popular songs claim to express inner experience directly, this metaphor can represent anything that shapes or opposes that experience from the outside. Every listener is able to flesh out this rhetorical figure with a personal interpretation. Talking Heads' first single, "Love —> Building On Fire" (alternatively known as "Love Goes To Building On Fire") deals with "two loves":

When my love stands next to your love,
I can't define love when it's not love.
It's not love, it's not love.
Which is my face, which is a building, which is on fire.

Talking Heads' second album, aptly titled *More Songs about Buildings and Food* (1978) includes "The Big Country," a song that is the negative counterpart of "Don't Worry About The Government":

I see the shapes I remember from maps.
I see the shoreline, I see the whitecaps.
A baseball diamond, nice weather down there.
I see the school and the houses where the kids are.
Places to park by the factories and buildings. . . .
(AND I SAY): I wouldn't live there if you paid me.
I couldn't live like that, no siree![55]

These lyrics are primarily meant not to be read but to be sung and heard, which adds the qualities of a voice, which in turn is embedded in music. All this produces a persona that the listener may enter for the few minutes that the song

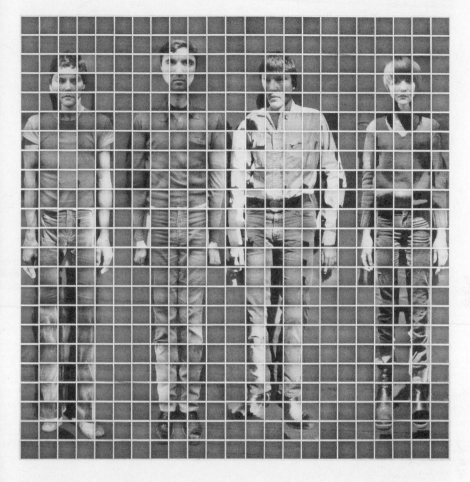

Figure 4 Life-size photomosaic of Talking Heads, David Byrne, 1978. 529 Polaroid SX-70 prints, 7.5 feet × 7.5 feet. Rephotographed by Jimmy DeSana for the album cover of *More Songs about Buildings and Food.*

takes. The songs suggest mental states, or fragments thereof, without resolution or conclusion. Making sense of them, deciding what is spontaneous and what manipulated or repressed, is up to the listener; this need for interpretation stands in the way of direct emotional identification.

A parallel to this link, positive or negative, between persona and surroundings, is given with the cover that Byrne designed for *More Songs about Buildings and Food.* The front cover consists of a grid of 23 × 23 Polaroid photos of the band members, each photo presenting one detail. As these snaps almost, but not quite, fit their neighbors, due to small changes in framing and lighting, the result is a recognizable but uneasy, rifted group portrait; a photographic, cubist grid.

The back cover reproduces *Portrait USA*, a computer-processed synthesis of satellite photos — also a kind of photomontage — that shows the entire land-mass of the U.S.A. in a single smooth image. This first color photomosaic of the United States was originally produced by General Electric with the assistance of the National Geographic Society and NASA. The juxtaposition — the ordinary image of four persons made problematic, the image of a huge country presented as if it could be taken in in a single glance — forms a fitting backdrop for the song's characters who are struggling with role models. Several covers for later albums would present variations on this theme.

So far, the discussion has concentrated on the songs and given no attention to the recording. Recording is crucial to popular music, even for songs that have been developed, rehearsed and performed outside the recording studio. The recording characteristics, the use of sound effects and filters, extra instrumental and vocal overlays, and the final mix of instrumental and vocal tracks can transform a song completely. *Talking Heads: 77* was produced by Tony Bongiovi. He had been suggested to the band by their record company as someone who might give their unusual and somewhat weird sound a more accessible form. Bongiovi let the band make endless recordings of single instruments, and tried to persuade them to add instrumental elements to their songs, trumpets, steel drums and a cello, to dress up their sparse sound. To Byrne, however, all this determined conventionality was more restricting than liberating, even to the point of feeling threatened that Bongiovi's advice might smother the elements of alienation and eccentricity that he wanted his songs to put across.[56]

Brian Eno produced *More Songs about Buildings and Food*, and he brought a completely different approach to the process of recording. He considered the developments in recording technology as opening up whole new artistic pos-sibilities. The new electronics gave access to an unprecedented range of ways to modify the textures and timbres of sound, and to the creation of virtual acoustic spaces. To him, the exploration of these possibilities was as much an original creative act as writing songs or playing musical instruments; it was a new form of composition.[57] Eno and the members of Talking Heads, especially Byrne and Harrison, had met each other in 1977, and discovered immediately that they shared a passionate interest in conceptual and cybernetic approaches to music and the other arts. Eno had already gathered considerable experience in using the recording studio as a creative tool, reversing the relationship between creative songwriting and secondary, contextual recording in his work with Roxy Music, Robert Fripp, David Bowie, and others. In 1975, in collaboration with a painter friend, Peter Schmidt, Eno had also published a set of conceptual and/

or managerial statements to use in the course of any creative process to ensure a degree of formal distance from the subjective routine that will often set in when people have to work under pressure. The *circa* 100 statements, titled "Oblique Strategies," were each printed on a playing card, to be used either at will or at random. The statements, such as "The tape is now the music," "You are an engineer," and "Honour thy error as a hidden intention" are a highly condensed and abbreviated, and therefore slightly surreal, version of the cyberneticist's formalizing and contextualizing approach to self-conscious thinking. The purpose of the cards, as Eno has written, is "to try to derail normal thinking habits when they've proven ineffective, and to suggest new ways of approaching problems."[58]

Eno described the texture of Talking Heads' music as rhythmically situated between pop and soul. His aim was to use the studio to enhance and sharpen the contrasts and imbalances that defined their sound. Even while the rhythm section was "perfectly poised between pop and soul," the band was defined by contrasts: strong and solid drumming, sonorous and wavy bass lines, spiky rhythm guitar with screeching and disturbing outbursts. "It created a field of charged rhythmic space — stark but tense, always slightly off-balance and therefore always moving forward."[59]

Eno's working method in the studio (in the days before digitized and computerized recording) was to reserve a few of the 24 available tape recording tracks for his own sonic experiments, while the band laid down instrumental and vocal tracks. On the spare tracks, Eno fed in an instrument of his choice to treat its sound electronically, feeding the signal through synthesizers, filters, delays, and other effects. In 1978, such detailed coloring of timbres, adding a range of small sonic gestures to songs (in contrast with the all-over psychedelics of "progressive rock") made listeners prick up their ears.

A characteristic result of Eno's method can be heard in Talking Heads' cover version of (Reverend) Al Green's hit "Take Me To The River." In his song, Green had managed to combine soul with gospel, erotic longing with religious desire, tying it all up in a single effervescent metaphor: "Take me to the river. Wash me in the water." While recording their version, Talking Heads decided to use only the recorded basis tracks of their instruments. Instead of the usual adding of extra instrumental tracks, they chose to add only single notes to the already recorded instruments. Eno then treated these additions with a synthesizer in the same way he had treated the snare drum, giving it a delay, an echo, to produce an "underwater" sound.[60] Just as typical is an irregular tinkling, jangling sound on the song "Warning Sign" that was accidentally recorded along with Byrne's vocal: he danced around with keys in his pocket, and their sound was registered. Other producers would have insisted on re-recording, but not Eno — it was just the kind of error that could be turned to good use. "It fits the rhythm so we left it on there," Byrne said.[61]

As the final step in this discussion of the first two Talking Heads albums, one or two aspects of their wider context deserve pointing out. In 1977, rock and roll, R&B, rock, and related styles had been successful for over 20 years, and in that time the elements of rebelliousness, counterculture, political opposition, and adolescent consumerism had been co-opted by the industries of music, television, and film. The entertainment industry had made rock possible in the first place; but now the sounds, textures and styles were channeled into well-defined genres, easily identifiable in order to be easily marketed. Sound textures and sentiments became inflated: symphonic rock, heavy metal, but also the smooth unified sounds of bands like Abba, Fleetwood Mac, and the Eagles were the outcome. The raw, unsentimental and deliberately unpolished sound of the bands associated with CBGB, Television, the Ramones, Richard Hell, the Patti Smith Group, Blondie, as well as Cleveland's Pere Ubu, were a reaction against that process. The reaction was often a romantic renewal of rock's authentic capacity. In this environment, Talking Heads stood out by questioning what directness in music is. The songs of *Talking Heads: 77* convey an intuitive experience, but that experience is made up of frankly conflicting and uncontrollable emotions, as well as outside forces. Byrne's lyrics and vocals suggested that rock's rebellious aesthetic of spontaneous and direct expression was insufficient.

4 ETHOLOGICAL AND NEUROLOGICAL ASPECTS OF MUSIC

As discussed above, both Byrne and Eno read their way into cybernetic literature, investigating the ramifications of the foundational idea of cybernetics that the flow of information in both animals and machines is regulated by feedback loops, by biological or technical control mechanisms. Most relevant for them was, of course, the question of which control mechanisms determine the functions of music. Music communicates, partly unconsciously, but how precisely does it manage to do so? If music can change a mood, bring to the fore some aspects of personality while other aspects recede into the background, how does that work inside the human nervous system? Byrne and Eno looked for answers to these questions in a number of books that provide an introduction to this complex and mysterious field, where biology and anthropology mix and mingle with psychology, neurology, and musicology. One of the fields they were interested in was sociobiology, the proposed synthesis of sociology and biology that attracted a great deal of attention and debate in the 1970s and

80s, especially after publication of Edward O. Wilson's *Sociobiology: The New Synthesis* in 1975. Both Byrne and Eno also read *The Imperial Animal* (1971) by Lionel Tiger and Robin Fox,[62] a book that Byrne preferred over Wilson's, since its approach is based more on the social sciences, and accordingly puts more emphasis on the social and cultural capacity for conscious change.[63]

It is easy to see how ethology and sociobiology fit in with the general outlook of cybernetics. Tiger and Fox write: "The human organism is like a computer that is set up or 'wired' in a particular way. It is always in a state of readiness — at successive points in the life cycle — to process certain kinds of information and to produce certain kinds of information."[64] What they add to this general insight is an evolutionary perspective. Their overview of human ethology, human behavior studied with biological methods, combines Darwin's theory of evolution with insights in human behavior and culture that have been developed in cultural anthropology and sociology. They point out how human behavior is still characterized by the fact that *Homo sapiens* is a mammal from the order of the primates, even if man has evolved further than the other primates because his forebears went out hunting. The demands of the hunt on the individual and on the tribe have favored the development of the cerebral cortex, which made possible an elaborate language and culture, as well as more complex tools. "Natural selection has produced an animal that has to behave culturally, that has to invent rules, make myths, speak languages, and form men's clubs, in the same way that the hamadryas baboon has to form harems, adopt infants, and bite its wives on the neck."[65] All of recorded history is only a moment on the timescale of evolution, which means it has not influenced our hereditary qualities. Truly modern man is still as he was tens of thousands of years ago: "*agricultural and industrial civilizations have put nothing into the basic wiring of the human animal. We are wired for hunting* — for the emotions, the excitements, the curiosities, the regularities, the fears, and the social relationships that were needed to survive in the hunting way of life."[66] As a result, human behavior consists of a standard repertoire. Regardless of the society in question, there are always "myths and legends, dancing, psychosis and neurosis, adultery, homosexuality, homicide, suicide, loyalty, desertion, juvenile delinquents, senile fools, and various shrewd practitioners to cure or take advantage of the various ills from which communities and people suffer."[67] Tiger and Fox's description of the function of music is noteworthy in this context. They start from the (in itself hotly debated) notion that in prehistorical times the hunt was reserved for men, which has led to a physical but also emotional predilection for this kind of behavior in men. This preference may be sublimated in economical activities, but also in music:

It appears still to be the case that the uncertainty and particular sensitivity of the hunt and its metaphor galvanizes men more than women, and boys more than girls. It is the band of men who play music like warriors, who worry a melody, turn it around, pass it back and forth, hide from it altogether, pair up, split up, combine to chase it, come crashing or singing around, and then drive to some utterly expert and exhausted point of rest when the improvisation is done and when the millisecond mutual awareness has paid off in a satisfaction only an improvising musician can understand as an essential luxury for his being . . . This is an almost pure emotional analogue of the hunt; music is not only the food of love but of predation too.[68]

Tiger and Fox's view on music is tied to their analysis of the position of male adolescents. In baboon societies, adolescent males have to make a difficult transition from their position as children, with the females of the group, to their new role as mature baboons. Since the older males have monopolized the power over the group and over the women, the adolescents have no other alternative than to take a place in the (dangerous) periphery of the group, trying to acquire a place among the powerful from that margin. This in-between-roles position is inherently full of tensions:

Adolescent males suffer confused instructions from the old program: become mature; remain dependent; show affection to girls and hardness to boys; accuse the dominants of being too powerful, yet admire their power; and perhaps begin dimly to shape out some way of reproducing. The job of reproducing is easy and fast and also immensely pleasurable. But reproduction, like justice, must not only be done, it must be seen to be done. Some social analogue of the actual or potential copulation must be established — the fraternity pin, the hibiscus behind the ear, the exchange of love fetishes or food.[69]

Tiger and Fox write in the assumption that scientific insight into the wiring (they use the term "biogrammar") of the human animal may help to produce a more balanced and civil society. They express their concern about the ongoing worldwide arms race, reminding their readers that man has the same propensity to aggression and violence as other primates, but has added tools and language, weapons, and concepts. In primate societies, aggression can be curbed: "Ethologists speak of the 'ritualization of aggression' — but the aggression has to be ritualized because it is so real. And ritual does not always work."[70] In human society, such ritualization has to take on a new dimension. Tiger and Fox insist that mankind must invent and institute new forms of ritual to deal with global problems of religious differences, economic inequality, etc.

And just like the causes of conflict, these new ritual forms of control will have to be highly symbolic.[71]

The Imperial Animal contains nothing that even comes close to a recipe for music and art; all the book has to offer is a general evolutionary perspective on the functions and meaning of art, music and ritual, which encompass all human cultures by stressing the fact that there is a single underlying human nature. The importance of this perspective is mostly that of a warning, namely not to forget that humans have not only verbal languages, but also behavioral languages,[72] just as cultures inevitably have to be expressions of human nature. Like evolutionary psychology, and like the older "archetypes" of Jungian psychology, the "behavioral languages" and the "biogrammar" of Tiger and Fox are not hard factual entities;[73] but they may help to grasp the complexity and heterogeneity of both human nature and culture.

Byrne was fascinated by the mythologies and rituals of mankind. He read Carl Jung's psychoanalytical studies of dreams and myths, and Joseph Campbell's studies in comparative mythology. The idea that all men share a common propensity for mythical thinking became increasingly important in Byrne's work. The influence of these authors who write about myth is discussed in the next chapter, in connection with Talking Heads' African and funk-influenced albums, where they can be seen clearly. But first, some other sources of inspiration for *Fear of Music*, Talking Heads' third album, deserve mentioning. These sources are a few medical studies that deal much more directly than Tiger and Fox's book with the complex ways in which the brain processes musical information.

The album title *Fear of Music* was inspired by a collection of highly specialized studies on the neurology of music, *Music and the Brain*.[74] One of these studies relates a case of fear of music that demonstrates how the brain is "wired" for music, and how we may only begin to perceive this neurological basis of normal experience, usually taken for granted, when these wires get crossed. The relevant case study is as follows: in the beginning of the twentieth century, a well-known Russian music critic named Nikonov was watching an opera by Meyerbeer. During the third act,

> he became tremulous, sweated profusely, and his left eye began to twitch. Then came a violent pain in his head, and consciousness was lost for a while. Thereafter Nikonov became a prey to similar attacks, each one brought on by music and by no other factor. Gradually his sensitivity seemed to increase, so that even distant, subdued music became epileptogenic. As a consequence, the victim was tormented by a veritable phobic dread of hearing music. If out of doors the sound of an approaching military band reached him, he would stop his ears, and seek refuge in a back street or any

handy doorway or shop. He was so interested in his own malady, that he wrote and published a pamphlet about his condition which he entitled "Fear of Music".[75]

Byrne was just as interested in the famous books of medical case studies published by Oliver Sacks, extraordinary accounts of the experiences of some patients with severe neurological disorders: *Awakenings* and *The Man Who Mistook His Wife for a Hat*. These books contain remarkable insights into the physical requirements that make it possible for human beings to enjoy music, narrative, and ritual; they also give many examples of the indispensability of these arts for human well-being and physical functioning. Sacks wrote on these matters:

> What we see, fundamentally, is the power of music to organise — and to do this efficaciously (as well as joyfully!), when abstract or schematic forms of organisation fail. Indeed, it is especially dramatic, as one would expect, precisely when no other form of organisation will work. Thus music, or any other form of narrative, is essential when working with the retarded or apraxic — schooling or therapy for them must be centred on music or something equivalent. And in drama there is still more — there is the power of *rôle* to give organisation, to confer, while it lasts, an entire personality. The capacity to perform, to play, to *be*, seems to be a 'given' in human life, in a way which has nothing to do with intellectual differences.[76]

One of the mechanisms that make this organization of the personality possible is the proprioceptive sense. Sacks introduces this as "our secret sense, our sixth sense"—that continuous but unconscious sensory flow from the movable parts of our body (muscles, tendons, joints), by which their position and tone and motion is continually monitored and adjusted, but in a way that is hidden from us because it is automatic and unconscious.[77] This sensory flow was named "proprioception" by C.S. Sherrington, to distinguish it from the five senses and from introspection, but also "because of its indispensability for our sense of *ourselves*; for it is only by courtesy of proprioception, so to speak, that we feel our bodies are proper to us, as our 'property', as our own."[78] Sacks underlines that the sense of proprioception is "the fundamental, organic mooring of identity — at least of that corporeal identity, or 'body-ego', which Freud sees as the basis of self."[79] This includes one's vocal identity: the modulation of speech is normally proprioceptive, as speech is governed by inflowing impulses from all vocal organs.[80] Sacks has written about the extraordinary symbolic and mythical properties of the patients whose fate he describes, whose rare factual conditions of the brain caused them to live through fabulously foreign experiences.[81] His essays bring out with unusual clarity how music and ritual may give indispensable structure and perspective to proprioceptive experience, and thus to human identity as such.

5 EXPERIMENTS WITH RHYTHM, TEXTURE, AND PERSONA

Fear of Music was recorded in 1979, again with Eno as producer. The album documents a moment of transition in Byrne's songwriting. He adopted a distancing approach to lyrics, writing instructions to himself to write a song about a certain subject, applying what he called "non-rational logic": starting with an irrational premise and proceeding from there as if it made sense.[82] Such an approach to making art was in line with what Sol LeWitt, a key figure in conceptual art, had written in his widely influential *Sentences on Conceptual Art*. Take LeWitt's sentences 1 and 5: "Conceptual artists are mystics rather than rationalists. They leap to conclusions that logic cannot reach." And "Irrational thoughts should be followed absolutely and logically."[83] Byrne's song "Animals," for example, was written "to disagree with the idea that animals are noble savages, living in harmony with their surroundings and with each other. I thought I'd present a contrary point of view of animals as obstinate beings with lots of problems."[84]

> I know the animals are laughing at us
> They don't even know what a joke is
> I won't follow animal's advice
> I don't care if they're laughing at us

Other lyrics adopt similarly illogical, dream-like premises, while often referring to the meaning and uses of music. The chorus of "Heaven" states: "Heaven is a place where nothing ever happens"; the verses suggest that everyone tries hard to reach such a place of eternal fulfillment — be it a bar, a party or a kiss. The song also contains the lines "The band in heaven plays my favorite song / They play it once again, they play it all night long." "Electric Guitar" presents the guitar, often the personification of the hero in rock music,[85] in troubled situations:

> An electric guitar is brought to a court of law.
> The judge and the jury (twelve members of the jury)
> all listening to records
> This is a crime against the state
> This is the verdict they reach:
> Never listen to electric guitar

"Life During Wartime" mentions roadblocks, truckloads of weapons, graves and gunfire — an atmosphere that is familiar from the TV news and from films. This is combined with a protagonist who explains his situation in a series of everyday impressions: changing passports and looks, staying away from the window, burning his notebooks since they won't help him survive. He also mentions his personal concerns: no longer being able to go to discos and clubs, to stay in college, or to play records. The lyrics are so indeterminate that they can be interpreted as a casual evocation of low-intensity guerilla warfare in an American city, as a metaphor for an adolescent identity crisis, or — why not? — as both together.

The songs on Talking Heads' first two albums had mostly been fully developed before they were recorded. Now, to avoid repeating himself, Byrne began to rely on the opportunity to construct a song in the process of recording, by breaking down a musical texture into separate tracks that can be erased and replaced at will, and by applying electronic effects to any selected sound. As Byrne explained this deliberate cut-and-paste process:

> There was a song that we used to perform live, "Electricity", which we re-arranged for the album with Jerry [Harrison] playing guitar instead of synthesizer; but it still didn't translate to tape. Brian [Eno] and I listened to it over and over again and then I suggested starting to remove things from the mix. First, my vocal came out, and then all the other parts, and all we were left with was the snare drum and some of my guitar. The problem was that, since the old parts were ingrained in our heads we couldn't come up with anything new to replace them. So what we did was work on the parts simultaneously but without each other's knowledge. Brian would play half a bass part and I would play half a bass part and then we'd put them together as if it was one part. We did the same with the guitars and came up with some chord progressions that I wouldn't have been able to come up with otherwise.[86]

Byrne also experimented with his voice, writing the melodies to "Heaven" and "Air" by singing the words phrase by phrase into a tape recorder and trying to make each syllable stretch over two or three notes.[87] For another song, "Drugs," he exercised until he was out of breath and then sang while jogging in place. He tried singing the lyrics of "Electric Guitar" as if he were mentally retarded, exaggerating so much that he had to record it again.[88]

Byrne was by no means a natural on stage. For a long time his tense and nervous mood was almost tangible. He sang out of need: "I was so painfully shy that strangely it was the only way I could express myself. So it was cathartic and powerful, but hardly what you would call pleasure."[89] That he was nevertheless experimenting with such unusual and awkward manners of singing shows his dedication to his work, as well as a conscious knowledge of what nervous awkwardness may add to the depth of communication.

"I Zimbra," the song that opens *Fear of Music*, is a typical product of studio composing. Byrne had been listening to records of African popular music and drumming, and wanted to construct a song in a similar way. He worked on seven guitar riffs, rhythmic and melodic patterns, and worked on them until they could conceivably proceed from one to another — only to find that this kind of music no longer lent itself easily to the chorus-and-verse format. Eno, who had worked with Dadaist nonsense poems by Kurt Schwitters and Hugo Ball in art school,[90] and who generally doesn't care much for writing meaningful song lyrics, proposed that instead of writing his own lyrics, Byrne could use "Gadji Beri Bimba," a *Vers ohne Worte* or poem without words by Hugo Ball. Ball was the organizer, poet and dramaturgist of the Dada movement. Ball wrote this text in 1916, describing it as a form of poetry in which "the balancing of the vowels is gauged and distributed only to the value of the initial line."[91] Talking Heads renamed the poem "I Zimbra" after its last words, used by Byrne as a summarizing and explosive shout:

> gadji beri bimba clandridi
> lauli lonni cadori gadjam
> a bim beri glassala glandride
> a glassala tuffm i zimbra[92]

To the resulting song, Eno added the "psychedelic" effects that occur when dramatic "vocal" qualities like straining, groaning, and stammering are electronically added to instrumental melodic phrases. *New York Times* critic John Rockwell described the outcome as "a hyper-sensitivity in which every little sonic gesture has dizzying ramifications."[93]

How to interpret the use of this nonsense poem? Hugo Ball's phonetic poem epitomizes Dada, the reaction to the breakdown of reason in World War I by a small group of artists who promoted nonsense as an antidote — and found that nonsense was able to provide a meeting ground for the artistic avant-garde and political protest. The text stands for the breakdown of conventional language. It is revealing that in June 1916, the month in which he performed "Gadji Beri Bimba" for the first time, Ball wrote and performed an avant-garde nativity play that also consisted only of meaningless sounds.[94] When language is reduced to mere vocalizations, to meaningless sounds, that implies a demand for a new source of meaning.

The overall atmosphere of *Fear of Music* is spooky and melancholic. The personae of its songs are stuck in obsessive patterns of thought, isolated from their surroundings. For Byrne, it was the product of a period of transition, in which he was redefining his position towards rock music. During his collaboration with Brian Eno, he gradually turned away from the standard formats of rock. They did this not only by using the studio as a tool for composing songs, dissecting and reassembling the crude but catchy exuberance of rock — they combined their practical work on Talking Heads' music with a search for a more philosophical understanding of popular music. For that purpose, Eno and Byrne looked mainly at the African tradition of music and art. They listened to African and Oriental music, often buying LPs with only the sleeve design as an indication of what kind of music they might contain, and studied ethnomusicological literature. Eno went on a musical field trip to Ghana; Byrne visited Bali, where he witnessed some religious and musical rituals.

For Talking Heads as a band, it was most auspicious that the less theoretically inclined members were investigating African music and its Latin and Afro-American derivations in a more direct way. In 1979, Chris Frantz and Tina Weymouth, the band's rhythm section, traveled about the Caribbean, where they witnessed musical Vodun rituals in Haiti and visited the famous reggae musicians and producers Sly Dunbar and Robbie Shakespeare in Jamaica. They brought a large set of Haitian drums home to New York to practice. Around the same time, Jerry Harrison worked as a producer for singer Nona Hendryx and bass player Busta Jones, Afro-Americans who would later play in the expanded version of Talking Heads.[95] While Byrne and Eno were assembling a conceptual framework to reinterpret and articulate the African musical tradition within their own Western context of art, mass media, and pop, Harrison, Weymouth, and Frantz were already preparing to play it.

Chapter 2

A Wider Musical Community

1 MUSIC AND DANCE AS SOCIAL EXCHANGE

Continuing their exchange of ideas, Byrne and Eno explored several other theoretical models for a new musical paradigm. In 1980, when Talking Heads issued their fourth album, *Remain in Light*, Byrne added a small bibliography to the press handout, hoping that it would encourage music journalists to write more interesting interviews and reviews.[1] The bibliography, which was briefly discussed in the Introduction to this book, lists four books:

- John Miller Chernoff: *African Rhythm and African Sensibility. Aesthetics and Social Action in African Musical Idioms.* University of Chicago Press, 1979.
- Robert Farris Thompson: *African Art in Motion. Icon and Act.* University of California Press, 1974.
- Christopher Alexander: *The Timeless Way of Building.* Oxford University Press, 1979, together with:
- Christopher Alexander and others: *A Pattern Language. Towns, Buildings, Construction.* Oxford University Press, 1977.

In each of these books, an art form — music, sculpture, architecture — is analyzed and interpreted as part of a wider system, an ongoing exchange with a community in which people who are not musicians, sculptors or architects do have a functional and at times decisive influence on the work of art. In other words, these books discuss art not as the work of a single artistic genius, but as an element in a wider circuit. If a cybernetic approach is redefined with some nonchalance as the perspective that insists on understanding the individual conscious mental process as part of a wider system, all these books

55

may certainly be seen as a prolongation of Eno and Byrne's fascination by cybernetics. Together, these books present the outline of an artistic paradigm beyond the borders of rock music, a paradigm that emphasizes the exchange of arts with the community, and the exchange of music with other forms of art.

Byrne explored this paradigm in a series of four consecutive albums, which are closely interconnected. He began working with Eno on tracks, almost all of which included "found" vocals, and recorded the musical assemblage *My Life in the Bush of Ghosts*, that would be released in 1981. When the first version of this album was recorded, but before it was issued (getting copyright clearance for all the used vocals proved to be problematic and time-consuming), Talking Heads and Eno recorded *Remain in Light* (1980), an album that explored the same method of assemblage, but with vocals by Byrne. Then Byrne recorded a solo album, *The Catherine Wheel* (1981), a ballet score that had been commissioned by Twyla Tharp. In recording this album, he collaborated once more with Eno, and also with John Chernoff, one of the authors whose work had influenced him. Finally, in 1983 Talking Heads recorded *Speaking in Tongues*, an album on which the band demonstrated how thoroughly they had digested the collage of theoretical and practical impulses and made them their own.

Of the three authors mentioned by Byrne in his press statement, only architectural theorist Christopher Alexander was directly connected to cybernetics. Alexander is something of an iconoclast in architecture, as he is convinced that the problems posed by modern design problems are simply too complex to be solved by architects. Instead of rational solutions, which they are incapable of producing, architects come up with idiosyncratic, "artistic" solutions, playing the role of the genius who can provide a master plan, a blueprint. In an earlier book, *Notes on the Synthesis of Form* (1964), Alexander set out a formal, cybernetics-inspired approach to organizing all possible relevant issues for a design — any design — into sets and subsets, a task that computers might help with. The outcome would then guarantee a rational and orderly way of working, and effectively restore the innocent and organic approach to design that modern architects have lost. In his later books, those recommended by Byrne, Alexander removed cybernetics and the computer from his method. In this version, a pattern language, a series of sets of architectural archetypes put into the hands of the community, guarantees a slow emergence of organic order in architectural design, whether the task in hand is a simple shed or an entire city. There will be more to say about Alexander's design philosophy later in this book, where Byrne's own take on design is discussed. For now, it is enough to take note of Alexander's advocacy for a design process that puts responsibility into the hands of those who actually use a building, instead of the architect. The other authors Byrne recommended bring forward similar points of view, but focus on dance, art, and music, which are the subject of this chapter.

Robert Farris Thompson, author of *African Art in Motion*, was professor for African and Afro-American art history at Yale University. Part anthropologist, part art critic, part musicologist, part student of religion and philosophy, Thompson is able to explain how African arts are anything but primitive, informed as they are by aesthetic, social, and metaphysical traditions. This has made him a groundbreaking historian of Afro-American art and aesthetics, and a forerunner of an art history that takes non-Western art as seriously as the developments in Paris and New York. The subject of *African Art in Motion* is the unity of the arts in Africa, a demonstration of how all forms of African art, music, sculpture, textiles, architecture, religion, and idiogrammatic writing, are part of an ongoing exchange of influences. Thompson celebrates this approach, which never absolutely emphasizes any single medium, as highly sensible. *African Art in Motion* is the catalogue for an exhibition in the National Gallery of Art in Washington, based on Thompson's concept, where African sculpture was presented in the context of aesthetic performance. Thompson included film, video, and recordings in the exhibition to demonstrate how African art can only be understood properly "through a grasp of African dance and ritual and in the special language of body motion: implied, arrested, or expressed."[2] Thompson insists on the importance of the exchanges between activities and forms that have been defined in Western culture as separate art forms.

> Sculpture is not the central art, but neither is the dance, for both depend on words and music and even dreams and divination. Music, dance, and visual objects are all important, separate or together; and if motion conveys stature to music and art, sculpture deepens motion by condensation of several actions into one. These unities demand that we start with the shared norms of performance.[3]

Thompson explains how these norms are united in the aesthetical concept of coolness, "a matrix from which stem ideas about being generous, clear, percussively patterned, harmonized with others, balanced, finished, socially perfected, worthy of destiny."[4] "Coolness" is a metaphor of right living, of moral perfection, an "all-embracing positive attribute which combines notions of composure, silence, vitality, healing, and social purification. Composure intersects with silence; vitality intersects with healing in the sense of restoration of shining health; the body politic is 'healed' in social reconciliations."[5] Such moral perfection and conscious balance can only be the result of a lively exchange in which extremes and excesses are avoided. Thompson points, among other aesthetic rules, to a form of representational balance, which he calls "mid-point mimesis": imagery that is not too realistic and not fully abstract either, but stabilized between these extremes. And he points at patterns of call-and-response and solo-and-circle in performances of song and dance to show how they serve a similar purpose, as sung-and-danced judgments of the quality of social interaction and cohesion.[6] This last subject, the aesthetics of rhythm, music and dance in Africa, has been explored in greater detail by the third author mentioned by Byrne, John Chernoff.

Chernoff's *African Rhythm and African Sensibility* is a study of the social meaning of music and dance in West African societies, as well as a reflexive autobiography and travelogue of an American anthropologist who spent ten years, mostly in Ghana, being trained as an African drummer. The book, which describes African drumming as a community of interlocking parts, is a remarkable combination of scholarly discipline with personal candor. David Byrne recommended it as "one of the few books I know of that talks of the political, social, and spiritual meanings of music. I was moved. It was so nice I read it twice."[7]

Chernoff begins his book by admitting that African music does not require a theoretical interpretation.[8] The basic assumption of the African aesthetic is exactly that its meaning depends on joining, on contributing something to the event, for example by dancing or by clapping one's hands. Without such participation, there is no meaning.[9] This is a fundamental difference with Western classical music, which presupposes the detached attitude that is traditionally seen in the West as a requirement for aesthetic pleasure.[10] Rhythm is at the heart of the music, "the diverse rhythms establish themselves in intricate and changing relationships to each other analogously to the way that tones establish harmony in Western music."[11] In African music there are always at least two rhythms going on that are not unified by a single main beat or basic meter. In musicological terms, it is essentially polyrhythmic, or, more correctly, polymetric, because the different instruments of an ensemble have to be notated in different meters. As one rhythm contrasts with another, it accentuates certain aspects of it, thereby giving it contour and meaning. Within a single ensemble, African drummers play apart from each other, allowing their rhythms to intertwine, to clash and conflict. There is a common beat, for otherwise the music would be impossible to play — but this common, unifying beat is not accented, in fact not even played at all: it is kept hidden, perhaps clicked with the tongue or in some other way demonstrated with a part of the body, i.e., "danced."[12] This leaves the music incomplete: the organizing ingredient still has to be added, a task that falls to the audience, the dancers or listeners. And this means that African music is not a self-encompassed, "absolute" art, but is essentially music for dancing. "The assumption by an African musician that his audience is supplying these fundamental beats permits him to elaborate his rhythms with these as a base, whereas the European tradition requires such close attention to their concrete expression that rhythmic elaboration is limited for the most part to mere ornament."[13] African music can be understood by dancing to it: then the music, although it may be played by a full orchestra, is transformed into an accompaniment for dancing. In Chernoff's words: "The listener must be *actively engaged* in making sense of the music; the music itself does not become the concentrated focus of an event, as at a concert."[14]

In this music, the heart of the composition is the basic organization of rhythms with their shifting accents and emphases and with patterns of "question and answer" known as call-and-response. The master-drummer or singer, if there is one, can add further interest to this weaving of multiple cross-rhythms by placing different accents. Although dances are fixed by tradition, their organization does leave room for improvisation. The individual rhythms, each of which is beaten on a specific drum, all know several variations, and drummers are expected to vary their rhythms to suit the occasion. A good drummer has to keep the dance interesting for the dancers by adding enough variations, but he also has to take care not to exhaust their energy.[15] The musicians and their audience share a responsibility for making the occasion a pleasant one, and in that context the music also has to fulfill its responsibilities by demonstrating the proper behavior. This responsibility is increased by the fact that the drummers can literally use their drums to talk.[16] Drummers of traditional dances can weave proverbs into their music, or comment on the dancers, or drum proverbial names of the ancestors of those present, and this gives them an important function in ceremonies such as weddings, funerals, and the inauguration of a new chief.

Considered separately, many of the rhythms of African music are not exceptionally difficult. They can very well be copied by Westerners, even though these have grown up in a quite different musical environment. What is difficult for Western ears is to hear and to distinguish the different rhythms and to appreciate the complex rhythmic structure that is woven out of them. The aesthetic ideal is not that of a perfectly performed composition, but rather to create a wealth of possibilities for combining and crossing rhythms: "the music is organized to be open to the rhythmic interpretation a drummer, a listener, or a dancer wishes to contribute. The music is perhaps best considered as an arrangement of gaps where one may add a rhythm, rather than as a dense pattern of sound."[17] The best drummers do not distinguish themselves by the intensity or the capriciousness of their improvisations, but by their ability to clarify and enrich the complexity and the movement of the whole musical event.[18] The stylistic criterion is not musical virtuosity as such, but the use of musical style to respect and if possible improve the dynamics of the musical and social relationships. This requires balance and restraint. Without these qualities, "the African musician loses aesthetic command, and the music abdicates its social authority, becoming hot, intense, limited, pretentious, overly personal, boring, irrelevant, and ultimately alienating."[19] Music, in this context, consists in finding and maintaining an interesting and dynamic balance between the varying rhythms, and at the same time between the diverse participants in the occasion, be it a ceremony or a feast. Chernoff quotes R.F. Thompson to explain this more fully:

> Multiple meter essentially uses dancers as further voices in a polymetric choir. The conversation is additive, cool in its expressions of community. The balance struck between the meters and the bodily orchestration seems to communicate a soothing wholeness rather than a "hot" specialization . . . Dialogue in apart performing . . . [and in] call-and-response . . . [is] a means of putting innovation and tradition, invention and imitation, into amicable relationships with one another.[20]

Thus to perform music and dance is finally to establish a community, which means that a moral edification message can go hand in hand with entertainment, excitement with decorum. His conclusion is that this traditional way of drumming has to be accompanied by an explicitly ethical or moral sense of purpose. "Music-making in Africa is above all an occasion for the demonstration of character."[21]

Chernoff contradicts the nostalgic bias that regards so-called traditional societies as determined by stable patterns of culture, patterns that are uncritically accepted and that serve to make every event richly meaningful. Instead, he stresses that life in African societies is characterized by diversity and discontinuity of experience. People often build their identities from elements that may seem mutually exclusive in Western eyes: nationalistic and tribalistic, Animist and Christian or Muslim, traditional and Westernized identities are combined. This music is not necessarily confined to small village communities either, but functions in situations determined by rapid change, urbanization, congestion and noise, poverty, unemployment, uprootedness, and family dispersion.[22] In such situations, according to Chernoff, "Equanimity with multiple rhythms and the silent beat can and does serve to inform social relations with a cosmopolitan attitude of toleration, rationality, and pragmatism."[23] Within this musical context, "singlemindedness of purpose would be equivalent to poverty of expression."[24] This African form of music promotes, and is in its turn favored by, a truly pluralistic sensibility.

Eno and Byrne were trying to copy and translate Chernoff's model of African music in their own work. This music essentially has to be performed live, based as it is on a direct and meaningful exchange with the audience. It is therefore questionable whether it is possible to imitate this communal model of musical meanings in Western popular music, since that usually separates playing and listening.

Evan Eisenberg's sociological description of the processes of making and hearing popular music in the West points to some of the problems that such a translation has to confront:

The glass booths and baffles that isolate the musician from his fellow musicians; the abstracted audience; the sense of producing an object and of mass-producing a commodity; the deconstruction of time by takes and its reconstruction by splicing — these are strong metaphors of modern life. Their mirror images in the listener's experience are solitude; the occlusion of the musician; the use of music as an object and a commodity; the collapse of a public architecture of time and the creation of a private interior design of time. Since they contradict everything that music-making once seemed to be, they are paradoxes.[25]

2 ISOLATED VOICES EMBEDDED IN RHYTHM

The first album of Byrne's that is related to this communal paradigm of music is *My Life in the Bush of Ghosts*. Remarkably enough, the album approaches the African model of coolness and active communal dialogue from the opposite practice of heated and isolated individual voices. Eno was, at this moment in his career, no longer interested in using his own voice, and preferred to use voices of others, radio voices and such, whose speech patterns would sometimes have interesting musical and/or emotional qualities.[26] Both he and Byrne had made tapes of highly emotional voices from U.S. radio stations, and added moving, lamenting voices found on recordings of Arabian singers, until they had a collection that contained "found voices" of preachers, exorcists and singers from the United States and the Arabian Middle East. They edited all these vocals by isolating and repeating significant fragments, and embedded each resulting vocal in a texture of rhythms and small sonic gestures. These textures were constructed in the studio, where they used guitars, basses, synthesizers, and drums, as well as a range of "found objects," including an amplified guitar case and studio floor as well as "coiled spring over car muffler" and plastic water buckets.[27] A series of invited guest musicians added percussive parts to the ongoing recordings.

The record presents those impassioned and entranced voices embedded in a texture of syncopated rhythms. Each album track was made by overlaying many layers of mostly small rhythmic motifs, combined with vocals to create a single emotional arc. This collage has an "ethnic-funk psychedelic" overall sound, as

Byrne described it,[28] and can be enjoyed as a series of intriguing patterns of voice and rhythm. But the record contains other levels of meaning that disclose themselves when the listener tries to identify with the vocal, an identification that is the norm for popular music. This attempt is bound to fail; in this respect these collages may be compared to the songs on *Fear of Music*, which repudiate direct identification with the personae of the lyrics. Yet on that album, Byrne's energetic deliverance, his central mediating role as a singer, together with his storytelling lyrics, invites the listener to consider the presented personae as real in a naturalistic sense, as recognizable, passing mental states. The organization of those songs in chorus-and-verse format also created a unified perspective by alternating direct emotional approaches (in the choruses) with more distanced perspectives (in the verses). "I Zimbra," the song that prefigured the collages of *My Life in the Bush of Ghosts*, was the exception to this.

My Life in the Bush of Ghosts is different. There is no single unifying voice, the lyrics do not outline a persona in a situation, and the music is not always organized in a chorus-and-verse pattern. The lyrics and voices as such do not solicit a direct identification, and there is no conventional organization of emotional perspective. These are voices that have been lifted out of their context, and seem to have lost their aesthetic command and their social authority. To borrow Chernoff's words for such music, they are hot, intense, overly personal and pretentious.

The opening track of the album, titled "America is Waiting," is a good example. It reproduces the voice of someone who is referred to on the record sleeve as an "unidentified indignant radio host, San Francisco, April 1980." An outraged male voice exclaims: "America is waiting for a message of some sort or another." Later on in the track, the same voice is heard to say, "No will whatsoever. No will whatsoever. Absolutely no integrity," and similar condemnations. The editing of this recorded voice by Byrne and Eno, with its alienating use of fragmentation and repetition, emphasizes the peculiar qualities of the speaker's statement. The speaker's moral indignation seems to require that the entire American nation must emotionally identify itself with his position to make reconciliation possible. This is a request of mythical dimensions. The title of the album, *My Life in the Bush of Ghosts*, suggests that we live in an environment that is filled with such messages. Eno and Byrne adopted this title from a novel by Nigerian writer Amos Tutuola. His book is a ghost story that tells of a defenseless little boy who travels through the jungle, where he is time and again caught by ghosts that subject him to hair-raising experiences on a journey where logic and continuity are time and again suspended. The unmistakable implication is that the media landscape may have a similar effect on an unprotected or destabilized audience.

Perhaps the texture of rhythms and sonic gestures that were added by Byrne and Eno can provide the sense of perspective that makes it possible to understand the extreme emotions that are projected by the voice fragments. The musical texture may be considered as an environment that envelopes those dis-embodied, trance-like voices, helping them to relate to their surroundings. This interpretation would be in keeping with Chernoff's exposé of the aesthetic and spiritual meanings of such rhythmic patterns: they are an invitation to join the dance and thereby the community. This invites an interpretation of the album as offering a rhythmic invitation to such hot, uncomfortable, pretentious voices in the media landscape to be cooled in a communal and musical celebration; this seems to me the only interpretation that is in keeping with the African aesthetic as explained by Thompson and Chernoff. As Thompson quotes some African spokesmen, "it cools the town when you dance . . . when you finish . . . you are restored to repose . . . and reconciliation with your family."[29] Chernoff repeatedly emphasizes that the ideal character that is presupposed in African polyrhythmic music is calm, "cool" instead of "hot," showing collectedness of mind.[30] This kind of character is indispensable to mediate the different power-fully vital rhythms, as well as to take part in the potentially always-conflicting social situation.

This composure is not emphasized to deny that rhythms and dances are used to help participants enter a trance; it is meant to point out that the most important aspect of such a trances is that one may leave them, and join the community. Chernoff writes that:

> when Africans allow a person to become possessed or identified with power, as when they celebrate or praise a particular cult god whose rhythm "rides" or "comes up" to a dancer, they are using music and dance as a technique of religious experience, and as we noted, they do so most often under strictly controlled circumstances in the presence of a religious figure, a specialist at cooling down "hot" people.[31]

And: "One does not dance to go into trance but to come out of a trance, to join a diversified assembly with a separate contribution, for dancing is a reminder that one is only part of the whole."[32]

The voices presented by Byrne and Eno lack coolness: they seem possessed, entranced. The added rhythms mimic the overexcited qualities of those voices; but in doing so they provide these isolated vocal personae with a musical context, symbolic of a community that invites the singers and speakers to cool down. Of course, Chernoff writes about the cooling down of actual people, while Byrne and Eno deal with media representations. The dance to which Eno and Byrne enlist their selection of found voices is only performed as a hypothetical exercise, so to speak. Yet that exercise is not without importance, since we live possibly quite as much in a world of media voices as in an assembly of real human speakers. When they began the recordings for *My Life in the Bush of Ghosts*, Byrne and Eno were inspired for a while by the idea of making a record that would be based on an imaginary culture, and they fantasized about detailed liner notes that would specify the way music functioned in that culture.[33] The idea was dropped after serving its function. And yet, turned on its head, it may still be useful, for our culture is saturated with representations, voices, and images that function through the imagination, and to keep one's cool in this environment everyone has to find ways to include these influential mimetic presences in his or her experience.

That Byrne meant something along these lines can be seen in Bruce Conner's *America is Waiting* and *Mea Culpa*, two short films made to accompany the tracks of the same name on *My Life in the Bush of Ghosts*. Byrne acted as producer for these films. Conner (1933–2008) was a conceptual artist and experimental filmmaker who in 1958 had started to make experimental films, mostly using found footage taken from educational films, government information films, science films, and such, footage that he combined with music and used to create complex and ironic, often dark juxtapositions. His films have often been credited as forerunners of the music video.[34] Conner opposes the viewer's expected response to familiar footage to convey another, opposed meaning.[35] As visual accompaniment to Byrne and Eno's "America Is Waiting," Conner combined images of radar stations and rhythmically moving exploding clouds with shots of families entering bomb shelters, children playing with toy grenade launchers, operating impressive and enigmatic machinery, and similar, mostly innocent representations of war from American film and TV culture. In the final images of this film, a sheep is peacefully standing in a meadow, when suddenly a wolf, which had been hiding behind it appears. Evidently, the use of found footage is a direct parallel to the use of found voices; the films add other layers of meaning to the musical textures.

3   AT THE CROSSROADS: *REMAIN IN LIGHT*

Byrne and Eno were intent on combining the African musical practice, which relies on direct participation, with their own practice of recording music for reproduction, where relations between musician and audience are abstract. They investigated this paradox in *My Life In The Bush Of Ghosts*, and that record served as a laboratory for further experimentation for Talking Heads' fourth album, *Remain In Light*. When Talking Heads began work on that record, Byrne and Eno introduced the process of using various multi-track tapes as a medium for collage and composition. Byrne did not feel inclined to write songs and take them to the band for rehearsals. He proposed to the other members that the rehearsals should not be rehearsals of predefined songs, but a way to sharpen their skills, "one person coming up with something, somebody else coming up with a part that rhythmically locks in with it."[36] The recording process was similar to these preparations: developing an interesting and satisfying texture of repetitive tracks by adding new layers and deleting expandable older tracks.[37]

This process resulted in dense, overfilled rhythms that combine a steady accentuated beat with hectic fast percussive motifs that add frayed and gabbling accentuations. On top of this goes a dense texture of repetitive riffs on keyboards and guitars, filtered and treated with synthesizer technology. The vocals come on top of all this, and they are as frayed and dense as the other elements of the music.

Making a Talking Heads album implied that Byrne had to write lyrics, and as soon as enough basic tracks had been completed, he started working on them. He came up with compilations of material that he had gathered from diverse sources: phrases and rants of radio evangelists recorded in different parts of the U.S.A.; a record of John Dean's testimony during the Watergate trials; a record of ex-slaves telling stories; newspaper headlines; and the books by Chernoff and Thompson.[38] Byrne and Eno also reconsidered the relationship of the vocals to the music. Where Byrne's previous, conventionally organized rock songs created dramatic tension by changing the music underneath the vocal melody, now he needed to find another means to create drama, as the music basically repeated root patterns over and over again. Byrne and Eno put together layered vocal arrangements, group choruses and vocals going on top of other vocals, and added instrumental solos weaving in and out of the rhythmic textures.[39] Nona Hendryx, who had been successful in the glam-funk trio LaBelle, was invited to add vocals, and her strong, self-certain, and clear voice adds a reverberating contrast to the more reticent and muffled voices of Byrne and Eno.

The resulting songs resemble generic rock music, but are unmistakably different. The lyrics of "Born Under Punches (The Heat Goes On)," the opening song of the album, may help to make the difference clear. This song opens with an echoing shout, followed immediately by the onset of a driving rhythm that includes both steady and syncopated elements; this texture is punctuated by parrot-like squeaks, instrumental passages like the sound of electronic pinball machines (actually a guitar solo, locked into a Lexicon digital delay and then electronically divided into fragments and rearranged[40]), shouts of animals, and the like. While Byrne sings some of his lines in a voice that is close to hysterical wailing, he switches to a more authoritative voice to render intermittent comments (here printed in italics):

I'm not a drowning man!	
And I'm not a burning building!	*I'm a tumbler!*
Drowning cannot hurt a man!	
Fire cannot hurt a man.	*Not the Government Man.*

At the same time, a choir of forceful female voices repeats: "And the heat goes on — goes on — Where the hand has been — And the heat goes on — goes on —." While these voices continue, a choir of more timid male voices sings:

All I want is to breathe.	*Thank you. Thank you.*
Won't you breathe with me?	
Find a little space . . . so we move in-between.	*I'm so thin.*
And keep one step ahead of yourself.	*I'm catching up with myself.*

Again, the italic lines are sung by Byrne alone, with great emphasis. The result is a complicated balancing act, in which the models of traditional African drumming, and of funk music as its latest American derivation, are used as a medium for the interpretation of contemporary metropolitan culture, which includes individual introspection. The songs combine elements of "persona" (Byrne's familiar theme of the individual under stress) with elements of what literary scholars call "topos," the common meeting place, in its dense texture of individual voice and choirs. And the musical texture is the result of improvisations, audible in the call-and-response patterning of rhythms and signals, yet formally structured through the extensive use of recording studio technology.

The first five songs on *Remain in Light*, "Born Under Punches (The Heat Goes On)," "Crosseyed and Painless," "The Great Curve," "Once In A Lifetime," and "Houses In Motion", are located at an intersection of different forms of musical experience. (This makes them the signature songs of the album. The three final songs, "Seen And Not Seen," "Listening Wind," and "The Overload", are closer to regular ballads.) They combine the key elements of rock ballads with the key elements of funk/disco tracks, and this locates them at an interesting crossroads, where the high value placed on intensified inner experience that belongs to rock ballads comes up against the celebration of the moment that is the point of the pure and fast repetitive rhythms of disco and funk. These five songs are both fast and slow, which means that they offer a dramatic confrontation between the insistence of memory and the equally insistent pressure of the present moment.

Simon Frith, the most interesting theoretician to write about the meanings of rock and popular music, has attempted a description of the relations between music and the experience of time. He quotes a phenomenological analysis of

musical time that is based on concerts of chamber music, where attention
is focused on "inner time," the mental play of anticipation and recollection,
of expectations about the music that is to come, and reflections on what
has just been heard. This mental play adds to the ongoing stream of musical
sounds and builds it into a complex and rich experience of time. As inner,
phenomenological experience of musical time, music can be experienced in
two directions simultaneously: "The hearer, therefore, listens to the ongoing
flux of music, so to speak, not only in the direction from the first to the last bar
but simultaneously in a reverse direction back to the first one."[41] Composers
of art music, especially modern and contemporary composers, use this time
structure of music and its potential to produce multiple, paradoxical, and
contradictory experiences of "inner time," to make music that *confronts* time. In
popular music, Frith distinguishes between two opposed ways to project inner
time. Ballads or "slow songs" project a sense of the past, an attempt to envelop
everything that has already happened, while rhythm numbers, or fast songs,
project an enhanced and exclusive present that expands to fill the moment.
Fast rhythmic music emphasizes the present, the "now" of "moment time," a
duration that excludes content, or the memory of durations, making memory
impossible or at least irrelevant.[42] These distinctions may explain how *Remain
in Light* is situated on the fault line where opposing forms of experience meet
and clash: the inner time of slow songs, with its sense of (auto)biographical
memory, and the moment time of disco, driving out memory to make room
exclusively for the present "now."

Remain in Light was received well by critics and audience alike.[43] When the
album was released, critic Ken Tucker noted in *Rolling Stone* that Talking Heads
had managed to bridge the gap between white and black music, at a moment when
the audience for new wave and rock and that for disco and funk had very little
interest, if not open disdain, for each other's musical styles.[44] White and black
musical styles in popular music were considered, and were often experienced as,
each other's very undoing. Where rock stands for an intensity of inner feeling,[45]
disco can be experienced as superficial and mechanical mindlessness, and in the
other direction, where dance music is appreciated for its forceful and infectious
presence, rock can be experienced as neurotic and romantic self-absorption. Seen
in this light, the two have to be mutually exclusive. (Which helps to explain why
it just doesn't do to imagine the Velvet Underground jamming with Kool and
the Gang, or Donna Summer, or even James Brown, doing a guest appearance
with rock groups like Television or Patti Smith.)

Talking Heads' ability to cross this musical divide has to be explained on a
few levels. Important is that the members of the band always confessed to enjoying all kinds of black dance music, and included elements of that in their own

sound. Chris Frantz would explain the difference between Talking Heads and punk groups as follows: "We like K.C. and the Sunshine Band and Funkadelic/Parliament. You ask Johnny Rotten if he likes K.C. and the Sunshine Band and he'll blow snot in your face."[46] But crucial is Byrne's capacity as frontman of the band to enact not just the emotional roles that his songs demand, but to write and enact songs that showcase conflicts between emotional states. Simon Frith, to return once more to his analysis, has written that the great pop performers "don't so much enact emotional roles as hold their enactments up before us in fragments, so we can admire the shape of the gesture itself."[47] Byrne's vocal performance doesn't just enact fragments of roles, but emphasizes the conflicts between emotional states. On *Remain in Light*, this portrayal of emotional conflict combines with the fast and slow rhythmic texture to produce a struggle between the "inner time" of memory and "moment time." It is music that confronts time, not in the domain of musical composition, but in the domain of the mass media. The songs of *Remain in Light* should not be taken for direct personal statements in the tradition of rock as expressive Romanticism, but as structural organizations of emotional conflicts and compromises. The songs' characters are problematic unities that struggle to contain several mimetic impulses at once, including projections from the mass media. These personae are involved as accomplices in their own emotions, even as they try to suppress them, deny them, or appear to be overwhelmed against their conscious will. While most of these characters appear to be prey to inner contradictions, the album also includes a joyous hymn ("The Great Curve") to the transcending and divine power of sexuality and of nature.[48] Such lyrics can't be rearranged into coherent descriptive stories, but have to be accepted as force fields, groupings of illogical metaphors that sometimes reinforce, but often countermand, each other.

Critics have compared *Remain in Light* to Picasso's *Demoiselles d'Avignon*, singled out by art historians as the paradigmatic cubist painting and also the first painting to combine African and European pictorial traditions.[49] This comparison is helpful: as cubism combines irreconcilable perspectives within a single painting, so Byrne, Eno, and the other members of Talking Heads constructed songs that succeed in combining different perspectives on emotion within a single musical texture. The comparison is also instructive in other respects. Picasso rendered a sense of multiplicity without knowing at first just how he managed to do it,[50] and that may also have been true of Eno, Byrne, and the other members of Talking Heads. They certainly did not solve the contradictions between African musical face-to-face interaction and Western music technology, where separate tracks can be erased or modified with a push on a button, but like Picasso, they did manage to articulate the conflict in an innovative manner, producing a relevant take on the conflicts between diverging musical experiences, as well as those between the experiences offered by the mass media versus that of face-to-face relations.

In his lyrics for "Seen And Not Seen," Byrne addressed this explicitly:

> He would see faces in movies, on T.V., in magazines, and in books . . . He thought that some of these faces might be right for him . . . And through the years, by keeping an ideal facial structure fixed in his mind . . . Or somewhere in the back of his mind . . . That he might, by force of will, cause his face to approach those of his ideal . . . The change would be very subtle . . . It might take ten years or so . . . Gradually his face would change its shape . . .

These lyrics show a striking parallel to a text that conceptual artist Victor Burgin included in his *Framed* (1977). Like Byrne, Burgin was strongly influenced by the work of Art & Language. *Framed* is a photo of a desolate public environment (an underground subway passage or a similar space) that has a framed Marlboro advertisement on a wall, showing the rugged cowboy "Marlboro Man," and a text titled "Framed": "A dark-haired woman in her late-fifties hands over a photograph showing the haircut she wants duplicating exactly. The picture shows a very young woman with blond hair cut extremely short. The hairdresser props it by the mirror in which he can see the face of his client watching her own reflection. When he has finished he removes the cotton cape from the woman's shoulders. 'That's it', he says. But the woman continues sitting, continues staring at her reflection in the mirror."[51]

In another song, "The Overload," Byrne, Eno, and Harrison tried to emulate what they had read in the music press about the British band Joy Division, whose music they had not heard at that time.[52] This dark, droningly monotonous track lacks the inner tensions of vocal, lyrics, rhythms, and other musical gestures that are the album's signature. It is a throwback to *Fear of Music*. Had it been on that album, it would have been a tragically clear-sighted take on the post-punk "doom bands" that were fashionable in England around 1980, as Joy Division's suicidally depressed singer Ian Curtis did indeed suffer from the musicogenic epileptic fits that *Fear of Music* was named after.

A song that does represent conflicting emotions, and more visibly so than the rest of the album because Byrne made a video clip for it, is "Once In A Lifetime." Its lyrics evoke a sense of bafflement, a process of self-reflection that combines everyday routine with a feeling of spiritual panic:[53]

> And you may find yourself behind the wheel of a large automobile.
> And you may find yourself in a beautiful house, with a beautiful wife.

> And you may ask yourself — Well . . . how did I get here?
>
> . . .
>
> And you may ask yourself: What is that beautiful house?
> And you may ask yourself: Where does that highway go to?
> And you may ask yourself: Am I right? . . . Am I wrong?
> And you may say to yourself: MY GOD! . . . WHAT HAVE I DONE?

The clip features Byrne, dressed in a grey suit with bow tie and dark-framed glasses, impersonating a hybrid between a TV evangelist and someone undergoing religious conversion. He executes movements that send his body jolting and twitching in a physical vocabulary that he based on body movements and gestures of preachers and other people who go into trances. Choreographer Toni Basil helped him to formularize those spasms and movements and make them into a dance. As Byrne explained, "It took a lot of rehearsals, the dancing part of it was meant to be a sort of halfway point between dance and a series of muscular spasms."[54] Basil and Byrne had visited the film library of the University of California in L.A. to study footage of different styles of dance, of preachers and of people in trance. According to Toni Basil, they considered the result more as acting than as dance per se.[55]

Byrne used a number of devices to put this performance in context. First, the video image of his dancing is mirrored and projected in fourfold as its own background, which formalizes and distances the performance. Second, the movements that Byrne executes are shown to be copied from anthropological film footage of foreign cultures, as the "original" (authentic?) gestures are periodically shown on a screen in the background, in a didactic style of montage (which, by the way, is completely familiar since it is used daily by TV news magazines). Part of this anthropological footage was taken from *Studies in Nigerian Dance 2* by Peggy Harper; another sequence came from Japan. Third, Byrne is shown in very short sequences, now against a background of ominously lighted fog, now profusely sweating while his head is steadied by hands that come from above (whose?), now sitting quietly, dressed casually and obviously relaxed while lip-synching to his own voice. In a clip of only 3 minutes and 24 seconds, such repeated and diverse contextualizations produce uncertainty in the viewer, an effect that Byrne explicitly aims to create: "Lyrically or imagistically or musically, it's most exciting when you can't quite get a handle on it."[56]

In this clip, Byrne creates a performative field that is both constructed and spontaneous. The spectator cannot reach a final conclusion about Byrne's own position towards his lyrics and other material, and so misses a focus that might enable him or her to take up a definite standpoint towards the work. And yet at the same time Byrne lays bare his sources of inspiration, the artistic devices he uses to overstep the conventions of rock music. His interest in radio and television evangelists had provided him with ample material to reflect on the meanings of publicized emotional performances — something that rock singers have in common with tele-evangelists, who use the media to preach, testify, convert, collect money, and even to heal members of their audience, relying fully on the direct effectiveness of their media presence. Byrne observed the contradictions in their performances:

> "Sometimes their delivery is real ecstatic, but what they're saying is so conservative and moralistic. It's hard to reconcile the fact that these guys are going absolutely berserk while they're telling everyone to behave themselves. And they're madly raving, jumping all over the place. In that kind of preaching — like in a music piece — as much is said in the delivery and the phrasing as in the words. What's important isn't what's literally being said."[57]

Talking Heads decided to play the new songs in live concerts, a decision that was far from obvious since the material couldn't possibly be played live by only four musicians. Because of that, the group invited a number of musicians to join them. Nona Hendryx and Dolette McDonald sang back-up vocals; Adrian Belew, who had played with Frank Zappa and David Bowie, played lead and rhythm guitar; Bernie Worrell, former member of the influential funk groups Parliament and Funkadelic, played keyboards; Steven Scales played percussion; and Busta Jones was the second bass player. Talking Heads were now an unusual mix of a white rock group with a black funk band. On top of that, the funk musicians had a much stronger musical background and training than the former art students. The band was also composed of men and women — an unusual line-up for a pop group, an artistic and political statement in itself.[58] (There would be several changes to this line-up: in 1982, Dolette McDonald sang the backing vocals alone; later, Lynn Mabry and Edna Holt replaced Hendryx and McDonald. Alex Weir replaced Adrian Belew, and Raymond Jones sometimes replaced Bernie Worrell.) The experiment worked out very well. Tina Weymouth commented: "It was lucky, things falling into place. And I've never seen a bunch of people so happy onstage."[59]

David Byrne was even more enthusiastic in interviews:

> "The feeling onstage is nothing at all like performing rock or pop songs, which relieves me greatly. I think some of the other musicians feel the same way. 'Spiritual' is a sort of dangerous word to use because of the western definition of the word, but that is how I describe the music. A lot of spiritual music which has its roots in Africa is very exciting and people have a lot of fun dancing to it. It's casual, too."[60]

He explained:

> "There's just less of a feeling of a performer projecting his own ego to a crowd, which rock and roll seems to be about. For me, there's more of a feeling of community — a group of people working and playing together. The kind of thing we're doing now deals with a different series of metaphors than pop music . . . The nature of the music is to inspire a mystical communion among the musicians and the audience through repetitive rhythms and so on. On a good night, it can become a transcendent experience that is mainly to do with a lot of people feeling that they're locking together and fitting together into one thing which is very different from the other music."[61]

Byrne delighted in presenting characters that were caught up in contradicting forces within the context of Talking Heads' music because the music articulated the possibility of an alternative experience of mimetic projections. During performances he often imitated people in spiritual ecstasy, and as singer he mediated the emotional appeal of the music. When asked whether as a singer he wanted to assume a spiritual role, Byrne replied that he "didn't want to take on the role of being a prophet or a shaman onstage. That can turn into a caricature that gets hokey after a while. There may be elements of that, but I didn't want to set myself up as a prophet or anything like that. I just wanted to say that we are part of that and so are lots of other people."[62] The voices, gestures and roles that Byrne assumes as a singer, borrowed from TV preachers, politicians, shamans, and a range of others, are simultaneously enacted simulations and real personal experiences, presented as humorous and ironic demonstrations of the human propensity for self-creation and delusion.

This new approach to songwriting, inspired by African examples, gave Byrne a sense of freedom and enthusiasm that he had not experienced before while singing on stage. Both he and Brian Eno spoke about this to journalists with great fervor. In an attempt to explain why Chernoff's book had impressed him so deeply, in an interview Byrne contrasted the African aesthetic with the capitalistic context of rock music. He turned to the great sociologist Max Weber's famous 1906 monograph *The Protestant Ethic and the Spirit of Capitalism*, on the relation between religion and capitalism in the U.S.A., to explain how music and the economy are related:

> "[Max Weber] was attempting to explain how a peoples' spiritual foundations lead them to a particular economic way of life, how their religious and moral upbringing leads them to a social and economic attitude. I think this is true for rock musicians as much as anyone. They've grown up in a society that values competition, the whole dog-eat-dog beat-out-the-other-guy kind of thing. So they're bound to play music in

the same way: trying to out-solo the other guy, trying to play louder than the other guy, et cetera."[63]

In 1992, looking back on this period, Byrne recapitulated:

"The structure of the music was that the whole was greater than the sum of its parts and that each part was just a little piece — together they made something that was not evident in any one piece. What seemed wonderful about that idea was that it was a musical metaphor for a utopian community."[64]

4 COMPARATIVE STUDIES OF MYTH, ARCHETYPES, AND RITUAL

At the same time as he was immersing himself in the celebrations of African and Afro-American sensibility provided by Thompson and Chernoff, Byrne was also eagerly read classic works on comparative mythology and on the psychological functions of myth and ritual. He studied the works of Carl Gustav Jung, which were widely read in the 1960s and 70s, and Joseph Campbell's studies in comparative mythology. Their influence is often recognizable in Byrne's work, sometimes in a detailed way, and more often in the general outlook. Byrne has told interviewers that he likes a lot of the cross-cultural comparisons of myths and rituals that these authors make, and values the perspective that their theories provide.[65]

Jung and Campbell gathered countless myths from cultures all over the world, and from all ages of mankind. Their collections demonstrate that myths have accompanied mankind always and everywhere. According to Jung's version of psychoanalytical thinking, the effectiveness of mythic symbols to organize the human passions is grounded in archetypes, primary mental patterns shared by large groups of people, in what Jung has termed the "collective unconscious." Jung's theory of the archetypes is also part of the foundation of Campbell's work, which makes both *oeuvres* compatible. Since Byrne is interested in Jung's work on archetypes and symbols rather than in his psychiatric method, the theories of Jung and Campbell will be discussed in combination. According to Campbell, "a mythology is an organization of symbolic narratives and images that are metaphorical of the possibilities of human experience and fulfillment in a given society at a given time."[66] Following Jung, Campbell considered mythology to be a function of biology: "every organ of the body has a different energy impulse, an impulse to action, and the experience of the conflicts of these different energies inside, is what constitutes the psyche . . . mythology is the expression in personified images of these energies."[67]

Campbell points out that all children spontaneously form animistic conceptions, symbolic fantasies about the origin of their world and its inhabitants. Such animistic ideas can be elaborated and organized into myths, which give a symbolic form to some of the basic facts of human consciousness. In so far as these facts of life are biological and universal to all men (for example a child's dependence on its elders, the organization of the senses, the basic drives), myths from different cultures are analogous, which means it is possible to translate and compare them. And the same is true of forms of ritualization and sanctification which are, similarly, elaborations of symbolic fantasies. Mythology, considered in this way, is closely linked to the human psyche. But this leaves the question unanswered of what the relevance of mythology is for adults, especially adults in a modern society who pride themselves on their independence of nature.

To grasp the outlines of this ambitious project to provide insight into the relevance of myth in modernity, it is helpful to compare Jung's concept of the unconscious to that of Sigmund Freud, his colleague and at one time friend in the development of psychoanalytical theory. Freud was inclined to think that a healthy adult mind does not need a mythology. In Freud's theories the unconscious is but the product of the mental repression of thoughts and impulses which the conscious mind cannot accept. It follows that a healthy ego doesn't need to revert to this mechanism. Instead, a healthy adult relies on contact with other people, and on the experience of reality that is communicated in this exchange, to form his understanding of the world. According to Freud, religion is merely the accepted form of mythology in modern civilization; in due course, it should therefore give way to enlightened scientific realism, which is able to unmask all myths as mere illusion. Jung, on the other hand, considered myths to be a valid source of motivation, a common biological necessity instead of an individual biographical mishap. According to Jung, myths help to give shape to psychic energy throughout life, and the healthy adult mind is the mind that knows and accepts its own mythical foundations. For Jung, there are two fundamentally different systems of unconscious motivation: the personal unconscious, as recognized and treated in Freudian therapy, and the collective unconscious, a common reservoir of "primary images" or archetypes, the psychic expression of anatomically and physiologically determined human tendencies.[68] This theory of archetypes, as Campbell has summarized it,

> assumes that there is in the structure and functioning of the psyche a certain degree of spontaneity and consequent uniformity throughout the history and domain of the human species — an order of psychological laws inhering in the structure of the body, which has not radically altered since the period of the Aurignacian caves and

can be as readily identified in the jungles of Brazil as in the cafés of Paris, as readily in the igloos of Baffin Land as in the harems of Marrakech.[69]

In Jung's view, individual consciousness is thus always closely related to the collective unconscious experience of all of mankind, and creative fantasy shows this when identical or similar mythological images come up time and again. As he writes:

> Creative fantasy also draws upon the forgotten and long buried primitive mind with its host of images, which are to be found in the mythologies of all ages and all peoples. The sum of these images constitutes the collective unconscious, a heritage which is potentially present in every individual.[70]

Jung's psychology of the unconscious is directly derived from the Romantic philosophy of nature, which posits the organic unity of man and nature. In contrast to the rationalism of the Enlightenment, which separated body and mind, this Romantic thinking holds that the cosmos forms a unity that comprises both mind and matter, history and nature. The unconscious is seen as the location where the transition from animal to psychic life takes place. This philosophy of nature is organized around the idea of the organism that unfolds from its original seed, according to an inborn law. In Jungian psychology, conscious identity unfolds organically from the unconscious.[71] The unconscious is, for Jung, an early stage of the conscious mind: a stage which has to be overcome, but which also contains within itself the force to realize the overcoming.

Some biologists have concluded from the helplessness of newborn babies that all people are born, as it were, prematurely, since they lack the capacity to survive independently. In this context, Jung has called myth the second womb, which holds the prematurely born human being for a while within the realm of nature, until it is finally released into the historical and cultural world — a release which is, according to Jung, often paid for by regression.[72] The unconscious remains the fertile soil for all creative activity, as demonstrated by the history of religions, by mass psychology and by the psychic life of anyone who has ever hoped or striven for something. Still, for the average personality it is better that the whole gamut of associations which is based in the unconscious is curbed by consciousness.[73]

According to Jung, the mythical fantasies that arise out of the unconscious serve a real purpose, since they are the origin of thought that is directed towards reality. Archetypes and mythical symbols may help to achieve this inner development, as well as a successful passage through the transitions that everyone has to achieve in life, going from childhood to puberty, from maturity to middle and old age. This theory is the basis for Jung's method of "amplification," in which the therapist helps the patient by clarifying his or her symbolic representations by means of analog imagery from the history of mankind.[74] A crucial aspect of this method is that it emphasizes the similarity of psychotic delusions and the symbolism of myths and religions.[75] Jung wrote: "I am therefore of the opinion that in general, psychic energy or libido creates the God-image by making use of archetypal patterns, and that man in consequence worships the psychic force active within him as something divine."[76] According to him, "the genesis of this figure is a natural process with a teleological orientation in which the cause anticipates the goal. As it is a natural process, it cannot be decided whether the God-image is created or whether it creates itself."[77] Jung often wrote about archetypes as if they were real entities, ascertaining that "it is a psychological fact that an archetype can seize hold of an ego and even compel it to act as it — the archetype — wills."[78]

In his search for archetypes, Jung combined material from dreams, myths, fairytales, children's fantasies, delusions, spiritual traditions, alchemic teachings, and from the dogmatic formulations of revealed religions without regard for the different ways in which an individual believes in them. In response to this deliberate practice of lifting myths from their original context, anthropologists have pointed out time and again that symbols must be studied within the practice in which they function and have their value, if they are to be interpreted correctly.[79]

Joseph Campbell was well aware of this critical debate surrounding the concept of archetypes. He compared his own Jungian perspective to the ethnological and sociological viewpoint that was formulated by the influential anthropologist A.R. Radcliffe-Brown in his 1922 study *The Andaman Islanders*:

A society depends for its existence on the presence in the minds of its members of a certain system of sentiments by which the conduct of the individual is regulated in conformity with the needs of society. Every feature of the social system itself and every event or object that in any way affects the well-being or the cohesion of the society becomes an object of this system of sentiments. *In human society the sentiments in question are not innate but are developed in the individual by the action of the society upon him* [Campbell's emphasis]. The ceremonial customs of a society are a means by which the sentiments in question are given collective expression on appropriate occasions. The ceremonial (i.e. collective) expression of any sentiments serves both to maintain it at the requisite degree of intensity in the mind of the individual and to transmit it from one generation to another. Without such expression the sentiments involved could not exist.[80]

In reaction to this, Campbell wrote that "no one has yet devised an effective method for distinguishing between the innate and the acquired, the natural and the culturally conditioned, the 'elementary' and the 'ethnic' aspects of such human-cultural catalysts and their evoked responses."[81] Campbell concludes that that is reason enough to pursue a Romantic-biological approach to the world's mythologies. His own four-volume overview of the world's mythologies, *The Masks of God* (1959–68) bears witness to this conviction. The potential advantages of this perspective are readily seen, since the functionalistic perspective of Radcliffe-Brown and so many other anthropologists and sociologists remains unable to explain the content of rites and symbols.[82]

It is interesting to note that the very same opposition of the Romantic, psychological approach of archetypes and the functionalistic, sociological approach still holds sway over the critics writing about David Byrne's work. The release of *My Life in the Bush of Ghosts* immediately sparked a debate over the question whether Eno/Byrne's use of found voices from different cultural backgrounds was appropriate and legitimate. In a review in *Rolling Stone* entitled "Does this global village have two-way traffic?," Jon Pareles gave voice to the functionalist and sociological point of view, writing: "My Life in the Bush of Ghosts is an undeniably awesome feat of tape editing and rhythmic ingenuity. But, like most 'found' art, it raises stubborn questions about context, manipulation and cultural imperialism." Pareles decries the tracks "Help Me Somebody" and "The Jezebel Spirit" as trivializing, calling them "pseudodocuments," and accuses Byrne and Eno of falsifying the vocal rituals they made use of by truncating their development and thereby deforming the rhythm of the ritual itself.[83] In the *New York Times*, John Rockwell took the opposite viewpoint, enthusiastically underwriting the idea of the "fevered energy" of the aural collage that Byrne and Eno had put together. Rockwell appreciated the album as "enlivened by Mr. Byrne's own intense and bizarre imagination and inspired by the rhythms and vocal colors of both black and Arab Africa. It is a superb achievement and an intimation of the growing influence Africa is likely to have on Western musicians in years to come."[84]

How to decide which critic is right? Or, in a more general sense, how to choose between the perspective of the "mythical method" with its recognition of the enthusing force of myths, and the perspective that recognizes the great importance of functional contexts? There is, of course, no other solution to this dilemma than the recognition that both sides hold only part of the truth, and should not claim to have it all. To define all of social and historical reality in terms of individual myths and fervors is reductive and unhelpful — and so is the tendency of countless experts and bureaucrats to describe reality

exclusively in terms of contextual systems. John Chernoff, who, as anthropologist, is not unaware of the forces of circumstance but refuses to reduce
the dignity, courage, and sheer high spirits of the individual to all of that, has
described this as "the politico-economic techno-philosophical socio-historical
global-developmental backdrop."[85] (Chernoff points to Fela Kuti's song "Mr.
Grammatologylisationalism Is The Boss" as a source of inspiration for his great
chain of adjectives.[86])

The point of contexts is that they are rarely singular. The record *My Life in the
Bush of Ghosts* is one context; the "cultural imperialism" that Pareles mentions
is a context; Christian orthodoxy is a context; and so is Islamic orthodoxy.
(Christianity and Islam being sources of some of the remarkable vocals used
for the record.) The answer to Pareles' question as to whether this global
village has two-way traffic is yes, but the traffic isn't regulated and it streams
in more than two directions. The entertainment industry does try to create a
monopoly — and nearly succeeds — but artists and music-lovers each have
their own agendas, and so do representatives of Christianity and Islam. The
history of the album shows this: an Islamic organization in London — not in
Algeria — protested against the use of the voice of Algerian Muslims chanting
Qu'ran (Koran) by Byrne and Eno, and they removed the track, which had been
on the first pressing, from the record.[87]

Byrne's dealings with music and anthropology will come up again in a later
chapter that is dedicated entirely to this matter. At this point, just a few remarks
may throw some light on the question that haunts the study of myth, which
is: how to apply myths in a well-considered manner, how to give them critical
purchase on a specific historical situation? On this matter, neither Jung nor
Campbell is very helpful. They interpret the wide diversity of mythological
material, regardless of its social status and context, as immediately relevant.
What they offer is to some extent negative: they refute the notion that mythologies are no longer relevant in modernity. As Joseph Mali, a contemporary
scholar in the field of myth and modern history writes, the quest for the
"mythical" is in itself typically modern: it signifies disenchantment with the very
notion of modernity, with the "dissociation of sensibility" and the destruction of
the very notion of a durable and usable "tradition" that are themselves a result
of modernization.[88]

What function can art fulfill here? Jung wrote: "Therein lies the social significance of art: it is constantly at work educating the spirit of the age, conjuring
up the forms in which the age is most lacking."[89] This, in combination with his
notion of a collective unconscious, may be understood as an encouragement to
artists to make free with the archetypal energies of all of mankind, to borrow
and imitate whatever their enthusiasm calls for. It is the very opposite of the

artistic strategy that Byrne started out with, described in the last chapter as the tentative rejection of mimesis.

According to James Frazer's general sketch in *The Golden Bough* (a monumental work that Frazer kept expanding between 1890 and 1936) of the two principles of magic, the first principle is that like produces like, an effect resembles its cause, a principle that Frazer names homeopathic, imitative, or mimetic magic; the second is that things which have once been in contact continue to act on each other at a distance, which Frazer names contagious magic.[90] These principles, according to Frazer, underlie the effectiveness of mythical thinking. Byrne's artistic work abounds with examples of such mimetic imitation and contagion. He read Frazer together with choreographer Twyla Tharp, who noted how he responded to it by looking for the residue of ancient thoughts in the most up-to-date aspects of society.[91] How and if Byrne's findings "conjure up the forms in which the age is lacking" is a subject to which this book shall return repeatedly.

5 ARCHETYPAL CONFLICTS: "GOIN' BOOM BOOM BOOM"

After recording *Remain in Light*, the members of Talking Heads turned their attention to different projects. Jerry Harrison recorded a solo album, *The Red and the Black*. Chris Frantz and Tina Weymouth, who felt that the conceptualism of Eno and Byrne was exaggerated and ostentatious (Weymouth told the press: "*I* didn't read those books"[92]), started their own band, the Tom Tom Club, aiming to be as unpretentious as possible. Their happy and simple sound was an instantaneous success. "Genius Of Love" and "Wordy Rappinghood" were hit singles, and their first album sold more copies than any previous Talking Heads album. Eno and Byrne turned their attention to the completion of *My Life in the Bush of Ghosts*.

Byrne had meanwhile taken on a commission by choreographer Twyla Tharp to create a score for a new full-length ballet. The general theme of the ballet was to be humanity's capacity for estrangement, with topics like a horrible family, nuclear annihilation, and paradise lost—paradise regained.[93] Tharp freely mixed symbolism and naturalistic acting, abstract movements and expressionist elements in her choreography;[94] Byrne's music functions relatively independently of her theatrical ballet. The commission provided Byrne with an opportunity to write music and songs without the constraints of the pop-song format, and with ample room to deal with archetypical conflicts within both the family and society. The ballet was performed on Broadway in the fall of 1981. The accompanying record, *Songs from the Broadway Production of "The*

Catherine Wheel", was Byrne's first solo album. It was a continuation of his experiments with African music as a model.

A commission to compose and record ballet music naturally sets its own demands. Tharp, who had set choreographies to popular music before, from Scott Joplin and Sinatra to the Beach Boys, explicitly wanted to avoid having her dancers always moving to a straightforward beat, which she found constricting and predictable.[95] Responding to this, Byrne put together rhythms for Tharp to try in rehearsals. He sometimes watched a finished section of the dance and composed music that would give the impression of generating that movement. Moreover, he invited John Chernoff, the author of *African Rhythm and African Sensibility*, to record with him. Together, Byrne and Chernoff made a simplified version of West African polyrhythmic music — one of the tracks is titled "Adé," in tribute to the Nigerian Jújù musician King Sunny Adé — to achieve a strong connection between music and dance that opened up room for choreographic freedom. According to Byrne, "there were so many rhythms going on that, no matter which way the dancers moved, they seemed to be connected with the music. It wasn't a simple four/four boom-thud, boom-thud."[96] Chernoff played a variety of drums and other percussion on half of *The Catherine Wheel*'s 23 sections, and sometimes also played piano and guitar. He co-composed the music for four sections of the ballet, including the song "Big Business." Chernoff later told about their playful and experimental way of making music, influenced by John Cage's use of "prepared" piano:

> "On 'Big Business', I played the parts of a drum orchestra with pencil erasers on a guitar while [Byrne] worked the frets. On 'Combat', I played the parts of a different drum ensemble on a piano he had modified by wrapping masking tape around some of the strings. I could deal with any of that, but I realized that even the pop musicians I knew in Africa, who were so interested in developing a sound which could cross the ocean, might have been perplexed."[97]

The instrumental sections of the album show Byrne's strength and limitations as composer. The musical texture consists of layer over layer of small, rhythmic impulses. Drums and percussion as well as bass, synthesizers, and guitars all have a rhythmic function as well as — often — a suggestion of melody: two or three notes that suggest a direction, comparable to the way a large number of small compass needles can indicate the curve of a magnetic field. Every instrument is given its own accent and coloring, its own pulsating, often near-vocal qualities. Every instrument, every sound almost, functions not only as a part in a musical texture but also can be perceived as a performative or proprioceptive suggestion. Byrne's grasp of music is not that of a classically trained composer, a talent he has never claimed for himself, but his work demonstrates an ability to perceive music simultaneously as an independent structure and as a subjective driving force.

This is most clear when the suggestion of a musical persona is strengthened by singing, when voice and lyrics allow the listener to identify with the musical intention. In most popular music, melody and rhythm function solely as support for this level, the singer conveying his or her emotional persona. In Byrne's songs of this period, everything combines to eradicate this distinction between singing and music. This continuity is achieved by alternating the singing with wordless vocalizing, by organizing the vocal melodies in the short rhythmic fragments, and by giving intimate, voice-like qualities to most instruments. Not the vocals alone, but the whole musical texture functions as the song's persona. Byrne explained this: "The sound of the singing, the sound of the instruments and the sound of the rhythm, all those sounds together open a door through which the text can enter. In fact, when that door is not open, the lyrics do not matter very much."[98]

In the lyrics, Byrne sketched emotional situations and sensibilities that are so generic that they can resonate far and wide, suggesting general, archetypal relevance. The last lines of "His Wife Refused," a song about a quarrel between husband and wife, brings out this perspective by referring to the couple as king and queen, giving their spat a mythical, almost cosmic relevance: "Yes he's the king and she's the queen / Run in a circle around their house / Open the door and let them in / Inside a circle around their house." Another song, "What A Day That Was," also portrays a conflict of mythic dimensions, and a closer look at the lyrics helps to see how this is achieved. (To the lyrics I have added, in italics, a rendering of Byrne's wordless vocalizations and shouts. The orthography is vernacular, as printed on the inner sleeve of the record, as if to stress that this is the notation of a voice.[99])

Well I'm dressed up so nice
An' I'm doin' my best
Yes I'm startin' over . . .
Startin' over in another place

Lemme tell you a story
Big chief with a golden crown
He's got rings on his finger
And then he walks up, up to the throne

He's makin' shapes with his hands

An' don't choo dare sit down
Now don't choo dare jump back
And don't choo dare stick out!

> And on the first day, we had everything we could hold
> Ooh and then we let it fall
> And on the second day, there was nothing else left to do
> Ooh what a day that was.
>
> *aa-haaa*

There are 50.000 beggars
Roaming in the streets
They have lost all their possessions
They have nothing left to eat

Down come a bolt of lightning
Now an electrical storm
Starts a chain reaction
Go pull a fire alarm

I'm dreaming of a city
It was my own invention
And I put the wheels in motion
A time for big decisions

> And on the first day, there was nothing else left inside
> Ooh what they were looking for.
> And on the second day, I had everything I could stand
> Ooh what a day that was.

Oh a day that was.
Ooh that's the way it goes
There's a million ways — to get things done
There's a million ways — to make things work out.

> *ouou-haa-haa..i i i whóóó ahhaha*

Well I'm going right through
And the light came down
Well they're roundin' em up
from all over town

They're movin' forward and back
They're movin' backwards and front
And they're enjoying themselves
Moving in ev'ry direction

So if you feel like you're in a whirlpool
You feel like going home
And if you feel like talking to someone
Who knows the difference between right and wrong

And on the first day I had everything all at hand
Ooh who could've asked for more
And on the second day there was nothing left we could hold
Ooh — what a day that was.
aa-haa-..i i i whóóó mmmm i i i who -haha brrrr

We're go(in') boom boom boom That's the way we live
And in a great big room and That's the way we live. [repeat refrain 4 times]
aa-haa!

This text has some remarkable characteristics. First, there are repeated shifts in its implied perspective, as shown by the pronouns shifting freely between "I," "you," "we," "he," and "they." The perspective also shifts from solitary musings to storytelling, from factual observation (in the beginning of the 1980s, the number of beggars in New York City was indeed estimated to have reached 50,000) to dreaming. The distant present of a mythological "big chief with a golden crown" mingles with the here and now, as if all of mankind's history is relevant to the interpretation of every single event within that history.

That this effect is indeed intended is shown by the way every persona within the song is characterized by gestures and postures: one is dressed up nice, makes shapes with their hands, avoids jumping back and sticking out, lets fall what they hold, and roams through streets. "Well I'm going right through / And the light came down" also appears to evoke an intuitive experience, as does "They're movin' forward and back / They're movin' backwards and front / And they're enjoying themselves / Moving in ev'ry direction." Such gestures are appropriate for a ballet; moreover, they suggest that such experiences have a ritual, proprioceptive basis that belongs to the human condition.

In the last quatrain, the dizzying shifts of perspective, time, and space result in moral confusion. "So if you feel like you're in a whirlpool / You feel like going home / And if you feel like talking to someone / Who knows the difference between right and wrong" — this asks for reassurance, but the lyric has only a riddle to offer as its conclusion: "We're go(in') boom boom boom/ That's the way we live/ And in a great big room and/ That's the way we live."

This chorus is emphasized by a fourfold repetition, but even more by its rendition. While the whole song is accompanied by an engaging rhythm that supports the singing, as well as by choir-like synthesizer sounds that highlight Byrne's vocal, now his singing is intertwined with disrupting, plaintive synthesizer accents. This indicates that "going boom boom boom" is not just dancing to a strong rhythmic pulse, but rather like being thrown from one side of a room to the other, or being repeatedly thrown out of perspective — between a paradisiacal "first day" and a catastrophic "second day," or between the position of a king and that of a beggar.

This may amount to a conclusion — put into words, it would be something like: however disrupted, the situation is still open. The work of Chernoff and Thompson has once more been a source of inspiration. Where Chernoff writes that, within the development of Afro-American styles, songs continue to serve as guides in practical philosophy to the people who listen to them,[100] in his footnotes he quotes a most appropriate observation made by R.F. Thompson:

> When Justi Barreto wrote the *Newspaper Shirt* mambo in 1950 he succeeded in capturing what it felt like to live in the fifties. The scene is Mexico City in June 1950. A Negro man has fashioned himself a shirt out of newspaper. He studies the material of his shirt, and the cloth of scare headlines frankly worries him. His shirt tells him war is raging in Korea, and he summarizes the news with onomatopoeia: BEEM! BOMB! BOME! BOOM! Perez Prado [who recorded this song] undercuts his anxiety with a piano solo which tinkles with insouciance. Air raid sirens sound. In the heart of the crisis, the mambo builds up and, to a cowbell-stressed rhythm, blasts out its most affirmative sounds. The man chants praise of his shirt, a chorus answers in call-and-response fashion, and the mambo ends. A capsule allegory; the man does not recoil in fear though he is sensibly alarmed. "Look," he says, "life is delicious and to be savored in spite of doom."[101]

Boom boom — that explosive disruptions are characteristic of modern life has been noted throughout the twentieth century. I want to quote three or four instances that may resonate through Byrne's "boom boom boom."

This is Norbert Wiener's version: "There is no homeostasis whatever. We are involved in the business cycles of boom and failure, in the successions of dictatorship and revolution, in the wars which everyone loses, which are so real a feature of modern times."[102]

Another version can be found in architectural theoretician Charles Jencks'

The Language of Postmodern Architecture (1977). Its first chapter opens as follows:

> Happily, we can date the death of Modern Architecture to a precise moment in time. [. . .] Modern Architecture died in St. Louis, Missouri on July 15, 1972 at 3.32 pm (or thereabouts) when the infamous Pruitt-Igoe scheme, or rather several of its slab blocks, were given the final coup de grace by dynamite. Previously it had been vandalised, mutilated and defaced by its black inhabitants, and although millions of dollars were pumped back, trying to keep it alive (fixing the broken elevators, repairing smashed windows, repainting), it was finally put out of its misery. Boom, boom, boom.[103]

Or think of Tristan Tzara's *Dada Manifesto*, published in 1918, the last year of the "Great War":

> Philosophy is the problem: looking from any angle at life, god, the idea or whatever. Everything one looks at is wrong. [. . .] When I call:
> IDEAL, IDEAL, IDEAL
> KNOWLEDGE, KNOWLEDGE, KNOWLEDGE
> BOOMBOOM, BOOMBOOM, BOOMBOOM,
> this is a fairly accurate account of progress, the law, morality and all other beautiful qualities which all kinds of very intelligent persons have discussed in so many books to state finally that everyone has danced to the rhythm of his own boomboom and was right as far as his boomboom goes.[104]

Even though the perspective of Byrne's lyric shifts time and again, there is no real development. The different aspects combine to form one "inner theater": when the song ends, the result is a sketchy outline. Again, this reveals how for Byrne the essence of music is not the inner development of musical themes and forms, but rather a medium for personal and social experience, dramatic as much as musical. In Tharp's ballet *The Catherine Wheel*, "What A Day That Was" is followed immediately by "Big Blue Plymouth," a portrayal of emotional overwhelm; both are used as music to the concluding quarter of the ballet, "The Golden Section." Arlene Croce, dance critic for *The New Yorker*, called *The Catherine Wheel* a major event, and the final Golden Section "a dance apotheosis of astonishing beauty and power." Of Byrne's music, she wrote that it was "the first rock score to pull solid weight in a theatrical-dance context. It has real rhythm, not just a beat. [. . .] Byrne's brand of concert rock must, I suppose, be accorded the status of serious music."[105] As a result, Byrne's music has been used for a surprisingly high number of ballet and theater productions: probably hundreds all over the world. By 1997, the archives of the Theatre Institute of the Netherlands alone contained records of over 20 different Dutch productions that had made use of Byrne's music.

Brian Eno's involvement in *The Catherine Wheel* concluded his ongoing collaboration with Byrne, begun four years earlier when Eno produced Talking Heads' *More Songs about Buildings and Food*. Journalists have often written about the influence of Eno on Byrne, and on Eno's stamp on Talking Heads, especially on *Remain in Light*. This shouldn't obscure Byrne's prominent role in these collaborative efforts. Eno's approach to music remains mostly impersonal, almost managerial. Rather than writing songs, he analyzes them from a cybernetics-influenced distance. Byrne values this distance, too, but combines it with nearness, merging his own personality with the personality of the songs he constructs. He has explained this process graphically: "The act of singing live recreates the emotions that went into the songs in the first place, like adding water to freeze-dried food."[106] His willingness to recreate emotions culled from many sources, including such sources as the vocals of several tracks of *My Life in the Bush of Ghosts*, especially "Help Me Somebody," which Byrne has often sung live during concerts, adds a crucial dimension to his music.

6 *SPEAKING IN TONGUES*: PERSONA AS RITUAL TEXTURE

When recording *Speaking in Tongues* (1983), Talking Heads built on the experience and pleasure of playing live as a sizeable funk-and-rock ensemble. The album develops the style and thematic of *Remain in Light* and *My Life in the Bush of Ghosts* by moving away from the hectic rigor of those records, arriving at a more easily accessible, lyrical style of funk. Once again, the music is a dense and funky texture of small rhythmical motifs, interspersed with a good many quirky accents. This time, however, it is unified by an ongoing relaxed and steady beat, and Byrne sings in a voice that is less strained. The album was produced by the four original members of Talking Heads, making all the music together.[107] It was the first Talking Heads album to sell more than one million copies in the U.S.A.[108]

Speaking in Tongues was recorded in the studio, and the new songs were meant for live performance from the start. Looking back on his studio experiments with Eno, and comparing them to his later experience of playing live with excellent funk musicians such as Bernie Worrell, Byrne reflected:

"To some extent, we were rediscovering the wheel. [We] worked on things by layering little pieces of rhythm and sound and building up a rhythm piece by piece that in the end sometimes sounded like one good funk drummer, or one *mediocre* funk drummer! But it's very different to discover something by starting from the bottom and *re*-discovering it and putting all the pieces back together than by looking out the window and just seeing. It's like kids who take their car engine apart and then put it back together again."[109]

Byrne tried to write songs for the album that were as passionate as the vocals used on *My Life in the Bush of Ghosts*. He explained about the meaning of those vocals, many in foreign languages:

"The vocal can be quite moving without literally meaning anything. That alone implies a lot: the phonetics and texture of a vocal have their own meaning. I'm sure no one would disagree with that, but most people tend to think that lyrics are most important. . . . A lot of people don't realize that the sound of a voice, phrasing or phonetic structures are affecting them at least as much as the words. Usually lyrics that are a little bit mysterious, that don't quite come out and say what they mean, are the more powerful. They deal with things in a metaphysical way."[110]

This describes the task that Byrne set himself when writing the lyrics for *Speaking in Tongues*: to compose words that would allow him to convey with credibility a series of passions, a number of personae "moved by an inner spirit" or in a state of emotional transport that are beyond literal expression. The expression "speaking in tongues" of course takes its meaning from the Biblical story of the day of Pentecost.[111] Byrne has commented at length about "speaking in tongues" and about the lyrics he wrote for the album:

"On most songs of 'Speaking In Tongues' I wanted to show that you could use texts that *literally* made no sense at all. Groups of words that depicted something or evoked a certain mood or feeling. That was rather difficult, but I considered it to be an interesting challenge. It meant the words had to fit together on a purely auditive level. You had to extricate yourself from the idea they had to mean something, they went beyond that."[112]

I don't consider lyrics to be like poetry, they are a completely separate discipline.

I believe that people who speak in tongues are in a certain sense very happy that they are able to do something like that. It gives them an inner peace. It makes them feel somehow to be at one with the universe, or something like that. It does not matter how idiotic that may seem; when it works for them, who can tell me it is wrong. . . .

I am trying to use a kind of language as it occurs in mythology. Almost as if that language is a kind of code. As if someone were reading a magical text, using it to conjure an event. This time, I have concentrated on the lyrics more than ever before; I've worked harder on them than for 'Remain In Light'.[113]

A song that refers directly to speaking in tongues (or "glossolalia" as it is referred to by psychologists) and "holy rollers" is "Slippery People" ("holy rollers" is a nickname for Pentecostal[114] Christians, because their glossolalia often goes together with writhing movements on the floor):

> what about the time?
> you were rollin' over
> fell on your face
> you must be having fun . . .
>
> put away that gun
> this part is simple
> try to recognize
> what is in your mind
>
> God help us!
> help us loose our minds
> these slippery people
> help us understand

[chorus:]   what's the matter with him?   he's alright!
            I see his face   the lord won't mind
            don't play no games   he's alright
                      love from the bottom to the top

The songs on *Speaking in Tongues* are designed to convey a range of archetypical emotions. Loose, metaphorical phrases and slogans evoke such emotional states. To render these lyrics, Byrne added many effects to his regular, rather unsteady high tenor, contrasting it with a dramatically deep and strained voice, and with whispers, shouts, moans, and such. The songs do not necessarily convey mental states as specific as glossolalia or trance, but suggest ecstatic moods: falling in love head over heels in "Girlfriend Is Better"; trusting love in "This Must Be The Place (Naive Melody)." Although this is the most direct and intuitive love song that Byrne has written — in interviews he dedicated it to his wife Adelle Lutz — its lyrics are also a deliberate construction: the line "Sing into my mouth" was based on a picture of Eskimo's singing into each other's mouths, an image

Byrne found extremely beautiful; another line, "You've got a face with a view," was a conscious attempt to connect a face to a landscape, suggestive of the love of nature expressed by nineteenth-century landscape poetry.[115]

These songs do not present individual characters, but elementary and easily recognized emotional states: exuberance in "I Get Wild/Wild Gravity" and "Pull Up The Roots"; overburdening guilt in "Swamp." This song is Byrne's version of the experimental New York theater company Mabou Mines' production, *Dead End Kids: A Story of Nuclear Power*. Byrne's contributed a score to the film that was later made out of the play; it will be discussed in the next chapter.

The lyrics of "Pull Up The Roots" may be heard as an expression of Byrne's own excitement while performing these songs:

> colored lights and shiney curtains . . . I'll take you there, I'll take you there
> ev'rything has been forgiven . . . pull up the roots, pull up the roots
>
> well I have a good time . . . when I go out of my mind
> and it's a wonderful place . . . and I can't wait to be there
> and I hear beautiful sounds . . . coming outa the ground
> gonna take us a while . . . but we'll go hundreds of times

The song that opens the album is an energetic funk song titled "Burning Down The House"; Byrne designed and directed a video clip for this song, which was a hit single.[116] The lyrics begin as follows:

> watch out   you might get what you're after
> cool babies   strange but not a stranger
>   I'm an or-di-na-ry guy
>   burning down the house . . .
>
> There's your ticket pack your bags time for jumpin' overboard
>   the transportation is here
> close enough but not too far, maybe you know where you are
>   fightin' fire with fire

Byrne's commented on these lines:

> "The phrase 'burning down the house' I first heard at a P-Funk concert, I think. And I think I might have misheard something else, but that's what I *thought* I heard. It seems to me to imply letting go, and giving it up, tearing things up. It's kind of an old idea, that to transcend things you have to smash them. In this case, burn them up!"[117]

In a BBC television interview, Byrne explained the symbolic meanings of the song and the video:

> "The song's title (Burning down the House) was about projection and projected imagery, it symbolized rebirth and destroying some sort of transitory personality, and shedding a shell and coming out with a new one . . . So on one level, the video is about that and it's about one group of performers, us, being substituted by another, by a group of impostors. I get replaced by a little kid and the others get replaced by other people . . . the use of projection, a lot of projected images . . . is about one personality or one image being layered on top of another . . . That was meant to be the subliminal basis of that video."[118]

Two different covers were used for the album, and they deserve some special attention as related works in another medium that shed light on the album from another source. Byrne commissioned artist Robert Rauschenberg to design the album cover for *Speaking in Tongues*. Rauschenberg came up with a circular collage of color photos, separated for printing in its components cyan-blue, magenta-red, and yellow. The blue separation is printed on the back of a transparent plastic record sleeve, the yellow on the front, and the magenta on a plastic circle that is riveted to the sleeve but can be turned. This creates a "dial-a-picture" system, as the separate color components have been shuffled so that one has to turn the sleeve to get a clear, full-color picture — which is always only of a part of the collage. The photos that Rauschenberg used for his collage are a random selection of arbitrary objects, a bicycle and a garden hose, photos from magazines, advertising.[119] A parallel to Talking Heads' songs of this period is clear: as the photomontage is turned to form now one image, now another, so the songs slip from one half-ecstatic mood into another, from one archetypical (and thus quite common) worldview into the next. This suggests an everyday universe of commonplace myths, subjective states that are most of the time not registered consciously — Byrne's predominant theme.

This cover may be seen as programmatic for Byrne's work at the time. Rauschenberg was a living emblem of a tradition that was highly relevant to Byrne: the Black Mountain experimental approach of Cage, Rauschenberg, Cunningham, and Olson, as well as the anti-formalism of the 60s, pop art, conceptualism, minimal art, performance — all developments for which Rauschenberg helped open the door. Art critic Brian O'Doherty has written that Rauschenberg's work

> introduced into the museum and its high-art ambience not just the vernacular object but something much more important, the *vernacular glance*. [. . .] The vernacular

glance is what carries us through the city every day, a mode of almost unconscious, or at least divided, attention. [. . .] It tags the unexpected and quickly makes it into the familiar, filing surplus information into safe categories.[120]

Byrne became friends with Rauschenberg and his collaborators. After Rauschenberg's death in 2008, Byrne published a letter, a eulogy of Rauschenberg, in the *New York Times*:

> Being around Bob was often like being on some kind of ecstatic drug — he inspired those around him to not only think outside of the box, but to question the box's very existence. His openness and way of seeing was contagious and inspired others in their own work — not to imitate and make pseudo-Rauschenbergs, but to see the whole world as a work of art. As corny as that may sound, that's what he sometimes did.[121]

Rauschenberg's cover was hard to produce in a large edition, so that in the end only 50,000 albums were issued with that cover. Byrne came up with a design for the remaining million or so albums' sleeves: a painted circle in the center, with photos of overturned chairs in the four corners. His design resembles a mandala, a circular design which, according to Jung, symbolizes "nothing less than a psychic centre of the personality not to be identified with the ego."[122] For Jung, mandalas are "concerned with the images that refer directly and exclusively to the new centre as it comes into consciousness"[123] — which quite fits the idea of "speaking in tongues." In fact, Byrne's cover design was probably inspired by Jung, who described a mandala as seen in a dream that corresponds closely to Byrne's cover design: "A circular table with four chairs round it. Table and chairs are empty."[124] The interpretation given by Jung is that this mandala is not yet "in use."[125]

The formal quality of Byrne's montage, with its combination of photography and painting, does not correspond directly to Jung's concept of an image that refers directly to a psychic centre that emerges from the unconscious. And yet: what could be more fitting for an attempt to present archetypical textures in an album of recorded pop songs, to make them accessible for everyone's understanding?

Chapter 3

Ritual in Daily Life

1 INTRODUCING PERFORMANCE THEATER

After exploring the ritual and dramatic qualities of music in his work with Talking Heads and with Eno, Chernoff, Basil, Conner, and Tharp, the next step for Byrne was to explore these qualities more fully in theater and film. He had been impressed with the experimental theater that was made in New York City since he moved there in the mid-1970s, and now welcomed the possibility of working in theater himself. The popularity of Talking Heads continued to grow, which enabled Byrne to move into film, and the success of his score for *The Catherine Wheel* made the heads of many directors and choreographers turn in his direction. Over the course of the 1980s, he collaborated with Robert Wilson, Mabou Mines, Spalding Gray, and Meredith Monk, each of them influential in the downtown theater scene.

To place Byrne's work in film and theater against a backdrop, the main tenets of New York's so-called "performance theater" may be introduced through the theoretical work of Richard Schechner. Schechner (born 1934) has been one of the central figures in avant-garde theater. He has combined the roles of innovative theater scholar — he founded the Department of Performance Studies at New York University — with that of editor of *The Drama Review* (which he made into the leading journal of performance studies), the role of director of the Performance Group (which later, directed by Elizabeth LeCompte, morphed into The Wooster Group), and that of organizer (in the mid-70s, Schechner presided over a collective that included, among others, the Performance Group, Mabou Mines, Richard Foreman's Ontological-Hysteric Theater, and Meredith Monk/The House; the idea was to streamline the business aspects and to promote artistic exchanges).[1]

93

In his seminal books on performance, Schechner expressly mixes theorizing with detailed fieldwork observations, criticism, polemics, and his own personal and political reflections. His writing is always steeped in emancipatory politics, controversy, iconoclasm, experiments with unusual perspectives. It is a general strategy for understanding performance that revels in the whirling interplay of all its aspects, in stark contrast with the formalist, minimalist[2] approach of his colleague Michael Kirby (who alternated with Schechner as editor of *The Drama Review*), who was as fanatically opposed to the use of value judgments and polemic in performance criticism as Schechner was in favor of it. Performance, in Schechner's view, is an arena where general ideas clash and mingle with everyday reality, and he wants to provide detailed accounts of the resulting interplay. He describes how the universal presence of myths, dreams, the evocative potential of the body to present meanings, and the interaction of the individual with society, are actualized time and again in drama and ritual. To him, the ritual aspects of theater are at least as important as the narrative content of a play. In a sense, this connects him to the work of Jung and Campbell, but Schechner is much more contemporary and specific. His insights into performance as such, into the ethological aspects of acting, and in the liminal position of art, are highly relevant here.

Schechner considers conventional Euro-American theater to be severely limited. At best it is a somewhat eccentric example of what performance can accomplish. The Western theatrical tradition is typified by the central role of the text, a fixed text, which exists independent of its performance. Actors, staging, costumes, and so on are used to serve the text, to bring it to life. A typical Euro-American playtext will deal with the origin and resolution of a conflict, and the quality of its performance is judged by the spectators in relation to other performances, in terms of artistic value. "For too long, in theater at least, performance knowledge has been identified with knowing the great dramatic texts [. . .] What performers and directors did was acknowledged but segregated."[3] This separation is responsible for a theater that aims only at a temporary suspension of disbelief, transporting the audience for a short period to the make-believe world of the play, a few hours of enchantment, returning it afterwards to ordinary life without aiming at durable change.

Experimental theater, as Schechner understands it, is the attempt to abolish neat separations between reality and text, text and performance, performance and audience. Each element of the performance can take pride of place. Schechner presents a triangular model of theatrical elements, in which traditionally, in Euro-American theater, text and narration form the basis, while music, rhythm, and movement form one of the sides, and architecture plus scenography the other.[4] In experimental theater, each side of this triangle can form the basis of a production, generating radically different events. Each experimental performance has to be approached as "a braiding of various performance 'languages,' none of which can always claim primacy."[5] The full range of performances as Schechner understands the term includes "events like the Mass, professional football, psychodrama, whirling dervishes in devotion, Sumo wrestling."[6] Performances have to be understood and analyzed in their entirety, which he terms alternately the performance "text," "score," or "braid." Following the examples of Antonin Artaud, Bertolt Brecht, and Jerzy Grotowski, who looked to non-European forms of theater and ritual to support their own theatrical innovations, Schechner's outlook is cross-cultural. He brings in detailed observations of a wide range of events: Ramlila of Ramnagar, a 31-day ritual drama of north India; Kathakali performer training in southwest India; Noh in Japan; Balinese theater; Javanese Wayang Kulit; the Waehma festival of the Yaqui Indians in Arizona; Papua New Guinea dances. He combines these with examples of performance in the U.S.A., including many that are not usually considered to be art or theater: a Black church meeting in Brooklyn; re-enactments in historical theme parks; Shaker dances and their re-enactments; a sadomasochistic sex theater in Manhattan; street festivals, carnivals, and political demonstrations; TV news shows; sports events.

Schechner always underlines the "liminal" position of art, its position in-between categories, between science and mythical or magical thought. He quotes anthropologist-philosopher Claude Lévi-Strauss: "Art lies half-way between scientific knowledge and mythical or magical thought."[7] The "limen" is a threshold, a border, and Schechner writes about the border experience: "Artists intentionally exaggerate extend blow up elaborate make huge the limen . . . The 'work of art' is (in) the limen; and so is the 'work of' ceremony, ritual, and other operations of human behaviour that appear to have no 'good' (i.e., pragmatic) reason for existing (like religion)."[8]

Schechner describes this liminal zone as the meeting of two worlds,

> the only two realms performance ever deals with: the world of contingent existence as ordinary objects and persons and the world of transcendent existence as magical implements, gods, demons, characters. It isn't that a performer stops being himself or herself when he or she becomes another — multiple selves coexist in an unresolved dialectical tension.[9]

All behavior in this liminal zone or "play frame" is "restored behavior," which Schechner characterizes as behavior that has been treated just as a film director may treat a segment of film. Such "filmstrips" of behavior can be rearranged and reconstructed at will. This means that they are no longer dependent on the circumstances that brought them into existence the first time. Such segments of behavior function, to a degree, independently of psychological and social realities:[10]

> Put in personal terms, restored behaviour is "me behaving as if I am someone else" or as if I am "beside myself" or "not myself", as when in trance. But this "someone else" may also be "me in another state of feeling/being", as if there were multiple "me's" in each person.[11]

It follows that performance behavior is not free and easy, as the word "play" suggests; it is known and practiced behavior, often rehearsed and learned, or generated by rules that dictate the outcome, as in sports, or revealed during the performance itself by elders or gurus.[12]

A performer doesn't stop being himself when he or she assumes another identity; in performance, multiple selves coexist in an unresolved dialectical tension. The performance as such is usually embedded in other practices, to help the performer enter and leave the liminal zone with success. Schechner distinguishes as many as seven phases in a complete performance sequence: training, workshops, rehearsals, warm-ups, performance, cool-down, and aftermath.[13] Naturally, different genres and cultures emphasize different parts of the sequence.

In Schechner's perspective, there is a continuum of performances that stretches from strictly individual performances to acting, whether in drama, dance or ritual, and taking part in social actions and cultural performances, collective events that do not have their origin within a single individual but that feed back into the actions of individuals.[14] This links restored behavior to ordinary life like the two sides of a Möbius strip, each turning into the other.[15] (At this point, Schechner's own preference for theater that tries to overcome the separation of performance and audience through audience participation, environmental staging and attempts at collective creativity, everything with an undertone of psychoanalytical ritualizing, shines through.)

To Schechner, performing as a form of symbolic action is characterized by a peculiar double negativity; the performer executes elements of behavior that are "not me," but these elements become "me," while retaining a certain foreign quality, between self and not-self, which Schechner names "not not me." This shift between self and other may take place on all levels of the performance, including text, performer, environment, and audience. "The larger the field of 'between', the stronger the performance. The antistructure that is performance swells until it threatens to burst. The trick is to extend it to the bursting point but no further."[16]

A crucial distinction between different kinds of performances is whether the actors and the audience return afterwards to ordinary life in more or less the same place that they started from, or remain forever changed by the performance. Schechner calls performances that effect such lasting changes "transformations," as opposed to "transportations," temporary excursions to the performative world. Examples of transformations are initiation ceremonies, such as a wedding, a graduation, and a bar mitzvah. Often, theater is held to be a transportation (temporary "entertainment," however moving and uplifting), while ritual is held to be transformative, but Schechner shows in his analyses that transformation and transportation often coexist in one and the same event. During initiations for example, only the initiated are ritually transformed, while all other participants afterwards return to their ordinary life at the same point where they had left it.[17]

Physical training is often important in the preparation for a performance. In Western performance, this is the case in ballet, dance, and also in many popular entertainments (circus acrobats, living statues in busy streets, sports, and so on). Physical training helps to produce a specific state of alertness, a proprioceptive change, and that ability transforms the performer: "The performance text is put into the body of the performer through a training whose bases are integral parts of the performance text itself. Once in the body of the performer, the performance text is manifest during performances."[18] Such performance events can closely resemble religious possession, trance, and other ecstatic forms. In fact, several Western theater makers have devised methods to include liturgical forms of performance in their theater; Jerzy Grotowski (1934–99) is an example (both Schechner and JoAnne Akalaitis/Mabou Mines trained with him). Schechner writes about his way of working:

> Grotowski believes there are certain sounds, rhythms, gestures, and movements whose effects are "objective" — that is, based on physiological and/or archetypal systems. Heartbeat, breathing patterns, certain pitches and precise progressions of sound, certain facial displays, body and hand positions, and movements constitute for Grotowski an intercultural or universal performative system.[19]

Performance is relevant to so many reaches of culture that the question comes up whether it is typical for human nature as such. In his book *The Future of Ritual*, Schechner describes what he sees as ritual's ethological origin: "Ritual is ordinary behaviour transformed by means of condensation, exaggeration, repetition, and rhythm into specialized sequences of behaviour serving specific functions usually having to do with mating, hierarchy, or territoriality."[20] These are potentially dangerous and violent circumstances, and ritual behavior is full of repetition and exaggeration to send the "metamessage of 'You get the message, don't you!?!' (a question surrounded by emphasis)," to make clear what is very important yet problematic. Behavior of this kind is, according to Schechner, common to humans and to primates such as chimpanzees and gorillas, who also express and communicate feelings.[21] How, then, to combine the rational, cognitive qualities of human behavior, the need to construct plausible stories and explanations, be combined with the ritual propensity, which may short-circuit thought? Schechner answers this as follows:

> My own experience from running many performance workshops during the past twenty-five years, is that rhythmic activities — especially if movement and sound-making are carefully coordinated and maintained for long periods of time — invariably lead to feelings of "identical opposites": omnipotence/vulnerability, tranquility/readiness for the most demanding physical action. In other words, the narrative-cognitive stimulus works from the cerebral cortex down while the movement-sonic stimulus works from the lower brain up. Performing a ritual, or a ritualized theater piece or exercise, is both narrative (cognitive) and affective. These work together to form the experience of ritualizing.[22]

This ambivalence is crucial to performance: Schechner sees all human creativity as still working "this playfield betwixt and between the ethological, the neurological, and the social."[23] And as a result of this ambivalence, performers can't really say who they are; their "multiple selves coexist in an unresolved dialectical tension."[24]

One aspect of the neurological and ethological basis of performance deserves to be mentioned here because it resonates with Talking Heads' *Speaking in Tongues*. Schechner has written about neurological and anthropological research by Felicitas D. Goodman into the nature of glossolalia, or "speaking in tongues." Received wisdom on such trance states was that there are a number of different religious trances, but "since the early 1980s, researchers have come to realize that there is only one neurophysiological change which underlies a number of different religious experiences."[25] Studying glossolalia in different parts of the world, Goodman found that "accent and intonation patterns were not related to the native tongue of the speaker. [. . .] They were nonlinguistic in origin and instead of obeying rules of language, most probably were caused by the striking bodily changes that I observed . . . ."[26] According to Goodman, the "tongues" patterns are not only unrelated to specific languages, but are also not related to religions in the ideological sense. People are not made to speak in tongues by their beliefs; the opposite is true: the speaking in tongues is driving religious belief.

Such perspectives on human behavior are immediately relevant to Byrne's work. In an interview, he explained his interest in religious behavior:

"It has a huge influence on human behavior. [. . .] The kinds of music that are made today are based on religious music. Art in principle is religious or spiritual. And yet the source, religion in itself, is almost bankrupt. It has lost its meaning to many people. At a certain moment we have started to believe that things like rituals were for primitive people and that we might get rid of things like that through science, and might neglect them. But finally it turned out that we have simply replaced them by new things: science, pop music, art . . . communism (grins). But the structures and images that religions have produced are still there . . .

You might say that the creative process, the music, has become my religion. Perhaps I am somewhat naive in that way, but I believe intensely in the enormous forces and influences of music."[27]

To return to performance theater: Schechner traces the origin of the American theater avant-garde back to the legendary John Cage-Merce Cunningham-Robert Rauschenberg performance at Black Mountain College in 1952.[28] In the 1960s and 70s, a theater of complex performance scores was developed in the U.S.A.: "The dream of 'total theater' envisioned in Euro-American culture by Wagner was realized by artists as diverse as Grotowski, Laurie Anderson, Richard Foreman, Robert Wilson, Mabou Mines (Lee Breuer, JoAnne Akalaitis), Elizabeth LeCompte, and others."[29] But in this "total theater," a measure of Brechtian, and distinctly un-Wagnerian *Verfremdung* is injected. This alienation allows for reflection: "The distance between the character and the performer allows a commentary to be inserted; for Brecht this was most often a political commentary, but it could also be — as it is for postmodern dancers and performance artists — an aesthetic or personal commentary."[30]

Life is increasingly lived while shifting across the frames and rhythms of institutions, corporations and cultures. Performances that want to be relevant in such circumstances need to deal with these shifts, and one way to do that is to place acting and non-acting side by side. What may result then is a form of theater about which Schechner writes, mentioning works by Robert Wilson and by Spalding Gray as examples: "This kind of theater displays its ambivalence; it is explicitly reflexive."[31] All this had its influence on Byrne's work.

2 A CONCERT IN THE CINEMA: *STOP MAKING SENSE*

In so far as music is purely for the ear, records, CDs, MP3 players, and such are a fine way to capture and distribute it. But when "music" is meant to include dance and drama, purely auditive media can reproduce only a slice of the entire performance. During the 1980s, Byrne turned increasingly to film and theater to capture performances, and the combination of film with popular music brought Talking Heads their greatest popularity. It also allowed Byrne to experiment with the working methods of the performance theater he admired.

When Talking Heads had expanded to a group of eight or nine musicians, they gradually elaborated their live concerts. The Tom Tom Club often opened, with a set of infectiously rhythmical songs that were simple and refreshing. Talking Heads then played a selection of songs that spanned their development, from the tense rock of their first albums to the rhythmic density of *Remain in Light* and the lavish funk of *Speaking in Tongues*. New arrangements were rich in theatrical detail and added timbres, counter-voices, and swirls and curlicues to most melodic gestures. An example is the 1981 version of "Animals" as recorded on the live album *The Name of This Band Is Talking Heads*, which has a pleasant reggae-beat refrain tagged on at the end, the singers repeating "Go ahead, laugh at me," as if inviting ridicule were the only sensible way out of the song's predicament.

On stage, the band was arranged in two neat lines, with drums, percussion, and synthesizers elevated on black risers, to showcase the dramatic aspects of the concert. Byrne performed a series of routines to act out the personae of his songs; now jogging in place, now singing through a megaphone to make his voice sound tinny and distant, now running around the stage with seemingly unbearable excitement, disappearing behind the risers to come out again at the other side. When film director Jonathan Demme saw Talking Heads in concert in 1983, he was moved and excited by the cinematic qualities of the show. Byrne later contacted him with the proposal to make the concert into a documentary feature film. A budget of $1.2 million was put forward, and *Stop Making Sense* was shot in December 1983, over a series of four specially designed and lighted concerts at the Pantages Theater in Hollywood.

The idea of the film was to give a cinema audience the best possible experience of the concert as such. Distractions were avoided. No dressing room interviews, no "behind the scenes" peeks at a touring band, no comments from roadies, fans, or management. Demme also used restraint in the editing, presenting the musicians in long takes rather than in many quick cuts, and avoiding artificial means to generate excitement such as special effects and cutaways to enthusiastic audiences.[32] Instead, he presented the musicians as if each were a character that revealed itself in the course of the concert, and the band as a group of people with its own patterns of interaction. To help establish personal identities, he filmed most shots of the musicians from fixed positions, thus creating a series of stable perspectives for the film's audience.

By not always zooming in on lead solos, showing another musician's responses to that solo instead, the film presents the band as nine different characters responding to each other and enjoying themselves together. Byrne in particular is shown as having fun on stage, dancing with the others, mimicking their movements and being mimicked in turn. Even while the cinema audience misses the direct crowd experience of the live concert, it is presented with a more direct, intimate and close-up experience of the band than it would be able to have during many regular concerts. *Stop Making Sense* was widely hailed as the best rock film ever made, and won the prize of America's National Society of Film Critics for best documentary of 1984.

Another essential contribution to the film is Byrne's design for the stage presentation of the concert. In 1983, he had worked with theater director Robert Wilson, contributing a score to his hugely ambitious project *the CIVIL warS*. Byrne had followed Wilson's work for some time. In 1976, Wilson's *Einstein on the Beach*, with music by Philip Glass, had impressed him because of its deliberate slowing down of time, and because of its sense of theater as a plotless environment, an atmosphere you can leave and return to in the course of the performance.[33] Wilson often separates the visual elements from text and music. He then uses extremely detailed and formalized lighting to single out and frame the movements of a single actor, or to present a single prop or a backdrop in exquisite, individual light. For Talking Heads' 1983 U.S. tour, Byrne borrowed some elements of Wilson's methods. He approached each song as a separate little play, with its own detailed lighting design. The illusions created with light are shown parallel to the devices that create them: stagehands carrying lights, slide projectors, and screens are often on view, "baring the device," as this is called in theater.

Very "Bob Wilson-like" are the projections shown on screens behind the band during the second half of the concert. Three billboard-size slides are projected next to each other. Most of these projections combine three isolated words or groups of words: "DOLL FACE | PUBLIC LIBRARY | ONION," and: "VIDEO GAME | SANDWICH | DIAMONDS"; later followed by indications of time: "BEFORE | YOU'RE | AWAKE," by photos of arms, buttocks and knees, cityscapes, bookshelves. These words and pictures are not mentioned and remain unexplained. They draw attention, but withstand attempts at interpretation: they just serve as a reminder that here, as in life, a great deal of potential information necessarily remains undigested and not interpreted.

Byrne threw himself into finding gestures for his song personae, bringing to bear his growing experience with performance theater, even inviting director JoAnne Akalaitis of New York's avant-garde theater Mabou Mines to visit the rehearsals in Hollywood and give her advice on the continuity in the development of these personae.[34] The way in which Byrne represents his songs is central to the film. In "Psycho Killer," "Swamp," and "Once In A Lifetime," Byrne stumbles and staggers across the stage like a buffeted rag doll, as if thrown about by some irresistible force. During "What A Day That Was," lighting from underneath transforms Byrne's face into an archetypical mask, made up out of loose parts: chin, mouth, underside of the nose, and eyes form an impersonal, skull-like face that shudders and trembles. A similar effect is produced when the band is silhouetted against a backdrop, creating the illusion that there are two bands: one of shadowy giants and another of tiny humans. Towards the end of the movie, Byrne's personae find more happiness, in songs like "This Must Be the Place (Naive Melody)" and "Girlfriend Is Better." All in all, the development suggests an abstract story of a man who is overwhelmed by outside forces and suffers an identity crisis, but somehow finds a way of dealing with it through the music, and achieves a balance. Byrne later explained: "the implied story . . . was of this man who frees himself from his demons and finds release and salvation in his big suit . . . He can cut loose in this house made of a business suit."[35]

That this story is told indirectly, through a loose combination of songs and added images, none of which is directly biographical, implies a specific view on the status of "personality" as individual fixture. In a review for Artforum, critic Carter Ratcliff singled out this aspect:

> In a world of institutions, "lifestyles," and scenes designed to absorb the self, all selves with even a trace of authenticity must acknowledge that they are — but must also object to being — patched together. Selfhood is a state of resistance to the seemingly natural fate of absorption. Its first tactic is to admit that singularity lives by means of artifice: images, fictions, rhetoric. Next, the surviving self must acknowledge the shakiness of all that artifice constructs.
>
> Near the end of "Stop Making Sense" a shadow appears against the back wall of the stage — it is Byrne's body distorted by the light beam's angle. Then the giant suit looms into view, at least doubling the volume of his body, and you realize that the shadow was a distortion of a distortion. During a big-suit song, "Once In A Lifetime," Byrne arranges his left hand in the form of a duck's head and quacks it at his own face. "How do I work this?" asks the lyric. The singer is asking about himself, the creature he has invented for use in the world. Enforced by suit, stage, and camera lens, the general flatness insists that Byrne's self-images are definitely images, if not so definitely selves.[36]

Stop Making Sense succeeds in capturing such duplicitous combinations of musical enthusiasm with delusion and disillusion. The film demonstrates how enthusiasm and other forms of possession are not just artistic illusions, but form the ritual aspect of the interactions of the individual with his surroundings. Byrne had always approached songwriting as if he were making small mimetic arenas, theatrical performances in which voices and rhythms confront each other, interact, and sometimes harmonize. From now on, he would repeatedly turn to film as a medium that allowed him to elaborate and clarify such performances.

A *Stop Making Sense* soundtrack was issued, with a booklet of film photos. For this booklet, Byrne, assisted by designers Michael Hodgson and Jeff Ayeroff, wrote a list of enigmatic "conceptual" statements about the point of the music and the film. A few examples:

TIPS FOR PERFORMERS: Singing is a trick to get people to listen to music for longer than they would ordinarily. There is no music in space. People will pay to watch people make sounds.

LIFE ON EARTH: People look ridiculous when they're in ecstasy. Sound is worth money.

THE SPACE PEOPLE: The Space People think factories are musical instruments. They sing along with them. Each song lasts from 8 a.m. to 5 p.m. No music on weekends.

IN THE FUTURE: In the future, love will be taught on television and by listening to pop songs.

Such statements invite the reader to consider the meaning and the function of musical performance, and suggest that neither is quite as clear as it might have appeared. With the benefit of hindsight, it is remarkable how Byrne has repeatedly returned to some of these statements, turning seemingly facetious notions into reality. The idea that factories are musical instruments returns not only in his *True Stories*; in 2005 Byrne actually transformed a factory building in Stockholm into a single musical instrument in a project called *Playing the Building*. Buildings in New York and London would follow in 2008 and 2009.

The musical development of Talking Heads was captured so definitively by the film that after completing the *Speaking In Tongues* tour, they would not play live again. When the other band members asked Byrne to tour with the songs of his film *True Stories* in 1987, he suggested doing concerts that included "cinema" in their lay-out, by playing at drive-in movie theaters and having actors come onstage between songs.[37] The other band members did not agree. Nevertheless, after *Stop Making Sense*, Byrne would be as much engaged in the dramatic, ritual, and visual aspects of performance as in the purely musical.

3 MUSIC IN CONTEXT:
TALKING HEADS VS. THE TELEVISION

It takes a conscious decision to go to the cinema and see a movie, but watching something on television is often not a conscious choice at all. This difference is reflected in the TV documentary of a Talking Heads concert that was made by British director Geoff Dunlop, a documentary to which Byrne made an important contribution as artistic advisor. Byrne did not want to just put Talking Heads' show on television as it was, he wanted to address the specific qualities of television. This documentary was an opportunity to deal with the distracting flow of programming and channels. A comparison of the hour-long documentary, titled *Talking Heads vs. The Television*, with *Stop Making Sense* shows how Byrne tries to bring out the special performative qualities of every form in which his songs are presented.

Dunlop filmed a Talking Heads concert in 1984 in London's Wembley Arena. In direct contrast to *Stop Making Sense*, his documentary does include shots of the band in the dressing room and of the sound check, as well as interview scenes with Byrne: this time, the concert is interrupted on purpose to confront it with distracting contexts. This falls in with the casual experience of watching TV, where a program is as often as not seen within the context of other programs, and, more to the point, within the context of the viewer's own house and the lives going on there. Instead of neglecting these distractions, which inevitably frame the viewer's experience, Dunlop's documentary addresses them openly and thoroughly, a choice that makes *Talking Heads vs. The Television* as remarkable as *Stop Making Sense*.

Dunlop wanted to deal openly with the diverging performative situations of a live concert and of television viewing. Byrne agreed with this emphasis on television and the media environment, but insisted on including religious, anthropological and ethnographic material as well, thus continuing to work in the vein he had first explored in the video clip for "Once In A Lifetime." He helped Dunlop go through a great deal of existing footage, and suggested points where that footage would correspond to the concert. Byrne also convinced Dunlop to leave out anthropological or religious footage that made its subjects look foolish.[38] It took years to secure copyright clearance for all the footage used in the montage, which meant that *Talking Heads vs. The Television* was finally broadcast in 1989, five years after the concert had been filmed.

The documentary opens with white noise and images that represent the whole chain of production and reception of television: TV assembly lines, commercials for satellite TV, a flood of imagery and a TV host making a declamatory announcement: ". . . and receive all the television there is to see in North America!!" The concert venue is introduced in a similar way, connecting the Talking Heads concert to a number of comparable(?) spectacles: "The name of this place is Wembley Arena, venue for rock concerts, Horse of the Year show, Holiday on Ice, tennis, Harlem Globetrotters, 5-a-side football . . . ."

The first song that the band plays, "Life During Wartime," is placed firmly within the context of TV by illustrating it with found television footage. The lyrics present the interior monologue of someone, a spy, terrorist, guerrilla, or criminal, who is in hiding in a city and views his situation. He considers his resources: passports, visas, food rations, phone taps, partner, and thinks longingly of the regular life from which he has cut himself off: the world of parties and disco, of education in night school or college, of carefree fooling around and kissing. Ideas for these lyrics may well have come from television. During the thousands of hours of television viewing that are part of a regular upbringing, crime films and thrillers teach everyone what the world looks like from the position of the outlaw, the lone warrior or the spy. It is thus debatable whether the use of TV footage lifts the song out of its context, the Talking Heads concert, or returns it to its original context, the excitements and distractions of the home theater.

"Life During Wartime" is contextualized and illustrated by found footage in at least five distinct ways. Footage lifted from police series and thrillers is used to create an atmosphere of tension and excitement. Later in the song, the television sound of wailing police sirens replaces a screeching guitar solo. Some of the footage is connected to the words of the song. A breathtaking example of montage juxtaposes a spectacular camera movement, lifted from a car chase through a big city, when the camera swipes in a 180 degree tilt over tall building blocks, with a similar shot of Byrne singing ecstatically. And the soundtrack is interrupted completely by a brief documentary segment about inner-city warfare, with footage of ruined building blocks.

This approach is addressed in a voice-over by Byrne, which accompanies the introductory scenes that precede the first song:

> "I try to take ordinary things and make them be seen in a new light, by breaking them up into bits and trying to reorganize them . . . I wanted to make boring things seem dramatic, instead of dramatic things seem boring. An ordinary thing put into an extraordinary place isn't ordinary anymore. Like scratching your head in front of a few thousand people isn't the same as scratching it in front of your family . . . When the performance is successful, something transcendent happens, that has to do with the audience and the musicians losing their egos, immersing themselves into sort of one identity. It need only happen in a performance for thirty seconds or so, and that justifies the whole thing."

The contextualizing strategy of *Talking Heads vs. The Television* is developed by the use of ethnographical and religious footage: people from different cultures dancing in ecstatic trance; people dancing in Sub-Sahara Africa, Japan, Italy, an Arab country, and China; American citizens describing their personal experiences of a divine presence; and shots of television preachers who use the TV to broadcast healing rituals, shouting: "Put your hand against mine"; "Heal, in the name of Jesus!"; "It'll pour through that tube right into you." The footage of people in ecstasy is accompanied by Byrne's comments on the soundtrack:

> "I guess I might be considered religious in some sense. If most religions originated in a combination of a sense of awe and excitement, and a little bit of fear. People look ridiculous when they're in ecstasy, whether it's religious ecstasy or sexual ecstasy. They really look sort of distorted. People look ridiculous when they kiss . . . But, you know, people know that . . . they don't feel ridiculous."

This is continued a little later, following footage of several Americans who testify to their personal experience of God: "They take ordinary language and transform it into something exciting. It seemed like something that was very close to what I was doing." And after the song "Slippery People," which has been illustrated with footage of break dancers, acrobatic dancing in Africa, whirling derwishes, a highly disciplined dance in a mosque, and Chinese children waving flags while executing a dance, Byrne comments: "Some of my ideas about music in other cultures might be wrong, but I don't think that matters. In some way probably the misinterpreting other kinds of music and using it to my own ends, I think, is justified." This is a statement with far-reaching implications. The whole documentary implies that popular music should be considered simultaneously in the frame of the media industry, and in the frame of transcultural comparisons of musical rituals. It openly states that it can offer no secure point of view from where this interpretative quicksand could be overseen, and admits freely that mistakes and misinterpretations are inevitable. But the attempt has to be made, and counts for something.

Byrne shows his analytical, anti-mimetic tastes when he voices his opinion that "people look ridiculous when they're in ecstasy," and when he recapitulates the development of Talking Heads in pejorative terms of "artifice" and "pantomime": "When the band began, I think the band and myself wanted to strip away all . . . the artifice of performing. We wanted to, as little as possible, make it seem like we were putting on a show. We wanted to go on stage wearing our street clothes and not move around much. Gradually we ended up bringing things back in that were at one point unacceptable. I think it just became a matter of realizing that you are up on stage, that it is a pantomime."

And yet he presents himself while singing and dancing ecstatically, and mentions his conviction that a form of "transcendence" justifies Talking Heads' concerts. Byrne oscillates between an ironic and analytical approach and the enthusiasm that takes him over during the performance — and uses his theoretical interests to balance the two.

4 *THE KNEE PLAYS*: MUSIC FOR ROBERT WILSON

Parallel to his work on *Stop Making Sense* and touring with Talking Heads, in 1983 and 84 Byrne contributed music and ideas to a theater project by Robert Wilson. Wilson was preparing an enormous 12-hour-long pageant that would be part of the 1984 Olympic Arts festival in Los Angeles. *the CIVIL warS — a tree is best measured when it is down* was planned as an artistic counterpart to the Olympic Games. Just as the Games present sportspeople from all over the world, Wilson wanted to present wars, myths and historical figures from all over the world, woven into a single tapestry. His play would be built around the American Civil War, with Abraham Lincoln and Robert E. Lee as central figures. Wilson worked from the assumption that civil war is endemic to human history, almost an integral part of civilization: hence the typography of the title, meshing the words "civils" and "civil wars." The entire production was planned in five sections that were rehearsed and produced in five countries: France, Germany, Holland, Italy, and Japan. Each country contributed some historical and mythical figures: Frederic the Great, Voltaire, Mata Hari, Captain Nemo, Admiral Perry, Abraham Lincoln, Madame Curie, the Japanese sun goddess, Giuseppe Garibaldi, soldiers, the earth mother, animals, a forest, Hercules, and many others. These five sections were divided into 15 scenes, separated from each other by the 14 interludes or "Knee Plays" as Wilson likes to call them, to which Byrne contributed.[39] Other collaborators on this gigantic project were composers Philip Glass and Hans Peter Kuhn, and East German playwright Heiner Müller.

Wilson asked Byrne to make scores for a few different sections, but — due to time limitations — Byrne could do only one. He chose the "Knee Plays" because of their more economical scale, which might allow it to tour successfully and reach a wider audience.[40] Although each of the parts was produced separately, in the end Wilson could not find the financial backing he needed to complete his project. His play was never produced in its entirety, neither at the 1984 Olympics, nor later. The sections differed in quality; while the Italian and Dutch sections had a static and rather superficial quality, the German section was outstanding and fascinating. Before discussing the music Byrne made for him, Robert Wilson's theater deserves an introduction.

Robert Wilson, born in 1941, is one of America's leading avant-garde theater directors. His work cuts across traditional genres, continually challenging the conventional divisions of drama, dance, opera, and visual art. He has made over 100 productions; among the most important are the play without words *Deafman Glance* (1970), the mystical opera *Einstein on the Beach* (1976), and *the CIVIL warS* (1984), an attempt to decipher all of history in a single *Gesamtkunstwerk*. In his pieces, Wilson is interested in exploring perception, not in analyzing characters. His theater is a laboratory that experiments with perceptual barriers and discontinuities. He works hard to separate the visual, aural, and textual elements of his productions, treating each of these elements with a formal precision of its own, demonstrating in the process a strong predilection for simple repetition and permutations of isolated details.

The inadequacies of human perception and of human affection are the central theme of Wilson's work. In the early days of his career, Wilson made works in collaboration with Christopher Knowles, an autistic boy of about 14, who was partially cut off from the exterior world, and with Raymond Andrews, an 11-year-old deaf-mute boy. Wilson tried to create theater productions that dealt with reality in ways that were similar to their perception of the exterior world, asking Knowles to perform on the stage with him.[41]

According to theater scholar Theodore Shank, Wilson

> believes that everyone sees and hears on two different levels. We experience sensations of the world around us on what he calls an 'exterior screen'. But we also become aware of things on an 'interior screen' — dreams and daydreams for example. Blind people only 'see' things on an interior visual screen and deaf people can only 'hear' sounds on an interior audial screen. Wilson found that in his long performances the spectator's interior-exterior audial-visual screens become one. Interior and exterior images mingle so that they are indistinguishable. Wilson says that people sometimes 'see' things on stage that are not actually there.[42]

In his theater, Wilson tries to present an opportunity for inner reflection on the limits of our perception, by slowing down and formalizing the events on stage.

Wilson's trademark as a director is the slowing down of theatrical time, having actors execute specific tasks in extreme slow motion or repeating actions time and again with only minor but deliberate changes. His reasons for this have been explained as follows:

> Slow motion over such an extended period of time alters drastically the way we perceive the performance. It tends to carry one beyond boredom, beyond the point of

being irritated by the slowness, and one tends to adapt by slipping into a mental state that is less acutely conscious than normal. (One of the ingredients of boredom — a feeling of being trapped — is absent because spectators are told they should feel free to go in and out of the auditorium as they wish.) This state of reduced consciousness makes possible the intended mode of perception.[43]

Wilson applies the experience of perceptual barriers to every human being: "We have to be blind and deaf, as well as hearing and seeing all the time. [. . .] We're always shifting in and out of these interior/exterior audio-visual screens."[44] Wilson uses the theater to investigate the meeting ground of vision, hearing, body language and the conventional patterns of interpretation:

> "What I try to set up in the theater is a situation where I can hear, and where I can see . . . And so often I can't hear. Because what I'm seeing is interfering. And I can't see because what I'm hearing is preventing me from seeing . . . we try to set up a situation where there is simply time for interior reflection . . . What happens for me is that theater frequently becomes too aggressive . . . the box, the frame, is rigidly defined for the audio screen and the visual screen."[45]

For *the CIVIL warS*, Wilson planned *The Knee Plays* as 14 short vignettes, a series of poetic transformations that symbolize the entire history of mankind.[46]

Figure 5 A scene from *The Knee Plays*, designed by Robert Wilson and David Byrne with contributions by Adelle Lutz. The photo shows the modular boat designed by Byrne. During the scene, the boat is constructed on stage and then carried off-stage, accompanied by Byrne's song "The Sound Of Business." Photo: Glenn Halvorson for Walker Art Center, Minneapolis.

Byrne's first contribution was an idea for staging these transformations. At the first workshop in Tokyo, he suggested a modular construction, similar to Sol LeWitt's cubic structures (but then, grids and cubes are the default mode of all modern design), a system of folding and unfolding squares, which would make it possible to transform a boat into a book, a book into a tree.[47]

For his music, Byrne started from the requirements of the entire project. *The Knee Plays* was designed as five-minute interludes between the longer scenes of the opera: they would have to come onstage quickly, and "the music had to be percussive to cover up the noises of hammering or sawing or pushing big wooden props behind the curtain."[48] Byrne initially tried to work with Japanese kabuki percussionists, since Wilson's way of working as a director has been inspired by the traditional Japanese theater. But the results he got sounded too imitative, too Japan-esque, and also too much like a generic movie soundtrack. (This music has been added to the 2007 CD/DVD re-release). Byrne then chose a completely different approach, using brass band music. He was especially inspired by the Dirty Dozen Brass Band from New Orleans, a marching band that plays fast, syncopated versions of New Orleans traditional standards, but mixes these with modern jazz pieces by the likes of Parker and Monk. Byrne felt that such brash sounds would provide a counterpoint to Philip Glass' minimal music and to the ethereal, slow-motion drama of Wilson. Byrne rehearsed with the Dirty Dozen Brass Band, but found that their spontaneous way of playing did not fit his design for a completely written score (he also experimented with graphic musical notation, but in the end did not use it) that would be performed more or less the same every night.[49]

Almost half of the score for *The Knee Plays*, as recorded in 1984, consists of rearrangements for brass, drums, and percussion of the American traditional gospels "In The Upper Room," as arranged by the Baptist Methodist Choir Church of God, and "I've Tried" by the Swan Silvertone Singers. Lacking the training to read and write music, Byrne used an Emulator synthesizer to compose his own contributions, recording parts on tape that were later transcribed for the musicians. The result often sounds solemn and organ-like. Part of the lyrics Byrne wrote are unabashedly formal and abstract. See the use of random elements in "Things To Do (I've Tried)":

Number one:	Try to (walking quickly) be
Number two:	Count to ten, smile, count to ten
Number three:	Big shoes
Number four:	Watching big shoes
Number five:	Buying things and spending money

Byrne recites the long list without expression, leaving it up to the listener what it all means, and whether there is a meaning to it at all. Does it offer a deadpan view of the human condition or just a random collection of meaningless actions? Is there a difference? The strategy resembles the projected words in *Stop Making Sense*: random combinations such as "CABLE TV | AIRPLANE CRASH | BURNT TOAST" also put the audience's associative powers to the test.

The music for "The Sound Of Business" is more compelling than that of most of the "Knee" plays. A snare drum beats a constant, metronome-like four/four beat that is syncopated by simple, repetitive and insisting, descending brass themes, and by percussion, with an overall effect of relentless drive. The lyrics, not sung but recited, fit this sensation of compulsion. This is the full text:

> They were driving south on the highway. Their business was in another town, bigger than the town they were driving from. Business took place during office hours, in both towns. This drive was considered business. The feeling of passing other cars was also considered business: the feeling of business being done; the feeling of drifting slowly through a field of moving vehicles. This was the real speed: the speed of business. Mark the numbers on the speedometer!
>
> One of them was playing with the radio, slowly changing channels from one station to another, sometimes listening to both channels at once. On one channel a man was talking to another man on the telephone.
>
> The other channel was playing oldies:
>
> Gone for Good — Listening Wind — Puzzle Power — Beechwood Serenade — Sunshine and Sugar — Golden Windows — Taste of Believing — Carnival Girl — Love Walks Away — Wishing Well— Knew You Could — A Face Like That — Dark Highway — Shakin' Venus — Colored Wheels — Visit Me Quick — Lonesome Money — School of Heartache — Painted Smiles.
>
> The sound of business being done.

The situation is in every respect in-between: between towns, between cars, between radio stations, between conversation and music, between past and present (or between forgetfulness and memory), while the list of song titles descends from sweetness and light to the suggestion of sordid remorse. The experience of driving a car should be added to this: corporeal immobility combined with alert attention to the road and the surrounding countryside that speeds by, which irresistibly leads to a shifting of one's attention to and fro, inside and outside. This is an everyday experience (often singled out as the quintessential experience of the United States), but one that makes it hard to produce an intuitive grasp of inner and outer reality, since neither is quite able to do justice to this immobilized speeding.

"The Sound Of Business" demonstrates how even the most mundane of experiences, such as driving, contain layer over layer of aesthetic mediation. Cities, cars, radio stations, the telephone, conversations, pop songs: all these produce their own aesthetic experience. The overlapping layers are not centered or balanced by a notion of proprioception: the music is not dance music, and the external third-person perspective of the text, together with Byrne's neutral declamation, suggests detachment. After the last words of the text have been spoken, the music pounds on for three more minutes, as if to underline its independent, unrelenting quality.

The songs and instrumentals were developed independently from the stage production. That was a choreography of dancers in white lab coats, carefully lighted, manipulating in kabuki-style movement, props of a book, a boat, and a tree. It was all designed to resonate in many ways with the main sections of *the CIVIL warS*, but also to function independently. The choreographer, Suzushi Hanayagi, was a traditionally trained Japanese dancer who had also worked in New York's "Judson Church" dance avant-garde in the 1960s. In the manner of working of Cage and Cunningham, music and choreography were only combined at the latest possible moment, during the last workshop.[50] "The Sound Of Business" accompanies the methodical construction of a boat out of cubic modules. When the boat is completed, it is slowly carried off the stage by the dancers.

The stately quality of Byrne's score, using traditional gospels, clearly signals sanctioned religion. This effect is opposed by the lyrics, which describe mundane matters that are usually considered to be outside or below the sphere of religion. Apart from driving in a car, the lyrics deal with the selection of clothes for a social occasion ("Today Is An Important Occasion") and with choosing food in a supermarket ("Social Studies"). All in all, something of the solemnity of the gospels is transferred to Byrne's descriptions of the everyday, implying that such ordinary scenes do take on a ritual quality.

5 *LITTLE CREATURES*: TELEVISION'S NAIVETÉ

After working with Wilson and Demme, Byrne began to make plans for a feature film, which would become *True Stories*. The idea was to highlight aspects of conventional, everyday American life, to allow the audience to experience it as truly amazing. Like Robert Wilson's operas, the film should be a kind of "total theater," a *Gesamtkunstwerk*, to combine many forms of art and awaken a wide spectrum of feelings. He began to look for financing and to scout locations for the film, which was to be set in Texas. In 1985, he asked the three other original members of Talking Heads to record a series of uncharacteristically easy and melodic pop songs that he had written. Half of these new songs were to be included in the film, where they would be sung by actors. The rest were released as a Talking Heads album, titled *Little Creatures*. Byrne wrote and recorded these songs in the traditional country-pop format, with some minor gospel and Cajun influences. They are copied from songs that might be heard around the clock from country radio stations; a sound that represents parochial America, the "backbone of the nation."

The best introduction to the album, and perhaps to *True Stories* as well, is the song "Television Man." Its lyrics present the experience of watching TV as both intimate and overwhelming, in keeping with Robert Wilson's model of perception on interior/exterior audio-visual screens:

> I'm looking and I'm dreaming for the first time.
> I'm inside and I'm outside at the same time.
> And everything is real. Do I like the way I feel?
> When the world crashes in, into my living room
> Television made me what I am.
> People like to put the television down. But we are just good friends.
> (I'm a) television man.

The working title of *Little Creatures* was *In Defense of Television*.[51] The song shows the TV to be a kind of demigod, influencing the lives of mere mortals beyond their understanding, always ready to transport consciousness to distant scenes and places.

Television has aptly been called "our third parent": an authority that remains to some extent unquestionable because it has helped to shape our personality from the very start. As every viewer must somehow intuitively know, television tends to decontextualize every content, thereby forcing the viewer to give up his claim for fully conscious interpretation, to drink in and enjoy the transmissions instead. It is quite normal to meet more people on the screen than in real life. Moreover, these TV acquaintances have been produced and edited to make them more emotionally appealing. Thus, TV interprets the world for us, even while viewers are free to choose their own favorite networks and programs. This is the "Creation" that Byrne portrays in *Little Creatures*, the collective dreams of convenient emotion. The wide-eyed and frank celebration of humans as such deeply conventional creatures is somewhat unnerving. The lyrics are determinedly naive, and completely devoid of the sense of guilt and judgment that pervades so much country music. "Creatures Of Love," a song that is (already because of its title) programmatic for the album, tells about love in this way:

> A woman made a man
> A man he made a house
> And when they lay together
> Little creatures all come out
> Well I've seen sex and I think it's alright

The music projects a wide-open innocence and directness, which often results in a quirky humor. The drums are recorded unfiltered, with a prominent role for the snare drum; the guitars play sweet, melodious accents, joined by a lulling steel guitar, and Byrne's soft, straightforward singing is joined by Tina Weymouth singing second voice:

> We are creatures of love, We are creatures of love . . .
> A man can drive a car
> And a woman can be a boss
> I'm a monkey and a flower
> I'm everything at once

The album as a whole breathes surrender and acceptance. It brings them forward with an all-encompassing gesture that is hard to accept, and even confrontational, in so far as it suggests by its very sound alone that this atmosphere is — or should be? — the basic disposition of parochial America.

This perspective of innocence is put up front by the album cover, for which Byrne commissioned a painting from Reverend Howard Finster of Summerville, Georgia. Finster is a naive painter who is "part gifted self-taught artist, part visionary minister of the Gospel, part eccentric. His work embodies a contemporary paradox — it is admired by the art world and coveted by collectors, but it is created primarily as a way of conveying religious teachings."[52] Byrne sent Finster Polaroid photos of Talking Heads, but left the design up to him, although he did ask that the painting be square, like a record cover, and that it resemble one of Finster's previous, particularly colorful, works.[53] In an accompanying letter, Byrne described how he wrote the words to one of his songs, and how he thought the inspiration was similar to the way Finster made his paintings.[54]

The resulting painting shows the four band members in an imaginary landscape, full of spiritual admonitions. Byrne, front center, carries a globe on his shoulders, bearing captions like "world on my shoulder," "get under the load with me," and "who knows the world's weight?" The painting is signed in the lower right-hand corner: "David Byrne is now on T.V. I am listening to him while painting this art 3:15 past midnight April-12–1985. This is my

4000.411th piece of art work. By Howard Finster from God in visions of other worlds beyond the light of the sun."[55]

Several songs from *Little Creatures* were made into video clips, perhaps as an attempt of the band to compensate for not touring. Most critical attention went to "Road To Nowhere," a clip that was storyboarded by Byrne and directed by Byrne together with Steven R. Johnson. This was at the time a state-of-the-art video clip, jam-packed with stop-motion animated iconic images.[56] "Road To Nowhere" is a happy, inviting, sing-along song about being "on a road to nowhere": "We're on the ride to paradise." The clip opens with a long shot of the Hi Vista Community Hall, in what looks like a small town in the American Midwest. Inside the hall, a tracking shot reveals a group of women, men and children, looking non-professional and strictly "ordinary," who sing the opening lines of what sounds like a hymn. This moment cuts to an open road, stretching off into an open landscape. Now Byrne's voice takes over to lead the rest of the song, and the video continues as a series of rapid cuts of image sequences and iconic images, using computer techniques like Paintbox and chromakey to combine several images within the picture space. In a symbolic way, the flood of imagery is all-inclusive; for Byrne, it was not about alienation but about surrender.[57] Academic postmodern theorists have built extensive interpretations on this clip,[58] but it is better to consider it as a prologue for the much more ambitious *True Stories*. After all, that film too begins and ends with a shot of an empty highway in an empty landscape.

6 *TRUE STORIES*: A GENERIC *GESAMTKUNSTWERK*

While working on *Stop Making Sense* with Jonathan Demme, and after directing several music videos, Byrne began to develop a feature film of his own.[59] To get the required funding, he had to bank on Talking Heads' stardom. But the film he made is by no means a vehicle for a rock band. Byrne himself does play a role in the film, as the "Narrator," but his part is clearly a formal device, like that of an anchorman in a news show. And while the film does contain an album's worth of songs by Byrne, it is by no means a rock film or a musical. Instead, *True Stories* (1986) is an ambitious attempt to highlight the patterns and textures of ordinary daily life in the U.S.A. by contrasting a great many different forms of performance. At the end of the film, Byrne in his role of Narrator explicitly states that the film's ambition is to uncover American reality by circumventing settled notions:

> "Well . . . I've really enjoyed forgetting . . . When I first come to a place I notice all the little details. I notice the way the sky looks, the color of white paper. The way people

walk, doorknobs, everything. Then I get used to the place and I don't notice the place anymore. So only by forgetting can I see the place again as it really is."

In preparing the scenario of *True Stories*, Byrne began by developing a framework that was loose enough to incorporate all kinds of accidental contributions. His way of working was inspired partly by what he had picked up from Robert Wilson's habit of beginning work on a theater piece with an abstract visual structure, which can accommodate later additions of music and dialogue. He collected stories from a variety of sources: the sensational stories printed in the *Weekly World News*, which aim openly at the reader's wish for fantasy, together with the *New York Times*, *Newsweek*, and the *Texas Monthly*, as Byrne chose a small town in Texas as the setting for his film. He wrote songs to fit these stories, using the local idioms of country, gospel, rock and Tex-Mex to make the songs blend in with the film's environment. Even though the songs are prominent, the film is not a regular musical, where songs interrupt the plot. As Byrne explained,

> The songs expand on the personalities and characters and on the milieu in and around the town where the story is set. Although the songs don't necessarily advance the story line, they do give relatively placid people — like you or me — a justification for becoming vibrant and full of energy, for expressing themselves and exposing their insides to everyone else in the town.[60]

True Stories is about the lifestyles of people in Virgil, a fictional small town in Texas. To portray the town, Byrne freely combined elements and methods from New York's avant-garde in the performing arts with everyday "art forms" such as tabloid newspapers, TV soaps, karaoke singing, fashion shows, malls, parades, and architecture. The film contains so many ways in which everyday life is stylized, ritualized, or enacted that it is a veritable treasure trove of mimetic strategies. This enabled Byrne to produce a series of works: together with the film, he also published a book titled *True Stories*; a soundtrack, *Sounds from True Stories*; and, with Talking Heads, a *True Stories* album, which contains Talking Heads' versions of songs that in the film had mostly been sung by the actors.

Byrne dislikes plot-driven films: "Most movies show you something and tell you how you're supposed to feel about it."[61] In *True Stories*, he consciously avoided this narrow perspective: "You're dealing with little bits of feeling and impulses and impressions that are jumbled up in the mind, rather than putting them into a rigidly defined hierarchy. Maybe that is closer to the way things are actually perceived or felt."[62] To make a film that was accessible to the widest possible audience, but could include all kinds of found material, he worked with scriptwriters Beth Henley and Stephen Tobolowsky, revising the script time and again to get just the right amount of conventional plot and still have every chance to highlight the performances and rituals of everyday life. To this purpose, *True Stories* weaves two storylines together. The film documents the preparations for a "Celebration of Specialness" in an ordinary Texan town. It introduces key members of the community, shows the town parade to celebrate the 150th birthday of Texas, and a talent show in a prefab theater outside town. This provides many opportunities to showcase people, places, and performances in short semi-documentary vignettes, opportunities that Byrne has made much of. Byrne's role of Narrator, somewhat like the role of the Stage Manager in Thornton Wilder's *Our Town*, allows him to comment on matters like city development, the uses of music, shopping and architecture. The second storyline follows a self-proclaimed conventional man, Louis Fyne, on his search for a woman to marry. He meets and rejects several candidates, gets advice from a Vodun "curandero" or folk healer/psychiatrist, and finally meets the woman he marries through his appearance as a singer during the "Celebration of Specialness" talent contest.

The characters in this second storyline do not have the complexities of real people. They are archetypal exaggerations of generic qualities like stubbornness, laziness, or unfounded optimism, simplifications that Byrne lifted out of tabloid papers. Louis Fyne uses "The Bear" as his nickname, and describes himself as Mediocrity turned flesh; the women he dates are cast as Lazy Woman, Lying Woman and Cute Woman. The town of Virgil also features a male and female Civic Leader, a Computer Guy, a Preacher, a Healer, and a Slick Seducer.

The opening scene shows a dirt road in a completely flat landscape, the horizon exactly in the middle of the frame. In the distance, a little girl in a white dress is walking towards the camera. This scene recreates a solo performance by experimental theater director Meredith Monk, *Songs from the Hill*[63]; Monk herself taught the girl actress her performance. After this scene, the girl hums a melody, a repetitive motif that is picked up by the soundtrack, a 13-note sequence in four/four, vaguely reminiscent of the minimalist music of Philip Glass.[64] Then, a voice-over tells the history of Texas, a highly condensed and laconic tale.

This history moves rapidly from prehistorical sea, dinosaur and first woman (Eve instead of Adam?!) to the recorded history of Texas, told as a dance of genocide, subjugation and war, the last episode of which is the seizing of Texas by the U.S.A.

"'Texas' comes from the Caddoan word for friend. However, the Caddo were amongst the first to be wiped out by settlers. A group of Spanish settlers offered the

Indians the chance to become slaves. The Indians thought about it, decided it was not a good idea, and killed the Spaniards. The Spaniards were fighting the Mexicans. The Mexicans fought the Americans. The Americans were fighting the Wichitas. The Wichitas were fighting the Tankowas. The Tankowas fought the Comanches. The Comanches fought everyone.

Meanwhile, most of the people who now lived here spoke Spanish. Covert military operations to seize Texas for the U.S. of A. were begun in 1835. Eventually, they did get Texas."

After that, history is transformed into economic history with its rapid succession of booms. Finally, Virgil's "Celebration of Specialness" is placed in this succession. This telescoping of history is very similar to the perspective of natural history, with its uncanny timescale that radically surpasses personal experience. It may be compared to the "timescale of evolution" as presented by sociobiologists Tiger and Fox: "If we made an hour-long film to represent the history of tool-making man, industrial man would flash by in a few seconds at the end — he would barely be seen."[65] And if much of the history of mankind resembles a cruel and foolish merry-go-round, that, too, fits the perspective of natural history.

This history is shown in a rapid montage of old film footage and photos. A clip of a growling dinosaur from the classic *One Million B.C.*, directed by Hal Roach in 1940; a publicity photo of Raquel Welch decked out in "prehistoric" leather for the 1966 remake of the same film; a still from the TV show *Little House on the Prairie*, and so on.[66] In finding this material, Byrne was helped by New York advertising company M&Co., the office of designer Tibor Kalman, who had worked for Talking Heads since he helped do the cover for *Remain in Light*. Kalman's specialty was the irreverent juxtaposing of graphic design styles, an approach that suited Byrne very well.

This rapid montage of footage from unrelated sources is acceptable in the cinema, where long years of watching films, TV, and music videos pay off. The repetitive musical motif smoothes the sudden transition from the little girl to the dinosaur; the nutshell rendition of history is plausible and vaguely familiar, while the accompanying imagery oscillates between simple illustration and ironical distancing, as history is obviously shown here as it has been enacted for mass entertainment. The audience now knows that subsequent events may be presented from a variety of perspectives.

In this sequence, Byrne has managed to combine the glitzy decontextualizing style that is endemic on television, history reduced to bite-size entertaining samples, with its diametrically opposed counterpart: the "larger perspective" in which the majority of human activities appear as vain and idle. Neither style cancels or levels the other: like the voice-over and the images, they set each other off as necessary complements within a single orchestration. As Byrne has commented:

"I like that type of footage on the level that it sort of widens the movie out, takes it out of the sphere of just dealing with certain people or a certain relationship. Plus, stock footage and bits and pieces of found stuff bring in other times and places just by virtue of the texture. You can throw in other references and put the story through a prism or kaleidoscope."[67]

The main part of *True Stories* is a densely packed collage of generic American rites and performances. It comprises, along with a treasure trove of conversational clichés, interior decorating, architecture, city planning, popular music, fashion, shopping, television advertising, dating, economic developments, and religious meetings. The film ends after simple man Louis "The Bear" has found himself a wife (that is, when nature has run its course). At this point, the little girl from the opening scene reappears, once again imitating nature sounds, but now walking away from the camera. Over the film's end credits, a final song is heard: Talking Heads playing "City Of Dreams," a plaintive country ballad that summarizes the film in its lyrics:

> From Germany and Europe
> And Southern U.S.A.
> They made this little town here
> That we live in to this day
> The children of the white man
> Saw Indians on TV
> And heard about the legend
> How their city was a dream

This is the method of *True Stories*: to present ordinary American reality as it is created and sustained by dreams, by private and collective fictionalization, and to be open about it: showing and telling. To accomplish this, the scenario switches regularly from dialogue and interacting to private musing (or singing, or performing) by the characters and to commentary from outside (often by the Narrator). The result is a steadfast, carefully blended mixture of documentary and fantasy. Even the characters are made up of found material: Louis "The Bear" Fyne was created out of several magazine articles about bachelors;[68] the "Computer Guy" is a mixture of interviews by Steven Jobs (founder and later CEO of Apple Macintosh) and articles on computer buffs sending signals to outer space[69] (plus, perhaps, Byrne's old dream of working as an anonymous systems analyst); and so on. Throughout the film, open references to such sources are made, to make the people and their lives as transparent as possible. The Computer Guy tells the Narrator that

> "It's a lot like music . . . computers are something like that . . . you can never explain the feelings of the connections to someone else. Figuring something out that's never been understood before is a rhythmic experience . . . Steve Jobs said that, he used to be head of Apple . . . Computers are as much a means of expression as language."[70]

Louis Fyne, the central character, tells himself, in his country and western song "People Like Us," backed by "The Country Bachelors," the story that he is common man made flesh:

> In 1950 when I was born
> Papa couldn't afford to buy us much
> He said be proud of what you are
> There's something special about people like us . . .
> What good is freedom?
> God laughs at people like us . . .
> Millions of people are waitin' on love
> And this is a song about people like us[71]

This is not (or not only) a true sociological, religious, or autobiographical representation: it is truth only in so far as it is accepted by someone as a personal reality, and in consequence is made true by his behavior. Compare the character of the Lying Woman: all her stories about herself are obviously untrue. She is a factory worker, but in her stories she is constantly surrounded by the rich and famous: "When I was a nurse in Vietnam I was stuck out in the middle of the jungle with the real Rambo." "I just work at Varicorp for a hobby." "I believe that part of my extra psychic ability is connected up with my being born with a tail," and so on.[72] Blatantly untrue, stories like this are true in so far as they demonstrate the desire for a more exciting life.

Such definitions of truth as constructed, imagined, as opposed to given, have a prominent place in the social sciences, for example in the so-called situational analysis of William I. Thomas, who wrote: "If men define situations as real, they are real in their consequences."[73] The stories in *True Stories* do not represent an objective, impersonal reality; they are model scenarios for the ways in which people fashion their personalities. Such stories are a part of social practice. Used for self-definition and to shape intimate relationships, they are an important, ritual aspect of everyday life.

Another example of the archetypal quality of the film's characters is the role of Ramon, a Hispanic worker in Virgil's computer plant "Varicorp." While flirting with his co-workers, Ramon claims to be able to read the music of their soul, as if it were a radio station, and bursts into song: "Baby your mind is a radio / the receiver is in my head / Baby I'm tuned to your wavelength." A source for this idea is Jung's psychoanalytical theory, which holds that everyone's unconscious contains an inner figure of the opposite sex. This is a personification of the feminine psychological tendencies in a man (called the anima) and of male tendencies in a woman (the animus). The anima is for instance responsible for the fact that a man is able to find the right marriage partner. Jung wrote:

> Even more vital is the role that the anima plays in putting a man's mind in tune with the right inner values and thereby opening the way into more profound inner depths. It is as if an inner "radio" becomes tuned to a certain wavelength that excludes irrelevancies but allows the voice of the Great Man [the inner self] to be heard. In establishing this inner "radio" reception, the anima takes on the role of guide, or mediator, to the world within and to the Self.[74]

Or consider Byrne's commentary on a shopping mall, in a section that is marked off by a title card reading "SHOPPING IS A FEELING":

> Shopping malls have replaced the town square as the center of many American cities. Shopping has become the thing that brings people together. The music is always playing here. What time is it? No time to look back. . . .
>
> People here are inventing their own systems of belief . . . inventing it . . . selling it . . . making it up as they go along.

Visually, the film carefully maintains a generic quality. The open landscape with the central horizon functions as a visual theme, providing a neutral and transparent background.[75] Byrne used recent color photos by William Eggleston, Len Jenshel, Joel Sternfeld, and Stuart Klipper to define the visual aspects (set design, choice of locations and so forth) of *True Stories*.[76] Their focus, as shown by the photos by Eggleston and Jenshel in the *True Stories* book, is on the decor and the debris that surrounds people. When brought to the viewer's attention, such scenery — mostly neglected out of overfamiliarity — seems to function independently, not as the result of conscious human decisions, but as an influence that people only follow, the way chameleons mimic their surroundings. This theme, too, is explicitly broached, when the Narrator drives up to a club: "You gotta see this . . . it might be part of Virgil's Celebration of Specialness. Or it might not be . . . Maybe you've seen it on TV . . . Maybe you missed it . . . but it's different here . . . Hope you don't mind loud music . . ." Inside the club, a series of people lip-synch along with a Talking Heads song, "Wild Wild Life," imitating rock stars like Billy Idol, Prince, and Madonna. Byrne wrote about this scene:

> The song itself becomes a vehicle that can say anything they want it to. Some gestures and movements are obviously derived from well-known sources: television shows ... movies ... and, most recently, rock videos.
>
> Odd to think that some lip-synchers are imitating characters in videos, who are really musicians imitating other characters.[77]

This shows Byrne's awareness of the complex layering of performance in contemporary life, where life may imitate the media, as well as the other way round. The film itself is also part of this complex, especially where it brings together several well-known makers of performance theater, either in person or in quotations. In this context, the fact that Spalding Gray plays "civic leader" Earl Culver requires special attention: Gray's very presence signals that *True Stories* must be considered a highly self-reflexive film, a performance about performance.

Spalding Gray (1941–2004) was a member of Richard Schechner's "Performance Group." Together with director Elizabeth LeCompte, he was

Figure 6 Spalding Gray as Mayor of Virgil in conversation with Byrne in his role of Narrator in a scene from *True Stories*. Photo: Mark Lipson.

central in the transformation of the Performance Group into The Wooster Group. LeCompte and Gray made three pieces based on episodes of Gray's life, pieces that were both unnervingly autobiographical and rigorously intellectual in structure. This *Rhode Island Trilogy* established The Wooster Group as *the* outstanding avant-garde theater in the U.S.A.[78] Gray said about this work that "he did not want to study others as objects, he wanted to explore himself as other." In his work with LeCompte, and in his later autobiographical solo performances, Gray "wanted to perform his own actions and be reflective at the same time on stage before an audience." His work became a kind of "public confession of his reflectiveness. It became, 'Look at me, I am one who sees himself seeing himself.'"[79]

In the middle piece of the *Rhode Island Trilogy*, *Rumstick Road*, Gray and LeCompte explored the suicide of Gray's mother, Bette Gray. In the play, they included taped interviews by Spalding Gray with his father and grandmother. There is a moment when Gray turns to the audience and tells that his grandmother has asked him not to use the interview with her, and then he goes ahead and plays the tape anyhow. And in his autobiographical role of "Spud," Gray also recreates a telephone conversation with a psychiatrist who treated his mother. He performs his half of the interview "live" while the doctor's responses are played from a tape recording of the call made without the doctor's knowledge.[80] The psychiatrist tries to reassure Gray that his mother got the right treatment, defending the electric shock therapy he administered before her suicide. He even says: "And don't be frightened by a hereditary disposition . . . You may not necessarily get it."[81] LeCompte carefully structured this piece in a manner that emphasizes the disjunctions between life lived and life structured by others, by dividing the stage in three rooms, putting the sound booth in the middle, allowing the audience to see the ongoing use of tapes, records and other theater technology.

The play is an open act of transgression, and the use of tapes against the express wish of the speakers, a violation of their rights that is expressly pointed out in the play, received a lot of attention by theater critics. What LeCompte and Gray made clear is that there is no secure and fixed dividing line between "pure," "imaginary" representations and "real life." The psychiatrist is exploited since his professional secrecy is violated; the electric shock therapy he administered might also be considered a violation of personal security, in spite of the institution "psychiatry" that supposedly excludes violence; for Spalding Gray the suicide of his mother was a brutal shock, which he shares through the performance with the audience. The canons of art are consciously broken, since everything is considered as potential performance material, which means the canons of life are broken at the same time. The result is a painful, all-encompassing irony that includes the artists and the audience, making it clear that none of them is standing on safe ground from where everything else can be judged impartially. Irony and witnessing overlap and merge here,[82] making it clear that here is no simple straightforward authenticity beyond the domain of performance. Even though *True Stories* almost demonstratively stays away from violent subjects like sex, war, and trauma (that is, after the historical introduction), the entire film, including Byrne's presence in it, may be understood as a milder but no less insistent demonstration of the same insight. Byrne plays the outsider's role of Narrator, but together with the other members of Talking Heads, he is in a music-video-like collage of scenes from TV commercials (watched from her bed by the Lazy Woman), in which they are treated like the other commodities. While they lip-sync Byrne's song "Love For Sale," they are dunked in chocolate sauce, wrapped in brightly colored foil, to be finally unwrapped and eaten. That entertainment gets treated like every other product is clearly the message here.

Next to Spalding Gray, the influence of Meredith Monk and of Robert Wilson on *True Stories* has been mentioned. Noteworthy is that Byrne included a direct visual quotation of Wilson's theater. *True Stories* contains an isolated scene of an executive at the local computer plant, an older man in a grey suit, alone in a cube-like office at night, where he is dancing and twirling around. Both the formalistic layout of this scene and its choreography recall the "space ship" scene in *Einstein on the Beach*, the opera by Robert Wilson and Philip Glass.[83]

There is another short peripheral scene in which three men do a "gas station dance," a choreography of slow unusual movements. In the *True Stories book* this is described as follows: "Two kids being given a drunk test by Police in front of a 7–11 store. One walks backward with his arms outstretched, and the other, with his eyes closed, slowly attempts to touch the tip of his nose with his finger."[84] The scene resembles the vernacular, task-like pieces of New York's Judson Dance Theater, the kind of postmodern dance that displays "the practical intelligence of the body in pursuit of a mundane, goal-oriented type of action."[85]

Last but not least, Byrne's treatment of religion and myth deserves attention. Religion is supposed to bring a meaningful coherence to life, to protect what is sacred and to sanctify the community. Byrne's description of shopping malls, which "bring people together and let them invent their own systems of belief," fits this description. His film contains three other examples.

First, a conservative preacher sermonizing about the hidden relationships that cause the demise of morality, suggesting an all-encompassing conspiracy. His sermon mixes some ridiculous examples with suggestive remarks about government commissions and the CIA, and turns into a rendition by the preacher, a gospel choir and the congregation of Byrne's song "Puzzling Evidence."

In a similar scene, Earl Culver, the civic leader of the town (Spalding Gray's role) holds forth on the impact of the computer revolution. Using the food on the dinner table in front of him to illustrate his words with improvised diagrams, he explains the changes in the economy:

> "They don't work for money anymore, or to earn a place in heaven, which was a big motivating factor once, believe you me. Economics has become a spiritual thing. They're working and inventing because they like it! It's a whole new philosophy . . . I must admit, it frightens me a little bit. They don't see any difference between working and not working. Everything is a part of one's life. [Carried away, addressing his children:] Linda! Larry! there's no concept of weekends anymore!"[86]

And third, Mr. Tucker, "a black man in his fifties with a very calm, serene demeanor,"[87] who works as the home assistant for the Lazy Woman. At home, he has an elaborate altar that combines Afro-Atlantic iconography with statues and images of Christian saints.[88] There, he works as a "curandero," a Vodun folk healer. Louis "The Bear" Fyne turns to him for help when he fails to find a suitable partner. Mr. Tucker cures him by "discharging the negative forces he has received," telling him, among other things, to drink three soda waters a day, that is, to drink half and throw the other half away. He also places a Polaroid photo of Louis Fyne on his altar, which he will use later in a ritual prayer. Following the prayer, he starts to dance and sings:

> Now I'm gonna call,
> Gonna call on Legba.
> Get yourself a sign
> Get your love and desire
>
> Rompiendo la monotonía del tiempo
> Rompiendo la monotonía del tiempo
>
> Papa Legba, come and open the gate
> Papa Legba, to the city of camps
> Now, we're your children
> Come and ride your horse[89]

"Papa Legba" is another song by Byrne. Legba is an important god in the Vodun pantheon; when he takes possession of a disciple in trance, the god is said to "ride his horse."[90] The refrain of the song, "Rompiendo la monotonía del tiempo" (which translates as "breaking the monotony of time"), as well as the prescription to drink three soda waters and throw half away, were lifted directly out of an article about folk healers in the *Texas Monthly*.[91]

These religious manifestations are just shown in the film, not discussed, but they invite a comparison. First, it is interesting how shopping malls, a fundamentalist church, the computer economy and a Vodun ritual are all treated equally, without the traditional distinction between (Western) religion and (non-Western) superstition, and without the distinction between mythical belief systems and rational economic systems. As a detail, it is noteworthy how computers are introduced as producing new connections that are like music, "a rhythmic" experience. Yet in the "spiritualized" computer economy, "there's no concept of weekends anymore," the basic social order of time is erased, leaving a calendar without rhythm. "Breaking the monotony of time," as Mr. Tucker aims to do, is in comparison the more musical religion.

The release of *True Stories* was accompanied by a flood of media attention, as is to be expected when a rock star writes and directs a movie. *Time* magazine ran a cover story on Byrne, gave him the freedom to design his own cover (only Robert Rauschenberg had preceded Byrne in this), and named him "Rock's Renaissance Man."[92] Most film critics responded positively to the movie's visual and narrative smorgasbord, but more than a few critics who looked for a political relevance complained that Byrne's irony was too easy, or even condescending. Richard McKim wrote: "Byrne's running commentary as our guide is obviously ironical in its wide-eyed, deadpan enthusiasm. The question is, ironical in what sense?"[93] His answer was that Byrne appreciated the spark of original vitality in all his characters, but still adopted "the old 'noble savage' notion" towards the Texans he depicts.[94] In *Artforum*, Barbara Kruger called *True Stories* "a touristic glance at the 'other.'"[95] And in the *Washington Monthly*, William G. McGowan paired Byrne's irony with Susan Sontag's essay on camp and David Letterman's talk show humor under the title "Selling out with a Smirk."[96]

A very different approach was put forward by art historian Henry M. Sayre. In *The Object of Performance*, a book on avant-garde performance in the arts from 1970–90, he places *True Stories* in the tradition of Cage, Cunningham, and Rauschenberg, with their aesthetic of heterogeneity, complexity, and undecidability. Sayre places Byrne, together with Philip Glass, Steve Reich, and Brian Eno, in Cage's tradition of artistic collaboration without forced submission under a master plan, and of a renewal of the *Gesamtkunstwerk* that champions an attitude that Cage has called "polyattentiveness."[97] Sayre accordingly characterizes *True Stories* as "a film about performance — performance in everyday life, a vernacular *Gesamtkunstwerk*."[98]

Sayre's book is limited to developments within the avant-garde arts, and has comparatively little to say about the confrontation of the Cagean, high-art approach to *Gesamtkunst* with the "total environment" produced by commercial mass media, advertising, and marketing that is so typical of *True Stories*. The idea of the *Gesamtkunstwerk* as propagated by Richard Wagner is that such art provides a community with a mythology that gives it shape and purpose. Wagner's own nationalism and anti-semitism provide a most unhappy example of the force of such a notion. John Cage's heterogeneous version of the *Gesamtkunstwerk* puts forward the Zen-like ideal that everything is fine just as it is, simply ignoring the political and communal common reservoir of concepts and symbols. Byrne's film is unusual in deploying the means of the Cagean avant-garde to show the mythical aspects of American capitalist consumer society without offering an alternative, preferring to illuminate the production processes of private and societal mythologies.

7 A SOUNDTRACK FOR MABOU MINES' *DEAD END KIDS*

In 1986, apart from *True Stories*, three more feature films came out of New York's downtown art community: JoAnne Akalaitis' *Dead End Kids*, Laurie Anderson's *Home of the Brave*, and Jim Jarmusch's third movie, *Down by Law*. All these films and directors were part of the network of collaborations underneath the creative output of SoHo. The degree to which Talking Heads and especially Byrne were part of this network is shown by their connection to all these films. Jarmusch directed a video clip for the *Little Creatures* song "The Lady Don't Mind," after an idea of Chris Frantz and Tina Weymouth. Anderson's *Home of the Brave* is a concert film of her *Mister Heartbreak* tour, similar in some respects *to Stop Making Sense*, and featuring several musicians who had toured or recorded with Talking Heads: guitarist Adrian Belew, singer Dolette MacDonald, and percussionist David Van Tieghem. Jonathan Demme's 1987 film version of Spalding Gray's autobiographical performance *Swimming to Cambodia*, with a subdued film score by Laurie Anderson, is another example of this network.

Dead End Kids was an experimental theater piece that was made into a film, for which Byrne provided a modest soundtrack. The full title of the film and of the original play is *Dead End Kids: A Story of Nuclear Power*. The play was developed and directed by JoAnne Akalaitis and performed by Mabou Mines at New York's Public Theater during the 1980/81 season. Mabou Mines had been founded in 1970 by Ruth Maleczech, Lee Breuer, JoAnne Akalaitis, Philip Glass (who wrote music for several productions), and David Warrilow, to experiment with theater that goes beyond storytelling.[99] For *Dead End Kids*, Akalaitis used her experience with this kind of theatrical "bricolage" to construct a play about the history of physical science, its origin in alchemy, the development and use of nuclear weapons and nuclear power, and its ethical ramifications. The result is "a kind of alchemical grand guignol," as a character within the film describes it, a complex story of historical quotations, told in a multiplicity of forms, ranging from a nightclub act to a TV quiz show, 40s-style musical, Goethe's *Faust*, scientific lectures, and TV street interviews. Byrne had much admired the stage production. "Swamp," from *Speaking in Tongues*, was Byrne's own version of *Dead End Kids*, a song about the use of atomic arms written from the perspective of the devil, and of everyone implicated in the sins of war: "How many people do you think I am / Pretend I am somebody else?" "Pika Pika," a seemingly meaningless expression used in "Swamp," is Japanese for a "spic and span" place to live. Byrne used the term as a covert reference to the bombing of Hiroshima:[100] "risky business. All that blood will never cover that mess."

JoAnne Akalaitis had advised Byrne on his designs for *Stop Making Sense*, and when she made a (very low-budget) film of *Dead End Kids*, Byrne returned the favor by making a soundtrack and a little music. At the time, he had begun to put together a sound studio in his home, and Byrne saw the film as a chance to learn how to work the equipment, experiment with some new sounds, and have some place for it to go.[101] But the stage production did not translate well to film, and the movie was not released, although it did get shown at the Toronto Film Festival.[102]

Central to *Dead End Kids* is a double perspective in which historical developments in science are compared to spiritual developments. A title card, quoting Carl Jung, says as much: "Alchemy was the dawn of the scientific age, when the demon of the scientific spirit compelled the forces of nature to serve man to an extent that had never been known before." The film also quotes J. Robert Oppenheimer, the physicist who directed the Manhattan Project that produced the first atom bomb. In 1946, Oppenheimer said: "In some sort of crude sense, which no vulgarity, no humor, no overstatement can extinguish, we physicists have known sin, and that is knowledge we cannot lose." The film goes on to present post-World War II American pop culture surrounding atomic weapons and atomic power as a parade of vulgarities, humor, and overstatements. Examples are a song-and-dance musical routine about dropping the atomic bombs on Japan, and a 1950s high school exhibition about "atomic energy for peace", which includes an "atomic coffee-pot" and "atomic long johns." The summit of vulgarity is reached in the final scene in which a sleazy comedian pulls the carcass of a dead and plucked chicken out of his pants, and asks a girl from the audience to hold it for him, to help him demonstrate the effects of radiation on poultry. The scene opens up a maelstrom of meanings, in which the dead chicken stands for poultry, but also for the penis and the vagina (the comedian

Figure 7 A poster Byrne designed and had put up in Manhattan for the 1984 U.S. presidential elections between Ronald Reagan (who had initiated the "Star Wars" Strategic Defense Initiative) and Walter Mondale (who supported a nuclear freeze). In the original poster, the top photo of a city destroyed by bombs is black and white, the photo of flowers and trees in color.

asks his assistant/victim to "give the bird some head"), and for the human body. The actress playing the girl from the audience also plays Marie Curie and the lead singer in the musical routine; these doublings produce reverberating meanings around every detail of the filmed play.[103]

Byrne's soundtrack for *Dead End Kids* is unobtrusive and atmospheric: an insistent, metallic throbbing for the opening titles, the ticking of an alarm clock, some modulating organ chords to underline alchemical quotations. His involvement in the politics of nuclear warfare is also evident in a poster he designed and had put up in Manhattan for the 1984 elections.

8 *THE FOREST*: A BYRNE-WILSON PIECE

After *The Knee Plays*, Byrne once again worked with Robert Wilson, this time having more influence on the concept of the entire production. Wilson approached Byrne when the city of West Berlin asked him to put together a play to celebrate Berlin's 750th anniversary in 1988. Byrne suggested using the epic of Gilgamesh, a mythical story he liked, and setting it in Germany during the Industrial Revolution, around 1860. Byrne also wanted to turn the piece into a movie, which was to have its own scenario, quite different from the stage version. Robert Wilson did most of the design for the stage, while Byrne developed a scenario and visual ideas for the film.[104]

The Gilgamesh epic tells the story of Gilgamesh, two-thirds divine and one-third human, a harsh and despotic ruler over the city Uruk, in ancient Babylon. Answering the complaints of Uruk's inhabitants, the gods create a rival for Gilgamesh: Enkidu, a wild man and a creature of the forest. When Gilgamesh is told of the existence of this man, he sends a whore into the forest to seduce him, and this plan is successful. Enkidu then leaves the forest, confronts Gilgamesh and wrestles him. When neither can beat the other, the two become friends and set out on a series of heroic adventures, challenging the gods. In the end, divine vengeance causes Enkidu to fall ill and die, leaving Gilgamesh to mourn him. To transpose the Gilgamesh epic to the era of the Industrial Revolution amounts to an attempt to fathom the mythical dimensions of the nineteenth century. Byrne explained this attempt as follows":

> This tale speaks about the relationship between nature and culture, civilization versus animals in nature, and about immortality and death. The old story was kind of weaving together a number of themes simultaneously in a way that seemed fairly contemporary, and in a way that I thought had relevance to a lot of things that we're thinking about now.[105]

After the theater production had been done, he reflected:

> "The more I did research on Germany during the Industrial Revolution, the more
> it seemed that the whole concern is currently replaying itself, with the industrialists
> taking one side and the romantics taking the other. It was an education for me. A
> lot of what we tend to consider modern, Twentieth Century thought came about
> during that period."[106]

A basic collage that Byrne did to illustrate this aspect of *The Forest* combines
a magazine ad for Nike running shoes with an almost similar image in the
style of the foremost Romantic German painter, Caspar David Friedrich. Both
images present people silhouetted by backlighting (a style Wilson used in his
stage lighting design for *The Forest*), thereby producing a heroic juxtaposition
of man and nature that is still widely credited.

The unresolved questions of Romanticism and of the contemporary forms
and relevance of mythology would continue to inspire Byrne, who wrote:

> To me "The Forest" is less a piece than a process. A process of discovering what it is
> we are made of. What kinds of ideas, what prejudices, what propaganda fills us up,
> what we think is beautiful and what we think is ugly, what we consider Nature and
> what we think is God.[107]

Collage   Collage
David Byrne

Figure 8 A collage made by Byrne, from the theater program for *The Forest* by Robert
Wilson and David Byrne. The text of the Nike ad in the collage spells out the romantic
quest for a sublime experience of nature: ". . . surpassing yourself . . . running ahead of
a threatening thunderstorm."

Another aspect of this can be seen in a letter Byrne published in August 1992, when questions of forest conservation resulted in a heated political debate in the U.S. This is a fragment:

> A few years ago, I was hoping to make a movie in Europe called "The Forest". I needed to find an untouched, wild, old forest. The new replanted forests, among other things, don't look the same. They're boring. Like Muzak as opposed to Music. [. . .] Much of the same thing has happened in this country. There's only a little bit left of the original ancient forests in the Pacific Northwest. 10%. Ninety percent has been destroyed. Most of it in the last 40 years. Forty years is nothing. [. . .] These forests are not a renewable resource: at least, not for hundreds of years.[108]

The stage version of *The Forest* was written by Heiner Müller (using material from his older play, *Zement*[109]) and Darryl Pinckney, after thorough discussions with Byrne and Wilson. Wilson began work on the stage version by designing it as a silent production, making a video tape of a workshop with people where the staging was mapped out. Müller, Pinckney, and Byrne used that tape, the visual book of the work, to set their texts and music to.

The music was a consciously primitive version of the late nineteenth-century Romantic symphonic style. Byrne had immersed himself in the music of Wagner, Bruckner, Mendelssohn-Bartholdy, Mahler, Strauss, Janacek, and Sibelius (*Finlandia*),[110] but made no attempt to do justice to this music on its own terms. On the contrary, he tried to listen in a naive way: "I didn't go to music school and learn the ins and outs of musical composition. So when I was making this music, it was a naive take on it."[111] Byrne's wager was that his lack of specific musical knowledge might be compensated by the continuing presence of Romanticism in film music (John Williams' orchestral scores for the *Star Wars* films are based on the same late Romantic examples Byrne listened to) and in popular genres such as heavy metal.[112] Since the Gilgamesh myth came from the Middle East, Byrne also mixed in occasional musical references to the East. Byrne used electronic keyboards and guitars plugged into electronic keyboards to come up with orchestral parts. Then he worked with arranger and orchestrator Jimmie Haskell, deciding together which instruments would play which parts, and which harmonies would be expressed in which section. The music for *The Knee Plays* (interludes) of *The Forest* was improvised by the orchestra. As Byrne explained this process,

> I watched one of the dances that Suzushi [Hanayagi] had choreographed and for some reason I thought of the sound of a rollercoaster. So I drew a rollercoaster going up and down and put different chords for the orchestra at the tops and the bottoms.

The musicians were conducted when to go up and when to go down; they could choose any note they wanted within that chord, but they had to try to slide together. It worked out pretty well. This is music that was written with visual images in mind. Whether it stands on its own remains to be seen. Often it works best when it goes against the images, when it's telling us something different.[113]

Byrne wrote only a few lyrics for *The Forest*. The first one mixes mythical and primordial scenes of family life, pastoral beauty, and sudden violence with standard rock nihilism ("one and two and three and four, I don't care and I don't know"):

> I'm only nine years old and my mother makes me
> sing she gives me lessons it is money down the
> drain stand up (and) wipe your ass with pages
> from the times creep down the hallway see my
> daddy (die) this golden afternoon the green grass
> all around love peace and happiness in nature's
> groves resound(s) and this is why we fight and
> why we come to blows in this our universe God
> only knows[114]

In the play, this song is interrupted by texts provided by Pinckney and Müller: "I feel this because I feel nothing at all I think this because this is nothing nothing nothing part of night and silence and of the fact that I likewise am a nothingness negative and interspatial." And: "and I looked upon the characters of the rock and they were changed and the characters were S S SI II LL LL EN EN CE CE."

Wilson did not understand his version of *The Forest* as representing reality, but as an occasion for revelatory insight, saying: "Theater is not something we can comprehend; it's something we can experience. What's necessary in the theater is the audience. What happens in the audience is the mixing. It's different with each person. WE can't mix Heiner's texts and David's music and my images; the audience will do it."[115] Theater scholar and critic Bonnie Marranca, an admirer of Wilson's "theatre of images," wrote about the production that Wilson sweeps the dreams of different cultures and ages, in an attempt to make his theater into a global and historical archive.[116] Arthur Holmberg, another theater scholar and admirer, saw nostalgia in Wilson's work: "Wilson's *Naturphilosophie* (the origins of this tradition go back to Schelling) belies the hope to merge with nature, transcending this breach between subject and object. The knowledge of separation brings with it the nostalgia for union."[117]

The stage version of *The Forest* was shown not only in West Berlin but also in New York, but still only a restricted number of theatergoers could see the production. Wilson had used a very high budget of 3.7 million German Marks, thanks to a major financial contribution by the German state lottery. Byrne hoped to make *The Forest* into a film that could be seen by a wider audience, but ran into financial difficulties. Only the script that he put together for the film remains in his archives. Much more outspoken than Wilson's version, it is an interesting document of Byrne's outlook and method.

9 *THE FOREST* AS FILM SCRIPT

Byrne's plan for the film version of *The Forest* was to combine the ancient myth of Gilgamesh, set in nineteenth-century industrial Germany, with a science fiction-like storyline about mythical gods who try to control all events. The film would be told mainly through images, leaving the text and the music to work on other levels, in other layers. While most of the story of Gilgamesh and Enkidu would be shot on real locations, some scenes would be formally stylized and allegorical, producing the possibility for interplay between the story scenes and the more symbolic layer. The script gives several instances of real nineteenth-century pre-cinema practices of making and using images, practices that would allow shifts from "realism" to "mythology": a medical operating theater, a photographer's studio where Enkidu has his picture taken in a number of fanciful settings, after the fashion of the time, and a "Kaiser Panorama," a stereoscopic viewing system for several spectators at a time that was one of the predecessors of film.

As part of his research, Byrne read Humphrey Jennings' *Pandaemonium: The Coming of the Machine Age as Seen by Contemporary Observers*. Jennings, a literary scholar and filmmaker, had put together this historical anthology as a means to examine the transformation of imagination and of human emotions over the course of the Industrial Revolution. Jennings employs a distinction between "the means of vision," which he circumscribes as "matter (sense impressions) transformed and reborn by Imagination: *turned into an image*," and "the means of production — matter is transformed and reborn by *Labour*."[118] His perspective is more historical, and in that respect more realistic than that of Carl Jung and Joseph Campbell:

> In the two hundred years 1660–1860 the means of production were violently and fundamentally altered — altered by the accumulation of capital, the freedom of trade, the invention of machines, the philosophy of materialism, the discoveries of science. [. . .] Man as we see him today lives by production and by vision. It is doubtful if he can live by one alone.[119]

This question, how the emotional side of our nature interacts with an industrial society and with the technological production of mythical imagery, is thematic throughout Byrne's script for *The Forest*. That this is so is especially clear in the scenes in which the gods meddle with human history.

> Scene 41: The Gods Lab III — The Kaiser Panorama
> We are back in the space where the light comes from all over. The GODS' LAB. In the center of the room sits a curious contraption surrounded by beautiful chairs. It is slightly higher than the height of a man, and roughly cylindrical in shape, beveled into a series of planes, with a series of viewing devices mounted at what would be eye level if one were sitting. It is a futuristic device as envisioned by the mid-nineteenth century.
> A couple of the INHABITANTS enter the space and seat themselves, gazing into the viewing parts. More and more of them enter until all nine visible seats are taken. They all gaze into the little holes. Some of them occasionally laugh, some others growl, as if affected by what they are seeing. Some of them respond as if reading from an unseen text.

In Scene 49, the gods in their laboratory are watching Enkidu and Gilgamesh, yelling and laughing at their adventures:

> The camera pulls back, for the first time, and reveals these masters of the universe to be a bunch of adolescents. A bunch of irresponsible kids in their early teens, their whims, reason and desires ruled for the most part by the hormones that rush through their beautiful bodies.[120]

Many scenes make clear that the different protagonists are really mirror versions of each other, representations whose fate depends on their other self. Byrne's script version of *The Forest*, written in collaboration with Michael Hirst, functions halfway between Mabou Mines' politically explicit theater and Wilson's pure and apolitical visions. The script is close to *True Stories*, but it has a historical subject, and it aims at the mechanisms that help some myths to dominance, and thereby to produce history.

It had not been easy for Byrne to find the budget to make *True Stories*, which was somewhere between $2 million and $3 million. Warner Bros. turned down his script two times, and that film had an album's worth of Talking Heads' songs to help it find an audience. The estimated budget for the film version of *The Forest* was set at $7 million, more than twice as high.[121] Byrne's music for *The Forest* is lumpy and shapeless in comparison to most of his songs, as if to show that much symphonic Romantic music consists of big, bold, simplistic blocks of sound without rhythmic sophistication.[122] It is not music to pull an audience into a cinema, or to sway entertainment industry executives. On top of that, it was next to impossible to find good locations, as Germany has changed completely since 1860. As a result, the projected budget was way too high, only within reach if all kinds of commercial and populist adaptations were made, which Byrne refused to do. In the end, the film was never made. For two more years, Byrne kept looking into other possibilities, like a treatment for television, but nothing happened.

The Forest, in Byrne's version, would have drawn its poetic energies from two sources: the tremendous upheaval of the industrial revolution, and the uninterrupted stream of weird adolescent mythologies pouring out of film and TV studios, the likes of *Star Wars* and *Pokemon*, *Lord of the Rings*, *Thunderbirds*, and *Knight Rider*. The combination of the two would have been fascinating, but the plan was completely beyond the standards of commercial entertainment.

In an essay titled "Theater of Memory," Byrne wrote:

> It's a kind of memory theater, an attempt to prevent the present from lying, denying, and controlling the past, and a similar attempt to prevent the past from perverting, eating, and devouring the present, its own children. An attempt to make a poetic machine, a vast multimedia mnemonic contraption that will hold all this stuff like the imaginary memory rooms of Giordano Bruno [. . .] Only by identifying and recognizing this crap can we break the vicious cycle of lies, of endless reprisals, vengeance, and genocide. Only when the truth is accepted can we and all people move on, and unless that happens we remain trapped, trapped in the time of the myth's creation, building higher and higher walls and defenses to keep reality at bay.[123]

"Theater of Memory" is about the work of songwriter, artist and theater performer Terry Allen — but parts of it read as artistic autobiography in disguise, perfectly applicable to Byrne's own work on *The Forest*. This also forms the right context for one of Byrne's occasional forays into performance art, *Report from L.A.*, his contribution to The Kitchen's *Two Moon July* video compilation of SoHo's avant-garde performers and video artists. The clip shows Byrne jogging around in The Kitchen's gallery space, saying "Today is my birthday. I just flew in from Los Angeles this morning, business class, so naturally I am thinking about movies." While running in circles, he reads from an (in-flight?) magazine about new films, a long list of titles: "This year we'll be seeing: 'Battle of the Valley,' 'Demoniac,' 'Sword and the Cross,' 'Pirate Warrior,' 'Pirate of the Seven Seas,' 'Executioner of Venice.'" The list goes on, and although Byrne adds no comment, the titles speak for themselves, in their sensational use of mythical motifs, without an inkling of wider responsibility. Byrne's work in film and performance theater, his collaborations with several representatives of the theater's avant-garde, are a way out of this closed circle of entertainment mythologies.

Chapter 4

Rock Star and Ethnographer

1 THE ARTIST AS ETHNOMUSICOLOGIST

After making *True Stories*, Byrne shifted his interest to musical practices and cultural experiences outside the American mainstream. In 1988, Robert Farris Thompson published an interview with Byrne in *Rolling Stone* in which Thompson wrote: "one could say that David Byrne is nowadays as much ethnographer as he is rock artist."[1] Thompson, as a highly respected Africanist and art historian, bases his characteristic enthusiasm on an enormous scholarly knowledge of his subjects, and he was friends with Byrne so he knew what he was saying. Of course, the combination of rock music with cultural anthropology is anything but self-evident and simple, and in each instance it is worthwhile to ask if, and how, the two really go together well.

Anthropologist Arjun Appadurai has written an often-cited study on the cultural dimensions of globalization, *Modernity at Large*, in which he stresses that imagination everywhere is influenced by the mass media:

Because of the rapid way in which they move through daily life routines, electronic media provide resources for self-imagining as an everyday social project. As with mediation, so with motion. The story of mass migrations, both voluntary and forced, is hardly a new feature of human history. But when it is juxtaposed with the rapid flow of mass-mediated images, scripts, and sensations, we have a new order of instability in the production of modern subjectivities.[2]

Byrne, living in New York City and Los Angeles, was working in two of the major industries, film and music, that are responsible for turning the imagination into a cultural collage. Any ethnographer worth his salt would be interested in the organization and meaning of this collage, in the underlying relations of power, meaning, and ritual, to bring them out into the open for inspection. Before he could think of doing so, he would have to steep himself thoroughly in the contributing cultures. This is a good way to think about a good part of Byrne's musical activities. Over the course of the 1980s, he covered a wide range of musical cultures. Several genres of American popular music, from new wave rock to country, gospel and funk, have already been discussed, and Byrne had also incorporated impulses from several of the world's musical cultures: traditional West African drumming, Japanese kabuki percussion, New Orleans brass band, European nineteenth-century symphonic music, and of course the modern sound studio as technical and conceptual tool. Add to this list the Arabian singers and American radio preachers on *My Life in the Bush of Ghosts*, and it is clear that Byrne responded to many forms of musical behavior. He also looked at Chinese music, minimalist music, and salsa, in three collaborations that deserve some brief attention.

After seeing *Stop Making Sense*, film director Bernardo Bertolucci asked Byrne to contribute some music to the score for *The Last Emperor*. Using synthesizers and other electronic tools, Byrne put together several rhythmic and sober tracks, five of which were used in the final score. For this music, which had to help the viewer accept that he was seeing something in China, he imitated several Chinese instruments and styles, basing the music on records and cassettes of Chinese music. The result is serviceable enough, and adds musical atmosphere to Bertolucci's movie, but it can't stand on its own as commentary on the Chinese aesthetic and culture. It was simply "music for hire," as Byrne described it.[3] It is ironic that Byrne (with co-composers Ruichi Sakamoto and Cong Su) won an Oscar for this somewhat nondescript film music, when with *True Stories* he had proven his ability to make a much more meaningful film score.

When composer Philip Glass wanted to try his hand at composing songs, he asked Byrne to write lyrics. (Later, Glass also asked Laurie Anderson, Paul Simon and Suzanne Vega to contribute.) Byrne produced stanzas of loose verbal motifs and phrases, asking Glass to organize them himself, allowing them to sink into the texture of Glass's non-narrative music. The resulting two songs are on Glass's *Songs from Liquid Days* (1986).[4] Again, the lyrics are serviceable enough, but if the album title had raised hopes that the lyrics would reveal something of the strange sense of time induced by Glass's music, with its combined and parallel influences of Indian music, of being stoned, of stubborn focused repetition and avoidance of distraction, these hopes would not be fulfilled.[5]

Asked by Jonathan Demme to do a song for his movie *Something Wild*, Byrne agreed on the condition that he could do a duet with Celia Cruz, the Queen of mambo and salsa. Together with salsa legend Johnny Pacheco, he wrote a "salsa-reggae" song, a song that was mostly but not quite salsa, with lyrics that introduced the storyline of the movie.[6] Once again, the song did what it was supposed to do for the movie, but nothing more: the distance between Cruz and Byrne, in terms of voice, language, culture, age, what have you, remained mostly inarticulate.

Such contributions to other people's projects provided Byrne with opportunities to discover other musical traditions, but they were only casual, one-off attempts. A full exploration of the cultural collage, with its gaps and shocks, its countless forms of indifference and ignorance, would be something else entirely. Nietzsche wrote in *Beyond Good and Evil* that "the abyss gazes into you,"[7] and that is certainly true for the abyss between different sensibilities. Understanding a foreign sensibility means an encounter with one's own insensitivity, which means that a confrontation between cultural myths will not leave one's own preconceptions untried. In the uncertainty and confusion that are the result of any rigorous analysis of the cultural collage, the stringent demands of conceptual art and of performance theater can be a useful guide, which is why some of the arguments presented in this field are summarized in this section, to prepare for the discussion of Byrne's topical series of works.

Conceptual artist Joseph Kosuth, in his essay "The Artist as Anthropologist," argued that artists should try to make explicit the interpretative conceptions that allow them to encounter and incorporate artistic Western and other traditions.[8] This was after he took a year off, in 1971/72, to study philosophy and anthropology at the New School of Social Research. Kosuth's call to artists to reflect in their work on the many cultural frames that surround art did not go unheeded, so that 25 years later, art historian Hal Foster could summarize the results. In *The Return of the Real: The Avant-Garde at the End of the Century* (1996), Foster dedicated a chapter to "The Artist as Ethnographer." The ethnographic role has become a new artistic paradigm for "advanced art on the left," as Foster notes, a paradigm for art that involves its audience in a consideration of its own culture and community in the widest sense, for works which assume the form of an "ethnographic mapping of a given institution or a related community."[9] According to Foster, such works become problematic when they are commissioned and even franchised by art institutions; he is suspicious of the ironies which this institutionalization of the critique of institutions produces.

Foster presents an overview of twentieth-century theoretical positions in philosophy and art to make his point that, in the 1980s and 90s, there can be found a turn towards anthropology that values anthropology for five reasons: 1) because it is the science of alterity, with its potential for subversion and transformation; 2) because it is the science of culture, placing art in the wider social field; 3) because ethnography is contextual, which automatically guarantees a critical understanding of the wider relevance of art; 4) because anthropology is seen as interdisciplinary; and 5) because it is seen as reflexive.[10] His critical suspicion of this position is that "the quasi-anthropological role set up for the artist can promote a presuming as much as a questioning of ethnographic authority, an evasion as often as an extension of institutional critique."[11] He issues two general warnings: first, given the globalization of the economy, it can no longer be supposed that any culture exists in a pure "outside" that is no part of the world system; second, this is also true of cultural identities.[12] Artistic attempts to transcend one's own cultural presuppositions, to make the "self" into an "other," may easily "flip into self-absorption, in which the project of an 'ethnographic self-fashioning' becomes the practice of a philosophical narcissism."[13] The gist of Foster's critique is that museums and other art institutions may illuminate a great many cultural practices by making an ethnographic turn, putting up exhibitions that are ethnographically self-reflexive — but as long as such reflexivity is kept within the domain of high art, within its spotless white walls, it does not mean very much. The real cultural decisions are not made there, and sensibilities are often formed and overhauled in more barbarian circumstances.

Performance theater and performance studies as envisaged by Richard Schechner are inherently intercultural, and that orientation has led to a collaboration between Schecher and anthropologist Victor Turner, who found the role of the observing cultural anthropologist and that of the interfering theater director to be complementary. Turner wrote about theater as a means to understand a culture: "Actors are deeply aware of how the human body can be made by costume, cosmetics, and stylization a matrix of living meaning, at once epitomizing and evaluating the social life of the times."[14] Schechner, looking from theater at anthropologists, wrote about their work "in the field":

> The situation precipitated by the fieldworker is a theatrical one: he is there to see, and he is seen. But what role does the fieldworker play? He is not a performer and not not a performer, not a spectator and not not a spectator. He is in between two roles just as he is in between two cultures. In the field he represents — whether he wants or not — his culture of origin; and back home he represents the culture he has studied.[15]

The very presence of the fieldworker is, as Schechner remarks, an invitation to playacting,[16] and according to him the soft sciences are therefore, in the final analysis, extensions of the arts and humanities.[17]

The relations between anthropology and performance have also been explored from another angle by Jay Ruby, who considers combinations of anthropology with the mass media of recorded music and film. Ruby advocates a strict position: ethnographic filmmaking should be the exclusive province of academically trained anthropologists who are interested in making pictorial ethnographies.[18] This would necessitate a radical break with current practices of documentary and ethnographic filmmaking, since they are restricted by the standards of television as well as by incisive financial pressures. He suggests that in order to visualize the many theoretical distinctions that are necessary to document forms of cultural behavior, ethnographic filmmakers should ally themselves with experimental filmmakers, who are content to produce works with no commercial potential designed for a very small audience.[19] At this point, Ruby turns to the work of Schechner and others to introduce the concept of culture as performance, as improvised mixed-media scenario. As Ruby remarks, ethnographic filmmaking may resemble transformative rituals when the film does not document reality passively, but reveals culture by provoking new perspectives: "*ciné-trance*" is the term which filmmaker Jean Rouch coined for this. A diametrically opposed possibility is the filming of long stretches of daily life in which nothing dramatic happens, presenting social reality in its most prosaic aspects. Ruby disagrees with the conventional idea that anthropological research is best represented in the form of an article for a scientific journal: a dramatic performance, a dance, or playing a piece of music may accomplish more.[20] To explain this, Ruby points at performance artists like Laurie Anderson, Spalding Gray, Coco Fusco, and Guillermo Gomez-Pena. They are "able to interweave the personal/autobiographical as description with the theoretical in a way that resembles Geertz's notion of thick description."[21] Ruby advocates experiments, and concludes somewhat resignedly that the very situation of ethnographic filmmaking is so complex that no general theory is possible beyond a critical and reflexive attitude towards realism, narrative, and communication. Ethnographic filmmakers should show in their work that it is their representation of the social reality that they portray: "It is therefore necessary to consider ways to subvert audiences' assumptions about films' mimetic capacities."[22]

The gist of all these discourses around art, performance, electronic media, and ethnography is that they can't be neatly separated, so that stylistic changes and contrasts can be equal to conceptual distinctions, and myths and dreams can't be said to exist only in one cultural domain — they can wear both scholarly and popular masks. Byrne's work in film and theater thus formed an excellent preparation for his attempts to combine music and ethnography. The euphoria developed at the end of *Stop Making Sense*, which had audiences dancing in front of the cinema screen, and the mix of a Talking Heads concert with all kinds of anthropological footage in *Talking Heads vs. The Television* had succeeded in subverting assumptions about music films. But how to achieve a similar effect in music, without the many options provided by camera and montage?

2 *NAKED*: TALKING HEADS' MOST "AFRICAN" RECORD

In 1988, Talking Heads recorded their last album, *Naked*. (At the time of writing it seems unlikely that the members of the band will ever record together again.) Stylistically, the band returned to the mixture of rock, funk, and African influences evident in *Remain in Light* and *Speaking in Tongues*, the music they had played live with such success before they recorded the songs of *Little Creatures* and *True Stories*, material they had never played live. This time, next to rock and funk, Latin and African musicians were to have a prominent and direct input. The musicians who contributed something to the sessions were remarkably diverse. Wally Badarou (who had already played on *Speaking in Tongues*) was prominent on many funk and disco albums by Grace Jones, and Abdou M'Boup (percussion), Yves N'Djock (guitar), and Mory Kanté (kora) belonged to the community of African (Cameroon) musicians living in Paris. Two horn sections contributed: one arranged by Lenny Pickett leaning toward funk, the other Latin, arranged by Angel Fernandez. Then there were English contributors, guitarist Johnny Marr of the Smiths and singer Kirsty MacColl, as well as James Fearnley of the Pogues. The idea was that "the groove would be determined by the interaction of everybody . . . we really felt that we were jumping cultural boundaries," as Byrne said about the recording.[23]

In so far as pure sound is what constitutes music, the album is a complete success. The many different contributions each have their own stylistic identity, but they work together very well. John Chernoff, the author of *African Rhythm and African Sensibility*, wrote a review saying that this was an album that "you could take to Africa and play in a disco, and the people there would enjoy the grooves and be dancing to it. But it's Talking Heads, definitely and identifiably so."[24] Chernoff wrote that the music had maturity, developed from the band's musical explorations, and concluded that Talking Heads had mastered the African idioms, an unusual accomplishment. He compared *Naked* to Paul Simon's enormously successful album *Graceland*, with its mostly South African-derived sound: "Graceland isn't unified and true to its idioms like Naked is. David Byrne can create things that have the integrity of the idiom and yet still have a kind of modernized edge."[25]

Byrne's lyrics make it very clear that he worked to make the songs present the contrasts in sensibility and the mythical confrontations that are implicated in the diversity of genres. Each lyric reads and sounds like a scenario for a play or a movie, full of conflict. This time, politics, sex, and violence are not left out of the picture, as Byrne had chosen to do in *True Stories*, but included in very bleak sketches. This time, all personae in Byrne's songs seem to be caught up in violent and chaotic processes. In "The Democratic Circus," American voters get ritual flag-waving instead of debate. "Cool Water" reads like a verbal description of Sebastião Salgado's famous photos of Brazilian miners: "Our backs are breaking . . . Up from hollow earth . . . From end to end . . . The noise begins . . . In the human battle stations . . . And the big one's coming in. / Work, work, work, work." "Ruby Dear" quotes Romantic poet William Blake's heretical idea that "angels and prostitutes might look the same."

That the lyrics were imagined like scenarios is clear from Byrne's comments on "Blind," the song that opens the album (with a chorus in which Byrne over and over snarls: "blind! blahnnd!"):

> "It's pure imagination, but it comes out of reading the daily paper. It's a cry of anguish. It's a man crying, rather than a woman. And I think it's directed at the authorities. Someone has been killed, or badly beaten, and someone else is looking out a window. Terrible things are happening, civil strife. It definitely goes beyond lack of sight. The more it's repeated, the more references are implied and the more it resonates with all the meanings within that word or phrase. And you're asking yourself and the listener to be aware of all that."[26]

But while both the music and the lyrics of *Naked* are certainly more mature than that of most popular music, no single element of all these contrast-rich hybrids has a definite location. No reference has a firmly grounded context, which means that every meaning, every element of the cultural collage can collapse into the undifferentiated vortex of pop. Take, for example, the song "(Nothing But) Flowers," where Byrne intertwined his guitar solos with those by Yves N'Djock, and with a guitar part by Johnny Marr. All the parts combine in a natural and easy way, which is certainly an accomplishment. The lyrics for the song highlight the tension between nature and civilization without taking resort to a simple solution: "There was a shopping mall / Now it's all covered with flowers / If this is paradise / I wish I had a lawnmower." The video clip for the song, made by Tibor Kalman's M&Co., includes projections of the song lyrics and adds bits and pieces of information. The musicians are introduced with their place of birth, from Ft. Campbell, Kentucky and Coronado, California to Manchester, England, and Edea, Cameroon. Loose, more or less randomly collected statistical facts are also projected on the TV screen:

Acres of the world's tropical rain forest cleared every day: 76.320.

Number of privately owned machine guns in the United States: 183.895.

Number of times since 1979 that Britain has "refined" its method of counting the unemployed: 24.

Number of those "refinements" that have resulted in lower unemployment rate: 23.

If these facts combine into a single message, it is that the world is not a place to be trusted without reserve; but as context is absent, the result is nothing more than a vaguely dystopian sentiment. Compared to the best work Byrne had done, and held up against the standards of Robert Wilson and Robert Farris Thompson, with whom he was collaborating around the time he was recording with Talking Heads, the album can't be called a full success without reserve. In a sense, the combination of Western and African pop was too successful, the fusion too complete, the result too homogeneous to retain the differences of the diverging sources and traditions.

Talking Heads had been among the first Western pop musicians who had brought African music into their style, and Frantz, Weymouth, and Harrison wanted to tour and play this music live, to revive the excitement of the earlier tours — and also to make money. Talking Heads had been offered an opportunity to make $15 million net in a single tour, or even $2 million for two weeks of touring.[27] But Byrne decided not to, preferring to concentrate on his own projects instead. This, in fact, meant the end of the band.

3 *ILÉ AIYÉ*: A MUSICAL ETHNOGRAPHIC DOCUMENTARY

In 1988, Byrne went to the Brazilian province of Bahia to shoot a 50-minute TV documentary about Candomblé, an Afro-Atlantic religion. He had visited Bahia for the first time in 1987, when he was invited to present *True Stories* in the Rio de Janeiro film festival. Listening to Brazilian pop songs, Byrne had learned of Bahia's reputation as a source of music and creativity, and when he visited the region, he had the impression that it was as much like going to Africa as it was going to Brazil.[28] He had a little background knowledge on African-American cultures, through his friend Robert Farris Thompson, Professor of African and Afro-American Art at Yale University. Thompson had invited Byrne to visit a Haitian Vodun initiation ceremony taking place in New York City. (Ethnographers use the term "Vodun," instead of "voodoo," as the respectful way to refer to that much maligned Africa-derived religion.) In that ceremony, two blacks and two whites would pass a fire test, holding their hands briefly in a scalding-hot mixture without feeling anything, as proof of self-control and oneness with the spirit. The successful completion of this "canzo" ritual would be celebrated with dancing and spirit possessions.[29] In an interview by Thompson, Byrne explained that although he had only a little knowledge of Afro-American religions such as Haitian Vodun and Cuban and Brazilian Orisha deities, the common prejudice against such religions as sickeningly violent mumbo-jumbo is wrong:

> "Artistically, you notice that this is the route where a lot of music and sensibility and attitude finds its way into pop music and popular culture. . . . Even us white kids who grew up on rock & roll have a common linkage with rhythms from Kongo, and the orisha are not as distant as they might seem."[30]

When Byrne was approached to do a documentary with music for Japanese TV, he suggested Candomblé as the subject, because he considered it to be the most open, least secretive Afro-American religion; it was also the variety of this religion that was least oppressed by its government. Thompson provided Byrne with some helpful names, locations, and contacts.[31]

While in *True Stories* Byrne was very much present throughout as the "Narrator," providing the spectator with some distance from the presented scenes, in *Ilé Aiyé* he deliberately stayed out of the film. His presence, wandering around Bahia and sharing his personal impressions and excitement with the viewer, would have been a selling tool for the film; but *Ilé Aiyé* does not provide a single privileged point of view, no authority figure giving a brief historical overview, no voice-over.[32] Instead of all that, Byrne wanted his documentary to immerse the viewer in Afro-Brazilian culture. According to him,

> It is a culture that the Brazilians themselves have described as a mush, a stew, a blend of many sometimes apparently contradictory elements, and I wanted to convey this musical and cultural beautiful mess. I knew I wanted to use music video and other techniques to convey past and present at the same time, to show correspondences and connections visually, without a voice-over explaining everything. So the result was sometimes confusing for some people, but that's part of the feeling I wanted to convey.[33]

Simply showing the Candomblé rituals, costumes, drumming, its use of trance and music, and its festive offerings might be the best way to enable the viewer to pick up something of its experience. The information that is indispensable in order to grasp the meaning of the events is presented in subtitles, or is implied by combining a main image with an inset, or by the interweaving of forms of music on the soundtrack. There are voice-overs, as well, but only of voices of insiders and participants. Together, these convey a great deal of information, explaining how the slaves transported from Africa managed to keep alive their spiritual ceremonies:

> "Each of these ceremonies is dedicated to a specific god or Orisha. Orisha's have their own rhythms, which are played in a proper order. Everyone, led by the head priest or priestess, sings songs of praise. The initiated women and men dance, using gestures associated with the attributes of each Orisha. It is a poem in movement and song that speaks on many levels at once.
>
> Some of the initiates may fall into trance, filled with the energy and spirit of the Orisha that rules their head. It is a joyous moment when the honoured guest has arrived at his or her own party."

And a Candomblé priestess, Zézé, tells of her own experience: "It is wonderful to be able to receive another being in yourself, a being who comes to say something, a being who comes to heal."

The documentary also registers some aspects of the intricate cultural hybridization that formed Candomblé. It tells how, when "animistic" ceremonies were repressed by the Catholic government, Candomblé survived by associating the Orishas with Catholic saints. To complicate the situation further, there are also popular, secular expressions of Candomblé. *Ilê Aiyê* briefly portrays the "Sons of Gandhi," a carnival society that makes use of the same rhythms. Its members celebrate, and also try to imitate, the non-violent life of the Mahatma. Byrne also filmed preparations for the Candomblé ceremony, the washing of all the white ceremonial clothes, the cleaning of jewelry, the preparations in the "terreiro" or temple ground, scrubbing, leaves being strewn over the ground, and so on. And he shows a group of little children who practice sacred rhythms on buckets and other improvised drums. All this helps to establish a sense of how Candomblé is woven into the texture of the society. Byrne also included a good deal of footage from other filmmakers, using it to show something of Candomblé's long tradition: "The old black-and-white footage gives you that idea that this has been going on for a while — and that it happens in varying ways in different places."[34]

Byrne's documentary was shown on television in the U.S.A. as a part of PBS's *Alive From Off Center* series.[35] In Japan it was also made available on LaserDisc. In 1989, Byrne wrote liner notes for that edition, in which he enthusiastically embraces the spirituality of Candomblé:

> Candomblé is art, religion, music, theater, gastronomy, dance, poetry, and more all at once. If one looks at it (as an outsider) as an "instructive" play or dance then we see

art that fulfils its highest function: orienting us as to our place in the universe. And it does it in a very deep manner. It is a way of life that "instructs" without dogma (there are no written texts, sutras, torahs, or bibles). The instruction is almost by osmosis . . . one learns about balance of forces by listening, watching, and participating gesturally. It is a religion that, like the oriental principle of yin and yang, conceives not of an absolute good and evil or even a morality independent of circumstances, but of balance . . . of being in tune with the continuum of natural cycles and processes. . . .

Even the sacrifice and offering is a metaphor. In Candomblé, the sacrifice of an animal, fowl, or foodstuffs implies that we are at one with the food we eat. We are all part of the natural cycle of birth, death, decomposition . . . (where we become food for the living) . . . and life again. As we eat a plant or animal, it is with the knowledge that it has given its life for us and we are aware that we too will someday participate in that some aspect of nature's cycle. It is a more humble kind of spirituality than some of us are used to. . . .

Anyone who has grown up listening to rock and roll (or Latin music, gospel, bebop, etc., etc.) will not find the Candomblé experience that strange. Music that has grown out of the Afro-Atlantic tradition inspires, in those who enjoy it, an altered state of consciousness and a joyous release. Refined, intensified, and ritualized it becomes a religion . . . while in the secular sphere one gets a "taste", a brief moment when one is aware and conscious of being a part of something greater than itself.

If Candomblé instructs by osmosis, *Ilé Aiyé* attempts to do the same in an unassuming way. The use of the soundtrack to introduce the Orisha exemplifies this. Additions to the sound of drums beating out the rhythms clarify their meaning for the uninitiated viewer. An insistent metallic clanging portrays Ogun, the Iron Warrior; organ music helps define the presence of Omulu, the Earth god, reigning over health and sickness, who has become associated with Saint Lazarus; a small segment of a light, melodiously swaying pop song devoted to Oshun or freshwater, the god of sweetness and love, implies the wider influence of Candomblé in Brazilian popular culture. Spelled out in words, this kind of montage of sounds may take on the appearance of a laborious construction, but when heard while watching the film, it is a series of added musical perspectives that may help to bring one's own relevant associations to bear on the Candomblé ceremonies.

Byrne was glad that he had been able "to do something almost completely without irony: because I was looking at this other culture."[36] Not everyone liked that. Ed Siegel, television and theater critic for the *Boston Globe*, distrusted Byrne's enthusiasm for Candomblé: "Byrne shows none of the humor and irony that he has shown toward American evangelicals. Is ZéZé [a Candombléan] any different from [American tele-evangelist] Tammy Faye Bakker, and is

Candombléan culture any less an opiate than Western religions?"[37] The obvious answer seems to be that yes, there are great theological differences, and historical differences as well, as the documentary itself points out the importance of the Christian repression of this animistic religion. On top of that, the act of transporting a musical ritual electronically, taking it from direct interaction between living people to a widely dispersed, MTV-conscious television audience, has already so many highly ironic implications that an added ironic posture is unnecessary.

4 *REI MOMO*: INCORPORATING LATIN SENSIBILITY

In 1989, Byrne recorded a solo album of pop songs, his first: *Rei Momo*. The album took him outside rock, to the Latin music and community that are in many respects native to New York City,[38] but that were definitely foreign to Byrne. Latin rhythms were foreign to the more monotonous beat of rock, too. Of course, Byrne's work with Talking Heads had prepared him for this step, but there is still a remarkable difference between expanding one's own style by including Afro-American and African elements, and incorporating a style that has been developed mostly outside Euro-American culture, the Latin blend of traditional African rhythms with Western melody and harmony. Elements of Latin music have always been included in Western popular music, but when he chose to record and tour with a Latin orchestra rather than with Talking Heads, Byrne was taking a step that may be compared — without exaggerating, given the personal importance of music for him — to the transformation of an ethnographer who has begun to study a foreign culture from the outside, but finds that the culture has become so deeply and personally relevant for him that he "goes native."

The sensibility of Latin music differs from that of rock, because it is based on the communicative exchange of rhythmic patterns that characterizes African drumming and dancing. This is an exchange of differences, a blend of cultural elements, which includes the African drum ensemble, the European orchestra, and Caribbean culture; sometimes it also includes elements of flamenco, of Islamic culture, and more.[39] R.F. Thompson has written beautifully on mambo and salsa dancing in "the world of Spanish Harlem ballrooms, where Puerto Ricans improvise constantly varying steps — dancing apart while their partners maintain a recurrent movement. These men 'interrupt' the movement of their women in a call-and-response manner, for they begin a new step or flourish considerably before their partners have finished the execution of their basic movements."[40] In comparison, rock can appear limited. Of course, rock songs have been used to display many emotional textures, but the dominating, foursquare beat seems rather appropriate to convey emotions of passive acceptance, interiorized melancholy, or the diametrically opposed, explosive assertion of pent-up inner convictions. Latin music is less given to such moods, since its musical foundation is rather dedicated to the open exchange of dramatic action.

To someone who grew up with rock, Latin music therefore has to sound superficial, lacking force and depth of conviction. As Byrne wrote in 1988 about Brazilian pop music:

> "I first heard music like this about nine years ago. I didn't 'get it' then — I couldn't hear it for what it was . . . The 'lightness' of much Brazilian pop music is often mistaken or confused for American middle-of-the-road bland radio ballads. We have come to associate lightness, subtlety and easy rhythms with shallowness and music without guts. It is a mistake that can blind us to much of the world's great music."[41]

Having decided to make a Latin album, Byrne approached the influential and respected percussionist Milton Cardona to listen to his demo recordings and to suggest rhythms that would fit each particular song. Next to being a percussionist, Cardona is an ordained priest of the Afro-Cuban Santeria cult, an authority on the cult's ritual songs and rhythms. Afterwards, Byrne held forth on how each of these rhythms brought a complete musical framework with it:

> "There are usually at least three percussionists. If you say you're doing a certain kind of song, each of the percussionists knows what to do. When they get to a particular section, the song will have a chorus section and the bongo player will put down his bongos and pick up a bell and start playing a bell part. He knows what kind of part to play. . . . If you say the rhythm of a particular song is *montuno*, that tells you what each person plays, the kind of lines the piano player plays. If you want, it tells you what kind of brass parts there are and if the song is romantic or not."[42]

Afterwards, the songs were arranged by Angel Fernandez and Marty Sheller and played by an all-star selection of Latin musicians. Byrne would often suggest minor changes, and layer his own melodies and lyrics on top of the rhythms. The resulting overall sound is a deliberately crooked mixture. Byrne's voice is still nervous, slightly wavering, a deadpan delivery telling of private reservations, qualities that set it apart from the musical patterns, which are unreserved, sensuous and full of bravado. In hasty, generalizing terms: a white voice against black music.[43] "You're superwhite!" one of the musicians reportedly told Byrne.[44] On top of that, the studio production of the album used so many overdubs that the result in some places sounds studied and constructed.

On the other hand, a touch of wryness in the music fits Byrne's lyrics, which are as disjointed as ever, telling of the impossibility to resolve the contradictions that arise on all sides, sometimes ironic, sometimes painful. That some songs combine English verses with Spanish choruses is only fitting.

"The Call Of The Wild" presents three actions that have a common goal, to bring light into the dark:

> Albert Einstein wrote equations
> God told Noah "Build an ark"
> Johnny Mathis sings Cole Porter
> To bring light into the dark

This is what philosophers of science call incommensurability: who could suggest a common ground for these three kinds of illumination? Who could even claim a comfortable understanding of a single one? Einstein's General Theory of Relativity sketches a universe that has properties that refute our day-to-day experience and intuitions; the story of the ark is as much the story of God's willful extermination of mankind; Johnny Mathis is not an entertainer with whom either Byrne or his audience would want to identify — and yet, adding another ironic twist, Byrne did record a Cole Porter song, "Don't Fence Me In," just like Mathis.[45]

Other lyrics present half-surreal sketches of violence and repression mixed with longing ("Don't Want To Be Part Of Your World," "Carnival Eyes") or, in the album's opening song, "Independence Day," use a hodgepodge of quotes from children's songs, highway signs, colloquial expressions and advertising to express a hilarious sense of freedom and independence:

> This compass points in two directions
> And North and South are both the same
> We'll look forward to the good times
> Come our Independence Day
>
> Hey Lady! You make me giggle
> We'll squiggle like honeymooners do
> I'm struck by lightnin', it's frightnin'
> So excitin', on Independence Day

The album's title, *Rei Momo*, is Portuguese for "King Grin," the play-act king of Carnival, "King Mask." The Latin word for mask is "persona," a meaning that has developed into that of a personal character; originally, "per-sona" meant "sounding through," that through which a voice manifests itself. That this reference to the original meaning of the word "person" isn't too far-fetched is seen in the song "Make Believe Mambo":

> He can be a macho man
> Now he's a game show host
> One minute hilarious comedian
> Now he's an undercover cop . . .
>
> So how can we be strangers
> He's got no personality
> It's just a clever imitation
> Of the people on TV

This lyric shows a persona that borrows its personality directly from television, in swift acts of mimicry — a mechanism that anyone who has grown up in a consumer society knows intimately. Here, it is depicted with such blunt exaggeration (compared to the subtle treatment of the same theme in "Seen And Not Seen," on *Remain in Light*) that this seems to imply a strong condemnation, be it in political, aesthetical or religious terms. But the catchy chorus of the "Make Believe Mambo" invites the audience to sing along, expressing tolerance instead of disdain, implying that everyone is somehow included in this world of make believe:

> Oh — let the poor boy dream
> Oh — livin' make believe
> I can be you and you can be me
> In my mundo, todo el mundo
> Ev'ryone's happy and ev'ryone's free
> Todo mundo, mundo mambo

Byrne was well aware that *Rei Momo* was an uneasy experiment, "probably too Anglo for the Latin radio stations and definitely too Latin for the rock stations that used to play Talking Heads."[46] Together with his musical advisors, he also chose to neglect the traditional divisions that define that samba has to come from Brazil, merengue from Santa Domingo, cumbia from Columbia, and so on. Instead, they provided an overview of different Latin rhythms. Angel Fernandez, the musical director for the *Rei Momo* tour, said: "you would normally need fifteen bands to do what we do. You would have a salsa, or a merengue, and never the twain would meet."[47]

These are but a few aspects of the complications and divisions in the cultural arena that Byrne had entered. After all, the shared history of Latin America and the United States has been anything but harmonious. A white rock star singing in front of an orchestra of mostly colored musicians (there were musicians with a Latin background as well as Brazilians and Anglo-Americans) inevitably reverberated with echoes of imperialism, racism and disdain for the otherness of a foreign culture: the more so because Byrne presented his own version of traditional rhythms. It was easy to insinuate that Byrne was just adding a bit of exotic flavor to his image, like so many rock stars. At the end of the 1980s, Paul Simon and Sting worked with African and Brazilian musicians, as did Madonna, Peter Gabriel, and Malcolm McLaren. Byrne, with his intellectual and artistic affiliations, was perhaps the most vulnerable to accusations of cultural tourism and artistic exploitation. His strategy was to bring the underlying tensions, prejudices, and contradictions out into the open. That Latin music forms something of a ghetto in the U.S.[48] was not his fault, and Byrne could say that he had simply stopped to respect the lines of segregation:

> "Instead of saying, 'Let's go far afield and find something exotic, something that'll be a new gimmick, a new sound,' I can literally walk two blocks and see and hear a great deal of this music coming out of cars, coming out of doorways."[49]

With the help of Fernandez, Byrne put together an orchestra of 14 musicians, plus Brazilian singer Margareth Menezes, for a world tour. He ensured that the tour included not only Japan, North America, and Europe (usually the entire "world" of pop music), but also Central and South America. There, as Byrne explained, "audiences might be more familiar with the rhythms. I wanted them to hear first-hand what we were doing, and if there were to be any criticisms or complaints, I would be there to take them, face to face."[50] If the album was constructed and gave the music a quality that might strike a listener hungry for "authenticity" as studied, flat and therefore unconvincing,[51] the live performances were brilliant and simply exuberant.

Byrne afterwards published a *Rei Momo* tour diary,[52] which he had kept during the South American leg of the tour. In his diary he dealt with the complex questions surrounding the authenticity and legitimacy of the project. The basic idea throughout is that musical forms and rhythms are not limited to a single people, but can be played by others, too.[53] Byrne notices repeatedly how the music that he embraces is often neglected by the music industry in South America: "Throughout most of our South American jaunt we heard very little local music, and if we did, it often sounded like a copy of North American styles."[54] He gives a sociological explanation for the lack of Brazilian music on Brazilian radio stations:

There's a samba station in Rio, but you can't hear any Brazilian music, or very, very little in São Paulo and very, very little . . . in Pôrto Alegre . . . it's the pressure of the multinationals . . . but probably it's also that samba, the local music, is considered low-class, the music of the poor. But rock-and-roll and jazz and other kinds of music are "refined", partly because they're foreign, and they are the music of the middle and upper classes. So all the kids aspire to listen to the music that might put their listening habits in another class.[55]

A second theme throughout the diary is the history of political repression: Byrne mentions musicians who were killed or exiled from Chile, Argentina, and Brazil.[56] In Rio de Janeiro, he notes that due to the ticket price, he is playing to an almost entirely white audience, a very limited section of the population of the city.[57] In São Paulo, he records a remark of composer and musician Tom Zé about the people of the Brazilian Northeast: "for nine generations they've been undernourished and [had not] enough protein for their brains. Now if they make a little money, they receive more protein, and their brains become starved for stimulus. And what do they get? They get television, soap operas."[58] He also passes on a conversation with one of the Brazilian percussionists in the touring orchestra, Cafe, saying that he "felt he had to leave Brazil to play Brazilian music! That it was very sad, people turning away from the riches of their own culture."[59] Next to documenting some of the hassle of a touring band, problems with stage checks, fuses blowing out, air conditioning systems on fire, jam sessions, after-show parties, and all that, this *Rei Momo* diary openly and intelligently presents the cultural contradictions that surrounded the tour.

5 SOUNDTRACKS FOR ETHNOGRAPHIC ART DOCUMENTARIES

Byrne has contributed soundtracks to four ethnographic documentaries by director Philip Haas. *A Young Man's Dream* and *A Woman's Secret* document traditional sculptors in Madagascar and painters in Papua New Guinea. *The Giant Woman* and *The Lightning Man* are documentaries about two forms of Australian Aboriginal painting. These documentaries were presented as an appendix to *Magiciens de la Terre*, the great 1989 exhibition of artists from cultures all over the world in Paris' Centre Georges Pompidou. This exhibition, which combined contemporary Western art with traditional non-Western art, was hailed as a step towards recognizing the work of artists from non-Western cultures; at the same time, it was denounced by postcolonial academic critics for neglecting the influence of modernization on artists in non-Western countries, presenting only what seems like "untouched" authenticity.[60] Byrne's approach is interesting in this respect. He tells about his contribution:

> Philip asked if I wanted to do music for some of his documentaries that he was doing for the Magiciens de la Terre show in Paris, and I agreed, if I could do 'unconventional' type scoring. Which I did. The music for the aboriginal artists' film, for example, was inspired by a statement that the aboriginal artists made. When Philip asked them what kind of music they would like, they said Jimi Hendrix, and they usually liked the rave-up noisy drone-y ends of those songs better than the melodic parts. So I thought, hmmm, sounds like Glenn Branca style would be good . . . so I did the whole score with retuned guitars, played in various unconventional ways, droning on, creating textures. They liked it, and I was happy.[61]

Although this description might suggest a very loud soundtrack (Branca's loudness is notorious), Byrne's music is in fact unobtrusive and fits easily into the sober atmosphere of the documentaries.

For *A Young Man's Dream*, Byrne made music that is vaguely reminiscent of the instrumental passages of *The Catherine Wheel*. Remarkable here is that the music of the soundtrack, recorded in the studio by Byrne, sometimes mingles with the music that was recorded by Haas while filming in Madagascar. When a group of women is seen singing and clapping, Byrne adds a bass rhythm; and when men are playing a self-made three-string guitar, he adds some modest electric guitar notes. This mix of "authentic" music with — inauthentic? but in what respect? — musical elements made in another country, coming from another culture, can either be interpreted as a form of harassment, or as a willingness to engage directly with others, instead of keeping them at a safe, scientifically justified distance. Understood reflexively, this strange mixing of musical contributions that have never met in real life is a useful commentary on the performative status of these ethnographic documentaries, which combine forms of visual art in a similarly strange way.

6 LUAKA BOP

Around the time that he was filming *Ilé Aiyé*, and recording *Rei Momo*, Byrne laid the foundation for his own record label, Luaka Bop. From the perspective of record company Warner Bros., this was a vanity label, a perk for one of their stars; for Byrne, it was a means to share his musical interests. He had made it a habit to go into record stores and buy records blindly, without knowing what to expect, hoping to be surprised, or by following the advice of the shopkeeper. In the mid-80s, Byrne had picked up Brazilian records by Milton Nascimento and Caetano Veloso, which he found very inspiring. He made cassettes of his personal favorites to give to friends, and later produced a compilation album: *Brazil Classics 1: Beleza Tropical*. Anxious to provide the songs in their context, Byrne printed not only the original lyrics with their English translations and appropriate footnotes added, but also two small essays, one by himself and one by Arto Lindsay, a musician from New York's new wave scene who was born in Brazil. Lindsay provided historical and musicological background, mentioning the 1960s "Tropicalismo" movement around singers Caetano Veloso, Gilberto Gil and others, heirs of Brazil's 1920's "Antropophagia" avant-garde. Byrne expressed his delight with the sophistication of Brazilian pop, and emphasized that its sweetness should not be confused with superficiality.

> It is hard for us to imagine this music as being in any way dangerous, but the military regime that ruled Brazil during the late '60's and early '70's found it quite threatening. . . . Maybe these songs are a more human form of political pop than our rabble-rousing rock-epics which often sound too close to national anthems or marches for me.[62]

This record was followed by compilations of other Brazilian styles, samba and forró, presented with equal care. In the notes for *Brazil Classics 2: O Samba*, which presents samba as intimately related to Candomblé, Byrne wrote an enthusiastic eulogy, titled "Philosophy of Samba":

> Samba, like many other Afro-Latin music forms, propels and ignites the lower body — the hips, the butt, the pelvis, etc. — by letting the downbeat "float". By de-emphasizing the first beat of each measure a rhythm becomes more sensual and ethereal; one "floats" outside the time and space of earthly existence. Repetition creates a timeless, communal otherworld, a floating ethereal cycle that is both rooted in biological rhythms and in the beyond or meta-biological.
>
> Any activation of the hips-sex-butt-pelvis relates to the source of all life, the womb. This music is definitely a respectful prayer in honor of the sweet, the feminine, the great mother — the sensuous life-giving aspects of ourselves and our lives — and to the Earth, the mother of us all. To shake your rump is to be environmentally aware. . . .
>
> Like all art, it is what it is, but it's something greater besides.

Luaka Bop was, and is, a record label without a fixed policy; the policy is simply to follow up on the eclectic preferences and tastes of Byrne and Yale Evelev, the label's manager.[63] They do not look for "authentic" and exotic forms of music that remain unsullied by influences of the Western music industry, but for musicians who excel in connecting strands from different traditions, including the global presence of Western pop. Instead of giving in to the sleek superficiality that is promoted by the record industry, the musicians promoted by Luaka Bop present their musical experiences without effacing the inner contradictions. Their songs are more diverse, pungent, and bitter than hit parade songs, more politically realistic and honest about global modernization than most "world music." Anyone who has grown up with pop can find an entrance into these songs. Just having an entrance may be a long way from understanding their experience fully — but it is unusual anyhow to find, in the often isolationist medium of popular songs, the diversity and richness of contemporary history.

Cuban music is presented on three discs: one of *trovador* (troubadour) Silvio Rodriguez, one of Cuban dance hits of the 60s and 70s, and one of new directions in Cuban popular music, including versions of reggae and of hard rock that are usually not associated with Cuba, the birth ground of son, mambo, and salsa. Because Cuban music was banned from the U.S.A. from 1961 until 1988, when U.S. Congress allowed the importation of master tapes (it remained illegal to hire Cuban musicians, which was considered "trading with the enemy"), these collections helped to fill a gap in the tradition of pop.

Luaka Bop's version of Brazil was equally diverse. Samplers of samba and classic pop were followed by a collection of forró, rough and direct party music from Northeastern Brazil, and later by samplers of contemporary Brazilian pop hybrids. The following is an excerpt from Byrne's liner notes for *Beleza Tropical 2* (1998):

> Sadly not only in the musical arena, but also in economic and social aspects, the Brazilians outpace us; they are the future. The world becomes more Brazilian every day — the Brazilianization of the great first world powers like the U.S. and U.K. Some call it globalization, some neo-liberalismo: the growing gap between rich and poor, thrown into high gear by Reagan and Thatcher, and proceeding unchecked, the destruction and waste of natural resources, every politician up for sale to multiple nations — these are all symptoms — soon we'll catch up to Brazil. One can only hope that we'll catch up musically as well, and that their funky spirituality and inventiveness will also be emulated by each country in their own way.

Byrne was especially taken by the work of Tom Zé, a Brazilian composer and songwriter who was part of the 60s Tropicalismo renaissance in Brazil, and who combines and mixes influences from bossa nova to Schoenberg and from John Cage to Dada. More irreverent and disruptive than other Tropicalistas, Zé's career went downhill and he had stopped recording when Byrne found in him an alter ego from another hemisphere. Luaka Bop released a string of old and new albums by Zé, and Byrne promoted Zé's work in every possible way, publishing an interview with him, inviting Zé to arrange and play on one of his own songs ("Something Ain't Right," on *Uh-Oh*), and singing along on an advertising jingle for Tom Zé by himself and on an album of his songs ("Jingle do Disco," on *The Hips of Tradition*): "Tom Zé! Tom Zé! Shall grant you relaxation, high spirits and happiness!"

Luaka Bop also released albums by Susana Baca, a black singer from Peru who is also a researcher of the Afro-Peruvian tradition. Black slaves were taken to Peru as well as to the rest of the Americas, and Peru has a comparatively unknown tradition of black music, presented by Luaka Bop on *The Soul of Black Peru*. Susana Baca has used her international fame to establish her own institute for ethnomusicological research in Peru, called "Negro Continuo."[64]

In recent years, Luaka Bop has mostly issued albums by individual bands and singers instead of compilations. Bloque, King Changó, and Los Amigos Invisibles are angry, loud and energetic bands from Colombia, Mexico, and Venezuela. The U.S.A. are represented by, among others, Geggy Tah and Jim White (descriptions of their music might read "introspective Los Angeles funk surrealism" and "acid-folk Bible Belt angst"). Zap Mama, from Belgium, combines African and European melodies; Cornershop makes Britpunk with an Indian twang. Waldemar Bastos from Angola sings love songs for his war-torn country. Djur Djura, a Berber-Algerian woman singer living in Paris, sings of courage and love against the background of a repressive and fierce patriarchal tradition, civil war, colonialism, and exile. To accompany the release of her album by Luaka Bop, Byrne interviewed her in 1994, asking about the rising influence of Islamic fundamentalism and her own solution for living in two cultures at the same time.[65]

An attempt to synthesize the releases by Luaka Bop is hopeless. The mind boggles. This is the point: in the face of diversity, confusion is better than single-minded certainty. The label has even released three albums, one of Brazilian pop, one of California soul, and one of West African polyrhythmic funk, under the moniker "World Psychedelic Classics." This is world music that does not present the other's music as exotic and distant, as "mythic" and therefore authentic, while Western tradition is rational and commercial. Asked to do so by the *New York Times*, Byrne set his ideas about music on paper in an article titled "I Hate World Music," explaining his disgust for a label that sets the rest of the world apart from Anglo-American pop:

> To restrict your listening to English-language pop is like deciding to eat the same meal for the rest of your life. The "no-surprise surprise," as the Holiday Inn advertisement claims, is reassuring, I guess, but lacks kick. As ridiculous as they often sound,

the conservative critics of rock-and-roll, and more recently of techno and rave, are not far off the mark. For at its best, music truly is subversive and dangerous. Thank the gods.

Hearing the right piece of music at the right time of your life can inspire a radical change, destructive personal behavior or even fascist politics. Sometimes all at the same time.

On the other hand, music can inspire love, religious ecstasy, cathartic release, social bonding and a glimpse of another dimension.[66]

7 IN THE MIRROR: SEX 'N' DRUGS 'N' ELECTRONIC MUSIC

The critical demand that anthropology has to be reflexive, that an interpretation of a foreign culture has to be accompanied by an interpretation of one's own culture — who wants to know, and why? — applies to Byrne's work, too. This section is a compilation of three of Byrne's more self-reflexive works, ordered to follow that well-known trinity of American and European ritual, sex and drugs and rock and roll.

"Sex," or more properly sex-related customs, is the subject of Obie Benz's documentary movie *Heavy Petting* (1989), which is a description and an evocation of American sexual mores just before the sexual "revolution" of the 1960s. Benz uses footage from Hollywood movies and sex education films, and 50s teenage pop, and combines that with reminiscences of their teenage years by Judith Malina (co-founder of The Living Theatre), Abbie Hoffman, Allen Ginsberg, Spalding Gray, Laurie Anderson, William Burroughs, and others, mostly artists. Byrne contributes some memories of his own teenage experiences, of basement parties with slow dancing to music he couldn't stand, some guys who would brag to other guys about who they had felt up, and so on. He adds that a lot of it is probably chemical, that for years the hormones are like drugs. The film can be taken as just a nostalgic look at 50s kitsch, but it could more properly be called a contribution to historical enlightenment.

Drugs are the main subject of Byrne's liner notes for a Talking Heads compilation album, titled *Sand in the Vaseline* (after pop art painter Ed Ruscha's work of that title). It is a condensed, factual description of the drugs he has used over the years, covering a wide spectrum from marijuana to speed, cocaine, heroin, and a few other substances. He later explained in an interview that he wanted to be honest about his history, and that even though he did not go off the deep end, he had been a part of the rock-and-roll lifestyle, not a conceptually motivated bystander.[67] He concluded his notes with thoughts on drugs in general, shifting his perspective from one sentence to the next: "The wide spread use of drugs is a symptom of a sick society. The war on drugs is bullshit. Especially since the CIA is one of the biggest dealers around. Drugs raise money and keep young black males (mostly) docile."

Electronic music is the subject of a half spoof, half serious ethnographic essay titled "Machines of Joy: I have seen the future and it is squiggly," written by Byrne about the eccentric popular genre he calls "Northern European Blip Hop." Since Byrne was born in Scotland, and holds on to his British passport, it can also be read in an oblique fashion as a self-portrait; after all, electronic sound equipment has been crucial to much of his music. As the abstract says:

The author identifies a preference for obviously non-natural sounds, an avoidance of rhythms easily danced to and a disposition toward effects only achievable through computers (as well as the sounds of the malfunctions and failures of such technologies) as indicative of Northern European acceptance of this modern symbiosis. The long and dark winters favored a people who could look inward for months at a time and not go crazy. [. . .] Never comfortable with their bodies, due to years of wearing bulky warm clothes, and to infrequent social interaction, the Northern Europeans have developed elaborate rituals in order to facilitate the physical contact needed by all human beings. The football match and the disco have become the foremost among these.[68]

The essay can be read as a counterpart to Byrne's "Philosophy of Samba." The sampler contains tracks by electronic acts like Mouse on Mars and To Rococo Rot, but also a track by Zairian-Belgian singer Marie Daulne of Zap Mama, whose albums are released by Luaka Bop, as well as one track, "Pocket Monster," which Byrne made under the name "Vibulator." The essay was used as liner notes for Luaka Bop's sampler *The Only Blip Hop Record You Will Ever Need, Vol. 1 — Compiled by Luaka Bop in Conjunction with the International Center for Comparative Sound — Commentary in English, Wallonian, Estonian.* First of all, of course, it is a spoof of anthropological surveys, which have so often produced astonishing simplifications.

8 CRITICAL RESPONSES

Several academic anthropologists have written suspiciously about Byrne's adventures in ethnography, interpreting them as a form of exploitation. It seems to me, however, that Byrne is as aware of the exploitation and commodification that go on in the music and entertainment industry as his critics, and that his strategy of dealing with it may be more effective.

In his journalistic biography of Talking Heads, David Bowman has written about the payola, the bribing of disk jockeys, that helped to make "Burning Down The House" a hit for Talking Heads. Bowman notes how disillusioned Byrne was when he found out afterwards. He never quite recovered his faith in the audience.[69] "Business and pleasure / lie right to your face," he had sang on the same album *Speaking in Tongues* that also held "Burning Down The House," echoing the distrust of the mass media that is as common to conceptual artists as it is to many academics.

Entertainment is so widespread in modern societies that it is characteristic of modern culture as such. Clever productions that invite participation while they simplify their content in a debilitating, regressive manner are so common that a complex strategic scenario of disaffections and counter-enthusiasms is required to be able to deal with entertainment without giving in to its inanities. Is Byrne's work in this respect a valid scenario?

Music Grooves (1994) by Charles Keil and Steven Feld documents the combined efforts of two ethnomusicologists to grasp theoretically the impact of the participation in, and mediation and commodification of, music in different cultures. They share a Marxist perspective, emphasizing that music worldwide is less and less made live for direct participation, and more and more owned and controlled for reasons of profit.[70] They underline the crucial importance of participating in music, of "grooving," as expressed by James Brown:

> "Y'know, one thing about music: It's the key to *every*thing, the universal language of man's commitment to be together. . . . 'cause, see what the music is doing? It's so *vast*, so *beyond* our thinking, because it reaches your soul and you can feel before you can see, that it's mind over matter. You say 'ouch' and you don't even know where the pain is coming from, but the *feeling* is *real*."[71]

According to Keil, the varying kinds of textural discrepancies that characterize all kinds of music encourage an emotional and animistic sense of participation that is anterior to collective representations.[72] Ethnomusicologists should try to understand the participatory discrepancies of different musical cultures by looking at cultures as "patterns-in-experience" and by understanding musical works as "affecting presences."[73]

Following the popular success of rock and roll, pop has produced a mutual influencing of American and African popular music. Here, admiration and appropriation make complex patterns, for example in Mick Jagger's idolization of Muddy Waters, or in Paul Simon's use of South African pop styles on *Graceland*. Although both sides benefit from these collaborations, Keil and Feld point out that the playing field is far from equal: the complexities of authorship, copyright, and marketing result in benefits that are not evenly distributed.

When James Brown broke down complex African polyrhythms and incorporated them into dense funk and soul dance tracks, critics didn't speak of a powerful African-American star moving in on African musical turf. And when, ten years later, Fela Anikulapo Kuti seized the essence of the James Brown scratch guitar technique and made it the centerpiece of his Afro-Beat, critics didn't speak of a powerful African star moving in on African-American turf. That's because the economic stakes in this traffic were small, and the circulation had the revitalizing dynamic of roots. But when Talking Heads moved in on both James Brown and Fela Anikulapo Kuti and used scratch, funk, Afro-Beat, and jùjú rhythms as the basic grooves for "Remain In Light", something else happened. The economic stakes, however much attention was drawn to the originators as a result, were increased, the gap between the lion's share and the originator's share enlarged, and the critical discourse on race and rip-offs was immediate and heated.[74]

And yet in the end, as Feld acknowledges, pop stars can't do much about the near-monopolistic structure of the music business as such.[75]

Feld analyzes the emergence of "world music" and "world beat." First, the major record companies more and more dominate the independent labels, just as Western pop stars more and more dominate non-Western musicians. Then world beat, with its danceable pulse, dominates other forms of world music. As a result of such tendencies, third- and fourth-world musicians and first-world fans tend to fall into patterns of exhibitionism and spectatorship. The result is a struggle between homogenizing and heterogenizing forces: questions of authenticity, the dynamics of appropriation and musical ownership are increasingly politicized.[76] In this field full of tensions, pop stars like David Byrne, Peter Gabriel, and the Grateful Dead's drummer Mickey Hart are able to combine "curatorial, promotional, and collaborative roles, as well as entrepreneurial and appropriative roles," which makes it possible to understand how "in the critical discourse surrounding the production and circulation of world beat, assertions of altruism and generosity appear as frequently as accusations of cannibalism and colonialism."[77]

Feld places Byrne's compilations of Brazilian samba classics and Cuban music on the same level as "benign yet serious analyses of international pop genres."[78] On the other hand, he sarcastically dismisses Byrne's work in popular ethnomusicology. Feld writes about Byrne's *Ilé Aiyé*:

arty and stylish, yet very much in the conventional mold of PBS "documentary" (syrupy narration featuring nuggets of ancient wisdom of others, plenty of sunsets and gyrating bodies), the film predictably has no time or place for locating candomblé in local politics, economy, or society. Byrne the curator is so busy transporting us into a world of "purely musical being" that the question of musical control, as Amy Taubin pointed out in a typically acute "Village Voice" column (11 July 1989), only surfaces, in small print titles, at the very end: "Original score by David Byrne, performed by (long list of Brazilian musicians)."[79]

But as Feld does not make a detailed analysis of Byrne's documentary, his dismissal is unserious. To oppose Feld's opinion, one might analyze how Byrne used the soundtrack to do exactly what Jay Ruby asks of anthropological documentaries: the producing of a soundtrack that is the filmmaker's construction of the social construction of the actuality of the music and the people portrayed, an interpretation of someone else's interpretation. And one might point to the humorous scene in *Ilé Aiyé* in which a woman goes to the market to buy a goat for a ceremony. She haggles with the seller, and accuses him of trying to sell the goat at a higher price only because she is being filmed. Combined with Byrne's careful historical positioning of Candomblé in *Ilé Aiyé*, this shows that Feld's critique is unfounded.

George Lipsitz, a professor of ethnic studies, wrote in his *Dangerous Crossroads* (1994) about Byrne's involvement with Latin musical culture. He writes that Byrne' s enthusiasm and empathy, creativity, and curiosity may result in important reappraisals of commercial culture, a dismantling of Western popular music. But in his duet with Celia Cruz, "Loco de Amor," when Celia Cruz answers Byrne in Yoruba when she sings "yen yere cumbe," Lipsitz hears something glib: "In traditional Cuban music, Yoruba lyrics resonate with collective memories of slavery and racism, they reinsert distinctly African identity back into collective national culture. But in Byrne's song, Cruz's Yoruba passage signifies only primitivism, exoticism, orientalism; she is an all-purpose 'other.'"[80] The problem with this kind of critique is that what it grants to Cruz, with good right, namely a cultural background and a dignified tradition, is withheld from Byrne, who in fact had great respect for Cruz.[81]

Critics like Steven Feld and George Lipsitz seem to identify Byrne with his position as a celebrity in the music industry. For them, that seems to define the meaning of his work, more than his artistic development and his attempts to bridge cultural gaps. Yet Byrne is not a politician but an artist, who should be judged by his art, and by the way he deals with cross-cultural dilemmas in his dealings with different artistic cultures. In that respect, he deserves a lot of credit. After all, he immersed himself thoroughly in Afro-Latin culture, so much so that percussionist and Santoria priest Milton Cardona, who played congas in the *Rei Momo* big band, said how impressed he was by Byrne's knowledge of deities and ceremonial practices, demonstrating a deep involvement.[82] Byrne has taken part in Candomblé ceremonies:

"I've had shells thrown to find out what my orisha is . . . I've made offerings and done that kind of thing. I believe that the religion holds a lot of truths and its attitude and sensibility seem to embrace all aspects of human living. It doesn't just say that religion or spirituality is just something where you are quiet and somber. It can be sexy, for instance."[83]

Nevertheless, Byrne admits to a certain remaining distance and foreignness:

"I don't think you can appropriate a sensibility wholesale. You can't really transplant it. I think someone foreign can only absorb it on their own terms. You might be able to approach the way someone else feels about it, but you'll never get it in the same way."[84]

Some ten years later than Feld and Lipsitz, music critic Carol Cooper assumed that Byrne had crossed over to the non-Western side of the music world, saying that after his career with Talking Heads he had in fact reinvented himself as a third-world musician, rejecting the perks of the stylistic and commercial category of the Anglo-American rock star.[85] This is exaggerated, but more to the point than the academic insistence on the impossibility of overcoming the cross-cultural problematic.

The influential anthropologist Clifford Geertz holds that ethnographers can transmit thoroughly foreign experiences when they provide what he has called "thick descriptions," descriptions that are in many ways similar to the work of realistic novelists in showing the strands and flows that are combined in every cultural situation. We live more and more in the midst of an enormous collage of cultures, as Geertz said in 1985, and in that situation

the job of ethnography [is] to provide, like the arts and history, narratives and scenarios to refocus our attention; not, however, ones that render us acceptable to ourselves by representing others as gathered into worlds we don't want and can't arrive at, but ones which make us visible to ourselves by representing us and everyone else as cast into the midst of a world full of irremovable strangenesses we can't keep clear of.[86]

The most relevant conclusion to this chapter on ethnography and music is that Byrne's work provides thick descriptions of popular music, and does it where it matters most, namely in popular music.

Chapter 5

In the Visual Arena

1 THE ARENA OF VISUAL COMMUNICATION

We spend our lives trying to get our facial muscles to match our interior states. [. . .]
The two are never naturally in synch. We spend our lives listening to ourselves,
watching ourselves, seeing how we are reflected, how we are responded to by others,
and then we fine tune ourselves in order to project accurately what it is we think
we are. It is possible that for some people their faces — their muscles, their smiles,
their frowns, the twitch of a lip, a raised eyebrow — have absolutely no relationship
to the feelings hoping to be projected from inside. As if the puppet had all the
strings attached in the wrong places, and no matter how much the puppet master
emoted, the wrong things kept happening. We spend years learning how the wires
are connected.

This is a quotation from "Crossed Wires," a short text in Byrne's book *Strange
Ritual*. The text reads like an essay, but it also has some qualities of a prose
poem. What does it mean? Is it autobiographic? In the second half of the text,
Byrne writes:

I often sing with all my might, and find that all I've accomplished is to convey a sense
of energy being expended and a desperate need to communicate something. Often,
no one is able to figure out exactly what it is I'm trying to communicate. [. . .] Just
like all our facial expressions, my strings are attached in the wrong places.

An autobiographical interpretation may be tempting: "my strings are attached
in the wrong places" makes a fascinating personal statement from a rock star
whose public image is that of a nervous and slightly geeky person. Celebrity

self-disclosure, gossip, personal problems: a good part of the mass media is always out to publish just that kind of material.

But there are other fitting interpretations, at least one of which is quite formal and impersonal. "Crossed Wires" may be read as a straightforward translation and application of an anatomical structure that is important in cybernetic theory, especially in Stafford Beer's version of managerial cybernetics. The anatomical structure is, in mixed Greek/Latin terminology, known as an "anastomotic reticulum," a network of connections in which pathways are branching and reconnecting, like streams in a river delta, so that no pathway is exclusive and unique.[1] There is no way of tracing the route by which a particular amount of water in the sea has come out of the river. As Beer states, decision processes inside bodies and inside organizations work like this. Input and output of the nervous system are connected, but the connections are organic, and way too complex and intertwined to reduce by analysis to a fully known chain of switches, or of conscious decisions. The brain, as Beer describes it, has more potential states than can ever be analyzed, and the connectivity in the brain has to be organized, it has to form and reform itself into appropriate structures. In other words, the brain needs to learn. And the mechanism through which it learns is, in cybernetic terms, feedback, which uses the very complexity of the brain to produce new forms of organization. The potential for confusion is the necessary condition for this feedback learning. Errors and mistakes are important guides in the learning process.

In this sense, "crossed wires" are a part of everybody's autobiography. It is a highly general description of the workings of the human brain that doesn't pay attention to personality, and doesn't differentiate between conscious and unconscious processes. Learning to ride a bicycle, and learning to play guitar, are two familiar examples of the process or reorganizing conscious and unconscious forms of coordination. In both examples, what seems impossibly complex when you think about it can be done without thinking after a period of training. In the process, wires have been crossed and uncrossed, neural networks have interacted, the brain has learned new tricks.

Of course, the profession of a popular singer/songwriter is full of forms of feedback that the average person needn't worry about, and public scrutiny becomes even more intense when a singer attempts to convey a foreign sensibility, as Byrne does with so many of his songs. A pop singer is part and parcel of the song he sings, and the construction of the character of the song is crucial to the personal credibility of the singer.[2] It is as if the singer makes of himself, of his personality, a studio for the recording and montage of emotions. In the process, the smallest detail, even the twitching of an eyelid,[3] may come under close scrutiny. Ethnographer Clifford Geertz, following the example of philosopher Gilbert Ryle, chose the repeated twitching of an eyelid as the example to explain the meaning of ethnographic "thick description." The difference between an involuntary twitch and a conspiratorial signal is all-important; so is the difference between a conspiratorial signal, a parody of such a signal, and the rehearsal of just such a parody by someone who is uncertain of his mimicking abilities. Ethnographic description is "winks upon winks upon winks," according to Geertz.

Byrne's "Crossed Wires" text is printed in a single line that runs across the bottom of 16 pages of his first book of photos, *Strange Ritual — Pictures and Words*. The text accompanies photos of an Indian instructional bas-relief showing the three stages of life, and a series of photos of Indian film posters, portraits of movie stars. What the text draws attention to is that we know very well how to interpret what we see, where to see symbolic meaning and where not — although sometimes, as in these instances where Byrne rephotographed and recontextualized movie posters, some mangled or defaced with scribbled mustaches and other additions, our interpretative capacity is definitely challenged. Our interpretation may easily be mistaken, and Byrne's words point out that that may be the case even while we are not aware of it.

Geertz stresses that the difference between an involuntary twitch and a meaningful wink may be unphotographable. Since they are identical as movements, a camera could not tell the difference.[4] But then, a camera can't *see* at all. Photographs have to be seen to fulfill their function, and seeing depends on the sensibility, the conventions, the prejudices, and the training of the spectator, and on the context in which the photos are presented. The interpretation of a photo depends considerably on the available information about the photo, on the caption in the newspaper, as well as on the circumstances: photos are seen differently in a museum than in a book, or in private. And since more and more photos are present in the environment, reproduced on the sides of trucks, on notice boards, on identity papers and in hospital rooms, on boxes for cereals or washing powder, on TV, in magazines, and so on, most people have developed their own repertoire of responses to photographic images. Byrne's photography draws attention to this arena of visual communication.

Two perspectives on the interpretation of photographs are particularly relevant for Byrne's photoworks. One of these is the contemporary interpretation of photographs in terms of artistic performance. Such interpretations analyze photos in terms of a complex social interaction, in which several mimetic genres and poses combine and overlap: the private snapshot versus artistic formal quality, social reportage, scientific document, glossy publicity photo, and other mimetic projections have been investigated by many photographers working in the art world.

A second perspective that has influenced Byrne's photography is the Jungian interpretation of visual art, including photography, in terms of psychological symbolism. Jung's widely read book *Man and his Symbols* (1964) included hundreds and hundreds of reproductions of artworks and photographs to demonstrate that such symbolism can be found everywhere in the history of mankind. According to the Jungian analysis of symbols,

> The history of symbolism shows that everything can assume symbolic significance: natural objects (like stones, plants, animals, men, mountains and valleys, sun and moon, wind, water, and fire), or man-made things (like houses, boats, or cars), or even abstract forms (like the numbers, or the triangle, the square, and the circle). In fact, the whole cosmos is a potential symbol.[5]

In his photographs, Byrne uses both approaches, now combining them, now switching from one to the other.

The members of Talking Heads were involved in the visual presentation of their work from the beginning. Byrne designed the first two album covers. The use of NASA's *Portrait USA* for *More Songs about Buildings and Food* began a series of group portraits that use special image-processing technologies. Byrne and Harrison came up with a thermograph or heat-sensitive photo for the inner sleeve of *Fear of Music*; Weymouth and Frantz with computer portraits (at that time a rare sight) of the band's members for *Remain in Light*. Fourteen years later, for a solo album titled *David Byrne*, Byrne had photographer Jean Baptiste Mondino make a photographic investigation of his body that consisted of a regular studio portrait, studies of hands and feet, fingers and toes, an elbow, the neck and an eye, extreme close-ups of body hair and skin. The series was continued with X-rays of molars and chest, computer scan photos of different cross-sections of the spine, as well as a series of cell photos. This investigation obviously subverts the notion of the photographic portrait as revealing the intimate artistic personality, as by revealing more and more physical detail the photos become more and more impersonal. (Byrne didn't actually lie in a CT scanner himself; the medical pictures were supplied by the New York University Medical Center.)

The importance of photographers like Eggleston, Jenshel, Sternfeld, and Klipper for the *True Stories* movie has already been mentioned. In the book version of *True Stories*, Byrne combined their photos with his own photos, newspaper photos and clippings plus film stills, and a version of the script. He hoped that this mix would be an equivalent to the way we experience people and things in their environment:

Out there lots of different things are going on at the same time. You can change your focus from one thing to another and still keep the first thing in your mind. You can look through other people's eyes, or look with a changing point of view, at the same place. You can stand at one spot and focus on different things and really look at them in different ways simultaneously.[6]

Another way of combining diverse images was used for *What the Songs Look Like: Contemporary Artists Interpret Talking Heads Songs* (1987). Graphic designer Frank Olinsky came up with the idea to make this book, for which some 50 contemporary artists would illustrate as many Talking Heads' songs. Byrne embraced the idea, and helped select the artists: an unusual, international mix of fine artists, illustrators, photographers, and one advertising agency, Studio Dumbar from the Netherlands. An unusual mix, since fine artists are usually very careful to protect their creative originality, and often do not to like to be associated with illustrators who do commissioned work. But here, work by avant-garde luminaries like Robert Rauschenberg and Nam June Paik as well as work from a younger generation of artists such as Jennie Holzer, William Wegman, Jean-Michel Basquiat, Duane Michals, and Krysztof Wodiczko can be found on the same pages as that of illustrators Sue Coe, Joost Swarte, Glen Baxter, and Russell Mills. Byrne contributed a collage made of 20 Polaroid photos,[7] and wrote an introduction in which he addressed the ways in which images acquire meaning:

When the government or a corporation uses a picture, a specific meaning is intended. What are these pictures selling?

If you knew an atomic war had broken out and you had at the most a half-hour to live, what would you choose to look at?

If you were putting a personal ad in the paper and couldn't use a picture of yourself, what image would you use?[8]

When Lynne Cohen published her first book of photos, *Occupied Territory*, Byrne contributed a foreword. Cohen's black and white photos show interiors of institutional buildings, in a style that is precise, detailed, frontal, and deadpan. Human beings are absent, so that all attention is given over to the contemplation of office spaces, reception rooms, banquet halls, classrooms, observation rooms, and therapy rooms. Here, so the photos seem to say, is the decor of Michel Foucault's disciplinary universe, and here is the furniture for the real-life version of Jacques Tati's slapstick of disconnection.[9] Byrne's foreword for *Occupied Territory* zooms in on the meaning and the aesthetic, artistic appreciation that the viewer, willing or not, has to add to these photos. He notes that the cool and detached quality of the photos and of the rooms they show "is being flipped back on itself to look ridiculous, although it also has a nutty, cosmic elegance," and asks: "Is it possible to love science for its stupidity?"[10] Byrne also puts to paper a few of his own impressions: "The esthetic evidenced in these rooms has also brought us to the brink of World War III. [. . .] This is the flowering of our civilization, not Monet's water lilies, which now seems like a remnant of a prehistoric way of thinking."

2 PHOTOGRAPHIC REPERTOIRES

In 1989 and 1990, Byrne published and exhibited three photographic projects. He had been taking photos throughout his career, alongside other activities, but hadn't given a definite shape or meaning to that habit. Now, the context he chose for his photos, and the diversity of the work shown, proved Byrne's ambitions as a visual artist to be equal to his musical endeavors. He published projects in *Artforum* and *Parkett*, leading contemporary art magazines, based on two sides of the Atlantic, in New York and Zürich. As if that wasn't enough to launch a career as an art photographer, he also contributed to a project that was curated by Joseph Kosuth, with that other masthead of the conceptual movement, Sol LeWitt, participating as well. Could there be a better way to align one's work with the conceptual movement?

In 1989, Byrne published a photographic project, *We Eat We Are Eaten*, in *Artforum*.[11] On three double pages photos on the right pages show public places or sanctuaries — an ex-voto room in a Brazilian church, a concrete monkey in the Tiger Balm Gardens park in Hong Kong, a roadside shrine in Japan — while the pages on the left contain photographs of small objects. The objects are a bowl of feathers, a wrapped cloth bundle, and a metal block with a T-shaped recess. Each photo is identical in size; captions underneath the photos identify the subjects. Formally, the shapes of the objects more or less resemble shapes found in the photos on the opposite page, but their relation remains undefined. Are the objects as sacred as the church and the shrine? Or are these sanctified places as substantial, yet as opaque, as the objects? The title, *We Eat We Are Eaten*, places everything within the natural cycle of animal life, inviting the viewer to speculate on what is eaten here. Is meaningless presence eaten by the attribution of meaning? Is one meaning consumed by another, more powerful? Is the meaninglessness of random objects consumed by the search for sacred meaning? Is the search for meaning in artworks rebuffed by such windows on distant realities?

The title is related to Byrne's documentary on Candomblé, *Ilé Aiyé*. Byrne wrote that in Candomblé, "the sacrifice of an animal, fowl, or foodstuffs implies that we are at one with the food we eat. We are all part of the natural cycle of birth, death, decomposition . . . (where we become food for the living) . . . and life again."[12] Still, the precise relation between Candomblé and this cosmopolitan selection of imagery leaves much to the viewer.

In an insert in the Swiss international art magazine *Parkett* (1990), Byrne presented photographs taken in Tokyo and Hong Kong, of anonymously constructed sites: a lobby, TV sets, jumbled street scenery. There is nothing typically Japanese or Chinese in these photos. Printed alongside these photos are a few questions and suggestive sentences, remarks that dare the viewer to interpret the photos and the content they show, to think about the repertoire of meanings that they offer, reveal, or hide. What do these designs tell about the culture that produced them? Byrne writes: "What does concrete joined to rosewood mean? In what context? Who cares?" "Do materials and objects reveal more about us (and them) than our (or their) faces, which are always masked? Do photographs of faces hide more than they reveal?"[13]

Again in 1990, Joseph Kosuth invited Byrne to take part in a small exhibition he was curating, "Reproduced Authentic." This took place to celebrate the opening of a Tokyo gallery.[14] Apart from Kosuth and Byrne, Barbara Kruger, Sol LeWitt, Haim Steinbach, and Jeff Wall took part in the exhibition. LeWitt was very influential in early minimalism and conceptualism, while the others, including Kosuth, belong to a younger generation of artists, each investigating an aspect of the social force field of representation. The concept of the exhibition was very specific. Each artist was to send an image by fax from New York to Tokyo, where the receiving fax machine printed high-resolution images on acetate. These in turn were used as photonegatives from which single black and white enlargements were made and shown. Kosuth's concept was that the shared medium would question the authenticity of the final prints, resulting in a "philosophically shared space" in which the larger theme of authenticity and its relevance for contemporary art would be broached. Kosuth's own contribution, more a conceptual gimmick than an interesting take on Walter Benjamin's demanding philosophy of the historical relevance of art, was titled *Ex Libris, W.B. (Tokyo), 1990* and consisted of a line from Walter Benjamin's essay "The Work of Art in the Age of Mechanical Reproduction," translated into Japanese. In English, the line reads: "One of the foremost tasks of art has always been the creation of a demand that could be fully satisfied only later."[15]

David Byrne's contribution, titled *Evil Eye II*, was a photo of Diana the huntress accompanied by Cupids, painted on a dinner plate in a kitschy approximation of an eighteenth-century French style. The image is covered with flies, at which Diana seems to be swatting with her bow. The dinner plate is covered with a rough 3 × 3 grid of transparent glass or plastic squares, and on each of these, except the square in the center, is a Chinese character, respectively representing "violence," "envy," "hatred," "anger," "fear," "greed," "jealousy," and "lies." Perhaps Diana also swats at these.[16] More layered and messy than the other pieces in this small show, Byrne's work points at the simultaneous presence of several repertoires of meaning. Combined, these three projects, the Parkett insert, *Evil Eye II* and *We Eat We Are Eaten* define the conceptual space which Byrne's photographic work tries to map. It is an investigation, not unlike ethnography, of the networks of connections that give meaning to the visual environment.

As might be expected, especially since his approach is theatrical and ethnographic in its intentions, Byrne has tried out many different ways to show his photographs. Following a conventional route, in the middle of the 1990s, he began to show internationally in galleries and art centers, sometimes having as many as ten solo shows in a single year. Prices for his work reflect the respect for photos in the post-conceptual art world, plus, certainly, Byrne's celebrity as a musician: a single photo, in an edition of ten, cost $700 in 1994, and might fetch two or two-and-a-half times as much at art fairs in 1998. Composite works, like *Sleepless Nights II*, consisting of 20 cibachromes, printed in an edition of three, would be priced at $7000.[17] His work was included in the collections of the Massachusetts Museum of Contemporary Art and the San Francisco Museum of Modern Art.

Stepping outside the purely pictorial convention of photo exhibitions, Byrne made an audioguide with a soundscape to accompany his first solo museum exhibition at the Massachusetts Museum of Contemporary Art in 1996. He chose to include a miniature model of an American city in this show, with some 400 model buildings and a huge train set, which he had found in storage at the museum. He also exhibited photos in public spaces, using commercial billboards, lightboxes, advertising space in subway cars, and the like. In yet another approach, in a show in Track 16 Gallery in Santa Monica, titled "Elective Affinities (a trade show demonstration)," visitors were encouraged to select a thumbnail image from a computer screen, to have it printed on the spot on a state-of-the-art photo printer, in a quasi-assembly-line fashion. They could then choose to buy the photo, or to have it added to the gallery walls by an assistant.

This diversity of presentation forms reflects the manifold ways in which imagery is present in daily life, influencing the ways we see ourselves and our surroundings. The point of all these photo theaters is reflexive: to mirror some aspects of the viewer's habits of seeing. As Byrne remarked in the introduction to the *True Stories* book, such shifts of perspective are often easiest to achieve in a book, and so far he has published three books that give a prominent role to photography: *Strange Ritual* (1995), *Your Action World* (1998), and *The New Sins* (2001). They were followed by a trilogy of books with a more epistemological outlook, which will be discussed in the concluding chapter. The overall thematic of these books of photography and words is motivation, both sacred and profane. Byrne portrays scenarios of motivation, and does it indirectly, not by photographing people, but by showing the scenery, signs and scenarios with which they surround themselves. Each book could be defined as a series of photo-essays about "crossed wires."

3 *STRANGE RITUAL*: DOCUMENTS OF SACRALIZATION

Byrne's *Strange Ritual — Pictures and Words* book contains over 100 color photos, most of them filling either a whole page or two opposite pages, plus some series that combine 12 or 20 photographs, arranged in neat grids. The pictures present a wide range of subjects: religious imagery and icons from several of the world's religions, film posters, posters depicting traffic accidents, double exposures of bungalows, hotel room fixtures, stacks of supermarket articles, shop window displays, handwritten messages, and studio photographs of individual objects and books. These books have mysterious and hyperbolic titles, such as *The Secret Museum of Mankind, How to Do All Things* and *You Can Live Forever in Paradise on Earth*; the cover design of that last book has evidently been the model for the book design of *Strange Ritual*. There are no portraits or photographs of living people, but a good many people are depicted in the posters and in the religious images.

The photographs are interspersed with texts; *Strange Ritual* is a book of pictures and words, as its subtitle states. These words are as diverse as the pictures. The lyrics of "Strange Ritual" from his 1994 *David Byrne* CD open the book. General hypotheses about contemporary culture each run along the bottom of several pages, like ticker tape, asking puzzling questions like:

> When far from home, the New Yorker or Los Angelino, feeling a pang of homesickness, may desire Thai food rather than his or her indigenous corn on the cob and Jello. [. . .] The Japanese visiting Burma may long for McDonald's or fresh spaghetti. [. . .] Will our consciousness be a complete pastiche? A patchwork of sounds, smells, and tastes — colonized by whatever attracts us?

Then there are lists. Lists of potential houses for the Messiah, of gods and goddesses, of things that could be "at the center of my world," of things to worship, of ways to pay a debt. Four longer texts fill one or two pages: a short essay on the shifting of cultural and political meanings in Russia after the Cold War ended, two diary fragments, a piece on the cultural influence of an imaginary TV channel called "Lifestyle." An afterword is included, and an interview with Byrne about his photography. On top of this, there are many words, names, titles, brand names, inscriptions, and texts in the pictures.

It's possible to relate some photos to Byrne's career in music. Photos of hotel rooms date back to 1979, when Byrne toured with Talking Heads; scenes in Texas were taken while shooting *True Stories*. Photos made in a Berlin steel foundry relate to *The Forest*, just as pictures from Bahia and from a Candomblé temple are connected with *Ilé Aiyé*. Film posters from Madras can be connected to Byrne's label Luaka Bop, which issued an album of Indian film music. But *Strange Ritual* is no photographic travelogue, and to look at it as such is to miss its meaning. Byrne has pointed out that he has two ways of making photos, two working processes that are opposites. He works in a documentary fashion, recording what catches his eye, but he also arranges subjects, "either by combining some images, or setting something up in the studio, or taking a stock image and then putting a photograph on top of it."[18] According to an already classical distinction, proposed by John Szarkowsky, leader of the Department of Photography of New York's Museum of Modern Art, photography can be approached "as a means of self-expression (as a mirror)," and "as a method of exploration (as a window)."[19] Byrne freely combines both approaches, and casually erases the distinction:

> Windows are mirrors through which we see ourselves reflected. Our view is coloured by our prejudices, history, and class. We see reflected our perceptions of the landscape, the skyline, the people on the street, the weather, and what they mean to us. Photographs are also mirrors. In them we see reflected our own internal biases, our own assumptions, our own presuppositions. [. . .] What we don't see is a reflection of our face, we see instead a reflection of our interior. An X-ray mirror.[20]

This text runs under four double-page photos: one of *trompe-l'œil* painted doors, one of which has been ripped off to reveal a real door behind it; one of a wall in a hall, on which a simplified landscape has been painted; one of windows with luxurious draperies; and one of a wall mirror in which only a draped white curtain is reflected.

In this way, the photography is bracketed in language. While the pictures frame their subjects, they are framed in turn by words — challenging the reader to find their meaning mirrored in the photos. This framing and reframing suggests that everything in the photos is also framed, made meaningful on purpose, rhetorical and therefore theatrical. The ritual signification implies human involvement, about which Byrne would quote writer/critic Wright

Morris, who wrote in another context about this quality of photography: "Only in their absence will the observer intuit, in full measure, their presence in the object."[21]

Byrne's writing has been called heavy-handed,[22] too literary for a book of photography, too much burdened by theory for literature. To someone who believes in the powerful modernistic aesthetic of formal purity, pictures should be self-sufficient, as suggested by this description: "[Byrne] plays with lines, using his camera to give six pipes, a bright red rail and the joints between tiles almost a higher, abstract meaning. Straight and slanting fields alternate rhythmically."[23] But Byrne's conceptual approach considers a wider field than a narrow pictorial formalism can interpret. It takes into account that taking pictures, and combining them in books, also involves the photographed objects, and changes them by placing them in new surroundings, bringing them into new company. It seems useful to compare Byrne's approach to photography not only with that of Lynne Cohen, and photographers like William Eggleston, who influenced the photography of *True Stories*. There are also affinities with the Japanese "Provoke" group of photographers. (In 1991, Byrne participated in "Beyond Japan: A Photo Theatre," in London's Barbican Art Gallery, a photo exhibition that built on Daido Moriyama's 1968 photo book *Japan: A Photo Theatre*.) The Provoke group turned the simplified notion of photography — "I am looking at the world" — around: "the world is looking at me," attributing an importance to the independence of the pictured object. The most philosophically minded member of the group, Takuma Nakahira, tried to show in his work that taking a photograph consists of making its object communicate by placing it in the world.[24] To make and to publish photographs is to experiment with the symbolic aspects of reality.

Byrne's photos, like his texts, mix the sacred and the banal, the deliberate and the unintended, the collectively shared religion and the individual obsession, finding in all these a common denominator:

> It is as if, in the store windows and corners of rooms, minor sacraments are offered up to us, and we only need to squint through the viewfinder to see them. There is a crazy beauty in these places that I am compelled to document.[25]

Documentation, then, is perhaps the best description to apply to Byrne's writings: documentation for both the seen and the unseen sites of meaning, of investing matter with the immaterial, of "sacralization," as he puts it.[26] All things considered, *Strange Ritual* is overtly conceptual: less interested in visual qualities as such than in the complex relationships between people and their visual environment.

4 THE VOODOO OF THE BUSINESS WORLD

Byrne's next book, *Your Action World: Winners are Losers with a New Attitude* (1998), is the profane counterpart to *Strange Ritual*. If the book design of *Strange Ritual* resembles a diary or a serious, perhaps sacred book, the design of *Your Action World* imitates corporate reports, commercial texts and management training books. Byrne said about the material in this widespread genre:

> "These forms of literature that we encounter every day: catalogues, junk mail, instruction manuals and advertising, have a profound effect on our sense of the world, on our sense of our selves. More than half our daily reading material is made by hacks and corporations."[27]

Your Action World takes a long hard look at the mythology and rituals of the contemporary business world. The book consists of nine series, each a distinctive combination of photographic imagery and graphic design, made in collaboration with designer Stephan Sagmeister. The titles speak a hyped-up jargon: "Regular Achievement/Maximum Achievement," "Winners/Losers — Superego: You Are A Company And Its Product."

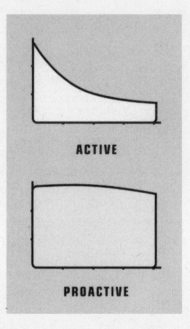

Figure 9 One of the page-filling logos that introduce each series in *Your Action World*.

The first series of images, "Better Living Through Chemistry," uses the smooth seductive visual language of advertising. Touristic photos (London's Big Ben, an immaculate azure beach with palm tree, the skyline of Hong Kong) are overlaid with small photos of drug paraphernalia against a white background, and with motivational slogans like "Winners are losers with a new attitude" and "You can't touch the stars and still remain at home." The implied meaning, suggested by the one-dimensional touristic icons combined with a bong, a coke snorter, and a syringe, is that the experience of reality advertised by this aesthetic is limited to the consumption of an already familiar sensation. A second series, "Affluence/Opulence — Stairway To Heaven," combines images of money from many countries with images of weapons in a similar fashion.

When these two series were publicly shown for the first time, it was in the form of picture posters mounted on lightboxes, like ads on the city streets. While planning this show, which took place in 1996 in the Massachusetts Museum of Contemporary Art, Byrne considered the very real possibility

Figure 10 Six panels from the photo-novel "Winners Never Quit/Quitters Never Win" in *Your Action World*. Text compiled and written by David Byrne, design Sagmeister Inc.

that the viewers might just take one quick glance at his pictures, employing the everyday neglect of visual communication that is a necessary part of the "vernacular glance." To counteract this, he made an audio guide soundtrack to accompany his visual work. This soundtrack was later released on a *Your Action World* CD,[28] and its text was used in a photo-novel that is part of the book, titled "Winners Never Quit/Quitters Never Win." This is a meeting ground of advertising and drugs, prosperity theology and gangsta rap, tourism, and talk show psychology, and the implications of these unexpected meetings deserve some looking into. What is the point of this combination? Do these ingredients have anything whatsoever in common?

The self-help ideas that are excerpted and mimicked in the soundtrack can be the point of departure for this inquiry. After all, mass media religion has been present throughout Byrne's work, from "Once In A Lifetime," and the preacher in *True Stories* who chants "Now I am the gun and you are the bullet" to the *Rei Momo* song "Lie To Me," where talk show religion is characterized in the lines "Making up stories that you know aren't true / But you know it's all right cause I know it too." *Your Action World* contains pronouncements such as "Live your life around your dreams and you live life like the movie it was meant to be." "You are your Superself and nothing can stop you now." "Take an island. Surround it with the beach — nearly 300 miles of it. [. . .] People it all with U.S. citizens, proud of their home [. . .] Picture Puerto Rico." On the CD, all texts are spoken by voice actors, with the slight exaggeration of happy conviction that is the familiar lingo of commercials, and backed by equally emphatic sweet sequences of stock music. The text mixture of new age self-help, popular management psychology, and prosperity theology is perfect, but by no means exaggerated; the genre is beyond parody in its boldly nonsensical anti-intellectualism. But it is also wildly successful, as a comparison of David Byrne's *Your Action World* with *The Secret* (2006) by Rhonda Byrne (no relation) shows. *The Secret* is a self-help book that claims to reveal an age-old secret, which would have been common knowledge to Plato, Galileo, and Einstein; it spouts such debilitating ideas as "Without exception, every human being has the ability to transform any weakness or suffering into strength, power, perfect peace, health, and abundance." Readers are told to compare themselves to "a human television transmission tower," and to raise their self-esteem, they are told that "The earth turns on its orbit for You. The oceans ebb and flow for You." The book was embraced and lauded by Oprah Winfrey on her talk show, made into a film, translated into almost 40 languages, and read aloud on CDs. The author is a former television producer. In other words, Rhonda Byrne's *The Secret* reads as if it comes out of David Byrne's *True Stories*. Reality exceeds parody.

Is all this just transparent exaggeration, stories that everyone knows aren't true? David Byrne combines the self-help blather with gangsta rap lyrics, quotes and pastiches of hip hop stars The Notorious B.I.G. and Cypress Hill: "I want it all, from the Rolexes to the Lexus. [. . .] I rob and steal, because the money's got that whip appeal." Read aloud in the sweet and clear voice of an old lady, this is puzzling and alienating: gangsta and self-help are made to appear just about identical. "Underground" criminal myth and consumer positivism meet and merge.

What they have in common is a thoroughly solipsistic outlook: only the conscious self really exists, everything else under the sun is just there to be consumed, to entertain, to serve, to fulfill each and every selfish wish. This aesthetic, this myth of an extremely reduced reality, is the common ingredient in trivial self-help literature and the equally successful gangsta lyrics, not because of some secret pact between the two unlikely bedfellows, but because it is an undercurrent that surfaces also in the yuppie lifestyle, in neo-conservatism and neo-liberalism. It is a worldview shaped by the refusal to accept the perspective of other humans, let alone other cultures, as real equivalents of one's own outlook and interests. A worldview where success is always clearly delineated and fully deserved, and within reach of those who dare to picture it and grasp it. (The analogy between aggressive rap lyrics and managerial rhetoric was also noted by Don DeLillo, the writer whose novels carefully detail how pop music and other mass media insinuate themselves into every nook of reality. In *Underworld*, DeLillo writes:

> In the bronze tower we used the rhetoric of aggrieved minorities to prevent legislation that would hurt our business. [. . .] Arthur [company CEO] listened to gangsta rap on the car radio every morning. Songs about getting mad and getting laid and getting even, taking what's rightfully ours by violent means if necessary. He believed this was the only form of address that made an impact on Washington.[29]

Your Action World demonstrates the facelessness of this aesthetic. Hotel rooms bear out a kind of hospitality without host, generic notices like "price does not include taxes" form a language that is not spoken by anyone of flesh and blood. A series of ethical test questions, printed alongside photos of security cameras, is based on the notion that ethics, a sense of duty toward others, and the need to reciprocate, can be switched on or off at will. "Hope/Despair" is a series of concrete, brick, and metal logos and nameplates of firms and institutes, located in a wooded area, bespeaking a relentless inapproachability. These business altars are best seen next to the altars of Africa and the African-Americas, discussed by Robert Farris Thompson in his book *Face of the Gods*; then they reveal themselves to be altars to the gods of facelessness, gods who uphold the

Figures 11 and 12 From *Corporate Signs: Rhône-Poulenc/Beauty*. David Byrne and Danielle Spencer, 2003. Photograph and digitally reworked photo.

laws of streamlined impersonality. That such a comparison is indeed intended can be seen in the lenticular images made out of these corporate signs in 2003 by Byrne and graphic designer Danielle Spencer. These images alternate company names such as IBM and Data General with such virtues as Courage, Trust, and Beauty, carefully presented on the same stones and in the same typeface.

Although *Your Action World* shuns all political rhetoric, and carefully remains on the surface where each picture and each sign retains something of its mantle of ambiguous excitement, the book as a whole demonstrates that such ambiguity is in the end debasing, as everything it touches is stripped of complexity and diversity. In terms of Jungian psychology, all archetypes are divested of unconscious qualities and reduced to one-dimensional, conveniently arranged outlines.

In their collaborative book design, Byrne and Sagmeister demonstrate how far-reaching the influence of this aesthetic is. Today, even colors are signs rather than just colors. To prove this, the bright monochrome and two-color pages at the front and end of *Your Action World* (mimicking the sponsor pages and ads in countless exhibition catalogues and art magazines) bear tiny captions, printed unobtrusively, upside-down, in the lower left corners of the page. They give the code for the colors: "Green and blue = Bell Atlantic. Red and yellow

= McDonalds. Green = Benetton. Red = Coke." All in all, *Your Action World* is the secularized and industrialized counterpart to *Strange Ritual*, a portrait of the aesthetic of commercial facelessness that has become ubiquitous.

5 *THE NEW SINS*: A NEW MYTHOLOGY OF CHAOS

In 2001, Byrne accepted a commission from the Art Bienal of Valencia, Spain. After *Strange Ritual*, with its general perspective that ritual simply is part of the human condition, and *Your Action World*, with its implicit condemnation of the rites and myths of the business world, the logical next step would be to come up with something resembling a positive, new mythology. The idea that artists may attempt to come up with a new mythology, a new universal form of communication, is at least as old as the Romantic current in Western culture, and Byrne's *The New Sins*, a bilingual English/Spanish book of text and photos that imitates religious literature, fits in this tradition. The book is made to look like the catechisms that are often presented at graduations and religious initiations. Pocket-sized, bound in wine-red imitation leather and with a cover that is lettered in gold, it looks like the kind of book one might find on a hotel room bedside table, or receive as a present from the Witnesses of Jehovah, the Christian Scientists, or followers of Scientology. But where does Byrne's contribution fit into the Romantic tradition of new mythologies? Before that question can be answered, a historical excursion to summarize that tradition is in order.

THE NEW SINS

scientific and logical, then faith—the ultimate illogical act—becomes the enemy. If materialism, data and things one can touch, see and hear are all important, then mystical, invisible forces are to be eradicated at all costs. These unquantifiable forces are dangerous, threatening, for they could topple the Order of the World.

IS IT POSSIBLE TO TRANSFER SINS?

If sins can be bought and sold, where does it end? Can anyone buy his way out of a cosmic jam? Do all rich men and women, or those who at least inherit their daddy's money, go to heaven?

Is God an entrepreneur?

So, if transfer of sin is a valid concept, is there a price list? Is there a discount store?

WHAT WE MEAN BY THE NEW SINS

The new sins described herein have emerged under cover, so to speak, of the old sins. They are usually mistaken for virtues. What are currently accepted by an older generation as virtues are revealed, upon closer examination, to be *vices*. Sins of the most insidious kind, for they pretend to be good for you—nice, sweet and cuddly. One would do well to be suspicious of all things sweet and cuddly.

That the new sins are disguised as virtues should not be surprising. Where would one least expect to find the

Figure 13 Two pages from *The New Sins* by David Byrne, design by Dave Eggers.

The idea that a new mythology was called for, as a meeting ground where science and morality, art, and philosophy can be freely mixed, was stated first by the group of early German Romantics, in the years 1795–1800, when Europe was in a state of political and spiritual turmoil following the French Revolution. While it may seem far-fetched to connect Byrne's work to these writings of over 200 years ago, the formal analysis and playfulness that pervades their work is very close to the basic tenets of conceptual art. Moreover, these Romantics were the first to analyze the consequences of the desire to apply rational analysis to all cultural spheres (including customs, religion, art) without reservations. These ideas were presented in the short anonymous text known as *The Earliest Program of German Idealism*, which presents the critical tendencies of early Romanticism as if it had been its manifesto.[30] This has been quoted in the Introduction, but is repeated here for convenience:

> We hear so often that the masses must have a *sensuous religion*. Not only the masses, but also the philosopher is in need of it. Monotheism of reason and of the heart, polytheism of imagination and of art, that is what we need!
>
> First, I will speak of an idea that, as far as I know, has not yet occurred to anyone

— we must have a new mythology, but this mythology must serve ideas, it must become a mythology of *reason*.

Until we make ideas aesthetic, that is, mythological, they are of no interest to the *people* and, conversely, until mythology is reasonable, the philosopher must be ashamed of it.

In this philosophy, mythology and religion stand for the possibility of universal communication, universal comprehensibility. According to the early Romantics, the mythologizing tendency of the human mind is a basic aspect of our nature, without which human experience would not be possible.[31] One of these thinkers, August Wilhelm Schlegel, explained: "The original action of the imagination is the one through which our own existence and the entire outer world gains reality for us."[32]

To create a new mythology, the early German Romantics felt that free experimentation with religion was called for. This amounts to a neglect of, and disrespect for, all dogma. Friedrich Schleiermacher, the theologian of the group of early Romantics, in 1799 defined religion accordingly as "feeling and intuition of the universe," and "the sense of the Infinite in the finite."[33] This feeling may be found anywhere, and the two greatest thinkers and poets of the group, Friedrich Schlegel and Novalis, put this conviction into words time and again. Novalis wrote: "There is no religion, that would not be Christianity."[34] And: "All our inclinations seem to be nothing, if not applied religion."[35] It is impossible to develop this apprehension of religiosity into a system: what remains of the knowledge of the absolute is only the momentary and fragmentary, point-like synthesis, in Romantic terminology the *Witz* or wit.[36] Novalis accordingly synthesized his own philosophy of religion in a single italicized word, published as a self-reliant fragment, built (as the German language allows) out of three concepts: *Experimentalreligionslehre*,[37] that is: experimental religious doctrine, or methodical experimenting with religion. In *Christendom or Europe*, Novalis characterized the content of the Bible as a "rough and abstract design of religion,"[38] and in his miscellaneous fragments *Pollen*, he noted that "If the spirit sanctifies, every true book is a bible."[39]

Friedrich Schlegel, who sometimes used quasi-mathematical abbreviations in his notebooks, once even went so far as to jot down a formula that defined both God and art. He used the operation of "dividing by zero" to indicate an idea that had been raised to an absolute level; so that $\frac{F}{0}$, for example, stands for the absolutely fantastical. The entire formula reads:

$$\text{The poetic ideal} = \frac{\sqrt[\frac{1}{0}]{FSM\frac{1}{0}}}{0} = \text{God}$$

In this formula, the letter F indicates fantasy, S indicates sentiment or feeling, and M is the mimetic power. The mathematical form of raising something to a higher power was used by the early Romantics as an expression for reflection. This formula expresses: the product of the absolutely Fantastic (F) with the absolutely Sentimental (S) with the absolutely Mimical (M, the ironical presence of the author in the work), raised to an infinite power (or: infinitely reflected) equals God. The divine, in other words, is the product of artistic sacralization. Friedrich Schlegel wrote in 1800: "Only he who has his own religion, an original view of the infinite, can be an artist."[40] And in a similar spirit Friedrich Schelling said in 1803 that "Every truly creative individual must himself create his own mythology."[41] Feeling that his age lacked a coherent mythology, Schlegel addressed the poets and artists of his time when he wrote:

> You above all others must know what I mean. You yourselves have written poetry, and while doing so much often have felt the absence of a firm basis for your activity, a matrix, a sky, a living atmosphere.[42]

This revolutionary aesthetic of Schlegel, Novalis, and their friends is known mainly to specialists in Romantic philosophy and in literary history, but its influence can be traced to later German Romantic thinkers and from them to Byrne. Friedrich Nietzsche's *Thus Spoke Zarathustra*, written between 1883 and 1885, is much more widely known; it is an obvious example of a new mythology, with its notion of the "Superman" (or "Overman") who overcomes the limitations of Judeo-Christian morality and is able to create his own morals. Nietzsche influenced Jung, who analyzed *Thus Spoke Zarathustra* extensively in one of his seminars; Jung's own interest in myth and archetypes comes close to a new mythology, as can be seen is his *Seven Sermons to the Dead*. Both examples were familiar to Byrne while he wrote *The New Sins*, as he had read Jung's works over the years. Another "new mythology" that was part of Byrne's reading can be seen in Gregory Bateson's combination of cybernetic theory with the Jungian idea of a collective mind. In his *Steps to an Ecology of Mind*, Bateson writes:

> The cybernetic epistemology which I have offered you would suggest a new approach. The individual mind is immanent but not only in the body. It is immanent also in pathways and messages outside the body; and there is a larger Mind of which the individual mind is only a subsystem.[43]

Byrne's approach to the idea of a new mythology is more oblique and more ironic than that of Bateson, Jung, and Nietzsche. It is closer to the witty work of Novalis and Friedrich Schlegel, as is already clear from the title, which may be understood as having identified "myth" with "sin," as rational science would have it. Byrne writes:

> God created Sins! . . . Sins are woven into the fabric of our lives. . . . To abandon and ignore sin is to ignore and reject God's handiwork. Sins are made by Him — to enjoy and use until they have been eventually understood.

And he continues:

> Each culture and the society make their sins — sins are not eternal, fixed and forever. They are constantly and eternally in flux. . . . Murder on the battlefield is an act of bravery, but in the home or in a public bathroom would be seen in a less flattering light. Is this a "bending" of moral standards for the economic gain of war, as the Marxists would have us believe? Or, as the Social Darwinists maintain, are we simply animals at heart, creatures of habit and instinct . . .?[44]

Imitating catechisms and other religious literature, the first page of *The New Sins* offers blank spaces where the giver may write to whom the book is given, by whom it is presented, and on which occasion. Other traits of such literature have been copied with equal care. The text is rife with "key words" printed in red, in capitals or underlined; many words and phrases begin with capitals, and ample use is made of rhetorical questions, non-sequitur arguments and bewildering admonishments and metaphors. The general drift of the text, however, is an appeal to the reader — the art-conscious, culturally reflexive, contemporary reader — to find structures of belief in unsuspected locations, outside the traditional framework of religion.

Explaining his notion of new sins, Byrne writes that they are usually mistaken for virtues.[45] He enumerates ten of these virtues: charity, sense of humor, beauty, thrift, ambition, hope, intelligence/knowledge, contentment, sweetness, honesty, and cleanliness. Each is characterized by a brief explanation and a photograph, mixing humor, religious metaphor, exaggeration and irony:

> Hope carries more weight than all the other sins put together . . . Hope allows us to deceive ourselves into thinking that life is parceled into discrete chunks — that our lives are stories with beginnings, middles and ends. That there IS narrative, linearity, and not chaos, chance and luck. *Chaos is beautiful.*[46]

A foldout page in the middle of the book adds some more categories of sinning, in the form of a hierarchic Inferno (after Dante): sins of extreme self-control (a category here seen to include "serious pop musicians"), sins of self-denial, sins of extreme logic, and sins of ideological adherence.

The New Sins combines several artistic strategies, the most prominent of which are its many imitative features. The front cover carries a legend stating "translated out of the original tongues with the former translations diligently compared and revised." The Old Testament is mimicked, in sentences like "The Heart is like the Sea, wherein dwells the Leviathan, and creeping things innumerable."[47] And apart from the graphic features, the juxtaposition of photos and text is often undermining any projection of symbolic meanings; or, in reverse, the photos prove that everything can assume symbolic significance, as was suggested by Jung.

As the text has it, "The pictures in this book will explain what the text obscures. The text is merely a distraction, a set of brakes, a device to get you to look at the pictures for longer than you would ordinarily."[48] One of the conclusions in the text, if it is that, may be taken as such, but not without reserve and caution: "We must think and feel AS NEVER BEFORE! . . . We must judge our own sins! We must take the joy, the chaos, the responsibility and the pain and make them our own."[49]

Like Byrne's other photoworks, but more emphatically, *The New Sins* deals with the projection of symbolic meanings. The book demonstrates reflexively, by imitating, how mimetic impulses coagulate into the substance of mythology. The text plays with the notion that symbols and myths might be superfluous:

> If the prevailing order in the contemporary world is scientific and logical, then faith — the ultimate illogical act — becomes the enemy. If materialism, data and things one can touch, see and hear are all important, then mystical, invisible forces are to be eradicated at all costs. These unquantifiable forces are dangerous, threatening, for they could topple the Order of the World.[50]

Against this modern credo, it reminds its readers that the history of mankind is one of ongoing re-enchantment: "The world has been beguiled, bewitched, enchanted, charmed, entertained, enthralled, delighted and captivated."[51] The greatest myth of all, so *The New Sins* implies, is to neglect this.

6 DRESSED OBJECTS AND OTHER FURNITURE

Another examination of mythical thinking is "The Wedding Party," an exhibition of large-scale photographs by Byrne that took place in 1998. The pictures portray dressed objects and sculptures that Byrne had made together with his then wife, costume designer and actress Adelle Lutz. The work is an attempt to inspire regular, everyday objects, like a radio, a vase with flowers, cutlery, an alarm clock, and a table, with an aura, to endow them with specific ritual and human qualities. To bestow to the ordinary the dignity of the unknown, is to romanticize it;[52] Byrne has repeatedly formulated the same idea as the underlying principle of his method: "I try to take ordinary things and make them be seen in a new light, by breaking them up into bits and trying to reorganize them.[...] An ordinary thing put into an extraordinary place isn't ordinary anymore."[53]

"The Wedding Party" was inspired by Byrne's interest in Afro-American religions such as Vodun, religions that ritually invest regular objects with sacred properties by wrapping or dressing them in fabric, or by feeding them with offerings. Inspired by an exhibition of the sacred arts of Haitian Vodun, Byrne asked himself:

> "What if this dressing process were applied to other objects? Would it give them life and a sense of power? [...] What if objects that already were somewhat anthropomorphic — furniture, for example, were dressed in this way?"[54]

Once his objects had been completed, Byrne found that they had indeed become animated, as he had intended, but in a different way. The everyday objects now seemed almost human, like caricatures of the qualities that can be found in any family grouping. Acknowledging that quality, Byrne titled his show of photos of these creatures "The Wedding Party."

Sacralization is a central theme is Byrne's work. It is nothing else than the realization of an indefinably wider subjectivity, as Byrne has explained several times:

> The impulse to attribute human attributes to objects is not stupid or wrong, as many scientists keep telling us time and again . . . we cannot be separated from the objects that surround us. They animate and imitate us just as much as we imitate objects and animate them. By breathing a soul into dead objects, we feel and understand that the world is truly alive, not just existing as an aggregate of dead objects and lifeless landscapes.[55]

This coincides perfectly with the ideas of the early German Romantics. Novalis, for example, wrote:

> Everything arbitrary, coincidental, individual may become our organ for the world. A face, a star, a region, an old tree, etc. may make an epoch in our interior. This is the great realism of the service of fetishes.[56]

Figure 14 *Molecule Chair* by David Byrne, 2005. Materials: cast zinc balls, steel dowels, powder-coating; 45 × 34 × 32 inches. This life-size armchair is solid enough to bear a grown person's weight. The author did not find it comfortable.

We think through projections, and to acknowledge those projections is not to undermine rational thought. To the contrary, it shows respect for its foundations.

David Byrne continued this game, adding anthropomorphic and animistic qualities to everyday objects in later art projects and exhibitions. In 2006 he showed a series of imaginative "chairs." Chairs are for obvious reasons already closely adapted to the human figure, which makes them natural candidates for the projection of all kinds of human qualities and human interests. The title of the show, held in New York's Pace/MacGill Gallery, was "Furnishing the Self — Upholstering the Soul," defining the exchange of qualities from furniture to person and the other way round. The emphasis on this ongoing exchange means, in vintage conceptual style, that the resulting furniture can either be executed or just imagined. Accordingly, some of these chairs/ideas are executed as real sculptural pieces, while others exist only as drawings or photographs. In 2008, Byrne added street furniture to his product range by designing nine bike racks in the shapes of a car, a coffee cup, a dog, a sitting pin-up, a dollar sign, a doodle (called "The MoMA"), and so on. They were executed in square steel tubes to resemble regular bike racks, and put up in New York City streets.

Chapter 6

Tropicalismo in New York

1 THE SINGER AS IMAGINARY LANDSCAPE

Leaving Talking Heads behind, Byrne had to rethink his role. The band had always provided him with a background and a history, and the demise of Talking Heads meant that in the public eye he was no longer part of a collective entity. Going it alone automatically placed him in the category of a singer-songwriter, a legendary position in the tradition of rock music, defined by the names of John Lennon and Paul McCartney, Bob Dylan, Joni Mitchell, Neil Young, Bruce Springsteen, and many others, singers whose songs are cherished by untold millions of people. The role came naturally to Byrne, who had a great portfolio of songs written and recorded with Talking Heads, but for him it came with an intriguing and delicious artistic paradox. Byrne's approach to songwriting had always highlighted the context of his songs' personae, insisting on a non-autobiographical perspective. But in the singer-songwriter tradition, singer and song are identified, the voice functioning as a guarantee for the heartfelt sincerity that is so often sorely missing elsewhere. Byrne set upon this paradox with energy and panache, and employed his new role to question its very foundation, in the best tradition of conceptual art. This entailed an ongoing search that shunned most readily available perspectives and positions, but nonetheless kept on struggling for sincerity.

> I'm just an advertisement
> For a version of myself
> Like molecules in constant motion
> Like a million nervous tics

Yo soy la nación
Soy la soledad
Lo particular
Soy la humanidad

These two samples of song lyrics are good examples of the questioning approach to the role of the singer-songwriter that is so typical for Byrne's solo career. The first example is taken from the song "Angels," from the 1994 album *David Byrne*. It is characteristic in its unnerving look at selfhood, taking up the idea that a steady personality is more often than not conditioned by the demands and opportunities provided by the environment; it is the very opposite of the myth of the self-made man. The second example is a song Byrne wrote in Spanish, putting himself at a distance from his native English: "Desconocido Soy" ("I Am Unknown"), from the CD *Look into the Eyeball*, released in 2001. The English translation is: "I'm the nation / I'm loneliness / I'm the particular / I'm humanity." A clear example of a song lyric in which the "I" stands for everything and nothing, for a position that can be held by an infinite range of subjects.

Just as these lyrics are impersonal, or rather questioning the very notion of personality, so did Byrne strive to develop a musical style that would go beyond his personal preference: "My own ambition is to write a song that sounds like I stole it, like 'I' didn't write it, but it has always been there. To get the 'I' out of the song is the ultimate compositional coup."[1] This ambition, to make music that isn't dominated by personal preferences and stylistic individuality, points directly to the example of John Cage, the artist and composer whose work exerted the greatest influence on the whole generation of artists to which Byrne belongs.

A well-known example of Cage's approach to composition is his *Imaginary Landscape No. 4*, a composition for 12 radios written in 1952. During this four-minute piece, each radio was played by two musicians who executed a carefully detailed score, one turning the station selector, the other controlling the volume and tone knobs. These musicians were, as Cage said, "like fishermen catching sounds."[2] Every sound they picked up was acceptable: the radio stations' musical and other programs, as well as static noise or silence.

In experiments such as this, Cage was disturbingly indifferent to the actual sound of his music, but very much concerned with the perceptual relationship between composer, piece, and audience. For him, music was never just sound, but an invitation to alter one's way of perceiving the world. Accordingly, it has not been through his music, but through his prose, where he could make explicit the "didactic element of my work," as he put it, that Cage has exerted his greatest influence.[3]

Through his writing, his innovative conceptual compositions, and his experimental collaborations with painter Robert Rauschenberg and choreographer Merce Cunningham, Cage became a pioneer of an aesthetic that wishes to include the listener's situation before and after a concert, to include daily experience with its heterogeneous stimuli. This has made him the leader of a musical movement and a model for the next generation of artists in every artistic discipline. Cage has become an icon: his name stands for an aesthetic of heterogeneity, complexity, and undecidability, for artistic collaboration without forced submission under a master plan, for a renewal of the *Gesamtkunstwerk* that champions an attitude that Cage has called "polyattentiveness."[4] This aesthetic was of great importance for the spirit of Fluxus and "happenings", and for the exchange between all forms and levels of art that began in New York's SoHo. To this artistic movement Byrne, together with composers Meredith Monk, Philip Glass, Steve Reich, and Brian Eno, has made substantial contributions.[5]

The lyrics of "Marching Through The Wilderness," one of the songs of *Rei Momo*, allude to the work of John Cage in a somewhat covert manner. The text to which Byrne alludes is the beginning of Cage's "The Future of Music: Credo" (1937), a statement of his artistic position that has become famous among experimental artists:

Wherever we are, what we hear is mostly noise. When we ignore it, it disturbs us. When we listen to it, we find it fascinating. The sound of a truck at 50 miles per hour. Static between the stations.[6]

In "Marching Through The Wilderness," Byrne sings:

Yeah, we are the noise
The noise between stations
Yeah it's a kinda strange
Oh boy! a strange situation

The change that takes place between Cage's manifesto and Byrne's lyric is telling. Where Cage states that "we" find the static between the stations fascinating, explaining a purely musical notion that undermines the authorship of the composer, Byrne transforms his statement into a much more radical notion: we *are* the noise between stations. What is undermined, is personality as such, the combined authorship and ownership of the person, and thus the sense of self. That the theme is dear to Byrne is also proven by another song, "A Long Time Ago," on *David Byrne*, where he sings:

in between stations I can hear
a million possibilities
it's only the singing of the stars
that burned out a long long time ago

Several of Byrne's conceptual musical pieces relate directly to Cage's work and example. In 1993, he contributed a track to *Caged/Uncaged — A Rock/Experimental Homage to John Cage*, compiled by the Institute for Contemporary Art in New York for the 45th Venice Biennale. The track was recorded in John Cale's home studio; Byrne used two of Cage's *Indeterminacy* stories and intertwined them with a story of his own, so that it is hard to tell where one story ends and another begins. The stories are presented against a chaotic background of sampled sounds underpinned by a steady rhythmic beat. The organizers behind the album hoped that it would enable the philosophy of John Cage to reach a wider audience.

Closer to Cage's own way of composing is Byrne's *Playing the Building* installation, which turns an industrial building that is no longer in use into a musical "instrument." The first installment of this project was realized in Stockholm in 2005; repetitions followed in Manhattan in 2008 and in London in 2009. In each case, a factory-size building is turned into a musical instrument by attaching motors, solenoids and the like to beams, girders and pipes to make them vibrate and resound. The switches of these electrical devices are controlled by the keys of a nineteenth-century pump organ or harmonium, which can be played by members of the audience. Even while the parameters of the music are defined by the building and the electrical technology, this instrument is far outside the range of regular music practice. The oblique link that connects the individual's desire to play music to the bygone era of industrialization is something that this installation has in common with *The Forest* by Robert Wilson and David Byrne, and the sounds that are elicited from the buildings appear to be related to the distorted version of the romantic symphony which Byrne composed for that project.

In 1990, Byrne composed "High Life For Nine Instruments" (sometimes called "High Life For Strings") for the Balanescu string quartet. The piece was commissioned by New Music America. Byrne used his guitar to write all the lines for strings, over a distantly African-sounding High Life groove. For someone who isn't quite trained in either tradition to combine African popular dance music with the classical European string quartet is obviously irreverent; Byrne made it even more so by writing nine parts, so that the quartet had to use overdubs (structurally similar to Talking Heads' *Remain in Light*, which required nine musicians to play the music that was recorded by a four-piece band).

A similarly irreverent approach to the iconic qualities of music and songs is apparent in two related video projects. First, Byrne interlaced a compilation of Talking Heads video clips, titled *Storytelling Giant*, with brief scenes of unrehearsed people telling anecdotes. These stories function as a context that places the clips in an unusual perspective, bluntly raising the question of how much of real life is based on anecdotal fantasies. Then, with David Wild as editor, Byrne re-used the footage of these interludes to compile a 2 ½-minute long selection titled *April 16, 1989*.[7] For this very short film, they selected and joined only the brief moments when the storytellers collect their wits before they begin to tell their stories. Each of these moments breathes a kind of willingness or readiness to communicate, but nothing is said; as if the bodily dimension of storytelling had been separated from the stories themselves to demonstrate a generic human willingness to exchange, or, in other words, to get the "I" out of the story. At the very end a woman whispers, "What are we gonna do, what are we gonna do, how are we gonna get out of here?"

That Byrne is quite willing to consider ideas that place the individual personality so far off-center that it becomes totally irrelevant, at least speculatively, can be seen in one of the entries in his internet journal, titled "Selfless." On January 25, 2006 he asked his readers: "What if there is no self? What if, and this is very convoluted, there are even parts of our brains that have evolved to convince us that each of us is unique — as a cover up or mask for the awful truth?" He then follows a speculative line of reasoning that perhaps the sense of unique individuality is a product of the natural evolution of mankind, a quasi-religious delusion that makes each human being see itself as exceptional.[8] It is an idea that goes together well with the anti-icons of himself that Byrne has repeatedly used. The prime examples of these are the David Byrne dolls, a series of four action dolls modeled after Byrne, reminiscent of Barbie, Ken, Skipper, and other toy store favorites. The dolls demonstrate four basic facial expressions: crying, angry, happy, and serious. Made by commercial model maker Yuji Yoshimoto, the dolls grace the cover of Byrne's *Feelings* CD and the *Your Action World* book.

Another anti-icon is the muscle suit, a suit looking like an anatomical textbook illustration of the human musculature, worn by Byrne for a few songs during concerts on his *Feelings* tour and also shown on the cover of his *The Visible Man* CD, bearing the biomedical caption "Contains the attenuated strain Salmonella typhi Ty 21a." It is relevant that this studio photo was made by Phyllis Galembo: her name links this photo of Byrne to the formal portraits that Galembo has made of priests, initiates, and devotees of Afro-Atlantic religions; Byrne contributed a foreword to her book *Divine Inspiration: From Benin to Bahia*.

Figure 15 Byrne dressed in his muscle suit. Studio portrait by Phyllis Galembo.

And finally there is robot Julio, an essay in uncanniness.[9] Byrne has lent his voice to this robot, constructed by David Hanson Labs to simulate human emotions. In Byrne's voice, the robot utters non-verbal phatic expressions and sings two very short songs. It was exhibited first in 2008 in Madrid's Reina Sofia museum.

All these conceptual projects are important and relevant to Byrne's work, but they are not as central as his songwriting. There, the influence of Cage makes itself felt in an approach that is more interested in frictions between sensibilities than in personal and musical identity. If Byrne's concerts may be compared to Cage's "Imaginary Landscape No. 4," then Byrne's persona, his projection of vocal personalities, is the radio, switching between channels. And just as Cage was at times indifferent to the actual sound of his compositions, so Byrne is often quite willing to let his voice take on awkward roles, including even blatant mismatches.

The core of Byrne's solo career is not in his songs, or in his albums, but in his work as a composer of sensibilities, putting chaos next to prettiness, euphoria next to discomfort, enjoying and shaping the resulting frictions. The result is a popular music that isn't easily summarized and packaged, an attempt to redefine the outline of popular music. Acknowledging and including sappiness and schmaltz as well as sarcasm, the frenzy of monotony as well as bubbling danceable grooves and soaring modulations, Byrne's music challenges the accepted notion of musical personality. This anti-style of musical masks that shift restlessly, lift to show the naked humanity that lies beneath, recombine and morph, is experienced best during live concerts.

2 BETWEEN THE TEETH

On Halloween 1992, one of Byrne's concerts was captured on film. Some eight years had gone by since Talking Heads stopped touring, and three years had passed since the recording of *Rei Momo*. In those three years, Byrne had developed several new songs and new arrangements for songs to highlight the distances between Latin styles, funk, and rock. The studio album *Uh-Oh* (1992) collects a dozen of these songs, but the live performance of some of these, next to material from *Rei Momo* and older Talking Heads songs, demonstrates with greater perspicacity how a meeting of popular genres entails a clash of worldviews.

The opening scene of the concert film *Between the Teeth* shows Byrne as he walks up to a single microphone, center stage. Accompanied only by an offstage rhythm box and lighted by a single lamp, he sings "Well" by Don Van Vliet, better known as Captain Beefheart. This setting is similar to the beginning of *Stop Making Sense*, where Byrne walked on alone to sing "Psycho Killer": a parallel that invites comparison with the successful older concert film. The choice of "Well," from Beefheart's notorious and uncompromising *Trout Mask Replica* album, indicates that *Between the Teeth* will be a raw, prickly, almost surreal concert, willing to consider the formlessness of reality by looking straight at it: "Light floats down day river on uh red raft o' blood" is the song's first line. The film's very title suggests as much: *Between the Teeth* is where the tongue, speech, and song have taken residence; it recalls the title of Byrne's pages in *Artforum* just a few years earlier: *We Eat We Are Eaten*. After "Well," Byrne picks up a guitar to accompany himself on "(Nothing But) Flowers," his bittersweet paean to a natural paradise that is inextricably connected to chain-store marketing, human second nature and biological nature mixed up for good. This is followed by "Girls On My Mind," a quirky tribute to countless clichéd flirtatious remarks, emphasizing them to the point where erotic pleasure unwillingly slides into sexual obsession. Halfway through the song, Byrne is joined on stage by violin player Lewis Kahn, adding the great musical cliché that equates the violin with romance to the lyrics' ironies. After this a curtain falls, and for the first time the entire band of nine musicians is visible, half of them on risers. All this still runs more or less parallel to the visual and musical build-up of *Stop Making Sense*, but the texture of the music is dramatically different.

The sound of *Between the Teeth*, rhythmic and muscular, punctuated by contrasts, is the key to the concert. It is a sound that is developed to bear out differences rather than to cover them up harmoniously: a mature sound, arranged to bring turmoil and bitterness out into the open. The potential of this style had dawned gradually on Byrne, while he was touring with the *Rei Momo* orchestra, which started out sounding much more mellifluent and traditional. In the middle of that tour, the orchestra was joined by a new drummer, Oscar Salas, and at that time Byrne noted in his tour diary how Salas' style, using more of the drum kit instead of Latin percussion, gave the rhythms a sharper flavor.[10] It was a rhythm that allowed Byrne to see the way to combine his love for Latin rhythms with the rock and the funk of his musical past. To him, the show at that moment was

> a culmination of working with the Latin musicians in "Rei Momo" and then mixing in funk musicians and some of my other things. Here was a time when it was all coming together. It was a show that had an identity of its own, not an identity that takes from all those traditions. So I thought, let's put this on film because after this I'll probably go and do something different.[11]

The personae that are presented here are contorted and interrupted by their surroundings as well as twisted by their own impulses, and as Byrne sweats and wipes his wet hair out of his eyes, sings, plays guitar, shouts, now hoarse, now almost crooning, producing a mad laugh where his lines demand it, his act seems to condense into a single statement. The song titles speak of a landscape of confrontation and violence: "Something Ain't Right," "Life During Wartime," "Women vs. Men," "Hanging Upside Down," "Lie To Me," "She's Mad," "Blind." Songs are interrupted by sharp breaks, shifting from a foursquare rock beat to the more open Latin rhythms and vice versa, which causes the dramatic situation to shift between melancholic inwardness and extraverted interaction. Tensions are displayed and emphasized, not resolved. "Something Ain't Right" is an example in case. The lyrics suggest the perspective of a child in a dysfunctional family, challenging and disavowing the right of a patriarchal father, or someone rebelling against an unjust god, and the music stresses the unease, with the brass section exchanging its instruments for a bevy of acoustic toy whistles to play a shrill intro that is halfway to a musicality, as arranged for the song by Tom Zé. "Blind," one of the songs dating from the last Talking Heads album, summarizes the frightening and only too topical quality of this musical landscape, its lyrics a collage of references to music and to media representations of violence perpetrated far away, yet brought to our living rooms:

> No sense of harmony, No sense of time, Don't mention harmony, say: What is it? What is it? What is it? [. . .] He was shot down in the night! People ride by but his body's still alive. The girl in the window what has she done? She looks down at me . . . says: "I don't want to die!"
> And I'm blind, blind, blind, blind

The "Make Believe Mambo" is another telling example. The song is no longer arranged as a unity, as it was originally. Instead, the two opening quatrains get a subdued organ accompaniment while the rest of the song is rendered full blast, combining a Latin swing with rock, with Byrne singing at the top of his voice, sometimes shouting and laughing sardonically. This is topped by a ripping Latin trumpet solo by Ite Jerez, and followed by a finale, an arrangement for the brass quartet of the band with metronome-like percussion, evoking Byrne's *Music for the Knee Plays*. This forms a clear break with the strained rendition of the song. The overall impression is of turmoil, of forces that refuse to be united in harmony. When interpreted as a commentary on "make believe," this performance stresses its painful inadequacy: its patterns of call and response are devoid of respect and of continuity.

This is not a concert film that works toward euphoria, as *Stop Making Sense* did so successfully. It is a struggle, an attempt to exorcize the false gods of smooth stylized sensationalism. *Between the Teeth* does not end with the whole band playing full blast; the last three songs are subdued and sparsely arranged, returning to the film's opening songs: just Byrne, his guitar, and a little added percussion. "Buck Naked," the penultimate song, was Byrne's response in song to the recent death from AIDS of his sister-in-law Tina Chow, a bitter meditation on the fact that we all are, in the long run, without protection against death, "buck naked in the eyes of the Lord," as the lyric puts it. "Road To Nowhere" concludes the concert, its naive wide-eyed optimism now tinged with sorrow.

Between the Teeth is not a concert film that aims for mass popularity in the way of *Stop Making Sense*, it aims at artistic maturity and independence, and it attains its goals as convincingly as the older film did.

3 NEW YORK TROPICALISMO

Over the last 20 years, David Byrne has recorded songs and incidentally performed live with a confusing array of musicians. As if the only idea is to leave no one out, to include all thinkable musical genres within reach, from country to rap to opera, from a choir of over-70- and over-80-year-old singers (the Young at Heart Chorus) to dance acts. The single most significant and lasting influence among all of these undoubtedly has been the Brazilian mixture of music, art, and irreverence for cultural separations that is known under the name Tropicalismo.

Tropicalismo, also known as Tropicalia, is the sophisticated blend of bossa nova with rock, psychedelic pop, and Afro-Brazilian elements that was developed in the second half of the 1960s by Gilberto Gil, Caetano Veloso, and a series of other songwriters and bands such as Tom Zé and Os Mutantes. Musically, Veloso and Gil were something like the Brazilian counterpart to the Beatles. But Tropicalismo also had links to the theater and to the visual arts; moreover, Gil and Veloso were also influenced by the concrete poetry of Augusto de Campos. Campos praised the inventiveness, the use of techniques of montage and fragmentation in the songs of Veloso and Gil, and associated them with the Brazilian avant-garde.[12] Tropicalismo was the 1960s successor of Brazil's 1920s modernistic movement, especially in the form it was given in 1928 by Oswaldo de Andrade in his *Manifesto Antropófago* ("Cannibalist Manifesto"). His manifesto mixes the influences of Futurism and Surrealism with the conviction that such European ideas have to be cannibalized, devoured, and digested, and mixed with non-European Brazilian culture to make them genuinely native and topical. "Tupi or not tupi, that is the question," is the best known line from the *Manifesto Antropófago*, and it mixes Hamlet's doubt with the Tupi tribe who reputedly once killed and ate a Portuguese bishop.

Tropicalismo aimed for musical as well as social freedom; freely mixing musical genres already implies that social boundaries between the social classes and ethnic groups that are associated with these musical forms can't be stable. "É Proibido Proibir" ("Prohibiting Is Prohibited") is a song which Caetano Veloso sang in 1968, inspired by the May '68 Paris protest slogan. All this was highly political at a time when Brazil was ruled by a military dictatorship, which responded in December 1968 by imposing a stricter regime of repression. Veloso and Gil were imprisoned, as the regime saw their irreverent and lighthearted music as a greater threat than that of more orthodox left-wing songwriters, who avoided all Anglo-American influences in their music and spurned electric guitars, just as the American folk movement had done in the first half of the 1960s. After three months of imprisonment, Veloso and Gil went into exile for two years in London before returning to Brazil where they continued their careers in spite of the regime's censorship. As musical "cannibals," Veloso and Gil "ate" the Beatles and Jimi Hendrix,[13] and in the 1980s Gil would "eat" Bob Marley and reggae to become Brazil's reggae superstar. Nowadays, Veloso is sometimes considered as a Brazilian counterpart to Bob Dylan, while Gilberto Gil held the position of Minister of Culture from 2003 to 2008 in Brazil's social-democrat government under President Lula, limiting his work as a singer to the weekends.

Caetano Veloso has written a partly autobiographical, partly essayistic, partly historical book on the history of Tropicalismo, published in English in 2003 as *Tropical Truth: A Story of Music and Revolution in Brazil*. Veloso describes Tropicalismo as a mixture of social, political, and economic concerns, together with existential, aesthetic, and moral questions, which were reflected in his songs. In Veloso's book, Byrne plays a minor but not unimportant role. Veloso and Byrne first met in Rio de Janeiro in 1986, a meeting that was, according to Veloso, "full of subtly decisive consequences for me and for our music." He continues:

> What fascinated me was David's growing interest in a type of musical production that had never attracted (nor ever would) the makers of jazz-fusion or sophisticated rock who would come to visit. The result, which I already had predicted, was that soon he would become involved as a producer of the *tropicalistas*. [. . .] Byrne's attention unsettled the Brazilian press, Tom Zé's life, and ours. And it opened a new track of international dialogue for our music.[14]

Veloso and Byrne struck up a friendship: every now and then they worked together on a song, gave concerts together, exchanged musical tips: cello player and arranger Jacques Morelenbaum, a long-standing collaborator of Veloso's, has also incidentally worked for Byrne. More important is the lasting influence on Byrne of the aesthetic of inclusion that is Tropicalismo. The cannibalism at its center is the appropriation and reclamation of intuition: instead of submitting to fixed standards of what is authentic and what isn't, this politics of inclusion maintains that forms of juxtaposition may be as authentic as forms of cultural purity, and insists that all forms of art are in principle accessible to everyone, regardless of barriers of race, class, gender, etc.

In 1991, together with a series of singers and actors, Byrne had a brief appearance in a 30-minute MTV special *Racism: Points of View*, hosted by hip hop singer Queen Latifah. He began by admitting that he harbored some racist notions, submerged prejudices that are part and parcel of growing up in a country with hidden but omnipresent racist attitudes. Racism, Byrne said, was something he was trying to overcome, but doing so was an uphill battle.[15] It is a subject to which Byrne has returned repeatedly. The deliberate choice of presenting himself as someone who is not entirely free of racist impulses, while he could have pointed to more than ten years of collaborations with black musicians to prove the opposite, demonstrates an awareness of the many ties that link the individual to the surrounding history, and of the deeper meaning of cultural mixing. This is part of the relevant background for Byrne's own ongoing adventures in musical miscegenation, both within and without Tropicalismo.

Definitely within the tradition of Tropicalismo is the song "Dreamworld: Marco de Canaveses," which Byrne and Veloso wrote together as their contribution to the *Red Hot + Lisbon* AIDS benefit album. Marco de Canaveses is the Portuguese village where samba singer and Hollywood movie star Carmen Miranda, who is probably known best for her outrageous banana headdresses, was born; Veloso is an admitted admirer of her gift for combining cliché with true wit. And equally within the range of Tropicalismo is Byrne's cover version, sung together with Marisa Monte, of Tom Jobim's classic bossa nova "Waters Of March" ("Águas de Março"), for the *Red Hot + Rio* album, another AIDS benefit. Byrne's preface for poet and rock singer Arnaldo Antunes' collection of concrete poetry is another example.[16] And Byrne's version of the forró classic "Asa Branca," a song about rural poverty and migration that was made famous by Luiz Gonzaga, also falls clearly within the canon of Tropicalismo. Byrne recorded it in 2006 with "Forró in the Dark," a New York-based group that features Brazilian-born percussionist Mauro Refosco, who has been part of Byrne's recordings and concert tours since the mid-1990s.

Not quite within the Brazilian tradition of Tropicalismo, and therefore of course all the more typical of its mentality, is Byrne's cover of the Peruvian song "María Landó," which was included on the Luaka Bop sampler *The Soul of Black Peru*. The song lyrics, written by poet César Calvo, tell the fate of a woman who is breaking from lack of sleep, who suffers because she has to work at all hours, while her work is all for others. The album opens with Susana Baca's Spanish rendition of that song, and it closes with Byrne's translated English version, which has no pretensions whatsoever to sound authentically Peruvian. According to Susana Baca, the song is a metaphor for all Peruvian working women who sacrifice themselves amid Peru's economic crisis: "There are so many María Landós. [. . .] She is the working woman, who works and works and earns four coins."[17] Byrne's performance of the song is passionate and dramatic, accompanied by strings that are reminiscent of film music, firmly opposed in style to Baca's much more sober and traditional version. Byrne's cover, with its obvious distance from Peru and from black Peruvian "authentic" experience, disrupts the album's claim for authenticity, but then again, it may serve as a reminder for its audience that the experience of poverty and exploitation, authentic as it is, should not be taken for granted.

Outside the tradition of Tropicalismo as such, but quite in keeping with its spirit, are Byrne's many duets and collaborations with other songwriters, from Richard Thompson and Rosanne Cash to Selena and Natalie Merchant with 10,000 Maniacs, his collaborations with producers and musicians like Morcheeba, X-Press 2, and his 2009 collaboration with hip hop duo N.A.S.A. and Public Enemy's Chuck D.

Most interesting is the influence of the Tropicalistas on Byrne's songwriting and singing. Once, in the 1970s, Byrne stopped taking singing lessons after a few weeks because he couldn't abide the idea of sitting at home singing showy standards like "Send In The Clowns." Now he began to use his voice to project lightness and prettiness, and allowed accessibility into his songs — although it is accessibility with a twist. As a songwriter, Byrne tirelessly produces balancing acts, juggling opposing moods and forces. A central theme is the notion that popular music functions as a new vehicle for mythology, but cannot really fulfill that task:

"Because if it's popular, it's just a commodity that goes into the record stores and marketplace. And it gets marketed and prostituted in every kind of way. And yet, this commodity really has deep meaning for people. In our economic system, culture and soul is bought and sold. And we often see something that means a lot in our lives, changed, bent out of shape, and prostituted as it is marketed, advertised and promoted, and that can really hurt us."[18]

Several songs deal with the queasy feeling that results from this exploitation. Take "Miss America," an allegorical song on the *Feelings* album of 1997:

> I love America
> Her secret's safe with me
> I know her wicked ways
> The parts you never see
>
> Oh Supergirl
> You'll be my Supermodel
> Although you pants are 'round your ankles

> And when you're down
> I'll be your Dirty Harry
> It will be just like in the movies.

"Miss America" may be compared to Gilberto Gil's song "Soy Loco Por Ti, América" of 1967, with its refrain that translates as "I am crazy for you, America / I am crazy for you with love." Gil's song paints a bitter love for a country and a continent where "the name of the dead man / may no longer be uttered, who knows? [. . .] the name of the man is people" ("El nombre del hombre muerto / Ya no se puede decirlo, quién sabe? [. . .] El nombre del hombre es pueblo"). Byrne's serenade to America does include some lines in Spanish, changing its perspective to that of the "other" America. But it does not refer to "the people": as if in the U.S.A. there is no such entity, no public sphere beyond the reach of marketing and commodification.

Another lyric takes the point of view of the neo-conservative extreme right that was so influential under the administration of George W. Bush, in a desperate attempt to turn its rhetoric against itself by showing it for what it is. The song is "Empire," from the album *Grown Backwards* (2004):

> Young artists and writers
> Please heed the call
> What's good for business
> Is good for us all
>
> And as it is in Nature
> So it is in life
> The weak among us will perish　(3×)
> The strong alone will survive　(2×)

Rather than just being ironic, in its wry echo of Bob Dylan's "The Times They Are A-Changin'" ("Come senators, congressmen, please heed the call"), the song admits that the cultural ecosystem has been devoured by falsely manipulated sentiments, and now it is an attempt at counter-cannibalism, defusing that cluster of emotions by devouring it in its turn. In 2003, working in tandem with liberal politicians who had turned against the War in Iraq, Byrne initiated a protest by popular musicians against it called "Music United to Win Without War." Supported by rappers Russell Simmons and Mos Def, as well as Rosanne Cash, Laurie Anderson, Caetano Veloso, and a long list of other popular artists, Byrne turned against the doublespeak employed by the Bush administration, and against its use of the media to exclude opposing voices and thoughts.

4 TV PRESENTER

In the 1998/99 TV season, Byrne expanded his role as promoter of musical diversity by acting as host of the weekly PBS live music television show, *Sessions at West 54th*, recorded in a studio on Manhattan's 54th Street. As presenter, Byrne took an interest in the selection process of the artists for the show, and found that even on public television the process was anything but free and easy:

> "Here is PBS, public television in the United States. Granted that it is the United States, there is commercial pressure everywhere, but I was surprised at how much other kinds of pressure there were on a show like this. [The show's producers] were under constant pressure from big record companies to put specific acts on, and under pressure from the subscriber stations. Each city decides whether they want the show that year or not. So they have to sell it to all these places, and some of them go: 'We don't want none of that rap music down here.' Or whatever. So they're under political pressures this way too. With a station that doesn't have advertisers and all that kind of thing, you would think that there would be a little bit more openness and freedom, but it is still very complicated."[19]

Given these pressures, the shows nevertheless included music from many genres and ethnic backgrounds, from the Afro-Cuban All Stars to folk singer Richard Thompson, from Burt Bacharach and Elvis Costello to Tori Amos, and from Indonesian pop singer Anggun to Phish.

One program in the series showcased two acts: Ozomatli, an ethnically mixed consort from Los Angeles playing an amalgamation of hip hop, ska, salsa, funk, and jazz, and David Byrne himself, performing with a small band, in combination with the Balanescu Quartet, playing three of Byrne's songs.

During an introductory chat with violinist Alexander Balanescu, Byrne asked him why he had decided to take the string quartet outside of the classical world. Balanescu replied that he wanted to address the body more, to get less exclusively intellectual. In an almost perverse opposition to this notion, Byrne and the quartet finished their set with a cover version of "The Model," a song by the German synthesizer band Kraftwerk, known for its coldness: a real challenge for the quartet, as Balanescu said, as they have to take care not to make Kraftwerk sound too warm, too nice.

Byrne then introduced Ozomatli, calling them "a revolution you can dance to" and asking some members of the band to explain their background, letting them tell how they had given their first concert during a labor conflict, a strike that was meant to start a union for poor inner-city youth in L.A. Musically, Ozomatli combines styles from Latin to dancehall, funk, and hip hop. To explain the point of this combination of music and politics, Byrne quoted Noam Chomsky: "to oppose the manufacture of apathy in the U.S.A."[20] Chomsky on a TV music show? Another example of the desire to work against exclusion, in line with the example set by Tropicalismo.

5 LIVE AT UNION CHAPEL

Live at Union Chapel, London is a David Byrne concert filmed for BBC television. It was issued on DVD in 2003. Compared to *Between the Teeth*, made some ten years earlier, the sound of this concert is definitely less aggressive, not just because the horn section of the former film is now replaced by a string section of six musicians, but also because more of the songs have a mid-tempo rhythm. The set list and arrangements witness Byrne's closeness to Tropicalismo cannibalism; they almost form an attempt to consume, digest, and regurgitate popular music in its entirety.

The accompanying musicians are strictly divided, in an unusual fashion. There is the rhythm section, made up by percussionist Mauro Refosco and bass player Paul Frazier, versatile musicians who have accompanied Byrne on several tours, plus drummer David Hilliard. And then there are the six string players, violins, viola, and celli. As there are no keyboards and synthesizers, Byrne has to maintain the musical unity between the two sections of the ensemble. To obtain this precision, the entire concert is carefully rehearsed, all musicians have in-ear monitors, and for most songs Byrne is handed a guitar that has been programmed to produce the required sounds. It is as if he were the radio in one of John Cage's "Imaginary Landscapes," being flicked from one station to another, changing the personality that his voice projects time and again. The songs are like emotional snapshots of mental states, and the ambition and a good part of the pleasure of this concert is in the precision with which unusual perspectives on emotional states are rendered. "To love human beings despite their failings, that is my sense of humor. To observe human beings as if you're from Mars — but to love them completely," as Byrne explains during one of the brief interview fragments that have been inserted between the songs on the DVD.

The concert is a mixture of Talking Heads and solo-career songs with songs for films and the theater, and these last songs provide the most remarkable perspectives. "God's Child" is a song Byrne recorded as a duet with Selena, the Texan Norteña music star. This, Byrne reminds the audience, was one of the last songs Selena recorded before she was murdered at age 23 by the president of her own fan club. As he adds, she is now (although the Pope doesn't know about this) sainted in Texas, where people have made shrines to her in their gardens.

Byrne also takes it upon himself to sing "Un di Felice," one of Giuseppe Verdi's arias from *La Traviata* — a song for which Byrne's voice is so obviously unfit that his version is more about the willingness to accept and include musical and mimetic impulses than about opera as such.

The last six or seven songs of this concert are ample proof of this all-embracing attitude. The lyrics of "U.B. Jesus," the song that opened Byrne's *Look into the Eyeball* album of 2001, combine the love for a girlfriend with the hope for a savior, a mixture that blends without further explanation into the language of commerce: "Baby you are the only car I drive." This is followed by "Life During Wartime," with its guerilla/terrorist/urban warfare persona, a song that Byrne announces as "written a long time ago, but it's more inappropriate now than it was inappropriate then." The next song is "Lazy," an international dance hit by X-Press 2 to which Byrne contributed vocals and lyrics that are a paean to laziness. Then, Byrne covers Whitney Houston's hit "I Wanna Dance With Somebody (Who Loves Me)," singing it with sincerity, but the sleek and over-familiar hit song is so far removed from his personality that the awkwardness can't be overlooked. "Ausencia," the following song, is a ballad about absence and loneliness, sung in Portuguese; it was sung by Cesaria Evora in the movie *Underground* by Kusturica. This in turn is followed by "The Accident," a song by Byrne that combines imagery of a car accident with that of the break-up of a relationship, a song that evokes and stresses the disruptive randomness of life, before the naive idyll "Road To Nowhere" concludes the concert. It is a set that pushes the envelope of credible imitation, a complex play in which all the roles of a television evening, male and female, young and old, silly and wise, a whirlwind of archetypes, are portrayed by a single actor.

6 CHOREOGRAPHED SONGS OF DAVID BYRNE AND BRIAN ENO

In 1999, Byrne wrote "Music Makes Dance — Dance Makes Music," a short text about his collaboration with choreographer Wim Vandekeybus. This formulaic title sums up Byrne's persisting interest in the connections between music and dance, between songs and the choreography of underlying impulses from which they arise. In 2008/09, Byrne toured the world for a year with *Songs of David Byrne and Brian Eno*, a concert of old and new songs that he had recorded with Brian Eno. These concerts were carefully choreographed, combining dance and music to produce a performance that was as much theater as popular concert. A first for Byrne, the tour party included three dancers/actors, who performed choreographies that often included Byrne as well as the three background singers. This attempt to give hands and feet to the inner impulses that define the songs is most characteristic of Byrne's work, but it brought with it a series of artistic, practical, and financial difficulties. For one thing, compared to popular music, theatrical performances reach only a small audience, and Byrne's artistic agenda insists that work must be accessible to the widest possible audience. Another aspect is that "ballet" gets booked in different, usually smaller venues than "rock music," which has financial consequences as well. And as a number of reviewers pointed out, a concert that is planned in every detail loses some spontaneity — although many others wrote of enthusiasm and rapture, feeling that the rich mixture of music, dance, and exchange formed a more than ample compensation for a spontaneity that is often more act than reality.

In the *Songs of David Byrne and Brian Eno* concerts, both Byrne's songwriting and his interest in dance and ritual came full circle with his old work with Eno and Talking Heads. The set list held a mixture of new songs that Byrne and Eno had just recorded, with old songs from the years when Eno produced Talking Heads' albums. This provided Byrne with an occasion to reinterpret his old songs, to return to the motifs that had inspired him some 30 years ago, approaching them from a new direction, based on his experience with musical genres and cultures from funk to country and from Candomblé to Tropicalismo.

Prior to this tour, Byrne and Eno released a new album, *Everything That Happens Will Happen Today*. The songs on the album were based on tracks originally recorded by Eno, for which Byrne provided the lyrics and vocal melodies to make them into songs. This was their first collaboration in 25 years, but it was no return to the working method that produced *My Life in the Bush of Ghosts* and *Remain in Light*. These new songs aren't built around alienating "found vocals" but are sung by Byrne, and they are anything but alienating in their resemblance to gospel songs, in that they are tuneful, harmonious, and accessibly structured with verses and choruses. Among the stylistic influences for the use of vocals was Phillip Bimstein, a contemporary American composer whose work combines folksy voice arrangements with the attempt to capture aspects of local history and landscape in his compositions.[21] "Gospel-folk-electronic" are the words Byrne uses in his liner notes to describe the combination of Eno's studio-built tracks with his own lyrics and vocals. The music is based throughout on simple major chords, and while Eno electronically treated and manipulated his tracks in ways that set them apart from regular folk and gospel, he avoided the more capricious and freakish sonic options. In Eno's words, "It's not clever music. It's music that's evolved to allow people to take part. David and I talked about music as a form of surrender, so you stop being 'me' and start being 'us'. It's the possibility of losing yourself."[22] As artistic ambition goes, there is something decidedly homely about this, as in the way

Byrne tells about joining a meeting of Eno's local singing group: "He invites a group of friends round. It's an a cappella type of thing with wine and cheese. They sing Hank Williams or Everly Brothers songs — easy songs to sing. No one takes the lead. Everyone finds their place."[23]

This resonates with the desire to use music as a metaphor for a utopian community, which had motivated the shared interest that Byrne and Eno showed in John Chernoff's study of African rhythms when they recorded *Remain in Light* and *My Life in the Bush of Ghosts*. But this time, utopia begins at home. While themes like fear, paranoia, and terror still linger in the songs of *Everything That Happens Will Happen Today*, they are no longer approached from the basis of a general distrust in one's own feelings. Byrne's formerly distanced stance to his own emotional processes and his general refusal to use personal experience as the sole foundation for songs and performances aren't dominant here.

The mood of surrender and inclusion that reigns over the album is strictly secular. Nature claims responsibility for human predicaments, as in Byrne's lyrics for "The Lighthouse":

> Heard nature say
> "I'm sorry —
> For stones and trees down below
> For those who tumble in God's name
> to an early grave
> into the sea and foam
> like ships tossed in a storm"

A similar perspective can be heard in the lyrics of "Everything That Happens":

> From the milk of human kindness
> From the breast we all partake
> Hungry for a social contract
> She welcomes you with dark embrace

The *Songs of David Byrne and Brian Eno* concerts add a great deal to this atmosphere of communality. Byrne opened these concerts by announcing what he calls "the menu," the set list of new and old songs, and by introducing himself with the words "I'll be your waiter." This metaphor is borrowed from one of the new songs, "The River," which opens with the verse "I'm standing on the stage / I'm working in a restaurant / I make a decent wage — and I — / Will sing into the microphone." Comparing food to music connects both, in an off-hand way, to an entire way of life; as Byrne once said about Celia Cruz, "In the sound of her voice you could sense the cuisine, the dancing, the clothes, the humor, and the sadness of a whole culture."[24] The same song has wider resonances. Its title recalls Al Green's "Take Me To The River," which Talking Heads covered successfully more than 30 years ago, and the shift from "Take Me To The River" to "The River" might be taken as a sign that Byrne has arrived at his destination. The song's lyrics briefly present Byrne's philosophy of cultural exchange, inclusion, participation, and reciprocity:

> The water's moving on
> Beyond the lies and hypocrites
> I'm thinking of a song
> I need you to remember it
> The forest is alive
> It asks us to participate
> We lifted up our eyes
> To promise and reciprocate
>
> We fell down on our knees
> For ev'ry human being —
> For one sad day I will fly away
> And one sad day I will tip toe away
>
> But a change is gonna come
> Like Sam Cooke sang in '63
> The river sings a song — to me —
> On ev'ry St Cecilia's day

The song Byrne wants his audience to remember is the flow of cultural exchange and participation. It may be Al Green's "Take Me To The River," and it certainly is Sam Cooke's "A Change Is Gonna Come," a song that opens with the line "I was born by the river." "A Change Is Gonna Come" has come to stand for the 60s civil rights movement, with its struggle against racism, poverty, war, and exclusion, and the ongoing necessity for this struggle is what Byrne's river sings of. (Saint Cecilia, by the way, is the patron saint of musicians.)

During the *Songs of David Byrne and Brian Eno* concerts, the choreographed exchange between dancers, singers, musicians, and songs produced a warm and embracing atmosphere, making this probably the most festive concert tour of Byrne's career. The exchange was emphasized by the all-over white clothing worn by musicians, singers, and dancers alike, by the mirroring of gestures between the dancers and between dancers and singers, and by the exchange of roles, as when dancer Steven Reker, background singer Redray Frazier, and percussionist Mauro Refosco all pick up a country-and-western type guitar to accompany Byrne in one of his more folksy songs, "My Big Nurse." In this concert series, Byrne still presented a number of troubled and contradictory personae, and the montage of personae that typifies the songs of *Remain in Light* got full treatment, as all five signature songs of that album were played, from "Crosseyed And Painless" to "Once In A Lifetime." But this time around the alienation that results from the incredibility of the TV preacher-persona of "Once In A Lifetime" gets quoted and reinterpreted in the choreography. In the 1980 video clip for "Once In A Lifetime," Byrne executed a repertoire of sudden twitching movements and gestures, one of them a rhythmic chopping with the right hand on the left forearm. In 2009, the three dancers, positioned to Byrne's left and right, one after the other make a similar but wider gesture, passing it on to each other so that the chopping movement runs across the width of the stage — bringing the twitching of an isolated persona into the sphere of social exchange.

The choreographies for the concert were made by four New York choreographers, each of them known for making contemporary dance that interacts with forms of theater: Annie-B Parson of "Big Dance Theater," Noémie Lafrance of "Sensproduction," and Sonya Robbins and Layla Childs of "robbinschilds." The choreographies they have made are an ongoing stream of danced and acted commentary on the songs and on the roles of the four singers on the stage. This effectively turns Byrne's songs into social games, emphasizing the festive character of music making. Now it is positions of hands and feet, now gestures of the entire body that may be executed by all three actor/dancers — Natalie Kuhn, Lily Baldwin, and Steven Reker — simultaneously, or in turns, in counterpoints of stillness and agitation, in jumps and leaps but also in such "unballetical" and mundane actions as lounging in a desk chair.

The danced accompaniment of "I Zimbra," Talking Heads' first "African" song with Hugo Ball's Dadaist nonsense-lyrics, is an eloquent example of this merger of dance and song. First, the dancers teasingly take away the microphone stands of the three background singers, placing them in a row behind Byrne. Later, playing a guitar, Byrne slaloms backwards through this line of microphone stands, while all around him dancing goes on; when one of the singers successfully imitates a twirling move performed by dancer Steven Reker, he smiles in congratulation. There is an ongoing exchange on stage of such teasing challenges and satirical routines, of gestures that are enlarged and passed on. While the vocabulary of dance movements is decidedly contemporary and vernacular, and has more in common with athletics than with classical ballet, the precision of the dancers stands out, so that the mirroring and the interruptions of the choreographed scenes produce a sense of montage that is equal to the density of video clips, as if the prerogative of technology is being repossessed, re-appropriated for live performance.

All this singing and dancing is guided by a demand for reflexivity and interwoven with conceptual input. "Strange Overtones," from *Everything That Happens Will Happen Today*, is a song about the making of a song:

> Your song still needs a chorus
> I know you'll figure it out
> The rising of the verses
> A change of key will let you out

The prominent role of choreography during this concert tour reflects the insight that emotion will often follow where gesture leads. As Byrne sang in one of the songs on an older album, *Look into the Eyeball*: "Every kid in every school / Knows all you've got to do is — smile." Emotion is often activated through movement, whether the movement is rehearsed or not, which means that rehearsal and spontaneity by no means exclude each other. Byrne's explains this non-dichotomy as follows:

> The line that separates "show" and deep heartfelt music is both real and imaginary. A performance can be moving, inspiring and therefore, we assume, heartfelt, when it is actually the craft at work — at its most subtle and hidden. [. . .] Deep feeling, intelligence, powerful emotions and sincerity are not mutually exclusive to stagecraft. In fact, pure emotion without stagecraft is often not very effective. It doesn't get communicated without the element of "show". A person crying or wailing is powerful, but it doesn't reach us, it's pure emotion with no way of connecting to us. It needs to be shaped, molded, crafted — and then we understand and can feel what the performer wants to communicate.[25]

This understanding, that emotion has important structural preconditions, is almost tangible during the concerts. It places emotional archetypes within a grid that includes the tragic sides of life as well as the formats of the entertainment industry and the forces of history. Innocence and surrender meet and mingle with alienation and manipulation. All in all, what Byrne's choreographed concerts communicate with the audience is a sense of personal humility vis-à-vis the wider human landscape, combined with a festive emphasis on shared responses and reciprocity.

7 HISTORY IN THE DISCO MIRROR BALL

The *Songs of David Byrne and Brian Eno* tour was not the first time in Byrne's solo career as a singer-songwriter that he had integrated his songs into a larger artistic ensemble. In 1999, Byrne collaborated with Belgian choreographer Wim Vandekeybus and his dance company Ultima Vez on an evening-length ballet. In Vandekeybus, Byrne found an artist who was driven by a fascination for the instinctive and the subconscious aspects of humans, and who was equally willing to pursue that fascination in collaboration with others, looking for synergies between the arts. Vandekeybus' background is not the balletic training of most choreographers; he studied psychology for some time, but finding himself disappointed by the purely theoretical approach he found in the university, he turned to the wordless experimental theater of Jan Fabre. After working there for some years, he set out on his own.

In making *In Spite of Wishing and Wanting*, Vandekeybus followed a few basic notions. He wanted to make a production with an all-male company, its guiding theme was to be desire, and the question it asked was to be "What can wishes provoke in our body?" As was his want, he set out to investigate this in intense and extreme ways; examples he gave in the beginning of the rehearsal process were "Jimi Hendrix giving a concert, or someone shivering while having a nightmare."[26] As another source of inspiration Vandekeybus used two short stories by Julio Cortázar, making them into a short movie that was shown on a screen that was lowered on the stage for the duration. Byrne's contribution to this piece was a score that was mostly atmospheric, a sonic landscape that "could lure the listener into a wind tunnel" as Anna Kisselgoff put it in her *New York Times* review. Into this soundscape, Byrne introduced remixes of two dance songs from his *Feelings* album: "Fuzzy Freaky" and "Dance On Vaseline."

Vandekeybus' choreography alternated long, almost static scenes with raw explosions when the dancers executed leaps and rolls, freezing suspended in mid-air to catch themselves, only to jump anew, and galloping like horses, clashing, head-butting and simulating fights with a near-frightening intensity and realism. Byrne's soundscape pulsated, sighed and ground, and the beat of his "superextended remix" of "Dance On Vaseline" forcefully involved the audience in the goings-on on the stage. What Vandekeybus' theatrical dance piece didn't address was the relation of the archetypical emotions that his dancers performed to real history. His cast, a group of dancers assembled from wide and far, from countries as far apart as Finland and Algeria, and the use made of English and French as well as Arabic, vaguely suggested a wider implication, perhaps South-North migration. But in the end, Vandekeybus' tableaux and film scenes were exactly that, a loosely arranged series of tableaux and scenes, full of an expressionist and surreal suggestive power that remains otherwise unspecified.

In 2005, Byrne began research for a project that was intended to combine the evocative potential of popular song with historic specificity.[27] Its subject was the life of Imelda Marcos (born 1929), former First Lady of the Philippines and widow of the dictator Ferdinand Marcos. Her life has Shakespearean dimensions: she went from rags to riches, was a beauty queen, and dated Benigno Aquino, who would later be Ferdinand Marcos' most prominent political opponent, before marrying and allying herself with Marcos. In the first years after Marcos had come to power in 1965, his politics may have benefited the country's economy, but later, as head of a U.S.-supported military dictatorship, the Marcoses exploited the Philippine economy as their private property, showing outrageous greed, corruption, and abuse of human rights. For Byrne, Imelda's story was an example of the timeless story of power, politics, and psychological needs (he was inspired in part by Ryszard Kapuściński's book-length reportage *The Emperor: Downfall of an Autocrat*, on Haile Selassie's regime in Ethiopia), but in Imelda Marcos' case the story came with a soundtrack of American disco music: she loved the glamour of discos, and had private discos built into her Manila palace and her New York mansions, where she could entertain powerful politicians and members of the jet set. Byrne planned a disco song cycle that would present the private mythology of Imelda's dreams and ambitions, and through that present something of the myths and images that guide the conduct of nations toward each other. Imelda's story is somewhat like Cinderella's, and in the beginning of their reign, Ferdinand and Imelda Marcos could be compared to John and Jackie Kennedy, young, glamorous, and benevolent rulers; at the same time, the Philippines were important allies to the U.S. in the Vietnam war, part of the frontier against communism that in American mythology could play as a re-enactment of the conquering of the Wild West. To cover all of this and more,[28] Byrne gave this project the title *Here Lies Love*, words that Imelda Marcos once mentioned to an interviewer as the epitaph she would like for her tombstone.

At the time of writing, *Here Lies Love* remains unfinished. As a project in comparative mythology, it invites comparison with *The Forest*; and as with *The Forest*, several aspects of *Here Lies Love* may well turn out to be unrealizable as Byrne originally conceived of them. Like *The Forest*, *Here Lies Love* is an attempt to demonstrate the presence of mythical forces in history, but its subject is contemporary. Conceptually, the piece calls for an unusual mixture of perspectives and genres, as the biographical and psychological reality of Imelda Marcos is combined with the political history of the Philippines, both shown partly from the perspective of the "special relationship" between the U.S. and the Philippines and from the perspective of the New York nightclubs of the 1970s that Imelda frequented and loved. In terms of theatrical genre, this requires an uneasy wedding between opera, disco, and theatrical experimentation — uneasy because Byrne initially hoped to allow the audience to dance to the music in a disco-like setting while at the same time following the unfolding of the story. Uneasy, also, because the material of *Here Lies Love* is decidedly wry and melancholy, centering on "the spectacle of nations, no less than individuals, helping each other along with their delusions,"[29] and this contrasts with the heady excitement of disco dancing.

In terms of New York City theater, *Here Lies Love* is neither Broadway musical nor Lincoln Center Opera, although Byrne had meetings and discussions with representatives of both.[30] *Here Lies Love* is situated in an artistic no man's land. For the musical side of the project, Byrne joined forces with DJ Norman Cook, better known as Fatboy Slim, who has a great deal of experience in remixing old hit songs. At the time this book was handed over to the publisher, a concept album version of the song cycle in which every song is sung by a different singer was about to be released; only time can tell whether that will be the final version of *Here Lies Love*.

Chapter 7

An Emotional Epistemology

1 CLOUD DIAGRAMS

> Lacking pictures of bald heads or phrenological diagrams, I used photos of cloud formations that I took over Arkansas to illustrate Karl Iagnemma's story ["The Phrenologist's Dream"]. I thought the photos could substitute for a phrenologist's diagram that locates emotions and feelings on a skull with an amorphous temporary blob in the sky that also could be seen as a fleeting diagram of the emotions, but one more wide and uncontrollable.[1]

The above is a quotation from a text Byrne wrote to explain his choice of illustrations for the 2003 Spring issue of *Zoetrope*, a literary magazine. The idea that a cloud could be used as a diagram is noteworthy. A cloud shows just about the opposite of every quality you would normally expect to find in a diagram. Stable geometric properties, clear delineations, and distinct values are conspicuously absent from clouds. Because of that lack, clouds make excellent screens for the projection of fantasy images, resembling animals, shapes from maps, and so on. And yet cloud diagrams are present in all of Byrne's recent work in conceptual art. There are several in his book *Envisioning Emotional Epistemological Information* (2003), and a few more in *Arboretum* (2006). Byrne's photos of clouds that are included in the *Zoetrope* issue are titled accordingly: *Epistemological Diagram: Cloud 4* and *Epistemological Diagram: Cloud 6*. And while the notion of a cloud as an epistemological diagram may at first seem to be unrealistic, flippant, and ironic, there is a perfectly serious side to it. That side comes up, for example, in a published conversation between Byrne and Daniel Levitin, a professor of behavioral neuroscience and music, who studied the ways in which the brain processes music.

Daniel Levitin: When we're imagining music, [the brain] uses the same neurons and circuits as when we're actually hearing it. They're almost indistinguishable. So when you're imagining or remembering something, it could be music or a painting or a kiss, disparate neurons from different parts of your brain get together in the same configuration then were in when you experienced it the first time. They're members of a unique set of neurons that experienced that first kiss or that first bungee jump or whatever it is that you're recalling. Actually, it's in the word 'remember' — you're re-membering them. You're making them members of this original set again. I think that's what memory is.

David Byrne: I agree that it's something like a network or a cloud.

Daniel Levitin: Yeah, it doesn't exist in one place. It exists everywhere.[2]

Scientists often have to reduce reality to a few strictly limited and controlled factors to be able to do meaningful research. Most scientific graphs and diagrams project one linear variable onto one or two other variables, to reveal the impact of one specific influence. In contrast to that, a "cloud diagram" would presumably reveal a whole host of influences and contexts simultaneously, mental and emotional states as well as external, physical phenomena, together with all their interrelations. It would be a visual representation that would sacrifice a good deal of clarity and simplicity to gain what scientists call "ecological validity," real-life relevance. Ultimately, this might mean crossing over from science into art and poetry, where what is lost in clarity and precision may be made up for in suggestiveness and stimulating associations. For that reason, Byrne's internet journal, which he began to publish in March 2004, may also be called an epistemological cloud, in that it freely switches between subjects and perspectives, following the flow of Byrne's experiences and interests. This is a list of the categories offered on Byrne's website to organize his published journal entries. (Many entries are filed in more than one category; typically, entries get filed under "Books, Music, Philosophical Musings, Religion, Travel," or under "Current Affairs, Politics + Economics, Tour/Show Reports, Travel, Web/Tech.")

Anthropology/Sociology
Art Projects
Books
Current Affairs
Dreams
Facts

Film
Food and Drink
Holidays
Music
Nature
Philosophical Musings
Politics/Economics
Religion
Reviews
Science
Tour/Show Reports
Travel
Web/Tech

This list makes it clear that Byrne refuses to let his perspective be dictated by the demand for mono-disciplinary specialization; he often turns established conceptual distinctions on their head or inside-out, ranging freely between seemingly unrelated fields and instances. He will, for example, compare his questions about the price and bandwidth of internet services to the history of sea fishing, with the attempts to regulate fleets, and with health care and insurance.[3]

There is no firm boundary between the books and journal discussed in this chapter and earlier books like *Strange Ritual* and *The New Sins*. There are, in fact, several photos of clouds and of landscapes with clouds in *The New Sins*. But in Byrne's more recent books, the emphasis has noticeably shifted to a more reflexive take on diagrams, conditions of knowledge, the use and abuse of categorical distinctions, and similar epistemological questions.

2 ENVISIONING EMOTIONAL EPISTEMOLOGICAL INFORMATION

In 2003, Byrne published *Envisioning Emotional Epistemological Information*, an art book that comes with a DVD. *E.E.E.I.*, as it will be called here for brevity, is a book in which most images were made with the presentation software program PowerPoint. The book, and especially the five clips on the DVD, are a portrait of PowerPoint when it is home alone, singing and dancing with abandon in front of the mirror. All the graphic tricks that PowerPoint has made accessible to everyone who owns a computer, all the icons, frames, background textures, bullet points, outsized letters, overlapping frames, and dissolves take part in a game of mimicry, a dance of visual rhetoric that suggests everything and nothing, oscillating between the bland and the uncanny. *E.E.E.I.* is a reflection that picks up where *Your Action World* stopped. The focus is not on the messages and mythology of business communication, but on the basic means that make it so easy to impose a visual order on anything and everything.

The sections of *E.E.E.I.* bear titles like "Architectures of Comparison" and "Sea of Possibilities," indicating that everything, regardless of its qualities and properties, can be ordered, compared, graded, divided, boxed. The cloud diagram, that composition of the utterly meaningless with the completely meaningful, is never far away from these pages. There is a diagram titled "Everything Is Connected," a narrow and very long horizontal spread that shows names of fashion brands combined with a random selection of terms and concepts (revenge fantasies, hardwood floors, book clubs, polytheism), each brand and term in its own little box, the boxes floating against a background of white clouds and blue sky and connected by arrows. (This was originally produced in 2002 as a public art piece, a 215-foot-long billboard covering the scaffolding on Saks Fifth Avenue.) A second cloud diagram plots cloud types against a fanciful selection of "-isms," such as fetishism, masochism, feminism, Romanticism,

Figure 16 One of the Venn diagrams in *Envisioning Emotional Epistemological Information.*

and fascism, producing a graph that rises and falls steeply to connect the cirrus cloud to sexism, and the mammatus formation to Romanticism.

"Physiognomies" is the section that deals most directly with the innate and irrepressible human propensity to judge the character of reality based on first appearances. It is a theme that pops up throughout Byrne's work, from the lyrics of "Seen And Not Seen" (on *Remain in Light*) to the "Crossed Wires" text in *Strange Ritual*. People do judge a book by its cover, and this tendency for quick generalization is also at play where graphic representations are used. Byrne wittily plays with the many ambivalences that are the result of many overlapping layers of this tendency in combination with its opposite, the retreat from this trusting belief in first impressions. This is where the emotional aspect of all visual information comes into play: we want to believe, to accept what we are shown, to fall in step, just as we are ready to distrust, to ridicule or to disavow; but in the end we'd like to be certain of where we stand.

E.E.E.I. combines the theme of emotional security with that of the clear visual representation of data, a combination that Byrne uses skillfully to keep his texts and visuals off-balance. He is, as usual, perfectly candid about this, for example in "Universal Language," an enumeration of ingredients or desiderata for such a language, each item — of course — is set apart and made more important by a bullet point. This is part of the list:

- Use of charts and visual language techniques to understand psychological processes
- Development of a language for better communication and evocation of nonverbal emotional and epistemological information
- Categorization of emotions as they relate to life decisions
- Naming the unnamable
- Leaving the unnamable unnamed

To get a better appreciation of what the notion of "emotional epistemology" entails, it is worthwhile to compare Byrne's *E.E.E.I.* with a book to which the title alludes, Edward R. Tufte's *Envisioning Information*. Tufte is an influential writer on the graphic design of information who puts forward what he sees as a universally valid rational analysis of visual design. Tufte, who began his academic career doing statistical research on the connections between politics and economics, insists on clear and distinct argumentation. Time and again he emphasizes that such thinking goes hand in hand with the use of clear and precise tables, graphs, maps, and other visuals: "When principles of design replicate principles of thought, the act of arranging information becomes an act of insight."[4] He insists that it is possible to develop universal principles of analytical design, and presents his readers with many definitions and rules-of-thumb for good design, such as "Graphical excellence is that which gives to the viewer the greatest number of ideas in the shortest time with the least ink in the smallest space," and "For non-data ink, less is more. For data-ink, less is a bore."[5]

Byrne admires Tufte's books on design, but his approach has little or nothing in common with Tufte's insistence on the rational analysis of data. Interestingly enough, in 2003, when Byrne published *E.E.E.I.*, Tufte published a vehement attack on PowerPoint in a pamphlet titled "The Cognitive Style of PowerPoint," which sparked a series of journalistic comparisons between the two very different takes on PowerPoint. But before going into that, it will be helpful to compare the two approaches in general. Tufte clearly represents a rational approach to design that presupposes that most everything can be divided in logically independent units, which can then be charted, counted, measured, and connected: he stands for enlightened science. Against Tufte's rationalism, Byrne's "emotional epistemology" stands out as Romantic — but here it is good to keep in mind that Romanticism does not automatically imply a sentimental anti-Enlightenment befuddlement; historically speaking, Romanticism has also been a critical self-correction of enlightened thinking, insisting that critical analysis should also encompass those aspects of human experience that do not lend themselves to the quasi-mechanical treatment that is so characteristic of the Enlightenment.

In "The Cognitive Style of PowerPoint," Tufte claims that "the popular PowerPoint templates (ready-made designs) usually weaken verbal and spatial reasoning, and almost always corrupt statistical analysis."[6] He denounces PowerPoint for having a very low resolution, and generally for promoting a style that dilutes thought by valuing format over content. Tufte sees this pushy style as inherently connected to the large commercial bureaucracy of the software design firms, where hierarchy and smarmy marketing rhetoric override all concerns for the directness, clarity, precision, and detail he so values.[7] In *E.E.E.I.*, Byrne's approach is in some respects remarkably close to Tufte's, especially in the introductory "Exegesis," where he writes that

> every piece of software comes with its own set of biases and tendencies. [. . .] The way that PowerPoint is structured and the various options provided have not only been limited (this can actually be a good thing) but they have been designed assuming, a priori, a specific world view. [. . .] You are rewarded for behaving and thinking like a software designer.[8]

But where Tufte's diatribe against PowerPoint suggests that the faults and weaknesses of PowerPoint are well contained, so that anyone who is forewarned can rationally identify and avoid them, Byrne does nothing of the kind. Instead of suggesting a clear alternative to PowerPoint, as Tufte does, he emphasizes the performative and theatrical qualities of PowerPoint presentations. While Tufte argues for a culture of rational representation, Byrne does not provide a similar clear-cut argumentation. Thrown in relief by Tufte's work, Byrne's pieces make the point that rhetoric, non-verbal communication and emotion can't be banned from the sphere of representation, because they belong to its very substance.

Following the publication of *E.E.E.I.*, Byrne did a short lecture tour, *I* ♥ *PowerPoint*, speaking at art institutes and universities. He gave his talk in a loose way, sometimes close to standup comedy, and included a good many examples of PowerPoint spoofs, such as "translations" of *Hamlet* and *Lolita* into generic PowerPoint graphs, as well as some seriously intended presentations on religion and marriage that bring out the tendency of some people to use PowerPoint to over-simplify. Mentioning the attacks on PowerPoint by Tufte and others, however, Byrne took the line that PowerPoint certainly has restrictions as a tool, and that many criticisms aimed at it have some accuracy, but that the simplifications and the illusion of content where not much is actually being said are part of a more general trend, and not to be blamed on PowerPoint as such.

Crediting Jamie O'Neil, a professor of digital media arts, as a source, Byrne gave special attention to the non-verbal and affectionate aspects of PowerPoint presentations. A presentation slide is not a book page; it is accompanied by a speaker, and related to both the speaker and his audience. Byrne quotes O'Neil (who quotes someone else in turn) on the notion that a good deal of information, between 63 percent and 95 percent, is received through non-verbal means, adding with deadpan comedy (who really knows what to make of such figures?) that that is more than half. But he elaborates on the theatrical aspect of presentations, comparing them to Asian theater, like bunraku puppet theater and Brecht's plays, where the attempt to create an illusion of naturalism is explicitly undercut. An image from Robert Wilson's theater piece *A Letter to Queen Victoria* serves as an example of how many contemporary theater makers do not aim for naturalism, which means that PowerPoint, very much the poor relation in the world of computer programs, can at least boast of a few respectable connections to the arts world.

3 *ARBORETUM*: THE GARDEN OF CORRESPONDENCES

Just as *Envisioning Emotional Epistemological Information* plays with PowerPoint and with the notion of analytical design, and demonstrates how easily and imperceptibly the rhetoric of clear-cut argumentation and conviction turns into its opposite, so Byrne's next book, *Arboretum*, published in 2006, plays with logic and with systems of logical classification. The book consists of 92 numbered diagrams, pencil-drawn and handwritten, carefully printed to include smudges and rubbings. Most diagrams are modeled more or less closely after the model of a tree with branches and roots, but there are also several flow charts, circle charts, and Venn diagrams. Each diagram is presented individually on a page spread, drawing on the right page and title on the left. In the back of the book is a four-foot-long foldout guide with densely printed background information to most of the diagrams.

Just as an arboretum is a collection of trees and tree-like plants for the purpose of scientific study and taxonomic classification, so *Arboretum* is a collection of categorizations. It is conceptual art in its primordial state, an attempt to surprise and capture concepts at the moment of birth, or in the middle of the process of mutating.

Unsurprisingly, the cloud diagram makes its appearance once again in this book. Not only do many trees resemble clouds, even the cloud diagram that plots cloud types against a selection of "-isms" is reprinted, identical with the version in *E.E.E.I.*, but now pencil-drawn. This time around, it bears the title "Psychosexual clouds," and it comes with an explanation:

Almost any defined set — behaviors, objects, names, numbers, colors or sounds — can be mapped onto any other group given a common means of measurement. For example, cloud classifications mapped onto sexual practices and perversions.

First, assume that thoughts and desires have a shape. A physical dimension. A "cloud" of desire is a specific set of neural connections and links that settles over an array of ganglia in a specific region of the brain. For each distinct behavior and desire the net of connections and potential links takes a slightly different form. The nets overlap, but each thought has its own shape. The elongated cirrus-shaped network that touches both the pain centers and the pleasure centers might constitute the "cloud" that is masochism, for example.

We currently classify these desires by their attendant behaviors, but we could just as easily classify them by the shapes of their neural nets, clouds of connections — if we had a way of seeing those, something recent technology is now making possible, and soon these webs will be tangible, almost concrete. Eventually, once the correspondences become familiar, we will associate the clouds in the sky with specific states of mind, ideas, and sexual feelings, not just with puppy dogs, dragons, boats or dead presidents.

The common means of measurement applied in *Arboretum* is the tree. Roots, trunk, branches, and twigs provide a notion of order, causality, and hierarchy: the trunk is more important than the branches, and the branch in its turn is

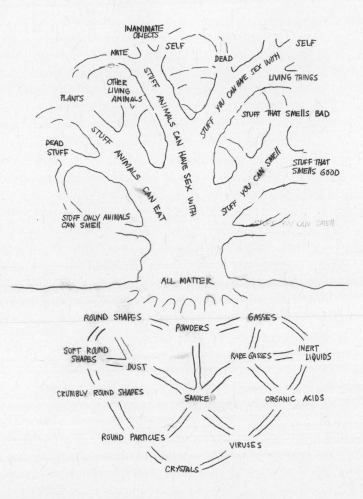

Figure 17 *The Evolution of Category,* one of the diagrams in *Arboretum.*

more important than the twigs. And the roots, underground, must provide the tree with its causal elements, even if they undergo a transformation when they rise above the soil. And all this doesn't really require an explanation: the visual logic is infective. Moreover, popularized science in magazines, newspapers, books, TV programs, and so on has taught everyone to expect the unexpected and the counter-intuitive as soon as diagrams and cumbersome logical explanations are wheeled out. *Arboretum* has aptly been described as a combination of earnest philosophical digressions and party tricks, and a closer look at the way in which Byrne manages this combination takes us to the very heart of the book.

The logic in each drawing is implied by visual means: a tree shape, or a flow chart. Anyone who inhabits contemporary reality, saturated as it is with the products of technology and with the "social engineering" of bureaucracies and institutions, is trained to manage the traffic of logical distinctions, to avoid the painful clashes that result from category mistakes. Machines and bureaucracies have to be addressed in the right order, on the correct level, at the pre-set moment: these are the facts of life. Each scientific discipline also imposes its own set of axiomatic categorical distinctions, its own logical system that is impervious to all impulses that are merely personal, subjective, mimetic.

The tree diagram stands for this logic in its most imperious form, as it imposes a clear-cut hierarchy on whatever it orders, dividing it into neatly separated classes and subclasses. Under the influence of cybernetic theory, all learning has been described as "an arboriform stratification of guesses about the world."[9] The influence of the tree diagram has been so pervasive throughout the modern sciences that architect/mathematician Christopher Alexander once took it upon himself to write an essay to explain how "A City Is Not a Tree"[10] (he proposed, instead of the tree, a somewhat more flexible and less hierarchic mathematical model for city planning, that of the "semi-lattice"). Such logical diagrams are invariably meant to shield clear thinking from digressions; they are supposed to be "not subject to the bias of language and experience," to quote Christopher Alexander once more.[11] And apart from the logic of tree diagrams and decision trees, trees also borrow from the authority of nature (the two combine in Darwin, whose *The Origin of Species* recapitulates all of evolution in one single tree-like diagram) and of religion (the tree of knowledge in the Garden of Eden).

What Byrne does in *Arboretum* is to wed the tree diagram, without further ado, to the most biased, subjective, and illogical forms of language and experience, especially to non-verbal experience. Next to all kinds of musical genres, styles of design, and corporeal gestures, the diagrams are full of the human, all-too human stuff that is usually supposed to be beneath the dignity of logic, so that dandruff on shoulders and pimple patterns come into a transformative relationship with urban planning and nanotechnology ("Pattern Recognition"), and crumbs in bed, stains, and used tissues somehow hook up with melodic fragments, partially read books, and photographs ("Selective Memories"). The physical experiences and fleeting preferences, prejudices, and mental associations of daily life are reconnected with the terminological hubs and spokes of the sciences, the humanities, and corporate business. The results are as funny as they are unsettling, in part because Byrne had the staying power to draw so many diagrams; the sheer amount adds to their power of conviction. It is as if all of the history, or rather, all of the myriad histories of mankind could be accommodated in this tree park.

David Byrne's own career certainly resonates in these diagrams. He had already used Venn diagrams in conceptual art pieces in the mid-1970s; he used Venn diagrams in *E.E.E.I.* and again in *Arboretum*. In his "Appendix A" in *E.E.E.I.*, Byrne writes about people (and emotions) being shaped by their surroundings:

> We assume that PEOPLE make organizations smart, when to our surprise it is more often the other way around. The idea that the cake results at least as much from the shape of the pan, the cooking and the timing than from its ingredients may run counter to some of our assumptions, but this idea is bolstered by numerous recent studies largely focused on the corporate world. [. . .] The revelation is that Organization is content.

Venn diagrams prove how circles, squares and blobs may suggest a new shape to the meaning of words. The way in which Byrne uses Venn diagrams to mold words into concepts that cover a certain shaped domain (known in mathematics as "sets"), which then can "logically" intersect and overlap with other sets, shows very well how the application of a logical-mathematical form can be simultaneously an act of what Frazer in his study of comparative mythology called "contagious magic," which is magic based on the principle that things that have once been joined must remain forever in a sympathetic relation.[12] Extrapolating, switching active and passive positions, and suggesting manifold connections between sublime and banal categories are other means that Byrne employs repeatedly in *Arboretum*.

Quite a few entries in the book are explicitly reflexive and self-reflexive. In the explanation that goes with Diagram 63, "The Evolution of Category," Byrne quotes Borges and Lévi-Strauss on the use of categories to introduce the point that "The way we categorize and perceive the world is sometimes based on what seem like arbitrary criteria." And he goes on:

> For example, there could be intersecting layers of categories: brown things, brown things that are alive, brown things that will hurt me, brown things that make nice pants material. One imagines a kind of plaid semi-translucent three-dimensional Venn diagram representing these categories and their intersections. The number of categories in the world is, therefore, larger than the number of things in the world.[13]

The phases of Byrne's career, from the beginnings of Talking Heads up to *Arboretum* itself, can also be recognized in these diagrams. Diagram 80, "Club Makes Culture," could apply to the experience of Talking Heads at CBGB and other clubs — or at least to Byrne's musings about CBGB as shaping the music in his essay "The Creative Algorithm." Byrne's commentary with Diagram 70, "Ideological Struggle," recalls the mall episode in *True Stories*: "Implicit in strip malls' bland packaging of retail opportunity is a belief that everything should be molded, shaped and presented within a clean modular shape. Implicit is a notion that THIS is democracy — in retail consumable form." Diagram 22, "Roots of War in Popular Song (Forest of No Return)," may easily be connected to Byrne's work with Robert Wilson, just as Diagram 57, "New Corporate Galaxies," might belong to *Your Action World*.

While *Arboretum* is an artistic experiment, the classifications of reality that it plays with are not without their political implications. The flexibility and reflexivity that *Arboretum* brings to its subjects cannot help to bring to light some domains where the rigid refusal of reflexivity is standard practice, and Byrne has certainly pointed out a few of these. "State Formalization of Obfuscation" (Diagram 79) is a tree of laws, declarations, and deal memos; its roots have names like "avoiding the subject," "confusing the issue," and "willfully misunderstanding." Byrne's pithy commentary in the back of the book is: "The laws that govern us, the constitutions and legal precedents, are often little more than elaborate rationales for avoiding the issue of how we shall live together." The tree diagram of "Ideological Struggle" (Diagram 70), mentioned in the previous paragraph, suggests that the culture of Happy Meals, Walt Disney, the Olsen twins, Hallmark cards, and more provides the fertile ground for the tree of U.S. military operations, with such reassuring names as "provide comfort," "desert shield," and "just cause." "Democracy is nothing if not the exercise of the will of the majority, an often ignorant, belligerent and naïve crowd," is the most pertinent part of Byrne's commentary. And while "The Roots of Consensual Science" (Diagram 23) is a diagram that suggests that respectable sciences like cybernetics, economics, and string theory have grown out of the domain of faith healers, fire walkers, and palm readers, Byrne writes in his comments that

> Economics, a fairly well established "science", might be said to be on the verge of heading the other way — of joining the horoscope readers, diviners and psychic readers that lie beneath and outside the realm of scientific acceptability. Economics' principal axiom, that people behave both rationally and in their own best interests, has been disproved time and again in recent years.

In *Arboretum*, such remarks are not elaborated, but in his journal Byrne often speaks out on the abuse of power that these remarks only touch upon.

4 THE REPRESENTATION OF POLITICS

In April 2001, Byrne organized a small exhibition of 20 news photos, "Gesture, Posture, and Bad Attitude in Contemporary News Photography." The show took place at Apexart, a small artspace in downtown Manhattan. Apexart stages monthly exhibitions, inviting a new artist or curator to organize each show, which should somehow challenge the received opinions about art. Byrne's concept for the exhibition was simple: he chose regular recent news photos that he had all enlarged to more or less the same size and printed in black and white, to help the viewer to see them as belonging together. The photos in themselves were unremarkable to anyone who reads newspapers. A dozen photos portray presidents and other political leaders shaking hands, making speeches, or exchanging a few words, immaculately suited and untouched. A few more photos show people in tumultuous, disorderly and dangerous scenes: South American Indians, dressed in loincloths, walking in a field of cut down trees; men pushing each other, running away from a cloud (tear gas?); a little girl smoking a cigar (is that a rifle behind her?). Such news photos are run of the mill, and as they are being shown without captions, without journalistic background information, they resemble the thousands of pages that we scan without reading, looking for something more interesting.

In an accompanying leaflet, Byrne explains his curatorial concept: "The photos I have chosen represent a documentation of a sort of choreographed performance. A dance of politics." His proposal is to consider his selection of press photos as if they represent an elaborate contemporary performance, taking place in over 100 cities. This imaginary production would be run simultaneously in all the world's capital cities (Robert Wilson's *the CIVIL warS* may come to mind, or an update of Edward Steichen's "Family of Man" exhibition). Like many postmodern choreographers, Byrne proposes to understand routines that are part of everyday life as dance forms with their own formal requirements. In the leaflet, Byrne writes:

The idea of a hidden choreographer whose company is entirely politicians and newsmakers might seem to be some ridiculous invention of mine, but maybe there is another kind of truth revealed here. Maybe there is a preferred set of gestures for use in politics — a set of movements that are not written down or described in any book, instruction manual or party pamphlet — but are nevertheless adopted by all who assign themselves to this profession. [. . .] Movements which obscure, obstruct, disguise and distract from the subject, from the text. Movements which say either what they mean, or exactly the opposite — sometimes the movements are the true content, and the speech or text is a mere distraction, a diversion.

Just as singers have stereotypical moves and gestures, so do those whose profession is the art of politics. It is learned by studying one's peers, one's predecessors and countless hours of TV viewing. Viewing with a special eye — for the ordinary member of the public seems to be completely unaware, at least consciously, of the staging and work that has gone into their news programs.

Byrne's small exhibition invites spectators to reconsider the presentation of politicians by the mass media. His subject is far from new. "Powerful people strut, and though the notion of power is as offensive to some as the strutting, there continue to be powerful people who continue to strut," is what sociobiologists Tiger and Fox write on the very first page of *The Imperial Animal*.[14] As another example, in 2002 Richard Schechner summarized the received wisdom about the public appearances of figures such as the American President:

> By now, everyone knows these kinds of activities are staged in every detail. Today's American Presidency — at least its public face — is a totally scripted performance. The President's words are written by professional speechwriters, the backdrops and settings are carefully designed for maximum effect, the Chief Executive himself well rehearsed. [. . .] Each detail is choreographed, from how the President makes eye contact (with the camera, with the selected audience at a town meeting), to how he uses his hands, dresses, and is made-up.[15]

The press photos Byrne selected for his small exhibition suggest a few things. Powerful people no longer strut so much as Tiger and Fox suggested: instead, they present themselves as respectable, trustworthy, calm, and reassuring. And news photographers have learned to capture the moments of this official presentation that show at least a semblance of spontaneous emotion and interaction. Their photos find momentary gestures in meetings that might be too dull to reproduce without the passion such gestures suggest — with the effect that politicians appear as both dignified and truly human. As a result, everyone else whose photograph gets printed in a political context cannot help but look unrestrained, awkward, and out of it, simply by contrast. The message, on the level of the choreography, is that their problems have to be their own fault, and that the causes and political positions they represent can't be as just and as dignified as those of the political leaders. The playing field is tipped in favor of those in power, putting everyone else at a disadvantage. "I believe that anyone who goes into politics should be treated with suspicion"[16] is Byrne's own conclusion.

Some six months before "Gesture, Posture and Bad Attitude in Contemporary News Photography," Byrne made two posters that related to the U.S. presidential elections. The posters showed big white plastic representations of the two

Figure 18 Byrne's posters of Bush and Gore masks put up on Manhattan's 16th Street in 2000.

contestants, Al Gore and George W. Bush; one the former vice-president, the other the son of a former president. Both white faces, each with small black eyeholes and wide photo-opportunity smiles, were photographed against a white background. Printed in bold letters on the bottom of each poster was just the word "Huh?"

Byrne photographed not actual masks, but the white supports that keep rubber masks from flopping around in their packages. This all-white version seemed less cartoony to him than the actual Halloween masks. He paid to have the posters put up, preferably in pairs next to each other, on walls and scaffolding on the streets of Los Angeles, Chicago, and New York.[17] In the context of Byrne's own work, these posters refer to his 1984 political posters (Next to the "CHOOSE/VOTE" poster, there was one with a photo of Ronald Reagan, with just the word "ACTOR" printed underneath), as well as to his artwork dealing with faces and dolls, and his "Crossed Wires" text about facial muscles that are pulled by a puppet master. The implied message is: these faces are really masks, look for the machinery beneath the surface. Explaining why he launched a poster campaign, Byrne said he felt voiceless in the present political and economic world, adding: "The system stinks. We should stop just accepting it and tell these plastic men to get lost."[18]

Figures 19 and 20 *Itsy-Bitsy Democracy/Big Fucking Democracy*, two photomontages by David Byrne and Danielle Spencer with the "Votomatic" used in Florida for the contested presidential elections of 2000.

Four years later, in 2004, designer/art director Danielle Spencer and David Byrne made another elections-related piece: *Itsy-Bitsy Democracy/Big Fucking Democracy* as part of "The Voting Booth Project."[19] For this show, organized by the Parsons School of Design, 50 designers and architects each remade or redesigned a "Votomatic," an aluminum suitcase that folds out into a booth that was used for the 2000 presidential elections in Florida. Since Bush and Gore came extremely close in that state, the confusing design of the Votomatic played a role in the highly controversial process deciding which candidate had won the Florida vote and the presidency. Spencer and Byrne made two photomontages of this voting machine in a precinct room. In one, the booth is so small it has to be meant for use by pre-schoolers only, in the other it is so tall that it is out of reach; the combination of the two makes for a mordant comment on a democratic process that oversimplifies all issues, and threatens to deliver the real processes of deliberation and decision into the hands of party oligarchs and sponsored lobbies.

5 WHO OWNS OUR EYES AND EARS?

Art has been at war with its own commodity character, to borrow a phrase of Walter Benjamin's, for a long time.[20] What is beautiful, interesting, or just

fascinating to look at has value, and is often made into exclusive property and used for profit, in the interests of some and not of all. The interest that many conceptual artists have shown for this struggle is just the latest phase in this history. In Byrne's work, two different aspects of this struggle stand out. On the one hand, there is the issue of reproduction and of copyright. This is a matter of great importance to Byrne:

"Almost everything I have experienced in my life: books, art, music, film, magazines, cars, furniture, clothes, fast or frozen food, even people sometimes, have been in reproduction. Copies. . . . But of course, this IS the authentic for my generation. The idea of an aura of authenticity surrounding an object is strange and foreign to us."[21]

Byrne has repeatedly taken a public position on matters of copyright, and on the influence of individual artists in a public sphere that is dominated by industrial media. But there is a crucial aspect of perception and reproduction that lies beyond the legal and economic issues of copyright, which Byrne describes as follows:

We tend to believe that it is the eye that sees, and the ear that hears. But those organs are merely the input devices — it is the brain that "sees" and "hears". The brain can, in this case, choose to ignore obvious imperfections and evidence and see only what it wants to see. I don't mean this in a metaphorical way — I mean it in an absolutely literal way — the brain only sees what it wants to see and disregards the rest. One can stare right at something and simply not see it. The contradictory information is simply not acknowledged. I don't mean "seen and later denied", but simply not seen at all. Denial is a built-in ability we have, it is essential for our survival.[22]

The circuits formed by these two forms of ownership are at the very heart of Byrne's work, going back to his earliest pieces and songs, such as his idea for a "Nielsen Rating System for the Arts." An explicit formulation of this circuit, but in the form of fiction, is the text "Lifestyle" in Byrne's book *Strange Ritual*. "Lifestyle" plays with the idea of a television channel that is dedicated completely to broadcasting the life of a single individual. (In 1998, three years after the publication of *Strange Ritual*, the Hollywood movie *The Truman Show* was built on similar premises. The success of TV "reality shows" where the camera follows groups of people like an omnipresent "big brother" is another example.) Byrne's text subtly turns on itself and becomes reflexive when a paragraph opens with "We shift our perspective and see the show from the point of view of various audience members." "Lifestyle" oscillates between fiction and philosophy, like the TV channel it depicts with the words "It's exploitative and metaphysical at the same time — the best of both worlds." Byrne emphasizes not the production of the program, but its reception: "The TV Audience talks about The Man — The Subject — all the time. He's a surrogate life. People begin adopting his mannerisms as their own." When he realizes the effect of his televised presence, the man begins to play with his power, which affects the habits of his audience and finally changes the very reality of the nation, even after the man has stopped appearing on television:

> The irrationality of the new life has extended beyond the personal, social, and political into the realm of time and space, which, for these individuals [those who did not personally take part in the "Lifestyle Revolution"] no longer behave as they once did. The physical world itself has become altered, and not just in the minds and behavior patterns of The Viewer Nation. The abstract has infected the concrete. Once seemingly exclusive properties flow with similarities. Where once there were no connections at all, now amazing interactions take place.

Over the course of his career, Byrne's work has become increasingly explicit about this circuit (vicious circle? hermeneutic circle?), to the point where it pervades all his work. As he wrote in his internet journal, there are

> campaigns, paid for by corporate clients, to raise the awareness and profile of a product by getting a small army of "agents" to drop a mention of the product into

casual conversation, carry it (in the case of a book) prominently displayed on the subway, write reviews to Amazon, ask for the product at shops, all without revealing that one is promoting it. [. . .]

And who knows, the same techniques and maybe the same companies use this process for inserting ideas, political opinions and "factoids" into normal society?

Do I sound paranoid? I'm not making this stuff up. I'm merely extrapolating, trying to determine the repercussions of this phenomena and what it means. [. . .]

Surprisingly, the ordinary people who are recruited to talk up the product are usually unpaid — they usually just get some free samples, and not enough of that to really financially compensate for all the time and effort they put in. But they're proud and thrilled to be the chosen ones, to be influential.[23]

This is the background against which Byrne's support for initiatives that try to give artists more authority over their work is best understood. One instance of this is his support for Creative Commons in 2004, contributing a song, "My Fair Lady," to a CD that was included in an issue of *Wired* magazine, together with the Beastie Boys, Chuck D, and a number of other musicians, including Gilberto Gil.[24] Gil and Byrne together also gave a benefit concert for this cause. Creative Commons is the attempt by Lawrence Lessig and others to introduce an alternative to the existing copyright, which in most instances has benefitted media corporations with legal departments much more than individual artists. (An example of the effects of copyright in practice is the story behind the Luaka Bop album *The Story of Black Peru*, as told by Heidi Carolyn Feldman. Some of the featured artists complained afterwards that Byrne had exploited them, since they never saw any money from this international release of their work.[25] Feldman writes about this: "The blame should not fall on David Byrne's shoulders but rather on the recording labels with which Lucila Campos and the other Peruvian artists originally signed their contracts."[26] The recording companies had bought all rights to songs in perpetuity, meaning they owned the material forever, so that when a new international audience was created for black Peruvian music, the responsibility to give the artists their share fell to them.) The existing practice of copyright also threatens to stifle forms of creativity that depend on the creative and transformative copying, sampling, and remixing of the copyrighted stuff that forms such an important part of the public environment — which amounts to a subtle form of censorship.

"David Byrne's Survival Strategies for Emerging Artists — and Megastars," an article Byrne published in the January 2008 issue of *Wired*, takes a stance that is close to that of Creative Commons: there is a middle ground between the artist signing away all rights to a big company, and having to take care of every aspect of one's work oneself. In the article, Byrne describes a range of six models for artists to work with record companies. These range from the "equity deal" model, in which the company has control over the full package, from recording to manufacturing, distribution, marketing, career advice, touring, and accounting, to complete self-reliance. Given the changes in technology, which have made recording and distribution easier and cheaper, Byrne proposes that artists should consider options in-between, options in which they control their own recordings and copyrights, and perhaps distribution and touring as well, according to their needs and possibilities. In the end, that could help artists to integrate their music in the social fabric, which is where it belongs, as Byrne writes.

From Byrne's point of view, fine art is as intertwined with business as music is. As he has expressed this, in New York "it seems fairly clear that despite the dream that art exhibitions, whether in galleries or in museums, are forums for complicated feelings and for new ideas, they are possibly more like car showrooms, where the latest models are paraded and applauded."[27] Accordingly, Byrne does not espouse the notion that viewing art is somehow morally uplifting and good for the viewer.[28] Nor is making art necessarily a directly inspired endeavor; "once an artist succeeds in branding his or her name, the system seems to favor steering the artist towards the repetition of that object, with slight variations, for decades. [. . .] With success, creativity often (not always) comes to a halt, and production begins."[29] Seen in this light, art is not categorically different from advertising. The two need to be redefined over and over again.

Two art projects made in 2003 by Byrne in collaboration with designer Danielle Spencer give examples of this process. *Corporate Signs* provides another look at a series of photos of corporate "tombstones," which was already included in *Your Action World*. This time, using Photoshop, the company names have been replaced by virtuous words like kindness, fairness, trust, hope and courage, in the same typeface the company uses. Both images, the original photo and the tweaked version, are then combined in a lenticular image, a process known from novelty cards and the like, which switches between the two images when the viewer changes his perspective slightly. The result brings out the grandiose pomposity that lurks half-hidden in so much corporate communication strategies. The *Corporate Signs* series was shown as part of "Illegal Art: Freedom of Expression in the Corporate Age," a travelling exhibition organized to highlight the ways in which copyright interferes with art. As a curatorial statement to the exhibition explains,

The laws governing "intellectual property" have grown so expansive in recent years that artists need legal experts to sort them all out. Borrowing from another artwork — as jazz musicians did in the 1930s and Looney Tunes illustrators did in

1940s — will now land you in court. If the current copyright laws had been in effect back in the day, whole genres such as collage, hiphop, and Pop Art might have never have existed.

The irony here couldn't be more stark. Rooted in the U.S. Constitution, copyright was originally intended to facilitate the exchange of ideas but is now being used to stifle it.

The Illegal Art Exhibit will celebrate what is rapidly becoming the "degenerate art" of a corporate age: art and ideas on the legal fringes of intellectual property. Some of the pieces in the show have eluded lawyers; others have had to appear in court.[30]

A series called *Fake Books*, also made by Byrne and Spencer, presents a humorous and slightly dizzying take on the art books on display in museum bookshops. It is a small series of covers for non-existent books, such as *The End of Reason: Essays in Non-Rational Logic*, edited by H. S. Perswary; the back cover presents a list of contributors and articles. These spoofs, mixing imaginary and real artists and authors, play on the authority of museums, museum bookshops and intellectual art discourse to provide anything and everything with an aura. They are also closely related to Byrne's own "epistemological" art books, *E.E.E.I.* and *Arboretum*, with their peculiar mixture of irony and seriousness.

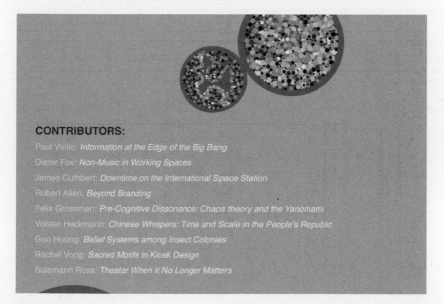

CONTRIBUTORS:

Paul Virilio: *Information at the Edge of the Big Bang*

Dieter Fox: *Non-Music in Working Spaces*

James Cuthbert: *Downtime on the International Space Station*

Robert Allen: *Beyond Branding*

Felix Grossman: *Pre-Cognitive Dissonance: Chaos theory and the Yanomami*

Volster Heckmann: *Chinese Whispers: Time and Scale in the People's Republic*

Guo Huong: *Belief Systems among Insect Colonies*

Rachel Vong: *Sacred Motifs in Kiosk Design*

Sulemann Ross: *Theater When It No Longer Matters*

Figure 21 Part of the back cover of one of the fake art books by Byrne and Danielle Spencer: *The End of Reason*. The colour-blindness tests included here are not recognizable in black-and-white.

6 PHILOSOPHY IN INSTALLMENTS

In March 2004, Byrne began to publish an internet journal, at http://journal. davidbyrne.com. It grew out of his habit of keeping a journal on tour, to send to friends, or, like the journal he wrote during the *Rei Momo* tour, for publication; but now he kept adding new entries, on tour or off. Written for a general audience, this is no intimate diary: it is the expression of a cosmopolitan life in music and art, with numberless reviews of concerts, exhibitions, and cities across several continents. Newspapers, scientific magazines, and books also provide Byrne with a good deal of input, widening the range of subjects so far that over the years, the journal has grown into a personal one-man encyclopedia. The casual format of a blog accommodates anything and everything, and sometimes Byrne just recounts stories or copies some fact that struck him. But many entries are carefully considered small essays, installments of an untiring philosophical questioning of the world that is by its very definition bound to remain unfinished and fragmentary: "I'm asking these questions of myself, how does this work, why does this happen, what's going on here."[31]

The journal is a mixed bag of museum shows, restaurants, cycling trips, movies, political commentary, Byrne's reportage of concerts, of the cities he visits: the charmed life of an internationally renowned artist. But underneath all this colorful diversity runs a questioning attitude, an insistent demand for reflexivity. And Byrne speaks his mind on politics without reserve. Before he took a stand against the U.S. invasion of Iraq in 2003, Byrne generally took the position that

> rather than feeling that to say something in a political way I have to speak the politician's language, I can say it in my own way. I don't have to say it in an article or statement about a specific policy or action, although I do occasionally, but for the most part it is in the work that I do. Political and social and cultural attitudes are in the work and that is where it should stay, that is the language I speak better.[32]

But in his journal, Byrne regularly gives vent to his disgust about the combination of neo-conservatism with big business that is so domineering.

Many entries read like the inside-out version of *Arboretum*: what was only indicated, suggested in the diagrams there is now discussed in full. Byrne doesn't take anything much for granted, and doggedly questions given cultural and mental frames, so that cognitive dissonance of some kind or other is the rule rather than the exception in his entries. He doesn't leave a subject alone until he has shown it in a light that makes it appear wondrously complex, quaint and eccentric, baring the projective devices that are typical of human psychology and of history. An example of this method is what Byrne notes about a visit to a Los Angeles TV studio, to the set where the *Big Love* series, for which he made music, was shot.

> I love these places — you're in the set and it's completely believable as a suburban home or an office and then you look up and there is no ceiling and huge AC hoses loom outside and the view through the window is a massive photo backdrop of the mountains that ring suburban Salt Lake City. These jarring juxtapositions are beautiful. In some ways they make what we consider homes, offices, bars — anything that can be turned into a set — seem completely hollow and superficial; they are mirrors of the real that make the real in turn seem fake. As if our comfortable notions of what constitutes the spaces that make up our lives are just made out of a familiar play of colors and shapes upon our retinas. Well, in some ways of course that's all our visual reality is, but we think of some of those spaces as "real" and we feel they are filled with the stuff of our real lived lives — but they are no different than these carefully faked copies. Especially out here where the built landscape is made of structures that are barely made to outlast a movie set. The mental dislocation is a wonderful feeling. It's somehow liberating.[33]

The journal entry in its entirety is only twice as long as this quote. It enfolds this methodological blueprint in the stuff of daily living, mentioning arrival at the airport, being picked up and driven to a hotel, taking a walk to get a feel of the suburban surroundings. Byrne describes that environment in terms that show it as fantasy turned into reality: there are no people to be seen on the sidewalks, the houses are new but suggest older styles, there is a shopping mall which imitates cozy village streets. Four photos, two taken outside and two inside, give the reader a visual impression of Byrne's trip, and they show the parallels between TV set and suburban reality: a photo of the real landscape is echoed by one of the studio imitation landscape, the real/fake streets in the shopping mall mirror a scene of trees in the studio, hacked off above the level that the cameras will show, backed by scaffoldings and studio lamps.

It is worthwhile to pick apart Byrne's description of this TV studio experience, to examine his conceptual moves up close. Point of departure is the set, beautiful because of its exemplary juxtaposition of convincing illusion and of the device, which both enables and undoes the illusion.

The next step is that he extrapolates from this demonstration: what goes for the studio set goes for every form of décor, every boxed-in version of reality, which gives it universal relevance: "the spaces that make up our lives" are at stake.

This, in turn, he connects to the nature of the human animal: "comfortable notions" of visual reality are not reality as such, they are mediated by the retina, shorthand for the biological and psychological propensities of the human eye and brain. Since Byrne invokes human nature as such, the problem he raises isn't a simple matter of truth versus illusion; visual reality is always in the end mediated by the eye; the Kantian "thing-in-itself" is forever beyond the grasp of human sight. The distinction between TV studio and outside reality is only gradual. Greater reality does not lie beyond illusion, but in the direction of the jarring juxtaposition of several illusions. Artistic standards of criticism are therefore applicable "out there."

Although he never confuses movie set and suburban cityscape, Byrne's method approaches both from an aesthetic perspective, which enables him to add their illusory qualities to each other. The result is a heightened sense of the symbolic qualities of human reality per se. And this heightened symbolic state, as off-hand as it is set down here, points in two directions, inside and outside. It points to the nature of the human animal (the retina, the play of colors and shapes) as well as to the nature of history (our real lives, the landscape out here). The "wonderful feeling" which is "somehow liberating" is the unsparing acceptance of this dislocation, which is both inclusive and alienating, and this sensation is found throughout the journal.

The main theme of the journal is the distortion of all kinds of meanings, by nature, by society, by individual delusion and denial. The play of these mechanisms of distortion, their combinations and interferences are endlessly absorbing, but when such distortions are combined and go unchecked, the effect may be disastrous.

The biological conditioning of human sensibility is a subject that crops up every so often. While this takes Byrne away from art and into the domain of the sciences, in the end such detours always add extra detail and contrast to the aesthetic and symbolic considerations that are his real concern. See for example the entry of June 9, 2008, when Byrne writes about the theory that people's brains contain "mirror neurons" that act in the same way when a person does something himself, or witnesses that same act performed by someone else. This allows people to understand another's mental state; they do not only decode the other, they also feel to some extent what the other feels. As Byrne summarizes this, "We feel for others because we become the others. Obviously, the neurons are not perfect mirrors, or we'd all be feeling way too much." Byrne then applies the notion of sets of mirror neurons to explain the work of actors, and the impression that dancers and sports athletes make on their audiences, and wonders to what extent computer-generated images might engage the mirror neurons of game players. Finally, he applies the idea to himself and his concerts, wondering whether his entire audiences sing with him? "Mentally at least, it appears they do [. . .] their vocal neurons firing with mine and yes, we become one hive mind. Sounds creepy, but that might be where the pleasure lies."

In an entry titled "Concepts & Sounds,"[34] Byrne copies two large chunks from a text by a professor of linguistics, John Whitman, describing several forms of onomatopoeia, words that imitate the sound of the thing they denote, as found in the Japanese language. Leaving out some examples, Whitman's text is:

> In addition to those onomatopoeia which imitate the sounds of nature, called gisei-go in Japanese, Japanese recognizes two additional types of onomatopoeia: one that basically suggests states of the external world (gitai-go), and another that basically names internal mental conditions and sensations (gijoo-go). There is some overlap between the two. [. . .] If the distinction between the external gitai-go and internal gijoo-go onomatopoeia isn't clear, there is good reason for this. While some of these forms are clearly descriptive of internal states, e.g., ira-ira "frustrated" (the Japanese press labeled the seemingly unending war between Iran and Iraq the "Ira-Ira War"), there are many which can be used to describe both external or internal states, for example, "gocha-gocha", which can quite accurately describe either the cluttered state of my office or that of my mind.[35]

Byrne's comment extrapolates from Whitman's observations in a characteristic way, suggesting that clear-cut distinctions between language, music, and reality are illusory:

> Can you imagine? States of mind have sounds?! Concepts have sounds!? Who'd 'a thunk it? It this a kind of synesthesia? So therefore a musical composition (musique concrete, most likely) COULD be a real map or analogy or model of a progression of concepts — a sonic map of a progression of thoughts . . . sometimes proceeding one after another, in traditional logical fashion, and sometimes overlapping, rushing onward, and sometimes happening simultaneously — as sounds certainly do, and maybe thoughts too?[36]

On a similar tack, reminding his readers that distinctions between seeing, mental representation and logic may be only provisional, Byrne adds the following notice to an entry on an unrelated subject:

> An interview in *Cabinet* magazine with a man who has invented a new form of symbolic logic. He also elucidates how symbolic systems like his (and like the Arabic numerals we use every day) make relationships visible and obvious — relationships that remain deep and hidden and obscure if we don't have the tools to help us visualize them.[37]

Another means that the human animal employs to organize reality, as basic in its own way as language and logic, is storytelling. Responding to a *New York Times* article that raises the question of why computer games aren't as emotionally engaging as older art forms and even myths, Byrne raises some further questions:

> Maybe narrative is like a religion — it is a way of explaining that things happen for a reason.
>
>   I wonder if there is a part of the brain that connects the perception of narrative to the amygdala — the center of ancient animal emotions like lust, pleasure and fear. Strands of connectivity that gives these forms their power . . . and their reason for existence. [. . .] Can there be such a thing as a narrative that emerges, by itself, from a seemingly random or chaotic structure or series of events?[38]

And after reading in *The New York Review of Books* about recent advances in evolutionary theory and embryology, which stress that relatively simple genes and genetic switches result in the growth of the endless variety of organs and organisms on the earth, Byrne comes to a conclusion that is the ultimate in inclusivity:

> Most life on Earth is, genetically speaking, one organism. I don't mean this metaphorically, I mean it literally. The various shapes and forms that life takes are ways that it, the über-organism, has found to occupy every available niche — but it is the always the same genetic framework that is being propagated everywhere, more or less.[39]

These entries, chosen from many examples that could also have served to make the point, present an alternative to some ingrained way of distinguishing between self and other, real and unreal, logic and illusion, and thus offer another "mental dislocation," another sense of heightened symbolic reality. This naturally leads to the question whether this heightened symbolic feeling is just a passing emotion, a fleeting sense of a wider reality. Can this well-rehearsed improvement on an overly narrow definition of consciousness, with its widening contextual circles, be put into practice? Within the journal, Byrne's answer to this question is formulated in response to a *New York Times* article, "Free Will: Now You Have It, Now You Don't,"[40] a review of current experiments by physicists, neuroscientists, and computer scientists that try to answer the question whether free will is just a human perception, in the final analysis an illusion, or a real material force. In his journal, Byrne first just mentions the article in passing, as he quotes with approval a metaphor used by the author, "that our conscious minds are like a monkey riding a tiger, who with powers of mind and reason, convinces himself that he is driving, is in control, when actually it is the massive tiger of the unconscious that will take little monkey for a ride."[41] Five weeks after this brief mention, Byrne published a long and well-considered text on free will, framing the subject in the context of the War in Iraq, which he opposed from the start. "Free Will, Part 2: Support Our Troops" is, at 3,400 words, 25 percent longer than the *New York Times* article: an essay rather than a diary entry.

Byrne begins by addressing the familiar arguments that allow responsibility to evaporate: soldiers have to follow orders, and the politicians who issue the orders to go to war cannot oversee the actions of individual soldiers who commit the atrocities that happen in war. He writes a harangue that piles up bitter and angry questions, addressing in turn the soldiers who actually pull the triggers, the workers in arms factories, the officers, the bureaucrats, and the top politicians, asking:

Do none of these folks bear any responsibility for their actions? Will Paul Brenner eventually step forward and say, "Oh, sorry, it was my fault, hang me too — I caused as many deaths as Saddam" —? Would Rummy [Donald Rumsfeld] take the heat? Will the gang who beat the war drums armed with lies and deception — Wolfowitz, Perle, Armstrong, Rice, Powell etc. — admit they hold responsibility for hundreds of thousands of deaths? Would Jeff Sacks admit he helped deliver the Russian people to the gangsters, KGB and oligarchs? Not likely.

I am reminded of the employees of most businesses whose owners are so distant that the employees never think or ask why they are doing something, how the product works, or just as often doesn't work, why a policy does or doesn't makes sense, or if a policy might even be counter-productive. Go into almost any store or office cubicle. Alienation, I believe Marx called it, based on his experience in Manchester during the industrial revolution. Most employees as a result of this disconnect simply cover their asses and have no personal investment in making things work better, knowing about the product they sell or how to fix it. It sometimes seems as if war, specifically the soldier, is the model for the alienated worker from his job. The workplace is modeled after the military. This can be a scary efficient machine, when all goes well.

[...]

How can the foot soldier, the poor grunt, the jarhead, be expected to be up on world politics, history, local culture and language — all the information one might need to weigh the morality of an action? The reporters and news media don't even do that, so how can the poor soldier be expected to be an informed citizen when the rest of the country isn't even made of informed citizens. The information to inform them is often so biased, skewed and spun that no intelligent decision can possibly be made. The citizens, here in the U.S. at least, are in a consumer trance most of the time anyway.

After giving his disgust and disappointment in the workings of the U.S. political and economic system a good airing, in the second half of his essay Byrne changes gear, setting himself the task of providing at least the seed for a positive approach. Under the heading "Circles of Responsibility," he sketches a contextualizing approach to the questions of free will and ethical action:

> If we assume that one does have some responsibility for one's actions then I ask myself how wide does that responsibility extend? [. . .] I would personally love to be more absolutist — to say that every person has a moral obligation to justify his or her own actions. To say that every person has an obligation to dig for the truth and then act accordingly. That every person is responsible for their own actions. All of them. Everyone is accountable. 100%. I would love to take an absolutist stance and say that we all have a duty to know what we are doing. However, I know that absolutism, black and white, good and evil — those hard, clear, simple divisions are how we get into the violent messes in the first place. [. . .] Morality and common sense are fuzzy — they're not forms of binary logic. They do exist, as concepts, and they do guide and inform our behavior, and their levels do seem to rise and fall. But they're slippery to define. The fever of war sweeps over a people and common sense, morality and reason sink to a frightening low. How do we discourage this fever, this disease, and keep the levels or common sense high and the social body free from infection? Is there such a thing as a psychology of nations, of people? Do nations get neurotic? Crazy? Sad and angry? Bitter and resentful? Proud and arrogant? I think maybe they do.

Byrne's conclusion can only spell out the underlying principle that supports his journal just as it supports his work as an artist: "Context, compassion, common sense and reason can be encouraged and even learnt."

And this is where Byrne sees the role of art in the wider scheme of things. Art has the capacity of shifting the center of attention, of transporting one from routine to heightened emotion, from the accepted scheme of things into the mythological perspective, the scientific view, the foreign culture, the disruptive logic that still can't be dispelled. Then, suddenly, the world and a song can illuminate each other. Little by little, by installment, participating in such temporary shifts of transportation may lead to a more lasting transformation, bring about a little more reason, more context, and more compassion.

7 *BICYCLE DIARIES*: A COMPARATIVE MYTHOLOGY OF CITIES

In 2009, Byrne published his seventh book, *Bicycle Diaries*. Illustrated with lots of black and white photos and a few drawings, this is his first prose book, grown out of his journals. The book's point of entry in the world is the liberating sensation of the cyclist: autonomous, out in the open air, faster than pedestrians, with more opportunities to look around and from a better vantage point than that of most car drivers. As Byrne took a bike with him on his tours and travels for almost 30 years, he can write from experience about cycling in cities almost throughout the world; *Bicycle Diaries* covers cities strewn across five continents.

The meat and potatoes of the book is Byrne's advocacy for cycling as means of urban transport. Throughout the book, he supports forms of city planning that give pride of place to cyclists and pedestrians, and encourage a lifestyle that is informal, and full of opportunities for everyone to meet and mingle, making cities more livable. As he recalls in the book, in 2007, working with *The New Yorker*, Byrne initiated a meeting in New York City's Town Hall to give a little push to making his hometown more bike-friendly. The planning of cities and neighborhoods is a far-reaching matter, which Byrne delves into with gusto. In a chapter on the many American cities that aren't bike-friendly but car-friendly, and thus frustrate anyone who looks for a more informal exchange, Byrne explains how this is the result of a hundred years of modern urban development based on car transport. It is a story that Byrne summarizes in no uncertain terms as "an undeclared civil war in which the car is winning. The losers are our cities and in most cases African Americans and Latinos."[42]

As a diary, the book veers away from cycling every so often, to go off on tangents about history, music, art, animals: anything that strikes Byrne's fancy. If there is an underlying theme, it is that cities are mythology made visible, and can be read as so many portraits of mankind. Byrne reveals his method of portrayal in a summary way in the introduction. Cities, he writes there, are

> physical manifestations of our deepest beliefs and our often unconscious thoughts, not so much as individuals, but as the social animals we are. [. . .] It's all there, in plain view, right out in the open; you don't need CAT scans and cultural anthropologists to show you what's going on inside the human mind; its inner workings are manifested in three dimensions, all around us. Our values and hopes are sometimes awfully embarrassingly easy to read. [. . .] Riding a bike through all this is like navigating the collective neural pathways of some vast global mind.[43]

Cities, as seen by Byrne, are compounded of mythic material. In Byrne's philosophy, there is no fixed identity: whatever subject he turns his attention to turns out to be determined at least in part by myth. This is true first and foremost of the modern city itself, influenced by the utopian visions of modern architects and city planners such as Le Corbusier, who presented themselves as purely rational. Modern architecture, found around the world, represents in Byrne's optic a collective desire for a fresh start, an emotional logic that wishes for an escape from the symbolic prison of history.[44] This logic has been common to both capitalism and communism: "These buildings represent the triumph of both the cult of capitalism and the cult of Marxist materialism."[45] As history continues, Byrne ironically describes these buildings now as "one vast global conceptual monument, whose parts and pieces are spread across the world's cities and suburbs."[46] Similarly, when riding through a suburban industrial park in Ohio, completely anonymous and perfectly manicured, Byrne notes that, while the "landscape has retained its surface familiarity, virtually, but the deep reasons for its existence — the social and sensual — have been eliminated," and he identifies such non-spaces with a form of religious fundamentalism.[47]

Just as cities are inherently mythical entities to Byrne, so are other basic categories. He insists that the idea that each human being is unique is an enormous self-deception;[48] in many important respects people are stamped by their culture, shaped by the infrastructure of their cities: "The city is a 3-D manifestation of the social and personal."[49] This porous, osmotic, mimetic exchange also means that people are more complex than they are usually imagined to be: "What we are is somehow simultaneously 'infinite,' but always similarly shaped."

Byrne accordingly presents people and their reality as infinitely interesting, an open-air cabinet of curiosities, or *Wunderkammer*, where everything is full of manifold meanings, and nothing belongs to only one simple category. "I wouldn't be surprised if poetry — poetry in the broadest sense, in the sense of a world filled with metaphor, rhyme, and recurring patterns, shapes, and designs — is how the world works. The world isn't logical, it's a song."[50] And he fully accepts the logical outcome of this, that most everything in the world can be experienced aesthetically, as a work of art:

> My definition of what is good art is, I'm afraid, pretty wide, and it isn't determined by the biography of its creator. I don't care who or what made it. For me the art happens between the thing — any thing — and the viewer's eye (or mind). Who or what made it is irrelevant.[51]

This confrontation of the modern city with a Romantic philosophy isn't without precedents. In the 1920s, surrealist novelist Louis Aragon described Paris, and the nineteenth-century shopping arcades that were at that time falling into disuse and disrepair, as reservoirs of modern mythology,[52] where every shop window could hold wondrous revelations. Walter Benjamin was very much taken by Aragon's novel, *Le Paysan de Paris* (*Paris Peasant*), and proceeded to write a history of nineteenth-century Paris, understood simultaneously as capital of the arts and showcase for the arts of capitalism, in *The Arcades Project*.[53] Byrne would most likely have no trouble at all in underwriting what Benjamin wrote about capitalism:

> A religion may be discerned in capitalism — that is to say, capitalism serves essentially to allay the same anxieties, torments, and disturbances to which the so-called religions offered answers. . . .
>
> Capitalism is the celebration of a cult *sans rêve et sans merci* [without dream or mercy]. There are no "weekdays." There is no day that is not a feast day, in the terrible sense that all its sacred pomp is unfolded before us; each day commands the utter fealty of each worshiper. . . .
>
> It adds to our understanding of capitalism as a religion to realize that, to begin with, the first heathens certainly did not believe that religion served a "higher," "moral" interest but that it was severely practical. In other words, religion did not achieve any greater clarity then about its "ideal" or "transcendental" nature than modern capitalism does today.[54]

Byrne mentions in his *Bicycle Diaries* how in the early 70s he was interested in hippie utopianism as embodied in the *Whole Earth Catalog*, but soon found that he was more interested in irony. Irony still is an important characteristic of his worldview, as he discerns myths in forms of human behavior that people usually prefer to think of either as purely rational or as incontrovertible truth. But it is important to acknowledge that Byrne's irony is structural, as the worldview he puts forward ranges everything under mythology. While irony is regularly associated with a condescending indifference, Byrne's irony produces the exact opposite: a greater involvement. This explains why Byrne's irony does go together well with his advocacy for bicycles as a serious form of city transportation, and with his insistence that the recent economic downturn might be an opportunity to create a better life, with better neighborhoods with many different kinds of people and businesses.[55] And he quotes Columbian politician and city planner Enrique Peñalosa:

> In developing world-cities, the majority of people don't have cars, so I will say, when you construct a good sidewalk, you are constructing democracy. A sidewalk is a symbol of equality . . . If democracy is to prevail, public good must prevail over private interests.[56]

If everything humans can see and do is pervaded by myths, all the more reason to bring forward those that point in the direction of happiness.

8 CONCLUSION

"The poet uses things and words like a keyboard,"[57] Novalis wrote, and his definition of poetry fits Byrne's work unusually well. It is Byrne's extraordinary accomplishment to sustain a style that consists of constant reinvention over the course of 35 years. His songs and videos, photos and books, films and writings, and installations and shows are all fragments of a single body of work. By making his art the medium for many different musical genres, visual icons, and myths, Byrne prefers the prosaic, level-headed quality that results from the comparison between styles over the enthusiasm and euphoria that a single exclusive style may evoke. In this respect his work coincides with the idea that was brought forward by many of the best Romantic artists and thinkers, from Novalis to Walter Benjamin, namely that prose can be the highest form of poetry.[58]

Byrne's portfolio of artistic comparisons challenges the fixed notions that are used to distinguish routinely between forms of art. By refusing to function within the fixed categories of the popular versus the artistic (or authentic, or avant-garde, or "high art"), Byrne's work often manages to scratch where it itches, where separations between categories and genres become uncomfortable and even painful. This hasn't escaped the attention of curators and musicologists, as the following three quotations of Byrne's work prove. The first of these appears in the catalogue of the great "Magiciens de la Terre" ("Magicians of the Earth") exhibition, held in Paris in 1989 to commemorate the French Revolution. "Magiciens de la Terre" combined pieces by contemporary Western artists with work of artists/sculptors/builders/shamans working in decidedly other traditions; the exhibition had the express intention of doing away with the insurmountable gap between Western artists and their non-Western (once labeled "primitive") counterparts. Such a historical gap can't be erased by a single exhibition, however ambitious in its dimensions, and "Magiciens de la Terre" was later debated extensively by art historians studying this disruptive field. What matters here is that Jean-Hubert Martin, chief curator of the exhibition, chose a line from Byrne's song "Totally Nude" (of the Talking Heads album *Naked*) as a motto for his catalogue essay: "So civilized / I guess you wonder where you are").

A second instance is found in *Politics-Poetics*, the catalogue for the tenth Documenta in Kassel, Germany in 1997. The thick catalogue is an extravagant attempt to condense the history of the arts (and of philosophy, and of urbanization, and of politics) after World War II. Page 88 shows a photo from Byrne's

Strange Ritual, one of the slightly chaotic scenes of urban life that he called "minor sacraments," "Corner vending machine, Tokyo."

A third example of such unobtrusive quoting occurs in an article by two musicologists, Susan McClary and Robert Walser: "Start Making Sense! Musicology Wrestles with Rock." The authors don't mention Byrne or Talking Heads, but there is no doubt that *Stop Making Sense* was on their mind, just as it is no accident that the title of their concluding paragraph is "Fear of Music." The fear of music as described by McClary (the intellectual prima donna of what is called "the new musicology") and Walser is the academic fear of the dance, the body, the infective gestures, heat, euphoria, and emotions that are an important key to the popularity of music, yet are by definition excluded from a musicology that analyzes music in terms of the written score. These examples speak of the reverberations of Byrne's work, the widening circles it draws around itself.

Byrne's work, in song and in other arts, is always an exercise in emotional contagion, comparison, and compassion. "Other people's problems, they overwhelm my mind," as a line has it in his song "No Compassion" from the first Talking Heads album. Some ten years later, Byrne's song "Television Man" deals with the same thematic: television viewing is described there as "the world crashes in, into my living room" (from the *Little Creatures* album). An ongoing question raised throughout is how, and when, people respond, and respond with compassion and empathy, to the signals they pick up from their surroundings. The generic question may be formulated as: the self is a cloud, and the circumstances are also a cloud: under which conditions does the inner cloud respond to the outer cloud, or even acknowledge aspects of it? Human beings need stories and songs, mythologies that put a face on otherwise nebulous circumstances; where such forms are absent or lacking, one cloud moves through the other without noticing it, without any compassion.

About the shyness, the reluctance to demonstrate empathy and compassion that are characteristic of people with Asperger's syndrome, it has been said that it may not result from a lack of feeling, but from excessive sensitivity, or "overwhelm":

> As regards the failure of empathetic response, it would appear that at least some people with autism are oversensitive to the feelings of others rather than immune to them, but cannot handle the painful feed-back that this initiates in the body, and have therefore learnt to suppress this facility.[59]

To Byrne personally, the self-fashioning aspect of this is his successful overcoming of his crippling shyness that he has compared to a form of Asperger's syndrome.[60]

Byrne's work puts forward that this goes for all people: what is noticed, seen, heard, and what goes unnoticed, remains unseen, evokes no compassion, is not at all a given, is not a fixed ratio. Context may be added, compassion may find adequate forms of expression, alternative mythologies can be brought to bear. By singing songs that do not give expression to everyday psychological verities, but that focus on patterns of compassion and denial, songs that inform emotional clouds of their circumstances and that provide the flow of pseudo-empathy that is aroused by television with an oppositional perspective, Byrne opens up reservoirs of compassion that might otherwise have remained unnoticed. His songs stand out as algorithms for new, reconfigured feelings.

Acknowledgments

This book would not have been possible without David Byrne's help, not only in answering my questions but also in providing me with catalogs, films, and other material that would otherwise have been inaccessible. At Todomundo, Byrne's offices, Danielle Spencer answered my seemingly unending queries, and helped me get the illustrations for this book and their indispensable copyright clearances. Rachel Edelman helped out to complete the bibliography of Byrne's writings.

Hans Kloos (Amsterdam) and Gregory Maass (Seoul) read my chapters as soon as I completed them and provided me with their commentary and friendship. David Barker and Katie Gallof of Continuum Books, New York, supported this project from the moment it reached their desks.

The process of writing has been unexpectedly long and sometimes tortuous, as it was interrupted time and again by other obligations, unforeseen delays, and illness. Through it all, Josh Moll gave me her encouragement and support, for which she has my heartfelt gratitude.

Notes

Notes to Introduction

1 *Untitled Patton/Byrne Piece*, directed by Wholphin, on *Wholphin No. 1*, published by McSweeney's, 2006.
2 Byrne, interviewed by Marco Puntin: *Il Progetto*, 4, Trieste, Italy, December 1998, p. 6.
3 Byrne: *Bicycle Diaries*, p. 194.
4 Byrne: *Journal*, May 20, 2008. Online: http://journal.davidbyrne.com/2008/05/index. html
5 Kosuth: *Art after Philosophy and after*, p. 91.
6 Cf. Roberta Smith: "Conceptual art," in Stangos (ed.) *Concepts of Modern Art: From Futurism to Postmodernism*, p. 260.
7 Byrne, interviewed by the author, February 22, 1999.
8 Howell: *David Byrne*, p. 14. See pp. 11–14 of that book and Miles: *Talking Heads*, p. 18, for descriptions of these concerts. The full name of The Kitchen was The Kitchen Centre for Video and Music; on its historical role, see Goldberg: *Performance Art: From Futurism to the Present*, p. 181.
9 Cf. Byrne: *Journal*, April 15, 2006, where he describes himself as he was more than 30 years ago, "a peculiar young man, borderline Asperger's, I would guess." Available online: http://journal.davidbyrne.com/2006/04/index.html
10 Byrne, interviewed by Marco Puntin: *Il Progetto*, 4, Trieste, December 1998.
11 On Byrne's solo album *Rei Momo*.
12 Byrne: *Journal*, August 22, 2005. Online: http://journal.davidbyrne.com/2005/08/ index.html
13 Eric Lorberer: "David Byrne Talking Back," *Rain Taxi*, 16, Winter 1999/2000. Available online: www.davidbyrne.com/art/yaw/about/rain_taxi_interview_yaw_sr.php
14 Beer: *Brain of the Firm*, p. 229.

15 Ibid., p. 25.

16 Ibid., pp. 9, 27, 62, and 113.

17 Eno: "The Studio as Compositional Tool," p. 129.

18 Eno: *A Year with Swollen Appendices*, pp. 293–97.

19 Quoted by Rick Poynor in Eno and Mills: *More Dark than Shark*, p. 101.

20 Byrne, quoted in Miles: *Talking Heads*, p. 41.

21 Miles: *Talking Heads*, pp. 47–48.

22 Davis: *Talking Heads: A Biography*, p. 134.

23 Schecter: "Beyond the Text: S(h)ifting through Postmodernism," p. 178.

24 Hebdidge: *Hiding in the Light: On Images and Things*, p. 234.

25 Derrida: *Of Grammatology*, p. 158.

26 Gombrich: Preface to the sixth edition of *Art and Illusion: A Study in the Psychology of Pictorial Representation*, p. xv.

27 Taussig: *Mimesis and Alterity*, p. xv.

28 Ibid., p. xvi.

29 Ibid., pp. xviii–xix.

30 Byrne, interviewed in Howell: *David Byrne*, pp. 82 and 83.

31 Rosen and Zerner: *Romanticism and Realism*, p. 5.

32 Ibid., pp. 18, 30, 35, and 38.

33 LeWitt, quoted in Heiser: "A Romantic Measure," in Heiser: *Romantic Conceptualism*, p. 137.

34 Verwoert: "Impulse Concept Concept Impulse. Conceptual Art and its Provocative Potential for the Realisation of the Romantic Idea," in Heiser: *Romantic Conceptualism*, p. 174.

35 Cf. Behler: *German Romantic Literary Theory*, p. 300. According to Friedrich Schlegel specialist Behler, the early Romantics anticipated and displayed many features of literary modernity, but it assumes a twisted posture toward modernism that is marked by a radical reflection on its conditions.

36 Andreas Michel and Assenka Oksiloff: "Romantic Crossovers: Philosophy as Art and Art as Philosophy," in Schulte-Sasse, *et al.*: *Theory as Practice: A Critical Anthology of Early German Romantic Writings*, pp. 158–59.

37 All the following quotations are from "Earliest Program for a System of German Idealism," in Schulte-Sasse, *et al.*: *Theory as Practice*, pp. 72–73. Likely authors of this text are Schelling, Hegel, and Hölderlin. It is generally considered to be a manifesto of early Romanticism. Cf. Braeckman: *De waarheid van de kunst*, passim.

38 Mittman and Strand, "Representing Self and Other in Early German Romanticism," in Schulte-Sasse, *et al.*: *Theory as Practice*, p. 51.

39 Frank: *Einführung in die frühromantische Ästhetik*, p. 222; author's translation of: "Ich nenne 'romantisch' die Philosophie, in der die Spekulation auf den Anspruch verzichtet, das Absolute durch Reflexion zu erreichen — und diesen Mangel durchs Medium der Kunst supplementiert."

40 Novalis: "Fichte Studies," in Schulte-Sasse, *et al.*: *Theory as Practice*, p. 108.

41 Cf. Frank: *Einführung in die frühromantische Ästhetik*, p. 300. The term "negative dialectic" refers to T. W. Adorno.

42   Tieck: "Eine gute Verwirrung ist mehr wert, als eine schlechte Ordnung." Quoted in Frank: *Einführung in die frühromantische Ästhetik*, p. 48.

43   Novalis: *Werke*, p. 334.

44   Novalis, in Frank: *Einführung in die frühromantische Ästhetik*, p. 270. Translations by the author.

45   Novalis: *Werke*, pp. 310–11.

46   Michel and Oksiloff: "Romantic Crossovers: Philosophy as Art and Art as Philosophy," in Schulte-Sasse, *et al.*: *Theory as Practice*, p. 174.

47   Ibid., p. 175. According to Novalis, art is the most substantial reality: "Je poetischer, je wahrer" ("The more poetical, the more true"). Novalis: *Werke*, p. 413.

48   Jochen Fried, in Behler and Hörisch: *Die Aktualität der Frühromantik*, p. 175.

49   Michel and Oksiloff, in Schulte-Sasse, *et al.*: *Theory as Practice*, p. 176.

50   Ibid., p. 177.

51   Quoted in Behler: *German Romantic Literary Theory*, p. 296.

52   Ibid., p. 237.

53   Ibid., pp. 239–40.

54   Cf. Schulte-Sasse, *et al.*: *Theory as Practice*, p. 291.

55   Benjamin: *Selected Writings, Volume 1*, p. 129.

56   Novalis, quoted in Benjamin: *Selected Writings, Volume 1*, p. 139, translation altered.

57   Schlegel, quoted in Benjamin: *Selected Writings, Volume 1*, p. 131.

58   Cf. Benjamin: *The Concept of Criticism* in *Selected Writings, Volume 1*, p. 195, note 216, on the wholly false modernization of Romantic doctrines. Thus, the suspicion that Romanticism is nothing but the subjectivation of aesthetics, based on Kant's concept of the genius, is unfounded. This fear has been expressed by Gadamer in the first part of his *Truth and Method*; cf. Frank, *Einführung in die frühromantische Ästhetik*, p. 127.

59   For a more extensive overview of this critical Romanticism, its continuation in the work of Walter Benjamin and Th. W. Adorno, and its relevance for the present, see my book *We Are the Noise between Stations*, pp. 239–321.

60   Byrne is not a philosopher, and has not written at length about his affinities with either Romanticism or postmodernism. But his *Journal* does contains reflections such as these: "I suspect that digital thinking, binary logic, the yes/no, pass/fail, good/evil legacy of the enlightenment in some ways fails to match the pragmatic needs of dealing with the real world. [. . .] But ultimately, breaking the world down into ones and zeros is a form of absolutism" (Byrne: *Journal*, February 7, 2007; online: http://journal.davidbyrne.com/2007/02/index.html) and "Advertising and branding breaks free from the Enlightenment Cartesian mechanistic view of the universe" (Byrne: *Journal*, February 3, 2005; online: http://journal.davidbyrne.com/2005/02/index.html).

61   Both are part of Byrne's *Envisioning Emotional Epistemological Information*.

62   Byrne: *True Stories*, p. 15.

63   Byrne, interviewed by Ken Coupland: *Graphis, International Journal of Graphic Art and Applied Art*, 313, 1998, p. 98.

Notes to Chapter 1: Stripping Down Rock Songs

1   Bowman, in *Fa fa fa fa fa fa*, p. 22, mistakenly writes that Byrne was admitted to MIT. Rectification David Byrne, mail to the author, September 30, 2009.

2   Byrne: "Autobiography." Available online: www.abc.net.au/rage/guest/2002/davidbyrne. htm

3   Ibid.

4   Ibid.

5   Byrne, quoted in Howell: *David Byrne*, p. 15.

6   Charles Harrison: "Art & Language: Enkele condities en interesses van de eerste tien jaar," in *Art & Language: De Schilderijen*, pp. 12–13.

7   On the history of Art & Language and Kosuth see Gabriele Guercio: "Introduction," especially note 15, in Kosuth: *Art after Philosophy and After*, p. xlii and p. 127, note 2.

8   Kosuth: *Art after Philosophy and After*, pp. 107–28.

9   Cf. Keesing: *Cultural Anthropology*, p. 537f.

10 Kosuth, quoting Scholte, in ibid., p. 119.

11 The letter stating this question is reproduced in Davis: *Talking Heads: A Biography*, pp. 85–86.

12 Ibid., p. 34.

13 Cf. Byrne: *Journal*, April 15, 2006. Online: http://journal.davidbyrne.com/2006/04/index.html. See also Jamie Dalglish's website: www.morphoglyph.com

14 Nielsen is the company that collects viewer ratings for the U.S. television system. (For an overview of the effect of such ratings on American mass media, see Herman and Chomsky: *Manufacturing Consent*, pp. 14–18).

15 Byrne, quoted in Miles: *Talking Heads*, p. 2. Quotation slightly emendated by Byrne, mail to author, 30 September, 2009.

16 . Byrne: introduction to *What the Songs Look Like*, p. 14.

17 Cf. "David Byrne Talking Back," interviewed by Eric Lorberer: *Rain Taxi*, 16, Winter 1999/2000.

18 See Heylighen and Joslyn: "Cybernetics and Second-Order Cybernetics."

19 Wiener: *Cybernetics*, pp. 25 and 164.

20 Wiener: *God and Golem, Inc.*, p. 36.

21 Alexander: *Notes on the Synthesis of Form*, p. 59.

22 Beer: *Brain of the Firm*, p. 25.

23 Ibid., p. 27.

24 Wiener: *Cybernetics*, p. 159.

25 In Beer's book, this figure represents the interrelationship between any coupling in a body or a firm between the four subsystems comprised of "internal sensory events," "external sensory events," "internal motor events," and "external motor events." Beer's original caption for this illustration is: "Ashby-type self-vetoing homeostasis operating between any two areas of figure 25. Each dot represents a total configuration of the system; dots contained in circles represent satisfactory states. The two systems are in equilibrium, because the trajectories of each (thick lines) remain within the circles." Beer: *Brain of the Firm*, p. 146.

26   Bateson: *Steps to an Ecology of Mind*, p. 132.

27   Ibid., p. 145.

28   Ibid., p. 136.

29   Ibid., p. 438.

30   Davis: *Talking Heads: A Biography*, p. 38.

31   Byrne, in "David Byrne Talking Back," interviewed by Eric Lorberer: *Rain Taxi*, 16, Winter 1999/2000.

32   Byrne: "The Creative Algorithm," in Kristal and Byrne: *CBGB & OMFUG*, pages unnumbered.

33   Beer: *Brain of the Firm*, p. 21.

34   Byrne: "The Creative Algorithm," in Kristal and Byrne: *CBGB & OMFUG*, pages unnumbered.

35   Byrne: *Envisioning Emotional Epistemological Information*, Appendix A.

36   Davis: *Talking Heads: A Biography*, p. 113, and Rockwell: *All American Music*, p. 238.

37   Howell: *David Byrne*, p. 12.

38   Bowman: *Fa fa fa fa fa fa*, p. 84.

39   On *Talking Heads: 77*; the song is "No Compassion."

40   Byrne: *Journal*, May 20, 2008. Online: http://journal.davidbyrne.com/2008/05/index.html

41   Byrne, quoted in Miles: *Talking Heads*, pp. 13 and 26.

42   Byrne, quoted in Miles: *Talking Heads*, pp. 30–31.

43   Byrne: mail to the author, 30 September, 2009.

44   Wayne Zieve, quoted in Davis: *Talking Heads: A Biography*, p. 43.

45   Weymouth, quoted in Miles: *Talking Heads*, p. 14.

46   Rockwell: "Talking Heads: Cool in Glare of Hot Rock," *New York Times*, Wednesday, March 24, 1976, p. 25.

47   Bowman: *Fa fa fa fa fa fa*, p. 82.

48   Miles: *Talking Heads*, p. 11.

49   Cf. the chapter on Randy Newman in Greil Marcus: *Mystery Train*.

50   Howell: *David Byrne*, p. 18.

51   See Davis: *Talking Heads: A Biography*, pp. 24–25, 29, and 45.

52   According to Bowman, *Fa fa fa fa fa fa*, p. 37, the song has part of its origin in an ironic/cheesy use of "psycho killer" as a description for all kinds of people. This irony, however, is no longer traceable in the song lyric.

53   Cf. Miles: *Talking Heads*, p. 30.

54   Some examples of lines: "I'm not a burning building," "Two different houses surround you," "I'm visiting houses in motion," "And you may find yourself living in a shotgun shack . . . And you may find yourself in a beautiful house, with a beautiful wife," all from *Remain in Light*; the song "Burning Down The House" on *Speaking in Tongues*; the many houses, rooms, homes, and cities on *The Catherine Wheel*, which also contains the lines "There's a train running through / Right through the middle of the house"; and Byrne's later solo album *Rei Momo*, containing the line "I walk like a building."

55   Byrne once compared this lyric to an Alain Robbe-Grillet novel: "just recording things
     . . . just description." Miles: *Talking Heads*, p. 37.
56   Davis: *Talking Heads: A Biography*, pp. 77–79.
57   Eno: *A Year with Swollen Appendices*, p. 293.
58   Ibid., p. 34.
59   Eno, quoted in Davis: *Talking Heads: A Biography*, p. 74.
60   Davis: *Talking Heads: A Biography*, p. 91.
61   Byrne, quoted in Miles: *Talking Heads*, p. 36.
62   Unpublished interview by the author with David Byrne, March 1990.
63   Byrne: e-mail to the author, May 14, 1999.
64   Tiger and Fox: *The Imperial Animal*, p. 15. Compare Edward O. Wilson: *On Human
     Nature*, p. 76: "An organism can be guided in its actions by a feedback loop: a sequence
     of messages from the sense organs to the brain schemata back to the sense organs and
     on around again until the schemata 'satisfy' themselves that the correct action has ben
     completed."
65   Ibid., p. 20.
66   Ibid., p. 22; italics in the original.
67   Ibid., pp. 14–15.
68   Ibid., pp. 122–23.
69   Ibid., p. 80.
70   Ibid., p. 110.
71   Ibid., p. 218.
72   Ibid., p. 5.
73   For a critical recent overview of evolutionary psychology and sociobiology see Steven
     Rose: "Escaping Evolutionary Psychology," in Rose and Rose (eds.): *Alas, Poor Darwin*.
     London: Jonathan Cape, 2000.
74   See Miles: *Talking Heads*, p. 40. Other sources of inspiration for the album *Fear of
     Music* that Byrne mentioned are Randy Newman's record *Good Old Boys*, Neil Young
     records, Oliver Sacks' book of neurological essays *Awakenings*, and records by the
     British new wave group Wire.
75   M. Critchley: "Musicogenic Epilepsy," in Critchley and Henson (eds.): *Music and
     the Brain*, p. 347. According to Critchley, one in ten million adults is the victim of
     musicogenic epilepsy, many of them with musical abilities above the average. Ibid.,
     p. 349.
76   Sacks: *The Man Who Mistook His Wife for a Hat*, p. 177.
77   Ibid., p. 42.
78   Ibid.
79   Ibid., p. 50.
80   Ibid., p. 48.
81   Ibid., p. xi.
82   See Miles: *Talking Heads*, p. 39, and Davis: *Talking Heads: A Biography*, p. 99.
83   "Sentences on Conceptual Art," reprinted in *Sol LeWitt*, MoMA catalogue, 1978,
     p. 168.
84   Davis: *Talking Heads: A Biography*, pp. 99–100. Byrne's view of animals' consciousness

may have been influenced by what Bateson writes in *Steps to an Ecology of Mind*: "dreams and animal behavior are similar in important respects, as both deal in opposites, have no tenses, have no negation, work by metaphor and do not pin their metaphors down" (pp. 57–58). This reads more or less like the formula for Byrne's lyrics on *Fear of Music*.

85   "The electric guitar, central sound of rock, has always been treated personally: the archetypical rock image is the guitar hero." Frith: *Sound Effects*, p. 161.

86   Byrne, quoted in Miles: *Talking Heads*, p. 39.

87   Miles: *Talking Heads*, p. 40.

88   Davis: *Talking Heads: A Biography*, p. 101.

89   Byrne: interview with Dave Eggers: *The Believer*, Music issue, June 2004, p. 81.

90   This is mentioned by Rick Poynor in Eno and Mills: *More Dark than Shark*, p. 124. See the text "The words I receive" therein on Eno's dislike for songwriting.

91   Goldberg: *Performance Art*, pp. 60–61; see also Teubner: *Hugo Ball*, pp. 148–53.

92   Ball's poem as printed on the inner sleeve of *Fear of Music*.

93   Rockwell: *All American Music*, p. 239.

94   The original title was "Ein Krippenspiel. Bruitistisch"; see Teubner: *Hugo Ball*, pp. 146–47. Ball's thematic was undoubtedly religious, as his later development shows.

95   Miles: *Talking Heads*, p. 40.

Notes to Chapter 2: A Wider Musical Community

1   Byrne, quoted in *Musician*, 32, April–May 1981, p. 46.

2   Quoted from the website of the National Gallery of Art in Washington, D.C.: www.nga.gov/past/data/exh388.shtm

3   Thompson: *African Art in Motion*, p. XII.

4   Ibid., p. 43.

5   Ibid., pp. 43–45. Cf. Thompson: "An Aesthetic of the Cool."

6   Thompson: *African Art in Motion*, pp. 26–28.

7   Byrne, quoted on the back cover of Chernoff's *African Rhythm and African Sensibility*.

8   Chernoff: *African Music and African Sensibility*, p. 1.

9   Ibid., p. 23.

10   Compare, for example, Anne Sheppard's *Aesthetics: An Introduction to the Philosophy of Art*: "It is still a widely accepted notion that one of the characteristics of the aesthetical way of seeing is distance, aloofness or disinterestedness." Quoted from the Dutch translation, *Filosofie van de kunst*, p. 80.

11   Chernoff: *African Music and African Sensibility*, p. 46.

12   Ibid., p. 50.

13   Ibid., p. 50, quoting Richard Waterman: *African Influence on the Music of the Americas*.

14   Ibid., p. 50.

15   Ibid., pp. 66–67.

16   Ibid., pp. 75–87.

17   Ibid., pp. 113–14.

18   Ibid., p. 121.

19   Ibid., p. 140.

20   R.F. Thompson, quoted ibid., p. 149.

21   Ibid., p. 151.

22   Ibid., pp. 155–56.

23   Ibid., p. 157.

24   Ibid., p. 158.

25   Evan Eisenberg, quoted in Frith: *Performing Rites*, p. 226.

26   See David Toop's liner notes for the CD reissue of *My Life in the Bush of Ghosts* by Nonesuch Records.

27   Miles: *Talking Heads*, p. 41.

28   Byrne, quoted in Miles: *Talking Heads* p. 41.

29   Thompson: *African Art in Motion*, p. 44.

30   Chernoff: *African Rhythm and African Sensibility*, p. 149.

31   Ibid., p. 169.

32   Ibid., p. 150. Cf. Schechner: *Between Theater and Anthropology*, pp. 126–27: "Extreme care is exercised in bringing the performer out of trance. This is so because trance exhibits qualities of both personality change and involuntariness: the trancer clearly needs help 'coming back' . . .."

33   David Byrne with Brian Eno: "The making of *My Life in the Bush of Ghosts*," liner notes for the CD reissue of *My Life in the Bush of Ghosts* by Nonesuch Records, April 2005.

34   Bruce Jenkins: "A Life in Two Parts," in *Artforum*, October 2008, p. 86.

35   See the interview with Bruce Conner in Macdonald: *A Critical Cinema*, pp. 244–56. Cf. Sklar: *Movie-Made America*, pp. 312–13.

36   Byrne, quoted in Miles: *Talking Heads*, p. 41.

37   The songs of *Remain in Light* were produced as collective collages. By improvising, every musician had contributed to the results; but both Byrne and Eno could claim something akin to the role of musical director. This resulted in quarrels within the band about the authorship of the songs. Finally the credits were distributed as follows: "all songs written by David Byrne, except David Byrne and Brian Eno on 'Crosseyed and Painless', 'Born Under Punches (The Heat Goes On)'; all arrangements by the musicians except vocal arrangements by David Byrne and Brian Eno." This is a confusing profusion of authors that shows how the recorded performative field was unusually widely stretched for a pop record. See Miles: *Talking Heads*, pp. 45–46, and Davis: *Talking Heads: A Biography*, pp. 119–21. The actual record label, however, mentions Eno as producer and states that all selections were written by Byrne and Eno, except for "Houses In Motion" and "The Overload," written by Byrne, Eno, and Harrison.

38   See Miles: *Talking Heads*, pp. 41 and 44. *Musician*, 32, April–May 1981, p. 45, mentions that the chorus of "Born Under Punches" ("And the heat goes on") was a *New York Post*

headline at the time of recording. Bowman: *Fa fa fa fa fa fa*, pp. 172 and 184, mentions influences from Thompson and Chernoff.

39　Ibid., p. 44.

40　Paul Colbert: *Musicians Only*, December 13, 1980, p. 9.

41　Alfred Schutz, quoted by Frith: *Performing Rites*, p. 146.

42　Frith: *Performing Rites*, pp. 145–49. Frith constructs his argument carefully out of quotations and comparisons between Alfred Schutz and John Chernoff, Keir Keightley, and Jonathan Kramer; his chapters on rhythm and time in *Performing Rites* are an almost rhythmically textured succession of rewarding insights.

43　The clip for "Once In A Lifetime," directed by Byrne and Toni Basil, was included in the collection of the Museum of Modern Art. In 1997, *Rolling Stone* magazine included the album in its list of the 200 all-time great popular records. Other examples from the press: "From 1982 [. . .] to 1987, when U2 hit their stride, Talking Heads were clearly the best band in the world, both on record and in concert. They set out to be modern, and 16 years later, they still sound it." Tim de Lisle, *The Independent on Sunday*, January 5, 1992, p. 15. Compare the cover of *Rolling Stone* magazine, January 15, 1987: "TALKING HEADS — Is America's Best Band Byrned Out?," and page 34: "The world's smartest rock group . . ." In 1984, *Esquire* magazine named Byrne as one of 373 Americans under 40 who were changing contemporary society; he was the only "rock" star to be included. See Davis: *Talking Heads: A Biography*, p. 125.

44　Ken Tucker: review of *Remain in Light*. Available online: www.rollingstone.com/artists/talkingheads/albums/album/300989/review/5942524/remain_in_light

45　Compare Andrew Chester's "Second Thoughts on a Rock Aesthetic," on the "intensionality" of rock in Frith and Goodwin: *On Record*, pp. 315–19.

46　Frantz, quoted in: Michael Aron: "Talking Heads, beyond safety pins," *Rolling Stone*, November 17, 1977.

47　Frith, *Performance Rites*, p. 215.

48　Byrne's explanation: "That [song] started off based on a riff we heard on a Fela [the Nigerian musician Fela Kuti] record. That started off the recording process, but never made it onto the finished song. And the words were inspired by some reading I had done about the Yoruba religion, or whatever you want to call it. I guess it's not a strict religion; I mean, it doesn't have a dogma. It's based on the cult of the Great Mother, the Great Woman. The only thing we have left of that kind of sensibility is our idea of Mother Nature. That's the only hold-over from that, but it's a very, very old idea." *Record*, 3(4), February 1984; p. 27.

49　I can't find the source of this comparison anymore, but I am certain (however much I regret it) that I did not come up with it myself.

50　On *Les Demoiselles d'Avignon*, see Robert Hughes' concise discussion in *The Shock of the New*, pp. 20–24.

51　Cf. Gauss (ed.): *Photo-Kunst. Arbeiten aus 150 Jahren*, pp. 262–63.

52　Bowman: *Fa fa fa fa fa fa*, pp. 178–79.

53　Compare Byrne's own laconic interpretation: "That's a song that juxtaposes the ordinary with the sublime. The choruses are about the sublime and submission and ecstasy, and the verses are about the ordinary and not about disliking the suburbs or something like that, as some people have misinterpreted. To me it's more about someone just being puzzled about the fact that they exist and they find themselves where they are." *Record*, 3(4), February 1984, p. 27.

54 Byrne, interviewed by Adrian Deevoy in *International Musician and Recording World*, August 1983, p. 43.

55 Davis: *Talking Heads: A Biography*, p. 134.

56 Howell: *David Byrne*, p. 60.

57 Byrne, interviewed in *Musician*, 32, April–May 1981, p. 46.

58 Talking Heads were by no means the first racially integrated band, but their line-up was still unusual. The video clip that Toni Basil directed for the *Remain in Light* song "Crosseyed And Painless" would never be played on MTV, since the channel deemed a clip with black breakdancers to be uninteresting for its predominantly white audience. Bowman: *Fa fa fa fa fa fa*, pp. 226–27.

59 Miles: *Talking Heads*, p. 47.

60 Ibid.

61 Miles: *Talking Heads*, pp. 47–48.

62 Howell: *David Byrne*, p. 40.

63 Byrne, quoted in *Musician*, 32, April–May 1981, p. 44.

64 Howell: *David Byrne*, p. 40.

65 Howell: *David Byrne*, p. 68.

66 Campbell: *The Hero's Journey*, p. 135.

67 Ibid., p. 159. Cf. Jung: *Symbols of Transformation*, p. 158: archetypes "correspond to the concept of the 'pattern of behavior' in biology." Such formulations suggest a degree of commensurability with the cybernetic approach to "control and communication in the animal," to paraphrase the subtitle of Wiener's *Cybernetics*, and indeed, Wiener and especially Bateson have expressed their positive opinion of Jung's work. See Wiener: *Cybernetics*, p. 149, on the consistency of psychoanalytical methods with the methods of cybernetics; and Bateson: *Steps to an Ecology of Mind*, pp. 455–65, on Jung as a source of inspiration to his version of cybernetic thought.

68 Campbell: *Primitive Mythology*, pp. 31–32. Campbell quotes from Jung: *Psychologische Typen*.

69 Ibid.

70 Jung: *Symbols of Transformation*, p. XXIX (Foreword to the second (German) edition).

71 See Vandermeersch: *Unresolved Questions in the Freud/Jung Debate*, pp. 39–42. The classical representative of this Romantic conception was E. von Hartmann, by whom Jung was profoundly influenced. Jung also referred explicitly to Fichte and Schelling in his exposition of the unconscious, see Jung: *Symbols of Transformation*, p. 29, footnote, and p. 176. Other Romantic influences were Goethe, Schopenhauer, and Nietzsche; cf. p. 43.

72 Cf. Frank: *Der kommende Gott*, p. 85.

73 Vandermeersch: *Unresolved Questions in the Freud/Jung Debate*, pp. 105–6.

74 Ibid., pp. 272–73.

75   Ibid., p. 276.

76   Jung: *Symbols of Transformation*, p. 86.

77   Ibid., p. 60.

78   Ibid., p. 66.

79   Cf. Vandermeersch: *Unresolved Questions in the Freud/Jung Debate*, pp. 276–77.

80   Radcliffe-Brown, quoted in Campbell: *The Masks of God I: Primitive Mythology*, pp. 33–34.

81   Campbell: *The Masks of God I: Primitive Mythology*, p. 41.

82   Cf. Keesing: *Cultural Anthropology*, p. 404.

83   Pareles: "Does this global village have two-way traffic," *Rolling Stone*, 2 April, 1981. Available online: http://bushofghosts.wmg.com/archive_press.php?id=3

84   Rockwell: "Africa's Influence on Jazz and Pop," *New York Times*, 8 February, 1981. Available online: www.bushofghosts.wmg.com/archive_press.php?id=1

85   Chernoff: *Hustling Is Not Stealing*, p. 12.

86   Ibid., p. 13.

87   Cf. also Byrne's commentary when interviewed by Chris Dahlen for Pitchfork Media. Online: http://bushofghosts.wmg.com/news_recent.php?id=4

88   Mali: *Mythistory. The Making of a Modern Historiography*, pp. 9–10.

89   Jung: "On the relation of analytical psychology to poetry," *Collected Works*, Vol. 15, p. 82.

90   Frazer: *The Golden Bough*, p. 11.

91   Tharp: *Push Comes to Shove*, p. 259. Later, Byrne stressed that he certainly didn't read all of Frazer, but had only dipped in (mail to the author, 1 October, 2009).

92   Davis: *Talking Heads: A Biography*, p. 113.

93   Cf. Tharp: *Push Comes to Shove*, pp. 257–65; Howell: *David Byrne*, p. 22; Davis: *Talking Heads: A Biography*, p. 126; and Byrne, interviewed by Elly de Waard, *Vrij Nederland*, July 17, 1982, p. 12.

94   Tharp also made a refashioned version for TV, which was issued on DVD.

95   Cf. Howell: *David Byrne*, p. 77.

96   Howell: *David Byrne*, p. 77.

97   Chernoff: *Spin* magazine, April 1988, p. 48.

98   Byrne, interviewed by Elly de Waard: *Vrij Nederland*, July 17, 1982, p. 12.

99   Dance critic Arlene Croce wrote about Byrne's lyrics: "When a word drifts out of the sonic haze, it strikes us as pre-articulate speech — closer to the sources of pain and emotion than normal speech is." Croce, in Carter (ed.): *Routledge Dance Studies Reader*, p. 109.

100   Chernoff: *African Rhythm and African Sensibility*, p. 73.

101   Ibid., p. 205, note 50.

102   Wiener: *Cybernetics*, p. 159. A similar interpretation might follow from Claude Lévi-Strauss' dictum that modern societies are different from primitive societies as much as a steam engine differs from a watch: modernity is in constant need of explosions to keep going. (The implicit suggestion that "primitive" societies have no history, however, is nonsense.)

103   Jencks: *The Language of Postmodern Architecture*, p. 23. Jencks was widely read. Theater

director Robert Wilson included filmed footage of the Pruitt-Igoe explosions in the German section of his *the CIVIL warS*.

104 Tzara: "Dada Manifesto," in: Drijkoningen, *et al.,: Historische Avantgarde*, p. 174. Author's translation.

105 Croce: "Oh, That Pineapple Rag!," in Carter (ed.) *Routledge Dance Studies Reader*, pp. 110–12.

106 See www.davidbyrne.com/music/cds/grown_backwards/grown_press/believer_04.pdf (p. 81).

107 This kind of explanation has been put forward often in reviews; for example by John Howell in his monograph on Byrne: *David Byrne*, pp. 142 and 144.

108 Davis: *Talking Heads: A Biography*, p. 131.

109 Byrne, interviewed by Anthony DeCurtis: *Record*, 3(4), February 1984, p. 28.

110 Ibid.

111 See Acts of the Apostles, ch. 2, vv. 2-9:

Suddenly there came from the sky what sounded like a strong, driving wind, a noise which filled the whole house where they were sitting. And there appeared to them flames like tongues of fire distributed among them and coming to rest on each one. They were all filled with the Holy Spirit and began to talk in other tongues, as the Spirit gave them power of utterance.

Now there were staying in Jerusalem devout Jews drawn from every nation under heaven. At this sound a crowd of them gathered, and were bewildered because each one heard his own language spoken; they were amazed and in astonishment exclaimed, 'Surely these people who are speaking are all Galileans! How is it that each of us can hear them in his own native language?'

112 Byrne, interviewed by Herman van der Horst and Bart van de Kamp: *Muziekkrant Oor*, 1, January 11, 1986, p. 12.

113 Byrne, interviewed by Herman van der Horst: *Muziekkrant Oor*, 13, July 2, 1983, p. 11.

114 The biblical episode of the Pentecost has always inspired forms of Christianity that stress a personal experience of God. A major example is twentieth-century Pentecostalism, founded in 1900 in Topeka, Kansas, by evangelist Charles Parham. Parham and his followers claimed to have recovered the ancient gift of speaking in tongues, or glossolalia, and founded their own church (or sect), stressing the role of emotion in religious worship. Pentecostal Holiness theology combines this freewheeling spiritual experience with a rigid and fundamentalist theology, claiming the absolute authority of husband over wife, inerrancy of the Bible and teaching the doctrine that at the end of the world, Jesus will hurl the unsaved into a lake of fire to suffer endless torture. Nowadays, Pentecostalism claims from 200 up to over 400 million adherents worldwide.

115 Byrne, interview with R.F. Thompson: *Rolling Stone*, April 21, 1988, p. 52.

116 The hit was — partly — bought with payola: Warner Bros. paid to get the song on playlists. Although this is common practice in the music industry, this manipulation of the audience meant a deep disillusion for Byrne, that was to have a lasting effect on him. See Bowman: *Fa fa fa fa fa fa*, pp. 257–58.

117   Byrne, interviewed by Anthony DeCurtis: *Record*, 3(4), February 1984, p. 27. A different version was told by Tina Weymouth, in the liner notes of the Talking Heads' greatest hits CD *Sand in the Vaseline*; according to her, Byrne heard the line first from Chris Frantz.

118   Byrne, quoted in Hebdidge: *Hiding in the Light*, p. 259, note 1.

119   Rauschenberg had made similar work in the 1960s. *Passport* (1967), screenpint on plexiglass, part of the series *Ten for Castelli*, made in an edition of 200 by Tanglewood Press, is bigger and more luxurious than the *Speaking in Tongues* cover, but in its concept identical. That edition was made for private collectors or museums, while the album cover was produced for a mass market.

120   Brian O'Doherty: *American Masters: The Voice and the Myth*, pp. 198 and 201.

121   *New York Times*, May 16, 2008. Available online: www.nytimes.com/2008/05/16/opinion/16byrne.html

122   Jung: *Psychology and Alchemy*, p. 98.

123   Ibid., p. 41.

124   Ibid., p. 186.

125   Ibid.

Notes to Chapter 3: Ritual in Daily Life

1   Schechner: *The End of Humanism*, p. 75, note 12.

2   Kirby was part of the circle around minimal artist Sol LeWitt in the early 1960s. See Lynn Zelevansky: "Ad Reinhardt and the younger artists of the 1960s," *Studies of Modern Art 1*, p. 19 (MoMA, 1991).

3   Schechner: *Between Theater and Anthropology*. p. 21.

4   Schechner: *The End of Humanism*, p. 20.

5   Schechner: *Between Theater and Anthropology*, p. 23. See also p. 221: "the theater of the 1960s and 1970s was not a theater of new plays, or literary texts interpreted at all, but a theater of new mise-en scènes — a theater of whole performance texts consisting of movements, stage placement and tableaux, music (and other sonic elements), visuals including settings, environments, costumes, projections, and a number of nonactor performers: masks, puppets, projections, films."

6   Ibid., p. 118.

7   Schechner: *The End of Humanism*, p. 80, quoting from Lévi-Strauss' *The Savage Mind*.

8   Schechner: *The End of Humanism*, p. 80.

9   Schechner: *Between Theater and Anthropology*, p. 6.

10   Ibid., p. 35.

11   Ibid., p. 37.

12   Ibid., p. 118.

13   Ibid., p. 16.

14   Ibid., p. 37.

15   Ibid., p. 14.

16 Ibid., pp. 111–13.

17 Ibid., pp. 125–26 and 130.

18 Schechner: *Between Theater and Anthropology*, p. 234. Cf. Steinman: *The Knowing Body*.

19 Schechner: *Between Theater and Anthropology*, p. 256. Cf. for example, Schechner's *The Future of Ritual*, pp. 13–14 and 245–50.

20 Schechner: *The Future of Ritual*, p. 228. Cf. also Schechner's *The End of Humanism*, pp. 77–92; *Between Theater and Anthropology*, pp. 213–60; *The Future of Ritual*, pp. 228–65.

21 Schechner: *The Future of Ritual*, pp. 229–30.

22 Ibid., p. 239–40.

23 Ibid., p. 263.

24 Schechner: *Between Theater and Anthropology*, p. 6.

25 Goodman, quoted in Schechner: *The Future of Ritual*, p. 241.

26 Ibid.

27 Byrne, interviewed by Herman van der Horst: *Muziekkrant Oor 13*, 2 July 1983, p. 11.

28 Schechner: *The End of Humanism*, p. 21.

29 Schechner: *Between Theater and Anthropology*, p. 221.

30 Ibid., p. 9.

31 Schechner: *Between Theater and Anthropology*, p. 98.

32 Demme did film audience shots, as is the custom for concert films, but later decided not to use them. Bowman: *Fa fa fa fa fa fa*, p. 264.

33 Byrne, quoted in Bowman: *Fa fa fa fa fa fa*, p. 91.

34 Years later, Byrne could not remember in detail: "At one point I got to know JoAnne Akalaitis, and I think I invited her to a rehearsal, to say, will you look at this and tell me what you think — if you think this is working." Byrne, interviewed by the author, February 22, 1999.

35 Byrne, interviewed by R.F. Thompson: *Rolling Stone*, April 21, 1988, p. 52.

36 Carter Ratcliff: *Artforum*, May 1985, p. 97.

37 Bowman: *Fa fa fa fa fa fa*, p. 311, and *Rolling Stone*, January 15, 1987, p. 58.

38 Byrne: e-mail to the author, May 14, 1999.

39 Wilson: *the CIVIL warS*, pp. 60–68, contains an overview.

40 *Record*, June 1985, p. 13.

41 Shank: *Beyond the Boundaries: American Alternative Theatre*, pp. 126–27.

42 Ibid.

43 Shank: *Beyond the Boundaries: American Alternative Theatre*, pp. 125–27.

44 Wilson: *The Forest*, chapter V, "Workshop."

45 Wilson, quoted in Cole: *Directors in Rehearsal*, p. 161.

46 For an overview see Wilson: *the CIVIL warS*, pp. 66–68.

47 Byrne, interviewed by Laurence Shyer: "The Forest: a preview of the next Wilson-Byrne collaboration," *Theater*, Summer/Fall 1988.

48 Byrne, quoted in Howell: *David Byrne*, p. 86.

49 Since Byrne's brass quintet is not accompanied by a piano, it depends on a highly

accurate rendition for its staccato punctuations. Cf. *DownBeat*, October 1985, p. 21.

50   Cf. Robert Stearns' essay from the Minneapolis catalogue for *The Knee Plays*. Available online: www.kneeplays.com/catalog/walker-essay

51   Bowman: *Fa fa fa fa fa fa*, p. 283.

52   Quoted from the book jacket of Turner: *Howard Finster*.

53   Byrne: mail to the author, 30 September, 2009.

54   Turner: *Howard Finster*, pp. 161–62.

55   It should perhaps be explained that this was no case of "rockstar exploits naive artist." Finster had an established career as an artist, was represented by New York gallerist Phyllis Kind since 1981, had received a grant from the National Endowment for the Arts in 1981, and was one of America's representatives at the 1984 Venice Biennale. Finster used the commission to further his own purpose: "I'm trying to reach more people now than I did when I was preaching. On the Talking Heads [album cover] there are twenty-six wholesome verses of mine. That album sold over a million copies. I had twenty-six million verses go out and reach the world. That's more than I ever reached in the forty-five years I was pastoring. The rock-and-rollers are my missionaries." Turner: *Howard Finster*, p. 162; see pp. 3–4, 116 and 158 for an account of Finster's career.

56   According to Hebdidge: *Hiding in the Light*, p. 235, the video was "frequently cited as one of the most technically complex and original micro-narratives yet produced for promotional purposes."

57   Byrne, interviewed by R.F. Thompson: *Rolling Stone*, April 21, 1988, p. 48.

58   See Hebdidge: *Hiding in the Light*, pp. 232–40, and Woods: *Beginning Postmodernism*, pp. 178–79.

59   Byrne began to collect material in 1983. The following is based in part on Byrne's "Introduction," *True Stories*, p. 9.

60   Byrne: *True Stories*, ibid.

61   Byrne: *True Stories*, p. 15.

62   Ibid., p. 64.

63   Cf. Henry M. Sayre: *The Object of Performance*, p. 265.

64   Ibid. This music of this "Road Song" was composed by Meredith Monk and arranged by David Byrne.

65   Tiger and Fox: *The Imperial Animal*, p. 50.

66   Sayre: *The Object of Performance*, pp. 265–66.

67   Byrne, in Howell: *David Byrne*, p. 68. As noted in *True Stories'* titles, the found footage was compiled for Byrne by M&Co., at that time a maverick advertising agency in New York.

68   Reprinted in David Byrne: *True Stories*, p. 40.

69   Ibid., pp. 39, 105.

70   The actual quotation from Steve Jobs appeared in a *Newsweek* article, reprinted in Byrne: *True Stories*, p. 39.

71   David Byrne: *True Stories*, pp. 176–78.

72   Ibid., pp. 34, 48, 50, 88.

73 This statement is known as the "Thomas Theorem." See Coser: *Masters of Sociological Thought*, p. 521.

74 Von Franz: "The process of individuation," in Jung (ed.): *Man and his Symbols*, p. 180. Another possible source for the mind as a musical radio can be found in Sacks: *The Man Who Mistook His Wife for a Hat*, p. 125ff; here Sacks tells the story of a patient who experienced a radio station in her head that played songs from her childhood in Ireland. According to Sacks, these transmissions were caused by epileptic transports which produced authentic childhood reminiscences (pp. 137–38). Byrne read both Jung and Sacks; he may even have combined both stories in his song.

75 For Byrne's ideas around this subject, cf. *True Stories* p. 42.

76 David Byrne: *True Stories*, p. 12.

77 Ibid., p. 50.

78 This trilogy is extensively discussed in Savran: *Breaking the Rules*, part II. About the pivotal importance of The Wooster Group, see Aronson: *American Avant-Garde Theatre*, pp. 144–211.

79 Shank: *American Alternative Theatre*, pp. 170–71.

80 Savran: *Breaking the Rules*, p. 92.

81 Ibid.

82 On the concept of witnessing as central to a good deal of contemporary art: Felman and Laub: *Testimony: Crises of Witnessing in Literature, Psychoanalysis and History*.

83 Also, another scene, "an illuminated stage in a barren field at night, seemed to pay homage to Wilson by alluding to the space ship in 'Einstein on the Beach.'" Jody Dalton in *EAR* magazine 11, 1988.

84 Byrne: *True Stories*, p. 56.

85 Sayre: *The Object of Performance*, p. 109.

86 Ibid., p. 100.

87 Ibid., p. 60.

88 A picture and a description of this altar are included in Byrne's *True Stories* book, p. 140. Similar altars and their meanings are discussed by R.F. Thompson: *Face of the Gods*.

89 Byrne: *True Stories*, p. 170.

90 A general introduction to Vodun that Byrne consulted is Maya Deren's *The Voodoo Gods*.

91 Byrne: *True Stories*, p. 143.

92 *Time*, October 27, 1986.

93 McKim: "*True Stories*," in *Cineaste* XV(3), 1987, pp. 44 and 45.

94 Ibid., p. 45.

95 Kruger: *Remote Control*, pp. 190–92; first published in *Artforum*.

96 McGowan: "Selling Out with a Smirk," *Washington Monthly*, March, 1986.

97 Sayre: *The Object of Performance*, p. 106.

98 Sayre: *The Object of Performance*, p. 266.

99 Cf. the introduction on Mabou Mines in Marranca: *The Theatre of Images*, pp. 113–18.

100 Byrne: *Journal*, August 26, 2005. Online: http://journal.davidbyrne.com/2005/08/index.html

101 Byrne: interview with the author, February 22, 1999.

102   My description of *Dead End Kids* is based on a video tape without end credits, given to me by Byrne in 1999.

103   Schechner: *The End of Humanism*, p. 118, gives his comment on the play.

104   Byrne: interviewed by Laurence Shyer: *Theater*, Summer/Fall 1988.

105   Byrne, in Rüter and Weber: *The Forest* (theater program), chapter VIII, "Music."

106   Byrne, quoted in Howell: *David Byrne*, p. 82.

107   Byrne, text in the booklet of *The Forest* CD, February, 1991.

108   Available online: www.talking-heads.nl/index.php/david-byrne-bio/david-byrne-archive/144–1992-letter-from-the-lumberjacks-friend

109   For other text sources, Edgar Allen Poe, and the Aztec "Florentine Codex," see Marranca: "*The Forest* as Archive," p. 39.

110   Byrne, interviewed by Manuel Bonik, *Wiener*, October 1988, p. 5; and John Rockwell, *The New York Times Magazine*, September 11, 1988, p. 86.

111   Byrne, quoted in Howell: *David Byrne*, p. 85.

112   Byrne, in Rüter and Weber: *The Forest* (theater program), chapter VIII, "Music"; and Byrne, interviewed by Manuel Bonik: *Wiener*, October 1988, p. 5.

113   Byrne, in Rüter and Weber: *The Forest* (theater program), chapter VIII, "Music."

114   Byrne's song as printed in the theater program for *The Forest*, Act 1.

115   Wilson, in Rüter and Weber: *The Forest* (theater program), chapter X, "Textwork."

116   Marranca: "*The Forest* as Archive," p. 43.

117   Ibid., p. 119.

118   Ibid., p. xxxviii.

119   Ibid.

120   These quotations are from an 80-page-long scenario in Byrne's archives, titled "The Forest, version for film," by David Byrne and Michael Hirst.

121   Howell: *David Byrne*, pp. 63 and 82. According to Q magazine, 3, December 1986, p. 29, "Despite being the leader of perhaps the most critically celebrated pop group in the world, David still had to peddle the script of *True Stories* round for a year till he'd raised the finance." According to the *Guardian* of September 16, 1986, Warner initially turned Byrne's proposal down twice.

122   See John Rockwell on the rhythmic backwardness of much symphonic material: *All American Music*, p. 51.

123   Byrne: "Theater of Memory," in: Allen, *et al.*, *Dugout*, pp. 170 and 173.

Notes to Chapter 4: Rock Star and Ethnographer

1   Thompson, *Rolling Stone*, April 21, 1988, p. 44.

2   Appadurai: *Modernity at Large*, p. 4.

3   See Howell, *David Byrne*, pp. 79–80.

4   Bowman: *Fa fa fa fa fa fa*, p. 284.

5   See Rockwell: *All American Music*, pp. 112–13, on the influences in Glass's music.

6   The Christmas after Celia Cruz' death, Byrne published a brief memorial in *Entertainment Weekly*, 743/744, December 26, 2003.

7   Nietzsche: *Beyond Good and Evil*, aphorism 146.

8   Cf. Kosuth: *Art After Philosophy and After*, esp. p. 119.

9   Foster: *The Return of the Real*, p. 172; the quote is from an earlier, more outspoken version of this text, Foster's "The Artist as Ethnographer?," in Fisher (ed.): *Global Visions*, p. 16.

10 Ibid., p. 182.

11 Ibid., p. 197.

12 Foster: "The Artist as Ethnographer?," in Fisher (ed.): *Global Visions*, p. 14.

13 Ibid.

14 Turner: "Foreword," in Schechner: *Between Theater and Anthropology*, p. xii.

15 Ibid., p. 108.

16 Ibid., p. 107.

17 Ibid., p. 109.

18 Ruby: *Picturing Culture*, p. 239.

19 Ibid., p. 244.

20 Ibid., p. 260. This debate is layered: I quote Ruby who quotes Conquergood who quotes Asad who quotes Walter Benjamin.

21 Ibid., p. 261.

22 Ibid., pp. 275–76.

23 Byrne, interviewed by Chernoff: *Spin*, April 1988, p. 50.

24 Ibid.

25 Chernoff, quoted in Bowman: *Fa fa fa fa fa fa*, p. 325.

26 Byrne, interviewed by R.F. Thompson: *Rolling Stone*, April 21, 1988, pp. 52 and 116.

27 Figures given by Bowman: *Fa fa fa fa fa fa*, p. 359.

28 See Howell: *David Byrne*, p. 53.

29 Ibid.

30 Ibid., p. 48.

31 Byrne: e-mail to the author, June 15, 1999.

32 Cf. Howell: *David Byrne*, p. 73.

33 Byrne: e-mail to the author, June 15, 1999.

34 Byrne, quoted in Howell: *David Byrne*, p. 74.

35 According to Howell: *David Byrne*, p. 33, *Ilé Aiyé* was also exhibited as part of "Magiciens de la Terre," the Parisian exhibition of 1989 that attempted to give an overview of artists working in different cultures all over the world. This is a mistake, perhaps due to the fact that two documentaries by Philip Haas, for which Byrne made soundtracks, were part of a side-program of "Magiciens de la Terre."

36 Byrne, interview with the author, February 22, 1999.

37 Quoted in Bowman: *Fa fa fa fa fa fa*, p. 336.

38 See Thompson: "Mambo: Microcosm of Black New York Creativity."

39 Ibid.

40 Quoted in J.M. Chernoff: *African Rhythm and African Sensibility*, p. 148.

41 Byrne, liner notes for *Brazil Classics 1: Beleza Tropical*, June, 1988.

42 Byrne, in Howell: *David Byrne*, p. 59.

43   This is too general, if only because some of the musicians are white; yet the general contrast is real.

44   *De Volkskrant*, June 13, 1997, p. 29.

45   Byrne recorded a cover version of Porter's "Don't Fence Me In" for a compilation of covers by several artists, *Red Hot & Blue*, an AIDS benefit.

46   Byrne: "The Rei Momo Tour Diary," in Howell: *David Byrne*, p. 107.

47   Quoted by Carl Hindmarch: *Elle*, January 1990, p. 35.

48   "Artistically and sociologically, [Latin music] is a ghetto." Rockwell: *All American Music*, p. 199. Angel Fernandez explained: "When I played Latin music, I played to people who spoke Spanish and you wouldn't see blacks or Anglos in the crowd very much. It was like a nation within a nation. Yet we all speak English; we've been bi-cultural for a long time. Many of us grew up in New York and played rock, jazz and funk as well as Latin." *Q*, February 1990, p. 38.

49   Byrne, interview with Craig Bromberg: *Rolling Stone*, January 11, 1990, p. 48.

50   Ibid.

51   This was the criticism of Jon Pareles in his *New York Times* review, quoted in Howell: *David Byrne*, p. 34. One of the presidents of Warner Bros., Byrne's record company, was of the same opinion; see ibid., p. 137.

52   In Howell: *David Byrne*, pp. 105–38.

53   Byrne: "The Rei Momo Tour Diary," in Howell: *David Byrne*, p. 131.

54   Ibid., p. 134; cf. p. 131.

55   Ibid., pp. 123–24.

56   Ibid., pp. 108, 126, 129.

57   Ibid., p. 119.

58   Ibid., p. 122.

59   Ibid., p. 125.

60   See for an introductory overview: Jan Nederveen Pieterse: "Multiculturalism and Museums: Discourse about Others in the Age of Globalization," in *Theory, Culture and Society*, 14(4), 1997, pp. 123–46.

61   Byrne: e-mail to the author, May 14, 1999.

62   Byrne: liner notes for *Brazil Classics 1: Beleza Tropical*.

63   For a self-portrait of Evelev: "A Nonmusician's Life in Music," *Leonardo Music Journal*, 12, 2002, pp. 67–69.

64   See an interview with Baca by Jaime Manrique (*Bomb*, 70, Winter 2000) in which Baca says: "There's a lot of hope. David Byrne's album of black Peruvian music was very important. It created a gateway for the rest of us. It generates interest; people come to Peru searching for our music. I hope doors will be opened for all kinds of music. Many people are doing things of great value in complete anonymity." Available online: www.bombsite.com/issues/70/articles/2295

65   Byrne: "Djur Djura," *Bomb*, 47, Spring, 1994. Available online: www.bombsite.com/issues/47/articles/1767

66   Byrne: "I Hate World Music," *New York Times*, October 3, 1999. Cf. Gilberto Gil's essay "The Music of the World Is Bigger than World Music" (1993). Available online: www.gilbertogil.com.br/sec_textos_view.php?id=1&language_id=2

67 Bowman: *Fa fa fa fa fa fa*, p. 350.
68 Byrne: "Machines of Joy," *Leonardo Music Journal*, 12, 2002, pp. 7 and 8.
69 Bowman: *Fa fa fa fa fa fa*, p. 258.
70 Keil and Feld: *Music Grooves*, p. 22.
71 James Brown, quoted in ibid., p. 24. Chernoff, too, insists that there is a philosophical dimension to some James Brown songs: *African Rhythm and African Sensibility*, p. 74.
72 Keil: "Participatory Discrepancies and the Power of Music," in Keil and Feld: *Music Grooves*, pp. 96–100.
73 Feld, describing the terminology of Robert Plant Armstrong, in his "Aesthetics as Iconicity, or 'Lift-up-over Sounding,'" in Keil and Feld: *Music Grooves*, p. 144.
74 Feld: "Notes on 'World Beat,'" in *Music Grooves*, p. 246.
75 Feld follows Simon Frith's analysis: the record companies work towards major hits which produce the major profits; major contract artists are only allowed to take economic and artistic risks in proportion to their record sales, and musicians are laborers selling their services in the marketplace. Feld, "Notes on "World Beat"", in: "Music Grooves", p. 245.
76 Feld: "From Schizophonia to Schismogenesis," pp. 269–70, in Keil and Feld: *Music Grooves*.
77 Ibid., p. 271.
78 Ibid., p. 271.
79 Ibid., p. 272.
80 Lipsitz: *Dangerous Crossroads*, p. 61.
81 After Cruz' death, Byrne wrote a brief memorial, published in *Entertainment Weekly*, 743/744, December 26, 2003.
82 Cardona, quoted by Richard Guilliatt: *20/20*, November 1989, p. 82.
83 Ibid., quoting Byrne.
84 Byrne, speaking about the sensibility of Candomblé, in Howell: *David Byrne*, p. 51.
85 Cooper, interview with Byrne: *The L*, October 2004. Available online: www.carolcooper.org/music/byrne-04.php
86 Geertz: "The Uses of Diversity," p. 271.

Notes to Chapter 5: In the Visual Arena

1 Definition based on Beer: *Brain of the Firm*, pp. 402–3.
2 Cf. Antoine Hennion: "The Production of Success. An Antimusicology of the Pop Song," in Frith and Goodwin: *On Record*, pp. 188–89.
3 Geertz: *The Interpretation of Cultures*, p. 6.
4 Ibid.
5 Aniela Jaffé, in Jung: *Man and his Symbols*, p. 232.
6 Byrne: *True Stories*, p. 12.
7 Jerry Harrison later told how he had convinced Byrne to leave out several of his own artworks that he had selected; Harrison thought it better that Byrne should not visually re-interpret his own lyrics. *Muziekkrant Oor*, February 13, 1988, p. 43.

8   Talking Heads and Frank Olinsky: *What the Songs Look Like*, p. 14.

9   I owe these comparisons to Laura Kleger's article "Inside, Accumulated" on Cohen.

10 Byrne, in Cohen: *Occupied Territory*, p. 15.

11 *Artforum*, December 1989, pp. 100–5.

12 Byrne: liner notes for the *Ilé Aiyé* DVD.

13 Byrne: "Insert," *Parkett*, 23, 1990, pp. 120 and 122.

14 "Reproduced Authentic" was curated by Joseph Kosuth for Galerie Via Eight on the occasion of the opening of Barneys New York. Tokyo, November 3–16, 1990.

15 As related by Azby Brown (AB): "Reproduced Authentic," in *Artforum*, February 1991, p. 141.

16 Cf. the description by Azby Brown, ibid.

17 Prizes as stated by Bart de Leenheer, Byrne's gallerist in Mechelen, Belgium.

18 Byrne, interviewed by Ken Coupland in *Graphis, International Journal of Graphic Art and Applied Art*, 313, 1998, p. 99.

19 This distinction was made by Szarkowski, for "Mirrors and Windows: American Photography Since 1960" (MoMA, 1978). Quoted in Sayre: *The Object of Performance*, p. 35.

20 From Byrne: *Strange Ritual*, pages unnumbered.

21 In a press statement, issued by Byrne's office.

22 Andy Grunberg, writing in a review for the *New York Times*, praised Byrne's photo's for their "distinctive and offbeat manner," but described his writing as "less sure than his eye." Quoted in *ARTnews*, October 1996, p. 122.

23 Moze Jacobs: "David Byrnes Amerika," *Vrij Nederland*, April 23, 1994, p. 41.

24 Chihiro Monato: "Japan and Photography: In quest of the other," in Frizot (ed): *A New History of Photography*, esp. p. 692.

25 Byrne: *Strange Ritual*, endnotes.

26 Ibid.

27 Byrne, interviewed by Elisabetta d'Erme: *Il Manifesto*, September 12, 1998.

28 At the occasion of an exhibition in Aktionsforum Praterinsel, Munich, Germany, titled "Glory! Success! Ecstasy!"

29 DeLillo: *Underworld*, pp. 119–20.

30 All the following quotations are from: "Earliest Program for a System of German Idealism," in Schulte-Sasse, *et al. Theory as Practice*, pp. 72–73. Likely authors of this text are Schelling, Hegel, and Hölderlin. It is generally considered to be a manifesto of early Romanticism.

31 Behler: *German Romantic Literary Theory*, p. 159.

32 A.W. Schlegel, quoted in Behler: *German Romantic Literary Theory*, p. 159.

33 In his book *On Religion: Speeches to its Cultured Despisers*.

34 Novalis: *Werke*, p. 531: "Es gibt keine Religion, die nicht Christentum wäre."

35 Ibid., p. 534.

36 Cf. Frank: *Einführung in die frühromantische Ästhetik*, p. 238.

37 Novalis: *Werke*, p. 530.

38 Ibid., p. 505.

39 Ibid., p. 348.

40   Schlegel, translation in Schulte-Sasse, *et al.*: *Theory as Practice*, p. 326.
41   Schelling, quoted in Schulte-Sasse, *et al.*: *Theory as Practice*, p. 147.
42   Schlegel, quoted in Behler: *German Romantic Literary Theory*, p. 161.
43   Bateson: *Steps to an Ecology of Mind*, p. 461.
44   Byrne: *The New Sins*, pp. 13–15.
45   Ibid., p. 23.
46   Ibid., p. 39.
47   Ibid., p. 47.
48   Ibid., p. 11.
49   Ibid., pp. 87–89.
50   Ibid., pp. 21–23.
51   Ibid., p. 59.
52   Novalis, quoted in Wanning: *Novalis*, p. 61.
53   Byrne, in the documentary *Talking Heads vs. The Television*.
54   Byrne: press release accompanying the exhibition "The Wedding Party" at the LipanjePuntin gallery, Trieste, Italy, November 25, 2000–January 31, 2001.
55   Byrne quoted on a leaflet of the "Aktionsforum Praterinsel," Munich, which accompanied his 1998 exhibition.
56   Novalis: "Fragmente und Studien 1799–1800," *Werke*, p. 560.

Notes to Chapter 6: Tropicalismo in New York

1   Byrne: "The Holy Grail of No Style," in Hall and Bierut (eds.): *Tibor Kalman: Perverse Optimist*, p. 87.
2   Cf. Sayre: *The Object of Performance*, p. 105.
3   My paraphrase of Rockwell: *All American Music*, pp. 53–54.
4   Cf. Sayre: *The Object of Performance*, p. 106.
5   Ibid., p. 113.
6   Cage: *Silence*, p. 3.
7   The film was shown at the New York Film Festival of that year.
8   Byrne: *Journal*, January 25, 2006: "Selfless." Online: http://journal.davidbyrne.com/2006/01/index.html
9   Cf. Byrne: "Julio the Uncanny." Available online: davidbyrne.com/art/art_projects/robot/index.php
10   Howell: *David Byrne*, pp. 125 and 138.
11   Byrne, interview with the author, February 22, 1999.
12   Perrone: "From Noigandres to 'Milagre da Alegria': The Concrete Poets and Contemporary Brazilian Popular Music," p. 61.
13   Veloso: *Tropical Truth*, pp. 153–63, esp. 156.
14   Ibid., p. 330.
15   I haven't been able to track the original MTV "documentary"; my source here is Byrne: *Journal*, August 7, 2004. Online: http://journal.davidbyrne.com/2004/08/index.html
16   Byrne: "Prefácio" to Arnaldo Antunes: *Doble/Duplo*. In his preface, Byrne clearly

places Antunes' work in the Tropicalismo tradition. Available online: arnaldoantunes. com.br/sec_livros_view.php?id=6&texto=1

17   Quoted in Feldman: *Black Rhythms of Peru*, p. 239. Feldman presents an extensive discussion of this song.

18   Byrne: "Rosanne Cash" (interview), *Bomb*, 44, Summer 1993. Available online: www. bombsite.com/issues/44/articles/1687

19   Byrne, interview with the author, February 22, 1999.

20   Compare "A Propaganda Model," the introductory chapter of Herman and Chomsky's *Manufacturing Consent*, pp. 1–35, and the paragraph on "Tone of negativism and apathy" in the same book, pp. 118–20.

21   Conversation with David Byrne, May 6, 2008.

22   Edward Helmore: "The business is an exciting mess," *Guardian*, 27 March, 2009. Available online: www.guardian.co.uk/music/2009/mar/27/brian-eno-david-byrne

23   Ibid.

24   Byrne: "Celia Cruz," *Entertainment Weekly*, December 26, 2003.

25   Cf. Byrne: *Journal*, October 23, 2005. Online: http://journal.davidbyrne.com/2005/10/index.html

26   All quotations are taken from the theater program for *In Spite of Wishing and Wanting*, Ultima Vez, Brussels, 1999.

27   For information on *Here Lies Love*, use was made of Byrne's website, especially the entry in his *Journal* about his research trip to the Philippines, the entry dated 25 December, 2005, and the similar chapter in his *Bicycle Diaries*, pp. 133–66.

28   A small anecdote that illustrates very well how pop music, neo-colonialism, racism, and exploitation are inextricably connected: Philippine culture is very much open to Western entertainment, and Philippino covers bands imitating Western pop acts can be heard in bars and nightclubs in the Philippines and around the world. Byrne considered the possibility of including one of these bands in his project, and phoned one of the agencies in Manila that handles the export and management of such cover bands. One of the first questions the agency asked him was what color he was interested in, meaning the skin color of the musicians; several skin tones could be ordered. Story told by Byrne to the author in 2006 in Bochum, Germany.

29   Byrne used this quotation from James Hamilton-Paterson's book on the Marcos era, *America's Boy*, to explain his fascination with Imelda's story. *Bicycle Diaries*, p. 132.

30   Related by Byrne to the author, conversation on May 6, 2008.

Notes to Chapter 7: An Emotional Epistemology

1   Byrne: "Notes on Images," *Zoetrope*, 7, Spring 2003, p. 98.

2   "David Byrne + Daniel Levitin: The singer/songwriter and the neuroscientist meet up to discuss music," *Seedmagazine.com*, April 30, 2007. Available online: http://seedmagazine.com/content/article/david_byrne_daniel_levitin/

3   Byrne: *Journal*, April 19, 2009: "Senigallia — You Get What You Pay For." Online: http://journal.davidbyrne.com/2009/04/index.html (What these three subjects have

in common is a problematic regulating system, discerning between private and public benefits.)

4   Tufte: *Visual Explanations*, p. 9.

5   Tufte: *The Visual Display of Quantitative Information*, pp. 51 and 175.

6   Tufte: *The Cognitive Style of PowerPoint*, p. 3.

7   Ibid., p. 13.

8   The pages of *Envisioning Emotional Epistemological Information* are not numbered.

9   O.G. Selfridge: "Pattern Recognition and Learning," quoted in Gombrich: *Art and Illusion*, p. 77.

10 Alexander: "A City Is Not a Tree," published in 1965 in *Architectural Forum*. Available online: www.patternlanguage.com/archives/alexander2.htm

11 Alexander: *Notes on the Synthesis of Form*, p. 78.

12 Frazer: *The Golden Bough*, p. 37.

13 Byrne's formulation here reads like an ironic take on Russell's paradox, which considers the set of all sets that are not members of themselves. Compare also Byrne's *Set Of All Goals* (Illustration 3 in this book). Diagram 68 in *Arboretum*, "Nambikwara Verbal Suffix Categories," is another excellent example of Byrne's interest in the reflexive effects of knowledge, "the watched watching the watchers."

14 Tiger and Fox: *The Imperial Animal*, p. 1.

15 Schechner: *Performance Studies: An Introduction*, p. 35.

16 As stated without explanation in a 2002 autobiography by Byrne. Available online: www.abc.net.au/rage/guest/2002/davidbyrne.htm

17 Byrne told *The New Yorker* he paid over 10,000 dollars for a sniping company to put up 3,600 posters. See Zev Borow: "Dept. of Talking Heads: The Man Behind the Masks," *The New Yorker*, November 13, 2000. Available online: www.davidbyrne.com/art/political_flesh/about/politcal_flesh_nyer.php. In the following months, Byrne showed photos in an art gallery made of the inside of similar masks, of George W. Bush, Yasser Arafat, and Saddam Hussein, under the title "Political Flesh."

18 Annie Nocenti: "And the Winner Is . . . the Middle-Aged White Guy," *Print*, November/December 2000. Available online: www.davidbyrne.com/art/political_flesh/about/politcal_flesh_print.php

19 For more information, cf. Gwenda Blair: "Designers Redefine the Political Machine," *New York Times*, October 7, 2004. Available online: www.davidbyrne.com/art/art_projects/voting_booth/voting_nytimes.php

20 For this formulation, cf. Benjamin: *The Arcades Project*, p. 895. For a more thorough discussion, see Steenstra: *We Are the Noise between Stations*, pp. 269–95.

21 Byrne: interviewed by Elisabetta d'Erme: *Alias*, a weekly insert with *Il Manifesto*, Trieste, Italy, September 12, 1998, p. 1.

22 Byrne: *Journal*, October 30, 2006, "The Secret Commonwealth." Online: http://journal.davidbyrne.com/2006/10/index.html

23 Byrne: *Journal*, December 8, 2004, "A Consumer Society." Online: http://journal.davidbyrne.com/2004/12/index.html

24 The *Wired* CD, titled *Rip. Sample. Mash. Share.*, was included in the issue of November 2004. See also "Sample the Future" by Thomas Goetz in that issue, p. 181–83, which

states: "Some artists got the idea and signed on in a flash, inspiring others to do so, too (thanks again, Mr. Byrne)" (p. 183).

25   Feldman: *Black Rhythms of Peru*, p. 232.

26   Ibid., p. 233.

27   Byrne: *Journal*, June 12, 2005: "Stockholm: Art & Sociology." Available online: http://journal.davidbyrne.com/2005/06/index.html

28   Byrne: *Journal*. See, among others, the entries of May 17, 2009 (available online: http://journal.davidbyrne.com/2009/05/index.html) and October 2, 2008 available online: http://journal.davidbyrne.com/2008/10/index.html).

29   Byrne: *Journal*, November 25, 2007. Available online: http://journal.davidbyrne.com/2007/11/index.html

30   This statement is available online: www.illegal-art.org/

31   Byrne: interview in *Pitchfork*, July 17, 2006, by Chris Dahlen. Available online: www.pitchfork.com/features/interviews/6382-david-byrne

32   Byrne: interview with the author, February 22, 1999.

33   Byrne: *Journal*, March 5, 2007, "Big Love (Spotting session)." Available online: http://journal.davidbyrne.com/2007/03/index.html

34   Byrne: *Journal*, August 26, 2005. Available online: http://journal.davidbyrne.com/2005/08/index.html

35   Ibid.; John Whitman's original text can be found at www.yourdictionary.com/library/japonoma.html

36   Byrne: *Journal*, August 26, 2005. Available online: http://journal.davidbyrne.com/2005/08/index.html

37   Byrne: *Journal*, August 14, 2005. Available online: http://journal.davidbyrne.com/2005/08/index.html. The interview he points to is "Crystal Clear: An interview with Shea Zellweger", *Cabinet*, 18, Summer 2005. Available online: www.cabinetmagazine.org/issues/18/crystal.php

38   Byrne: *Journal*, July 21, 2007, "Interactivity versus Storytelling." Available online: http://journal.davidbyrne.com/2007/07/72107-nyc-kneep.html

39   Byrne: *Journal*, April 29, 2006, "NYC: We're All One." Available online: http://journal.davidbyrne.com/2006/04/42906_nyc_were_.html

40   Dennis Overbye: "Free Will: Now You Have It, Now You Don't," *New York Times*, January 2, 2007. Available online: www.nytimes.com/2007/01/02/science/02free.html?pagewanted=1&_r=1

41   Byrne: *Journal*, December 31, 2006.

42   Byrne: *Bicycle Diaries*, p. 10.

43   Ibid., pp. 2–3.

44   Ibid., pp. 78–79.

45   Ibid., p. 79.

46   Ibid., p. 80.

47   Ibid., p. 31.

48   Ibid., p. 74.

49   Ibid., p. 245.

50   Ibid., p. 194; on categorization, see p. 193.

51 Ibid., p. 234.

52 Cf. Aragon: *Paris Peasant*, originally published as *Le Paysan de Paris* in 1926.

53 Benjamin wrote *The Arcades Project* in the years 1927–40.

54 Benjamin: *Selected Writings, Volume 1*, pp. 288 and 290.

55 Byrne: *Bicycle Diaries*, pp. 40–41.

56 Ibid., p. 284–85.

57 Cf. the "Conceptual Romanticism" section in the Introduction to this book.

58 Cf. in Benjamin's *The Concept of Criticism in German Romanticism (Selected Writings, Volume 1)* the section on the idea of art, which contains in important respects the real conclusion of that book.

59 Phoebe Caldwell: "Letters," *The Times*, December 30, 2005.

60 Cf. the Introduction to this book, Note 9.

Discography and Filmography

TALKING HEADS ALBUMS

Talking Heads: 77 (1977)
More Songs about Buildings and Food (1978)
Fear of Music (1979)
Remain in Light (1980)
The Name of This Band Is Talking Heads (1982)
Speaking in Tongues (1983)
Stop Making Sense (1984)
Little Creatures (1985)
True Stories (1986)
Naked (1988)

SOLO ALBUMS AND ALBUM COLLABORATIONS

My Life in the Bush of Ghosts (with Brian Eno, 1981)
Songs from "The Catherine Wheel" (1981)
Music for the Knee Plays (1985)
Rei Momo (1989)
The Forest (1991)
Uh-Oh (1992)
David Byrne (1994)
Feelings (1997)
The Visible Man (remixes of some songs from *Feelings*, 1997)
Your Action World (15-minute audioguide, 1998)
Look into the Eyeball (2001)

Grown Backwards (2004)
Everything That Happens Will Happen Today (with Brian Eno, 2008)
Everything That Happens Will Happen on This Tour (live EP, 2009)

SCORES FOR FILM, TELEVISION, AND BALLET

Sounds from True Stories (1986)
Dead End Kids: A Story of Nuclear Power (1986)
The Last Emperor (with Ruichi Sakamoto and Cong Su, 1987)
A Young Man's Dream and a Woman's Secret (1990)
The Giant Woman and the Lightening Man (1990)
In Spite of Wishing and Wanting (1999)
Lead Us Not into Temptation: Music from the film "Young Adam" (2003)
Big Love: Hymnal (2008)

CONCERT FILMS

Stop Making Sense (directed by Jonathan Demme, stage show designed by David
   Byrne, 1984)
Talking Heads vs. The Television (recorded 1984, directed by Geoff Dunlop for
   Channel 4, 1989)
David Byrne Live: Between the Teeth (recorded 1992, directed by David Byrne and
   David Wild, 1993).
David Byrne Live at Union Chapel (recorded 2002, directed by Janet Fraser Crook,
   2004)
David Byrne: Live from Austin Texas (recorded November 28, 2001, directed by Gary
   Menotti, 2007)

OTHER FILMS

True Stories (directed and co-written by David Byrne, 1986)
Ilé Aiyé: The House of Life (directed by David Byrne, 1988)
April 16, 1989 (a 2 ½-minute film, directed by David Byrne and David Wild, 1988)
Storytelling Giant (compilation of all Talking Heads' videos to date; seven directed by
   Byrne, 1988)

Bibliography of David Byrne writings

True Stories. London/Boston: Faber and Faber, 1986.

"Introduction," in Talking Heads and Frank Olinsky: *What the Songs Look Like: Contemporary Artists Interpret Talking Heads Songs*. New York: Harper and Row, 1987, p. 14.

"Foreword," in Lynne Cohen: *Occupied Territory*. New York: Aperture, 1987, pp. 14–15.

"It has been said that a myth is a dream . . .," chapter VIII, "Music," theater program for *The Forest* by Robert Wilson and David Byrne. Berlin: Theater der freien Volksbühne, 1988, pages unnumbered.

Scenario for the film version of *The Forest*, Copyright March 1988, by David Byrne and Michael Hirst. David Byrne Archives, unpublished, 80 pages.

"We Eat We Are Eaten," *Artforum*, December 1989.

"Insert," *Parkett* 23, 1990, pp. 119–29.

"Artist in Dialogue," in John Howell: *David Byrne*, New York: Thunder's Mouth Press, 1992, pp. 37–89.

"Funky Town," *Aperture*, 127, Spring 1992, p. 3.

"The Rei Momo Tour Diary," in John Howell: *David Byrne*, New York: Thunder's Mouth Press, 1992, pp. 107–38.

"Foreword," in Phyllis Galembo: *Divine Inspiration: From Benin to Bahia*. Albuquerque: University of New Mexico Press, 1993, pp. vii–viii.

"Tom Zé" (interview), with Arto Lindsay, *Bomb*, 42, Winter 1993. Available online: www.bombsite.com/issues/42/articles/1628

"Rosanne Cash" (interview), *Bomb*, 44, Summer 1993. Available online: www. bombsite.com/issues/44/articles/1687

"Djur Djura" (interview), *Bomb*, 47, Spring 1994. Available online: www.bombsite. com/issues/47/articles/1767

"Art . . . Qu'est-ce que c'est?," *World Art*, November 1994, p. 120.

"A Country Place," *Talking Pictures*, 1994, pp. 178–80.

"I first saw David Carson's work . . .," Introduction to Lewis Blackwell (ed.): *The End of Print: The Graphic Design of David Carson*. London: Lawrence King, 1995.

Strange Ritual: Pictures and Words. London: Faber and Faber, 1995.

Your Action World: Winners Are Losers with A New Attitude. Milan: Gotham, 1998.

"12 Moral Questions," *Pierogi 2000: Vol. 2*, New York: Pierogi Press, Fall 1998, pp. 24–26.

"The Holy Grail of No Style," in Peter Hall and Michael Bierut (eds.): *Tibor Kalman: Perverse Optimist*. New York: Princeton Architectural Press, 1998.

"Eulogy: Tibor Kalman," *Time*, Monday, May 17, 1999. Available online: www.time.com/time/magazine/article/0,9171,991005,00.html

"Crossing Music's Borders: 'I Hate World Music'," *New York Times*, Sunday, October 3, 1999.

"Music Makes Dance — Dance Makes Music," in the theater program for *In Spite of Wishing and Wanting* by Ultima Vez, directed by Wim Vandekeybus, 1999, pp. 22–23.

The Dance of Politics. Curatorial statement for "Gesture, Posture and Bad Attitude in Contemporary News Photography," curated by David Byrne. New York: Apex Art, April–May, 2001.

"A blip, a blob, a groove, and a curve," in Karim Rashid: *I Want to Change the World*, Universe Publishing, 2001, pp. 222–23. Also ran in *Men's Journal*, September 2000, 105–6.

The New Sins. New York: McSweeney's, and London: Faber and Faber, 2001.

"A Self-Made Man," in Rosanne Cash (ed.): *Songs without Rhyme: Prose by Celebrated Songwriters*. New York, 2001, pp. 1–24.

"(David Byrne Asks You:) What Is It?," *Pinspot, No. 13*. Santa Monica: Smart Art Press, 2002.

"As an adolescent I wasn't sure if I wanted to be a scientist or an artist." Available online: www.abc.net.au/rage/guest/2002/davidbyrne.htm

"Nostalgia for the Real — Or, Bad Is Good," in Juan C. Mena and Oscar Reyes: *Sensacional! Mexican Street Graphics*. New York: Princeton Architectural Press, 2002, pp. 9–12. Also ran as "When Bad Art Is Good," *Utne*, March–April 2003, pp. 84–87.

"Top Ten," *Artforum*, January 2002, p. 35.

"Machines of Joy: I have seen the future and it is squiggly," *Leonardo Music Journal*, 12, 2002, pp. 7–10. Available online: www.luakabop.com/comparativesound/home/homemain.htm

"Notes on Images," *Zoetrope*, 7(1), Spring 2003, p. 98.

"Pink," *Cabinet*, 11, Summer 2003. Available online: www.cabinetmagazine.org/issues/11/pink.php

Envisioning Emotional Epistemological Information. Göttingen and New York: Steidl and Pace/MacGill, 2003.

"Life During Wartime," *Arthur*, July 2003, pp. 22–26.

"Learning to Love PowerPoint," *Wired*, September 2003. Available online: www.wired. com/wired/archive/11.09/ppt1_pr.html

"Food," in John Baldessari: *Yours in Food*, New York: Blind Spot/Princeton Architectural Press, 2004, pp. 34–38.

(with Bruce Mau) "Interview," *Contemporary*, 69, 2004, pp. 28–37. Available online: www.contemporary-magazines.com/interview69.htm

"Theater of Memory," in Terry Allen, *et al.: Dugout*. Austin: University of Texas Press, 2005, pp. 167–77.

"The Creative Algorithm," Afterword in Hilly Kristal and David Byrne: *CBGB and OMFUG: Thirty Years from the Home of Underground Rock*. New York: Abrams, 2005, pages unnumbered.

"Most of David Byrne's notebooks have a random feel — ideas coming in and out of focus." Untitled contribution of diary pages to: Jennifer New: *Drawing from Life: The Journal as Art*. New York: Princeton Architectural Press, 2005, pp. 130–35.

"Foreword: sauntering meaningfully," in Robert Farris Thompson: *Tango: The Art History of Love*. New York: Vintage, 2006, pp. ix–xi.

"Pop Music and Contemporary Art," *The Limit*, May 2006.

Arboretum. San Francisco: McSweeney's, 2006.

"Things Are Going through You All the Time: The Art of Kiki Smith," *Zoetrope*, 10(1), Spring 2006.

"Strange and Wonderful: The Filipino Art Biennial exists on the street — get your ass out there," *Manila Envelope*, 2, 2006, pp. 60–77.

"David Byrne talks with Olivia Judson," *The Believer*, February 2007 (with Daniel Levitin). "The singer/songwriter and the neuroscientist meet up to discuss music," *Seedmagazine.com*, April 30, 2007. Available online: seedmagazine.com/content/ article/david_byrne_daniel_levitin/

"Space Junk," in *Bale Creek Allen*, Gerald Peters Gallery, 2007, pp. 7–9.

"David Byrne's Survival Strategies for Emerging Artists — and Megastars," *Wired*, December 18, 2007. Reprinted in *WOMEX Guide*, August 2008. Available online: www.wired.com/entertainment/music/magazine/16-01/ff_byrne

"Bob the Builder," *New York Times*, May 16, 2008. Available online: www.nytimes. com/2008/05/16/opinion/16byrne.html?_r=1&ref=opinion

"OurTube," in "Moments That Mattered," *New York Times Magazine*, November 23, 2008.

"Bike Messenger," *New York Times*, May 28, 2009. Available online: www.nytimes. com/2009/05/31/books/review/Byrne-t.html?_r=3&ref=review

"11.25.2007: Bubble Number One: It's Better because it Costs More," in Susan

Jennings (ed.): *THIS: A Collection of Artists' Writings*. New York: Right Brain Words, 2009, pp. 16–21.

Bicycle Diaries. London: Faber and Faber, 2009.

"A Talking Head Dreams of a Perfect City: Osaka's robot-run parking lots mixed with the Minneapolis lakefront; a musician's fantasy metropolis," *Wall Street Journal*, Life & Style, September 11, 2009. Available online: www.wsj.com/article/SB100014 240529702034401045744032930641 36098.html

Journal. March 2004–September 2009. http://journal.davidbyrne.com

LINER NOTES BY DAVID BYRNE, IDENTIFIED BY TITLE OR BY FIRST SENTENCE

"Tips for performers: Playing cards have the top half upside-down to help cheaters." *Stop Making Sense* booklet by David Byrne with Michael Hodgson and Jeff Ayeroff. Talking Heads: *Stop Making Sense*. Sire Records, 1984. LP.

"These songs represent but a small sampling of the fruits of a flowering in Brazilian creativity." Various artists: *Brazil Classics 1: Beleza Tropical*, compiled by David Byrne. Fly Records/Sire Records, 1989. LP.

"Philosophy of Samba." Various artists: *Brazil Classics 2: O Samba*, compiled by David Byrne. Luaka Bop/Sire Records, 1989. LP.

"The music of Tom Zé is unlike any other Brazilian music I've heard." Tom Zé: *Brazil Classics 4: The Best of Tom Zé*, compiled by David Byrne. Luaka Bop/Sire Records, 1990. CD.

"I first heard this music when I visited Salvador, Bahia, for the first time in 1986." Various artists: *Brazil Classics 3: Forro etc. Music of the Brazilian Northeast*, compiled by David Byrne. Sire Records, 1991. CD.

"How does one describe Silvio's music to someone who has never heard it (or the other singers of *Nueva Trova* [New Song]?" Silvio Rodriguez: *Cuba Classics 1: Greatest Hits*, compiled by David Byrne. Luaka Bop, 1991. CD.

"I grew up listening to this music . . . but I didn't know it." Various artists: *Cuba Classics 2: Incredible Dance Hits of the 60's and 70's — Dancing with the Enemy*. Luaka Bop, 1991. CD.

"It has been said that a myth is a dream that helps us find our place in the world." David Byrne: *The Forest*. Luaka Bop, 1991. CD. [Condensed version of Byrne's text in the program for the 1988 Berlin production of *The Forest*.]

"Yes, we all lived in the same 'loft' on Chrystie St." Talking Heads: *Sand in the Vaseline*. Sire Records, 1992. CD.

"Waldemar Bastos has created a first . . . something unique and surprising . . . a beautiful heartfelt lilting recording that includes and synthesizes Afro-Pop styles from all over the continent." Waldemar Bastos: *Pretaluz*. Luaka Bop, 1998. CD.

"Brazilians are the original masters of mixology, blend and hybridization." Various artists: *Beleza Tropical 2: Novo! Mais! Melhor!* Luaka Bop, 1998. CD.

"The late 60's in Brazil produced an explosion of creativity that is still reverberating throughout the world . . . and Os Mutantes (The Mutants) were the most outrageous band of that period." Os Mutantes: *World Psychedelic Classics 1: The Best of Os Mutantes: Everything Is Possible!* Brazil. Luaka Bop, 1999. CD.

"David Byrne and Jim White Talk and Talk and Talk." Interview, December 21, 2000. Available online: www.luakabop.com/jim_white/cmp/talk.html

"Machines of Joy: I have seen the future and it is squiggly." Various musicians: *The Only Blip Hop Record You Will Ever Need, Vol. 1*. Luaka Bop, 2002. CD.

"French Kiss Your CD." Various Musicians: *Luaka Bop présente Cuisine Non-Stop*. Introduction to the French nouvelle generation, compiled by David Byrne. Luaka Bop, 2002. CD.

"I go about my business, mostly here in New York, traveling from midtown to downtown and back up again, often to Brooklyn, less often to Hoboken or Queens." Also: four dream protocols, titled "Bread Shoes," "Animals Know," "Narrow Escape," "Faceless Denouement." David Byrne: *Grown Backwards*. Nonesuch, 2004. CD.

"Candomblé is art, religion, music, theater, gastronomy, dance, poetry and more all at once." David Byrne: *Ilé Aiyé. The House of Life*. Plexifilm, 2004. DVD; liner notes originally written for 1989 LaserDisc.

"The Making of *My Life in the Bush Of Ghosts*." Liner notes by David Byrne with Brian Eno, 2005. Brian Eno and David Byrne: *My Life in the Bush of Ghosts*. Nonesuch, 2006. CD.

"What's a Knee Play?" David Byrne: *The Knee Plays*. Nonesuch, 2007. CD. See also Byrne's 1983 notes, "Knee Plays::Music". Available online: www.kneeplays.com/ideas/music1.shtml#top

"A couple of years ago I passed through London and, having reconnected with Brian Eno during the Bush of Ghosts re-release, I popped round his office/studio to hear what he'd been working on." David Byrne and Brian Eno: *Everything That Happens Will Happen Today*. Todomundo/Opal, 2008. CD.

General Bibliography

Akademie der Künste (ed.). *SoHo — Downtown Manhattan*. Berlin: Berliner Festwochen, 1976.

Alberro, Alexander. *Conceptual Art and the Politics of Publicity*. Cambridge, Mass.: MIT Press, 2003.

Alexander, Christopher. *Notes on the Synthesis of Form*. Cambridge, Mass.: Harvard University Press, 1970.

——— *The Timeless Way of Building*. New York: Oxford University Press, 1979.

Alexander, Christopher, Murray Silverstein, Shlomo Angel, Sara Ishikawa, and Denny Abrams. *The Oregon Experiment*. New York: Oxford University Press, 1975.

Alexander, Christopher, Sara Ishikawa, Murray Silverstein, with Max Jacobson, Ingrid Fiksdahl-King, and Shlomo Angel. *A Pattern Language: Towns, Buildings, Construction*. New York: Oxford University Press, 1977.

Appadurai, Arjun. *Modernity at Large: Cultural Dimensions of Globalization*. Minneapolis: University of Minnesota Press, 1996.

Aragon, Louis. *Paris Peasant*. Trans. Simon Taylor. London: Pan Books, 1987.

Aronson, Arnold. *American Avant-Garde Theatre: A History*. London: Routledge, 2000.

——— *Looking into the Abyss. Essays on Scenography*. Ann Arbor: University of Michigan Press, 2005.

Art & Language. Eindhoven: Van Abbemuseum, 1980.

Art & Language. *De Schilderijen*. Brussels, 1987.

Asad, Talal. "The Concept of Cultural Translation," in J. Clifford and G.E. Marcus (eds.) *Writing Culture: The Poetics and Politics of Ethnography*. Berkeley, University of California Press, 1986.

Ault, Julie (ed.). *Alternative Art New York, 1965–1985. A Cultural Politics Book for the Social Text Collective*. Minneapolis/London: University of Minnesota Press, 2002.

Baldessari, John. *Yours in Food*. New York: Blind Spot/Princeton Architectural Press, 2004.

Bateson, Gregory. *Steps to an Ecology of Mind*. New York: Ballantine, 1983.

Baudrillard, Jean. *America*. Trans. Chris Turner. London: Verso, 1988.

Becker, Howard S. *Art Worlds*. Berkeley: University of California Press, 1984.

Beer, Stafford. *Brain of the Firm: The Managerial Cybernetics of Organization* (2nd edn). Chichester: Wiley and Sons, 1981.

Behler, Ernst. *Friedrich Schlegel*. Reinbek bei Hamburg: Rowohlt, 1966.

—— *German Romantic Literary Theory*. Cambridge: Cambridge University Press, 1993.

Behler, Ernst and Jochen Hörisch (eds.). *Die Aktualität der Frühromantik*. Paderborn: Schöningh, 1987.

Benjamin, Walter. *Gesammelte Schriften I-VII*. Frankfurt am Main: Suhrkamp, 1972–89.

—— *Illuminations: Essays and Reflections*. Ed. Hannah Arendt, trans. Harry Zohn. New York: Shocken, 1988.

—— *Reflections: Essays, Aphorisms, Autobiographical Writings*. Ed. Peter Demetz, trans. Edmund Jephcott. New York: Shocken, 1986.

—— *One-Way Street and Other Writings*. Trans. Edmund Jephcott and Kingsley Shorter. London: Verso, 1997.

—— *Selected Writings, Volume 1: 1913–1926*. Ed. Michael W. Jennings, trans. Jennings and Marcus Bullock. Cambridge, Mass.: The Belknap Press of Harvard University Press, 1996.

—— *Selected Writings, Volume 2: 1927–1934*. Eds. Michael W. Jennings, Howard Eiland and Gary Smith. Cambridge, Mass.: The Belknap Press of Harvard University Press, 1999.

—— *The Arcades Project*. Trans. H. Eiland and K. McLaughlin. Cambridge, Mass.: The Belknap Press of Harvard University Press, 1999.

Borow, Zev. "Political Flesh, Dept. of Talking Heads: the man behind the masks," *The New Yorker*, "Talk of the Town," November 13, 2000.

Bowman, David. "David Byrne at the Ear Inn," *Salon.com*, October 14, 1999. Available online: www.salon.com/people/lunch/1999/10/14/byrne

—— *Fa fa fa fa fa fa: The Adventures of Talking Heads in the 20th Century*. London: Bloomsbury, 2001.

Boxer, Sarah. "Slogans and Images, with Talking Heads Bending Your Ears," *New York Times*, Sunday, August 18, 1996, pp. 35–37.

Braeckman, Antoon. *De waarheid van de kunst: Over de rol van het esthetische in Schellings romantische modernisteitskritiek*. Leuven: Peeters, 1996.

Brecht, Stefan. *The Theatre of Visions: Robert Wilson: The Original Theatre of the City of New York from the mid-60s to the mid-70s*. Frankfurt am Main: Suhrkamp, 1978.

Breuer, Lee. "The Theatre and Its Trouble: An Essay," in Lee Breuer, *Sister Suzie Cinema: The Collected Poems and Performances, 1976-1986*. New York: Theatre Communications Group, 1987.

Bronson, A.A. and Peggy Gale. *Performance by Artists*. Toronto: Art Metropole, 1979.

Brown, Asby. "Reproduced Authentic: Galerie Via Eight," *Artforum*, February 1991, p. 141.

Byrne, David. See separate list of David Byrne's publications.

Cage, John. *Silence: Lectures and Writings*. London: Boyars, 1995 [1963].

Campbell, Joseph. *The Masks of God I: Primitive Mythology*. New York: Arkana/Viking Penguin, 1991 [1959].

—— *The Masks of God II: Oriental Mythology*. New York: Viking, 1962.

—— *The Hero's Journey: Joseph Campbell on his Life and Work*. San Francisco, etc.: Harper & Row, 1990.

Carter, Alexandra (ed.). *The Routledge Dance Studies Reader*. London: Routledge, 1998.

Cash, Roseanne (ed.). *Songs Without Rhyme: Prose by Celebrated Songwriters*. New York: Hyperion, 2001.

Chernoff, John Miller. *African Rhythm and African Sensibility: Aesthetics and Social Action in African Musical Idioms*. Chicago/London: The University of Chicago Press, 1979.

—— "Naked Heads: The Talking Heads explain their world to John Miller Chernoff, author of 'African Rhythm and African Sensibility'," *Spin*, April 1988, pp. 48–52, 76–78.

—— "Thoroughly Modern Music: The Evolution of Talking Heads," in *Music & Sound Output*, May 1988, pp. 40–48, 78.

—— *Hustling Is Not Stealing: Stories of an African Bar Girl*. Chicago/London: University of Chicago Press, 2003.

Cocks, Jay. "Rock's Renaissance Man," *Time*, October 27, 1986. Available online: www.time.com/time/magazine/article/0,9171,962640,00.html

Cohen, Lynne. *Occupied Territory*. With David Byrne, William Ewing, and David Mellor. New York: Aperture, 1987.

Cole, Susan Letzler. *Directors in Rehearsal: A Hidden World*. London/New York: Routledge, 1992.

Coser, Lewis A. *Masters of Sociological Thought: Ideas in Historical and Social Context* (2nd edn.). New York: Harcourt, Brace, Jovanovich, 1977.

Cotton, Charlotte. *The Photograph as Contemporary Art*. London/New York: Thames & Hudson, 2004.

Coupland, Ken. "All Over the Map with David Byrne," *Graphis, International Journal of Graphic Art and Applied Art*, 313, 1998, pp. 92–100.

Cox, Christoph and Daniel Warner (eds.). *Audio Culture: Readings in Modern Music*. New York/London: Continuum, 2004.

Critchley, Macdonald and R.A. Henson (eds.). *Music and the Brain: Studies in the Neurology of Music*. London: Heinemann Medical Books, 1977.

Dalton, Jody. "Robert Wilson: Seeing the Forest for the Trees," *Ear*, 11, 1988.

Davis, Jerome. *Talking Heads: A Biography*. London: Omnibus Press, 1987.

Dent, T.C., R. Schechner, and G. Moses (eds.). *The Free Southern Theater by the Free Southern Theater: A Documentary of the South's Radical Black Theater, with Journals, Letters, Poetry, Essays and a Play Written by Those Who Built It*. Indianapolis and New York: Bobbs-Merrill Company, 1969.

Deren, Maya. "Art and Anthropology: The Crossroads/From the Notebook of 1947," introduced by Catrina Neiman, in *October*, 14, Fall 1980, pp. 3–46.

—— *The Voodoo Gods* (original: Divine Horsemen, 1953). Frogmore, St Albans: Granada/Paladin, 1975.

Derrida, Jacques. *Of Grammatology*. Baltimore/London: Johns Hopkins University Press, 1976.

DeLillo, Don. *Underworld*. New York: Simon and Schuster, 1998.

Drijkoningen, F. and J. Fontijn, with M. Grygar, P. de Meijer, and H. Würzner (eds.). *Historische Avantgarde: Programmatische teksten van het Italiaans Futurisme, het Russisch Futurisme, Dada, het Constructivisme, het Surrealisme en het Tsjechisch Poëtisme*. Amsterdam: Huis aan de Drie Grachten, 1991.

Eggleston, William. *The Democratic Forest*. London: Secker & Warburg, 1989.

Eno, Brian. "Generating and Organising Variety in the Arts," *Studio International*, 984, November–December 1976, pp. 279–83.

—— "My own work in video . . .," *The Luminous Image*, 1984, pp. 112–13.

—— *A Year with Swollen Appendices: Brian Eno's Diary*. London: Faber and Faber, 1996.

—— "The Studio as Compositional Tool," in Cox and Warner (eds.). *Audio Culture*, 2004, pp. 127–30.

Eno, Brian and Peter Schmidt. *Oblique Strategies*. Originally published 1975. http://music.hyperreal.org/artists/brian_eno/oblique/oblique.html

Eno, Brian and Russell Mills. *More Dark than Shark*. Commentaries by Rick Poynor. London: Faber and Faber, 1986.

The Epic of Gilgamesh. London: Penguin, 1987.

Evelev, Yale. "A Nonmusician's Life in Music," *Leonardo Music Journal*, 12, 2002, pp. 67–69.

Farelly, Liz. *Tibor Kalman: Design and Undesign*. London: Thames and Hudson, 1998.

Feld, Steven. "A Sweet Lullaby for 'World Music'," in Simon Frith (ed.). *Popular Music. Critical Concepts in Media and Cultural Studies. Vol. II: The Rock Era*. London/New York: Routledge, 2004, pp. 62–85.

Feldman, Heidi Carolyn. *Black Rhythms of Peru: Reviving African Musical Heritage in the Black Pacific*. Middletown: Wesleyan University Press, 2006.

Felman, Shoshana and Dori Laub. *Testimony: Crises of Witnessing in Literature, Psychoanalysis, and History*. New York/London: Routledge, 1992.

Fisher, Jean (ed.). *Global Visions: Towards a New Internationalism in the Visual Arts*. London: Kala Press, 1994.

—— *Reverberations: Tactics of Resistance, Forms of Agency in Trans/cultural Practices*. Maastricht: Jan van Eyck Editions, 2000.

Foster, Hal (ed.). *The Anti-Aesthetic: Essays on Postmodern Culture*. Seattle: Bay Press, 1983.

—— *The Return of the Real: The Avant-Garde at the End of the Century*. Cambridge, Mass./London: MIT Press, 1996.

Frank, Manfred. *Der kommende Gott: Vorlesungen über die Neue Mythologie*. Frankfurt am Main: Suhrkamp, 1982.

—— *Gott im Exil: Vorlesungen über die Neue Mythologie II*. Frankfurt am Main: Suhrkamp, 1988.

—— *Einführung in die frühromantische Ästhetik*. Frankfurt am Main: Suhrkamp, 1989.

Frank, Manfred and Gerhard Kurz (eds.). *Materialien zu Schellings philosophischen Anfängen*. Frankfurt am Main: Suhrkamp, 1975.

Frazer, Sir James. *The Golden Bough: A Study in Magic and Religion*. Abridged ed. by J. Frazer. Ware: Wordsworth Editions, 1993.

Frith, Simon. *Sound Effects: Youth, Leisure, and the Politics of Rock 'n' Roll*. New York: Pantheon Books, 1981.

—— *Performing Rites: On the Value of Popular Music*. Cambridge, Mass.: Harvard University Press, 1998.

Frith, Simon and Andrew Goodwin (eds.). *On Record. Rock, Pop, and the Written Word*. London/New York: Routledge, 1990.

Frith, Simon, Andrew Goodwin, and Lawrence Grossberg (eds.). *Sound & Vision: The Music Video Reader*. London/New York: Routledge, 1993.

Frizot, Michel (ed.). *A New History of Photography*. Cologne: Könemann, 1998.

Galembo, Phyllis. *Divine Inspiration: From Benin to Bahia*. Foreword by David Byrne, essays by Robert Farris Thompson, Joseph Nevadomsky, Norma Rosen, Zeca Ligièro. Albuquerque: University of New Mexico Press, 1993.

Gauss, Ulrike (ed.). *Photo-Kunst: Arbeiten aus 150 Jahren*. Stuttgart: Cantz, 1989.

Geertz, Clifford. *The Interpretation of Cultures: Selected Essays*. London: Fontana, 1993.

—— "The Uses of Diversity," in Sterling M. McMurrin (ed.). *The Tanner Lectures on Human Values*. London, 1986, pp. 252–75.

Gil, Gilberto. "The Music of the World is Bigger than World Music," 1993. Available online: www.gilbertogil.com.br/sec_textos_view.php?id=1&language_id=2

Goldberg, RoseLee. *Performance Art: From Futurism to the Present* (rev. and enlarged edn.). London: Thames and Hudson, 1988.

Gombrich, Ernst H. *Art and Illusion: A Study in the Psychology of Pictorial Representation* (6th edn. with a new preface). London: Phaidon, 2005.

Gracyk, Theodore. *Rhythm and Noise: An Aesthetics of Rock.* London/New York: Tauris & Co., 1996.

Gray, Spalding. *Swimming to Cambodia: The Collected Works of Spalding Gray.* London: Pan Books, 1987.

Gray, Spalding and Elizabeth LeCompte. "Play: Rumstick Road," in *Performing Arts Journal*, 3(2), Fall 1978, pp. 92–115.

Hall, Peter and Michael Bierut (eds). *Tibor Kalman: Perverse Optimist.* New York: Princeton Architectural Press, 1998.

Halliwell, Martin. *Romantic Science and the Experience of Self: Transatlantic Crosscurrents from William James to Oliver Sacks.* Aldershot: Ashgate Publishing, 1999.

Handelman, David. "Are four heads better than one? The world's smartest rock group talks about confronting the David Byrne media blitz," in *Rolling Stone*, January 15, 1987, pp. 34–36, 54–58.

Harrison, Charles. "Art & Language: Enkele condities en interesses van de eerste tien jaar," in *Art & Language: De Schilderijen.* Brussels, 1987.

Hebdidge, Dick. *Hiding in the Light: On Images and Things.* London/New York: Routledge, 1988.

Heiser, Jörg (ed.). *Romantischer Konzeptualismus/Romantic Conceptualism.* Bielefeld/Leipzig: Kerber Verlag, 2007.

Herman, Edward S. and Noam Chomsky. *Manufacturing Consent: The Political Economy of the Mass Media.* New York: Pantheon, 1988.

Heylighen, Francis and Cliff Joslyn. "Cybernetics and Second-Order Cybernetics," in R.A. Meyers (ed.). *Encyclopedia of Physical Science & Technology* (3rd edn.). New York: Academic Press, 2001. http://pcp.vub.ac.be/Papers/Cybernetics-EPST.pdf

Holmberg, Arthur. *The Theatre of Robert Wilson.* Cambridge: Cambridge University Press, 1996.

Howell, John. "Robert Wilson and David Byrne, *The Knee Plays*, in Alice Tully Hall," in *Artforum*, March 1987, p. 131.

—— *David Byrne.* New York: Thunder's Mouth Press, 1992.

Hughes, Robert. *The Shock of the New: Art and the Century of Change.* Updated and enlarged edition. London: Thames and Hudson, 1991.

Inglis, David and Roland Robertson. "'World Music' and the Globalization of Sound," in David Inglis and John Hughson (eds.). *The Sociology of Art: Ways of Seeing.* Basingstoke/New York: Palgrave Macmillan, 2005, pp. 156–70.

Isler, Scott. "Going, Going, Ghana! David Byrne and Brian Eno bring Africa to Soho," in *Trousers Press*, 61, May 1981.

Jay, Martin. *The Dialectical Imagination: A History of the Frankfurt School and the Institute of Social Research 1923–1950*. Boston/Toronto: Little, Brown and Company, 1973.

Jencks, Charles. *The Language of Postmodern Architecture*. London: Academy Editions, 1991.

Jennings, Humphrey. *Pandaemonium, 1660–1886: The Coming of the Machine as Seen by Contemporary Observers*. Eds. M.L. Jennings and C. Madge. New York: The Free Press, 1985.

Johnson, Ken. "Report from North Adams: Back to the Future Again. After years of delays, MASS MoCA is now moving toward a 1988 opening date — with a radically revamped sense of audience and mission." Includes "David Byrne at MASS MoCA," in *Art in America*, October 1996, pp. 51–55.

Jung, Carl G. (ed.) *Man and his Symbols*. London: Aldus Books, 1964.

Jung, Carl G. *Symbols of Transformation* (2nd edn.). Volume 5 of the *Collected Works*. Princeton, New Jersey: Princeton University Press, 1990.

—— *Civilization in Transition* (2nd edn.). Volume 10 of the *Collected Works*. London/Henley: Routledge & Kegan Paul, 1970.

—— *Psychology and Alchemy* (2nd edn.). Volume 12 of the *Collected Works*. London/Henley: Routledge & Kegan Paul, 1968.

—— *The Spirit in Man, Art and Literature*. Volume 15 of the *Collected Works*. London/Henley: Routledge & Kegan Paul, 1978.

Kalman, Tibor, J. Abbott Miller, and Karrie Jacobs. "Good History/Bad History," in Michael Bierut, William Drenttal, Steven Heller, and D.K. Holland (eds.). *Looking Closer: Critical Writings on Graphic Design*. New York: Allworth Press, 1994, pp. 25–33.

Keesing, Roger M. *Cultural Anthropology: A Contemporary Perspective*. New York: Holt, Rinehart, and Winston, 1976.

Keil, Charles and Steven Feld. *Music Grooves: Essays and Dialogues*. Chicago/London: University of Chicago Press, 1994.

Kertess, Klaus. "In Robert Wilson's Forest," *Parkett* 16, 1988, pp. 56–59.

Kirby, Michael (ed.). *The New Theatre: Performance Documentation*. Drama Review Series. New York: New York University Press, 1974.

—— *A Formalist Theatre*. Philadelphia: University of Pennsylvania Press, 1987.

Kleger, Laura. "Inside, Accumulated: Lynne Cohen." Available online: www.laurakleger.com/art/writing/lynnecohen.html

Kosuth, Joseph. *Reproduced Authentic*. Tokyo: Galerie Via Eight, 1990.

—— *Art After Philosophy and After: Collected Writings, 1966–1990*. Ed. with an introduction by Gabriele Guercio, foreword by Jean-François Lyotard. Cambridge, Mass./London: MIT Press, 1991.

Kristal, Hilly and David Byrne. *CBGB and OMFUG: Thirty Years from the Home of Underground Rock*. New York: Abrams, 2005.

Kruger, Barbara. *Remote Control: Power, Cultures, and the World of Appearances.* Cambridge, Mass./London: MIT Press, 1993.

LeCompte, Elizabeth. "An Introduction" (to "The Making of a Trilogy: Three Places in Rhode Island"), *Performing Arts Journal*, 3(2), Fall 1978, pp. 81–86.

—— "Who Owns History?," *Performance Arts Journal*, 4(1), 1979, pp. 50–53.

—— "The Wooster Group Dances: from the Notebooks of Elizabeth LeCompte," *The Drama Review*, 29(2), Summer 1985, pp. 78–93.

—— "Notes on Form," originally published in the program for the Wooster Group's performance of *Fish Story* in 1993. Available online: www.e-felix.org/issue3/Lecompte.html.

Levitin, Daniel J. *This Is Your Brain on Music: The Science of a Human Obsession.* New York: Dutton, 2006.

LeWitt, Sol. *Sol LeWitt.* New York: The Museum of Modern Art, 1978.

Lipsitz, George. *Dangerous Crossroads: Popular Music, Postmodernism and the Poetics of Place.* London/New York: Verso, 1994.

Luria, A. R. *The Mind of a Mnemonist: A Little Book about a Vast Memory.* Cambridge, Mass./London: Harvard University Press, 1987.

Maenz, Paul and Gerd de Vries (eds.). *Art & Language: Texte zum Phänomen Kunst und Sprache.* Essays by Terry Atkinson, David Bainbridge, Michael Baldwin, Harold Hurrell, Joseph Kosuth. Cologne: Du Mont Schauberg, 1972.

Mali, Joseph. *Mythistory. The Making of a Modern Historiography.* Chicago and London: University of Chicago Press, 2003.

Manrique, Jaime: "Susana Baca" (interview), *Bomb*, 70, Winter 2000. Available online: www.bombsite.com/issues/70/articles/2295

Marcus, Greil. *Mystery Train: Images of America in Rock'n'Roll Music* (4th rev. Edn). New York: Plume, 1997.

Marranca, Bonnie (ed.). *The Theatre of Images.* Contains Robert Wilson: *A Letter for Queen Victoria.* Richard Foreman: *Pandering to the Masses: A Misrepresentation.* Lee Breuer: *The Red Horse Animation.* New York: Drama Book Specialists, 1977.

—— "*The Forest* as Archive: Wilson and Interculturalism," in *Performing Arts Journal*, 33/34, 1989.

—— *Ecologies of Theater: Essays at the Century Turning.* Baltimore/London: John Hopkins University Press, 1996.

Martin, Jean-Hubert, *et al.* (eds.). *Magiciens de la Terre.* Paris: Centre Georges Pompidou, Musée National d'art moderne, 1989.

McClary, Susan, and Robert Walser. "Start Making Sense! Musicology Wrestles with Rock," in Simon Frith and Andrew Goodwin (eds.). *On Record. Rock, Pop, and the Written Word.* London: Routledge, 1990, pp. 277–92. Originally published in 1988.

McDonough, Tom. "Making Sense of David Byrne: Talking Head analyzed on the occasion of his directing debut," in *American Film*, 12(1), October 1986, pp. 31–38.

McKim, Richard. "True Stories," *Cineaste*, 15(3), 1987, pp. 44–46.

Miles. *Talking Heads: An Illustrated Biography*. London: Omnibus Press, 1981.

Nederveen Pieterse, Jan. "Multiculturalism and Museums: Discourse about Others in the Age of Globalization," in *Theory, Culture and Society*, 14(4), 1997, pp. 123–46.

Nietzsche, Friedrich. *Werke*. Ed. K. Schlechta. Frankfurt am Main: Ullstein, 1980.

Novalis. *Werke*. Study edn., ed. Gerhard Schulz. Munich: C.H. Beck, 1987.

O'Doherty, Brian. *American Masters: The Voice and the Myth*. New York: Universe Books, 1988.

Parker, Ian. "Absolute PowerPoint. Can a Software Package Edit Our Thoughts?," *The New Yorker*, 28 May 2001, pp. 76–87. Available online: newyorker.com/archive/2001/05/28/010528fa_fact_parker.

Peckham, Morse. *Man's Rage for Chaos: Biology, Behavior, and the Arts*. New York: Schocken, 1967.

Perrone, Charles A. "From Noigandres to 'Milagre da Alegria': The Concrete Poets and Contemporary Brazilian Popular Music," *Latin American Music Review*, 6/1, Spring/Summer, 1985, pp. 58–79.

Puntin, Marco. "Intervista a David Byrne," *Il Progetto*, 4, May 1998.

Ratcliff, Carter. "David Byrne and the Modern Self: How Do I Work This?," *Artforum* 23, May 1985.

Rockwell, John. "An Epic grows in Brooklyn," *New York Times Magazine*, November 9, 1988, pp. 50, 51, 84, 86.

—— *All American Music: Composition in the Late Twentieth Century*. Reprinted with a new preface. New York: Da Capo Press, 1997.

Rose, Hilary and Steven Rose (eds.). *Alas, Poor Darwin*. London: Jonathan Cape, 2000.

Rosen, Charles and Henri Zerner. *Romanticism and Realism: The Mythology of Nineteenth-Century Art*. New York: Viking Press, 1984.

Ruby, Jay. *Picturing Culture: Explorations of Film and Anthropology*. Chicago: University of Chicago Press, 2000.

Russell, Bertrand. "On the Value of Scepticism," 1928. Available online: www.positiveatheism.org/hist/russell4.htm

Rüter, Christoph and Guntram Weber (eds.). *The Forest* (theater program). Berlin: Theater der Freien Volksbühne, 1988.

Sacks, Oliver. *The Man Who Mistook His Wife for a Hat*. London: Picador, 1986.

Savran, David. *Breaking the Rules: The Wooster Group*. New York: Theatre Communications Group, 1988.

—— "The Death of the Avantgarde," *TDR: The Drama Review* 49(3), Fall 2005, pp. 10–42.

Sayre, Henry M. *The Object of Performance: The American Avant-Garde since 1970*. Chicago: University of Chicago Press, 1989.

Schechner, Richard. *Essays on Performance Theory 1970–1976*. New York: Drama Book Specialists, 1977.

—— *The End of Humanism: Writings on Performance*. New York: Performing Arts Journal Publications, 1982.

—— *Between Theater and Anthropology*. Philadelphia: University of Pennsylvania Press, 1987.

—— *The Future of Ritual: Writings on Culture and Performance*. London: Routledge, 1993.

—— *Performance Studies. An Introduction*. London/New York: Routledge, 2003.

Schechner, Richard and Lisa Wolford (eds.). *The Grotowski Sourcebook*. London/New York: Routledge, 1997.

Schecter, Martin. "Beyond the Text: S(h)ifting through Postmodernism (Nick at Nite, David Byrne, and Kathy Acker)," *American Journal of Semiotics*, 8(4), 1991, pp. 173–86.

Schelling, F. W. J. *Texte zur Philosophie der Kunst*. Stuttgart: Reclam, 1991.

Schlegel, Friedrich. *Kritische und theoretische Schriften*. Comp. A. Huyssen. Stuttgart: Reclam, 1990.

Schleiermacher, Friedrich. *On Religion: Speeches to its Cultured Despisers*. Ed. and trans. Richard Crouter. Cambridge: Cambridge University Press, 1988.

Schulte-Sasse, Jochen, with Haynes Horne, Andreas Michel, Elizabeth Mittman, Assenka Oksiloff, Lisa C. Roetzel, and Mary R. Strand. *Theory as Practice: A Critical Anthology of Early German Romantic Writings*. Minneapolis: University of Minneapolis Press, 1997.

Shank, Theodore. *Beyond the Boundaries: American Alternative Theatre*. Ann Arbor: University of Michigan Press, 2002.

Sheppard, Anne. *Aesthetics: An Introduction to the Philosophy of Art*. Oxford: Oxford University Press, 1987.

Shyer, Laurence. "The Forest: A preview of the next Wilson-Byrne collaboration," *Theater*, Summer/Fall, 1988.

—— *Robert Wilson and his Collaborators*. New York: Theatre Communications Group, 1989.

Sklar, Robert. *Movie-Made America: A Cultural History of American Movies*. New York: Vintage, 1976.

Sontag, Susan. *Against Interpretation*. New York: Dell, 1969.

Stangos, Nikos (ed.). *Concepts of Modern Art: From Futurism to Postmodernism* (3rd edn., expanded and updated). London: Thames and Hudson, 1994.

Stearns, Robert. "The Civil Wars: The American Section." Available online: www.kneeplays.com/catalog/walker-essay-p1.shtml

Steenstra, Sytze. "Neutralizing . . . Now!," in Jean Fisher (ed.). *Reverberations*. Jan van Eyck Editions, Maastricht, 2000, pp. 126–29.

—— "David Byrne: Getting the 'I' out of Design," in *Dot Dot Dot*, 4, Winter 2001/2, pp. 63–69.

—— *We Are the Noise between Stations: A philosophical Exploration of the Work of David Byrne, at the Crossroads of Popular Media, Conceptual Art, and Performance Theatre*. Maastricht: Mixed Media, 2003.

Steinman, Louise. *The Knowing Body: Elements of Contemporary Performance and Dance*. Boston/London: Shambhala, 1986.

Talking Heads and Frank Olinsky. *What the Songs Look Like: Contemporary Artists Interpret Talking Heads Songs*. Introduction by David Byrne. New York: Harper and Row, 1987.

Tamm, Eric. *Brian Eno: His Music and the Vertical Color of Sound*. Boston and London: Faber and Faber, 1989.

Taussig, Michael. *Mimesis and Alterity: A Particular History of the Senses*. New York: Routledge, 1993.

Teubner, Ernst (ed.). *Hugo Ball (1886–1986): Leben und Werk*. Berlin: Publica, 1986.

Tharp, Twyla. *Push Comes to Shove: An Autobiography*. New York: Bantam, 1992.

Thompson, Robert Farris. "An Aesthetic of the Cool," *African Arts*, 7(1), Fall 1973, pp. 40–43, 64–67, 89–92.

—— *African Art in Motion: Icon and Act*. University of California Press, 1979.

—— *Flash of the Spirit: African and Afro-American Art and Philosophy*. New York: Vintage Books, 1984.

—— "David Byrne: The Rolling Stone Interview," *Rolling Stone*, April 21, 1988, pp. 42–52, 116.

—— *Face of the Gods: Art and Altars of Africa and the African Americas*. New York: The Museum for African Art and Prestel Verlag, 1993.

—— "The Medicine in the Imagining: Notes on Mambo," *First of the Month*, 1, 1998, 10–11.

—— "Mambo: Microcosm of Black New York Creativity," in Jean Fisher (ed.). *Reverberations*, Maastricht: Jan van Eyck Editions, 2000, pp. 164–73.

—— *Tango: The Art History of Love*. New York: Vintage, 2006.

Tiger, Lionel and Robin Fox. *The Imperial Animal*. Foreword by Konrad Lorenz. New York: Henry Holt and Company, 1989 [1971].

Tufte, Edward R. *Political Control of the Economy*. Princeton, New Jersey: Princeton University Press, 1980.

—— *The Visual Display of Quantitative Information*. Cheshire, Conn.: Graphics Press, 1983.

—— *Envisioning Information*. Cheshire, Conn.: Graphics Press, 1990.

—— *Visual Explanations: Images and Quantities, Evidence and Narrative*. Cheshire, Conn.: Graphics Press, 1997.

—— *The Cognitive Style of PowerPoint*. Cheshire, Conn.: Graphics Press, 2003.

—— "PowerPoint Is Evil. Power Corrupts. PowerPoint Corrupts Absolutely," *Wired*, Issue 11.09, September 2003. Available online: www.wired.com/wired/ archive/11.09/ppt2_pr.html

Turner, J. F. *Howard Finster, Man of Visions: The Life and Work of a Self-taught Artist.* New York: Knopf, 1989.

Tutuola, Amos. *My Life in the Bush of Ghosts.* London/Boston: Faber and Faber, 1981.

Vandermeersch, Patrick. *Unresolved Questions in the Freud/Jung Debate: On Psychosis, Sexual Identity and Religion.* Leuven: Leuven University Press, 1991.

Veloso, Caetano. *Tropical Truth: A Story of Music and Revolution in Brazil.* Ed. Barbara Einzig, trans. Isabel de Sena. New York: Knopf, 2002.

Wanning, Berbeli. *Novalis zur Einführung.* Hamburg: Junius, 1996.

Wiener, Norbert. *Cybernetics: Or Control and Communication in the Animal and the Machine.* (2nd edn). Cambridge, Mass.: MIT Press, 1985 [1948].

—— *God and Golem, Inc.: A Comment on Certain Points Where Cybernetics Impinges on Religion.* Cambridge, Mass.: MIT Press, 1963.

Wiggershaus, Rolf. *Die Frankfurter Schule: Geschichte, Theoretische Entwicklung, Politische Bedeutung,* Munich: Hanser, 1986.

Wilson, Edward O. *On Human Nature.* Cambridge, Mass.: Harvard University Press, 1995 [1978].

Wilson, Robert. *Der deutsche Teil von der CIVIL warS: a tree is best measured when it is down, im Schauspiel Köln.* Frankfurt am Main: Suhrkamp, 1984.

Woods, Tim. *Beginning Postmodernism.* Manchester: Manchester University Press, 1999.

WEBSITES DEDICATED TO THE WORK OF DAVID BYRNE AND OF TALKING HEADS

www.talking-heads.net
www.luakabop.com
www.davidbyrne.com
www.kneeplays.com
www.bushofghosts.wmg.com

Index